HOW
BALTHASAR
CHANGED MY MIND

HOW
BALTHASAR
CHANGED MY MIND

*Fifteen Scholars Reflect on
the Meaning of Balthasar for
Their Own Work*

Rodney A. Howsare
and Larry S. Chapp
Editors

A Herder & Herder Book
The Crossroad Publishing Company
New York

The Crossroad Publishing Company
16 Penn Plaza–481 Eighth Avenue, Suite 1550
New York, NY 10001

Printed in the United States of America

The text of this book is set in 11/14.5 Adobe Garamond.

Cataloging-in-Publication Data is available from the Library of Congress
ISBN-10: 0-8245-2569-8
ISBN-13: 978-0-8245-2569-9

1   2   3   4   5   6   7   8   9   10   12   11   10   09   08

Contents

Introduction   1
    Larry S. Chapp

1. A Reflection on Christ, Theological Method, and Freedom   9
    Robert Barron

2. How Balthasar Shaped My Mind   26
    Martin Bieler

3. And the Word Became Text: Materialism, the Culture   40
    of Despair, and the Spirit of Childhood
    Anthony DiStefano

4. The Message in a Bottle: How Hans Urs von Balthasar   58
    Changed My Mind
    Raymond Gawronski, SJ

5. A Few Words on Balthasar's First Word   74
    Michael Hanby

6. Being Lost: Hans Urs von Balthasar on Love and Hope   91
    Nicholas J. Healy

7. Not Peace, but a Sword: How Balthasar Changed My Mind   103
    Rodney A. Howsare

8. Truth Grounded in Love: Han Urs von Balthasar's *Theo-Logic*   123
    and Christian Pedagogy
    Francesca Murphy

9. How Receptivity Opens the Mind for Creative Collaboration   135
   Danielle Nussberger

10. I Am Not What I Am Because of . . .   151
    Cyril O'Regan

11. The Paradox of Hans Urs von Balthasar   172
    Russell Reno

12. A Catholic Appropriation of Romantic Themes   191
    Tracey Rowland

13. Hope and the Freedom of Philosophy   209
    David C. Schindler

14. Modernity and the Nature of a Distinction: Balthasar's
    Ontology of Generosity   224
    David L. Schindler

15. Every Thought Captive to Christ: How Balthasar Changed
    My Mind about Faith and Philosophy   259
    Adrian Walker

Notes   279

Contributors   303

Introduction
Larry S. Chapp

The idea for this book was conceived two years ago by my colleague Rodney Howsare. It was the centenary year of the birth of Hans Urs von Balthasar, and Rodney was thinking about a fitting way to celebrate that milestone. Remembering the book *How Karl Barth Changed My Mind,* he proposed that he and I produce a similar text on Balthasar. How fitting, we thought, to celebrate Balthasar's intellectual achievements with a text entirely devoted to the manner in which his thought has catalyzed the thinking of others. However, our interest is not merely that of the intellectual voyeur who seeks to peer behind the "psychology" of modern thinkers to learn how their intellectual autobiographies can be "explained" by the influence of another, more seminal, thinker. We are not interested, in other words, in a simple cataloging of the sycophantic opinions of mere epigones. Rather, our interests remain strictly theological in that we seek to demonstrate the truly fecund nature of Balthasar's theology by highlighting the manner in which it has been creatively appropriated in the thought of a variety of different contemporary scholars.

I will make no attempt here at an *Überblick* that neatly encapsulates the central themes of each essay. I prefer, rather, that those themes emerge on their own as readers either peruse systematically or free-range haphazardly the contents of the text. However, several common themes do emerge that, in my opinion, point to certain trends in the modern appropriation of Balthasar's thought.

First, and perhaps most important, the subtle relationship between the theology of Karl Rahner and that of Balthasar permeates several of the essays. What is striking is the manner in which the dialogue between Rahnerians and Balthasarians mirrors many of the great theological controversies that emerged in the wake of the Second Vatican Council. Clearly, the theological turmoil of the postconciliar period created, in the words of Tracey Rowland, an "explosive problematic" for the church pastorally that is still not completely resolved. Furthermore, no theology is ever conceived or received in a cultural vacuum, and the theologies of both Rahner and Balthasar are no exception to this rule. And so, for some, Balthasar was the antidote to the postconciliar, liberal-progressive "Rahnerian problem," while for others, Balthasar represented a romantic revisionist return to a discredited ecclesiastical past. Some of the essays in this book reflect this tension even while laboring to give it context. Others attempt a postmortem of the conflict and seek to analyze what theological steps forward, if any, can be discerned in the great historical meeting of these two rich streams of thought. However, what shines through in many of the essays is the singular importance of understanding the relationship between the thought of Rahner and that of Balthasar in order to truly appreciate the history of modern Catholic theology.

Related to this theme is, of course, the deeper question of the theological relationship between Transcendental Thomism and the school of theology that has come to be known as *Ressourcement*. What complicates the story of this relationship is precisely the fact that easy caricatures of these two schools of thought have brought more confusion than clarity to the discussion. To cite just one example, it is far too simplistic to say that Transcendental Thomism represents a "turn to the subject" as a starting point for theology while *Ressourcement* represents a "turn to Christ" in its attempt to reorient theology around a christological center. It is simplistic because it implies that Rahner was unconcerned with Christology and that *Ressourcement* thinkers were unconcerned with human subjectivity. And yet serious thinkers know this to be false even on the level of basic generalization in terms of what each approach "emphasizes." An astute Rahnerian can show quite easily that Rahner's entire transcendental approach is predicated upon an antecedent Christology that permeates his analysis of human subjectivity. In other words, an astute Rahnerian can show that Rahner's theology is not an attempt at a cheap foundationalism that proceeds with a naïve Kantian view of reason and with Christ somewhere in the rearview mirror as a vague memory. In like manner, one need only read Henri de Lubac's discussion of the Blondelian tradition and Balthasar's treatment of the historical, dramatic, and relational notion of truth in *Theo-Logic* to see that human subjectivity is a central theme in their thought as well.

Thus, the value of many of the essays in this book that treat this issue is that they clearly demonstrate a nuanced understanding of the relationship between these two schools of thought. What they bring out is that there are indeed important differences between Balthasar and Rahner, but that the differences are much deeper than a simplistic distinction between a "turn to the subject" and a "turn to Christ." What they show is that they both "turn to the subject" and "turn to Christ," but that they do so from differing theological premises and different anthropologies.

A second major theme that permeates many of the essays is a recognition of the uniqueness of Balthasar's approach to the tradition. Many of Balthasar's critics from the ranks of the neopaleo-Thomists are often quick to point out the strange, idiosyncratic character of much of Balthasar's retrieval of the tradition. There is great distrust, in particular, of the intellectual debt that he owed to the private revelations of Adrienne von Speyr, and questions linger about the methodological propriety of basing an authentically Christian theology, with its necessary "public" dimension, on such esoterica. Some (e.g., Alyssa Pitstick) go so far as to accuse Balthasar's theology of being so innovative that it is, in fact, heretical. While making no attempt to address these issues head-on, many of the essays in this book are frank in their acknowledgment of the shocking originality and freshness of Balthasar's analysis of several key aspects of the tradition. Thus, it seems that the dividing line between Balthasar's admirers and his detractors on the "right" is precisely how one is to characterize properly the unique aspects of Balthasar's vision: prescient genius who is repristinating the church's tradition through bold and original insights, or dangerous innovator who, though a genius, represents at best a bizarre and nonrepeatable (and certainly nonteachable!) theological system and at worst a seductive heresy that subverts the faith even while it purports to reinvigorate it. At the very least, all of this should give the lie to the notion that Balthasar was merely a kind of Tridentine-Germanic-Romantic intent on resurrecting a nonexistent ecclesiastical golden age.

However, what many of the essays in this book show is that Balthasar, following in the footsteps of Henri de Lubac and Romano Guardini, was not a hopeless Germanophile Romantic but rather offered analyses

of human and divine personhood, truth, historicity, subjectivity, experience, and metaphysics that anticipated many of the insights of postmodern
thinkers. Balthasar himself was most certainly not a "postmodern" thinker
in the vein of Jean-François Lyotard and Jacques Derrida, but his concern
for both the historical and relational nature of truth, owing to its rooted-
ness in the dialogical circumincession of the Trinitarian Persons, opens up
truly fresh intellectual pathways that bear some resemblance to the insights
of modern hermeneutical thinkers (think Hans-Georg Gadamer here rather
than Derrida). However, the original aspect of Balthasar's retrieval of the
tradition is that he rarely makes explicit reference to so-called postmodern
thinkers and focuses instead on a rereading of the church Fathers that makes
them sound shockingly contemporary in their concerns. In other words,
Balthasar's originality is not to be explained by reference to a postmodern
form of thought that he rarely, if ever, mentions; rather, the roots of his originality stem from his ability to read the Fathers with a fresh eye freed from
neo-Scholastic assumptions and with a desire to relate the Fathers to certain
theological themes that were prevalent in their day and have reappeared with
a vengeance in our own.

Thus, with regard to the idiosyncratic character of Balthasar's theology,
one needs to take into consideration that Balthasar's retrieval of the tradition
is not that of the antiquarian. Balthasar's retrieval of the past has a contemporary focus that animated his reading of the Fathers. In other words,
Balthasar's retrieval of the tradition is a creative retrieval and a unique appropriation of the past for the sake of the present. Once one takes into
consideration that Balthasar's chief intellectual project was (in my opinion)
the attempt to retrieve the tradition in such a manner that would inocu-
late it against the virus of Germanic neo-Gnosticism, then one begins to
understand his "peculiar" (and how "peculiar" was it?) frustration with the
dualistic language of neo-Scholasticism and its subsequent inability to deal
with this threat. It is often the case, therefore, that one's analysis of Balthasar's
retrieval of the Fathers will be determined first by whether or not one agrees
with Balthasar's diagnosis of the ills that plague modernity, and second by
whether or not one agrees that these were, analogously, the same theological
issues that confronted the Fathers.

Many of the essays that follow deal with this issue explicitly. In particular,
I draw the reader's attention to the essay by Russell Reno. Reno is actually

critical of Balthasar and the *Ressourcement* school of thought for being, perhaps, a little too harsh on neo-Scholasticism and a little too creative and innovative in their retrieval of the tradition. Reno's conclusion is that Balthasar in particular is so idiosyncratic that it is impossible to translate his thought into a "standard" church theology. Thus, Balthasar and others successfully destroyed neo-Scholasticism but replaced it with a brilliant, but unusable, theology that accounts for the current theological muddle that we are in. I do not agree with Reno's analysis (in fact, I very much disagree with it), but it cogently puts forward the critique of Balthasar's creative retrieval of the tradition and will perhaps generate a much-needed discussion of the topic.

A third common theme that emerges from these essays is the ability of Balthasar's theology to untie the multiple intellectual "Gordian knots" created by the encounter between classical and modern thought. Once Lessing's dictum that the contingent truths of history could not serve as an adequate vessel for the eternal truths of reason was adopted as an intellectual norm in Europe, then Christian theology either had to reject this idea and answer its critique or had to accommodate itself to it. The result was either a stale theological rationalism that accepted the Enlightenment's fact/value bifurcation or a wholesale retreat into some form of pietism. Balthasar, once again following in the footsteps of de Lubac and Guardini, was the master of paradox and understood that Christian revelation is neither the natural flowering of a generic human "religious consciousness" nor a pure supernatural miracle imposed upon a largely "secular reason." The stark contrast between "nature" and "supernature" that is so characteristic of modernity *is the true intellectual idiosyncrasy* that created the strangely denatured and titrated form of Christianity called "Liberalism." Liberals who were "conservative" held out hope that "natural reason" could somehow create a proper foundational propaedeutic upon which one could erect a proper theological edifice that was now grounded in "reason." Liberals who were "liberal" sought to ground the truth of the faith in some kind of generic inward religious experience that is open equally to all people of good will. But notice how in both cases the concern is with the universality of revelation understood as a pure function of some central feature of human nature generically conceived. The Enlightenment, following in the wake of the fragmentation created by the

Reformation, simply distrusted "historical" divine revelations and sought religious refuge instead in either the universal standards of reason, univocally understood, or the universal religious feelings generated by human nature, once again, univocally understood. Balthasar saw the deformations in Christian theology caused by this obsession with universality-as-univocity and sought instead to recover the true inner essence of revelation's "public" nature as precisely something that is rooted in the particularities of history. In order to do this, he had to get beyond many of the neo-Gnostic "antiflesh" assumptions of a rationalist modernity, with its "angelist" anthropological emphasis on a strangely disembodied reason.

Thus, as I stated, many of the essays in this book contribute to an understanding of how Balthasar's theology allows us to untie many of the intellectual knots created by modernity's strained view of nature and grace, time and eternity, flesh and spirit. As many of the essays in this book make clear, Balthasar's problem was not with "natural theology" or the methodological distinction between "faith and reason"; rather, his problem was with the nontheological nature of how the relation between faith and reason was grounded — pushing theology to find some "neutral" substrate (either cosmology or anthropology) with which to ground itself, thus making something extrinsic to revelation a judge of the ground rules for its public manifestation. Fortunately, the hegemony in modern thought of old-fashioned Cartesian rationalism was killed off by Darwin and Freud. But the tectonic subduction of the two plates of rationalism and scientific materialism have generated the tsunami of modern skepticism and nihilism, opening the door once again to a simple and uncomplicated reconsideration of precisely the historical claims of Christianity and the personal-dialogical form of reason that such a historical grounding for "Truth" generates.

Finally, since I offer no sustained essay in this book, here I would indulge in some autobiographical reflections of my own. In my case, discovering Balthasar was not so much the cause of a monumental theological revolution in my soul as it was the lifting of a kind of veil from my mind or scales from my eyes. I came to Balthasar in my youth while I was in minor seminary and was never quite satisfied either with my own theological account of how best to negotiate the intellectual shoals of the modern world or with what was being taught to me on the same subject by my teachers. But one of my teachers, Fr. Anton Morgenroth, CSSp, an acerbic, curmudgeonly German and a convert from Judaism, called me into his room one day and literally threw a copy of Balthasar's *Love Alone* at me. I asked him, "Who is this guy?" and he issued this unforgettable response: "Never mind that. Just read it. It will make you less stupid." He was right. I will never make any pretense to truly understanding the full scope of Balthasar's theology or the intellectual currents of thought to which he was responding. However, for me, Balthasar has always acted like an intellectual antihistamine that simply allows me to clear my mind of clutter and to see things more clearly. In that sense, Balthasar truly has had the effect of making me "less stupid," even if my own paltry intellectual resources have never reached into the full heights of the Balthasarian stratosphere. In other words, what struck me about Balthasar is his sanity and ability to create clarity. That might seem surprising to those who find his literary style daunting; but once mastered, his style is, at least for me, piercing and cleansing.

But what is it about Balthasar's theology, precisely, that had this clarifying and cleansing effect on me? It has to do with Balthasar's ability to take whatever theological topic he is discussing and intensify the focus of the question along strictly christological lines. Thus, even if one ends up disagreeing with Balthasar's conclusions, one cannot help but have the impression that the issue has been properly christologically "compressed" by Balthasar and the true issues that are at stake thus brought to the surface. Trained as I had been up to that point in my youthful education in a strict neo-Scholastic Thomism that was more in the tradition of the commentators than of Thomas himself, I often was dismayed by how "unevangelical" it all seemed, and how the whole focus was on answering propositional questions with rationalist and propositional Christian "truths" that themselves were only loosely grounded in the Gospels or even the writings of the Fathers or the church's liturgical-sacramental life. Thus, Russell Reno is at least half right: reading Balthasar destroyed this form of neo-Scholasticism in my mind once and for all. But where I disagree with Reno is in what happened in my mind after this: reading Balthasar opened me up to an "evangelical" reading of the church's tradition ("evangelical" here meaning a theology with an eye toward the manner in which the gospel is a "proposal" and not a "proposition") and liberated my mind from the straightjacket of theological rationalism.

I mention this piece of autobiographical trivia only because I suspect that it represents one of the main reasons so many theologians have found studying Balthasar to be beneficial: they share a common respect for the manner in which Balthasar's thought elevates the church's discourse through a simple process of clarification. And this, I think, is the fourth common theme that ties all of these essays together. Even where one might disagree with Balthasar on this or that point, one rarely gets the feeling that reading Balthasar has simply been a waste of time or that he has obfuscated an issue to such an extent that it has become hopelessly twisted and contorted with intellectual sophistry. What all of these essays show us is how Balthasar's theology has allowed a wide variety of thinkers from a wide variety of intellectual backgrounds to elevate their own thought even when they might not particularly agree with Balthasar on a particular point. In short, these essays demonstrate that Balthasar's theology is rather fecund because it allows us, as Raymond Gawronski concludes, to see old topics, no matter how many times we have been exposed to them, for the first time. It is our hope, therefore, that the essays that follow will help the reader to see, with Balthasar and the thinkers represented here, old topics with fresh eyes.

Chapter One

A Reflection on Christ, Theological Method, and Freedom

Robert Barron

I distinctly remember the first time I became aware of the theology of Hans Urs von Balthasar. It was in April 1986, and I was at St. Meinrad Archabbey on retreat in preparation for my ordination to the priesthood. Through a mutual friend, I made the acquaintance of Fr. Guy Mansini, a monk of St. Meinrad and an inveterate professor and theological writer. In the course of a lively conversation in Fr. Guy's office, I remarked on the number of Karl Rahner's books that lined his shelves. Much to my surprise, he made a sort of grunt of disapproval and then said, "Yes, I cut my teeth theologically on Rahner, but I don't read him much anymore. Now I'm reading Balthasar, and you should too." That kind of curt dismissal of Rahner was by no means common in the mid-1980s. In the course of my seminary studies, Rahner was more or less *the* voice in contemporary Catholic theology, a figure of almost magisterial authority. I must confess that I did not immediately follow Mansini's advice, but his particular juxtaposition of Rahner and Balthasar stayed very clearly in my mind as an intriguing indication that something was perhaps beginning to shift.

My first real exposure to Balthasar's writings occurred in the summer of 1989, when I was a doctoral student at the Institut Catholique in Paris. One day I found myself rummaging around in the theology section of La Procure, the best Catholic bookshop in Paris. I saw a number of texts by Küng, Schillebeeckx, Rahner, Kasper — the most popular authors of the time —

but then I noticed that two entire shelves were devoted to the books of Hans Urs von Balthasar. I saw *Herrlichkeit* in its entirety, French translations of *Mysterium Paschale,* even some English versions of Balthasar's collections of articles and writings on prayer. It was the way that Balthasar dominated the theology section of this French bookstore that impressed me and reminded me of that conversation at St. Meinrad. I decided to buy the French version of *Mysterium Paschale,* more, I must admit, to work on my French than to understand Balthasar. For the next several days I took the book down to the banks of the Seine, just behind Notre Dame Cathedral, and read it, puzzled both by the French rendering of Balthasar's German and by the novelty of the theology. I realized even then that the method employed was radically other than the one to which I had become accustomed.

In the course of my three years in Paris I participated in a number of doctoral seminars conducted by Fr. Michel Corbin, a Jesuit of the Centre Sèvres and a specialist in Hegel, Aquinas, and Anselm. Corbin usually structured his seminars as follows: the reading of texts by Aquinas on a given topic and then the study of texts by earlier figures such as Bernard, Anselm, or Augustine on the same subject, and finally a critical assessment of the thirteenth-century master in light of his predecessors. It soon became clear that what Corbin preferred in those earlier doctors was a scriptural density, unambiguous Christocentrism, and spiritual power that was at least relatively lacking in the more detached and philosophical Thomas. At the close of the first seminar I learned that Corbin had been a student of Henri de Lubac, one of the greatest advocates and allies of Balthasar, and as I plowed through more and more of Corbin's own writings, I found numerous references to Balthasar. A certain pattern and a certain style of theological thinking were becoming clearer to me.

When I returned from Paris to commence my teaching career at Mundelein Seminary, I resolved to undertake a formal and careful reading of this figure whose traces I had been following for several years. But given the press of my obligations — preparing a wide variety of courses, lectures, talks, and so on — I never managed to do it. Finally, I decided to compel myself. In the winter of 1994 I spoke to the academic dean and arranged to teach a course in the theology of Hans Urs von Balthasar the following fall. This rather rash move absolutely forced the issue, and I spent that winter, spring, and summer plowing through the Balthasarian corpus. That effort of working through literally thousands of pages of Balthasar's writings rather decisively changed my mind. Here I will explore this change in relation to three major issues: theological method, Christology, and theological anthropology.

Becoming Uneasy with Modern Experientialism

My theological formation, especially in the seminary, was largely modern in form and inspiration. By this I mean, above all, that experience was consistently construed as the starting point and interpretive matrix for doctrine. As I suggested above, the contemporary theologian who had the greatest impact on my thinking was Karl Rahner. By the time I finished my four years in the seminary, I had read through most of Rahner's major texts, and I had composed my STL dissertation on Rahner's interpretation of the Christology of the Council of Chalcedon. Moreover, in my earliest years as a professor at the seminary I had taken my own licentiate students through a careful reading of Rahner's early career masterpiece *Hearers of the Word*. I had come to recognize and appreciate the standard Rahnerian method of commencing, in the modern mode, with theological anthropology, more precisely, with the human experience of "standing in the presence of Absolute Mystery." In article after article, book after book, Rahner began with an analysis of the dynamic and self-transcending quality of every act of knowing and willing. By its very nature, Rahner argued again and again, the mind reaches out beyond any particular object to the infinite horizon of all that can in principle be known. Bernard Lonergan maintained, in a very similar vein, that the mind cannot be satisfied until it knows "everything about everything," until, in short, it grasps Being itself. And the will, Rahner said, has the same sort of restless and questing nature. Beyond any particular good that it desires or attains, the will wants the Good itself, all that can possibly be willed. This natural capacity of the human spirit to transcend itself in the direction of the infinite Rahner called "the supernatural existential," and he identified this dynamic as the foundational religious experience, the characteristic manner in which human beings stand in the presence of God.

Then, in regard to issue after issue — God's existence, human freedom, Jesus Christ, the nature of sin and salvation — Rahner interpreted doctrine in light of this fundamental religious experience. Thus, God is the "whence" of the self-transcending dynamism; Christ is the meeting point of the human tendency upward and the divine condescension in love and grace; sin is the refusal to respond positively to the lure of God; salvation is the restoration of this attitude of openness; sacraments are word-events that call out to the transcendental longing; and so on. In short, he consistently brought doctrine before the bar of subjective experience for adjudication, explanation, and evaluation, hoping thereby to convince a skeptical audience that Christian claims enjoyed a basic coherence.

In this fundamental approach Rahner showed himself to be a close ally of the contemporary Protestant thinker Paul Tillich, who also commenced the theological undertaking with an appeal to a basic and universal religious experience. Tillich argued that we are claimed by hundreds of concerns in the course of our lives, but that we can discern, under and through all of those particular interests, an abiding and unavoidable preoccupation, something that presses on us unconditionally. This he calls "ultimate concern." It speaks not to some superficial dimension of the self but rather to the "deepest roots of the ego," and its demands are absolute. This unconditioned concern can manifest itself as the Good, which undergirds all of moral activity, or as the Beautiful, which governs every action of the artist, or as Justice, which animates the work of the lawyer and the judge. Having named and awakened this experience, Tillich proceeds to interpret doctrine, dogma, and practice in its light. God is "what ultimately concerns us," or "the unconditioned"; creation is the rapport between conditioned beings and this infinite ground; revelation is the "shaking and turning" of the self that occurs when the unconditioned breaks into ordinary experience; Jesus is the definitive appearance of "the new being" under the conditions of estrangement; and so on. The theological method that Tillich practiced and defended is that of correlation, which is to say, the coordination of the "questions" that well up from human experience to the "answers" that come from the biblical and theological tradition. For too long, Tillich felt, Christian thinkers have been proposing answers to questions that no one was asking. Although it seems to presume a balance between the questioning subject and the answering tradition, the correlational method, in point of fact, favors the former. As any reader of the Platonic dialogues can attest, the one who poses the questions is always the one who determines the nature, flow, and finally the conclusion of the conversation. Thus, for Tillich, as for Rahner, religious experience is foundational and explanatory, the privileged criterion by which doctrine is assessed.

In these moves, of course, both Rahner and Tillich were the disciples of Friedrich Schleiermacher. At the beginning of the nineteenth century, Schleiermacher endeavored to reconfigure theology in such a way as to make the faith acceptable to the "cultured despisers" of religion, those Enlightenment-era rationalists who were gleefully predicting the immanent disappearance of Christianity. He did so by rooting the faith not in doctrine (about which there was endless dispute) or in metaphysics or in ethics or in received tradition but rather in personal, subjective experience. In his *On Religion: Speeches to Its Cultured Despisers,* Schleiermacher argued that all religious people, despite their differences in regard to dogma, cult, and ethical practice, have in common a "sense and taste for the infinite," a feel for Being considered as a totality. It is this sensibility that makes them, properly speaking, religious. In his later, more systematic text the *Glaubenslehre,* Schleiermacher articulated this grounding religious sense as "the feeling of absolute dependency." We are proximately dependent upon all sorts of things — from the air that we breathe, to the floor on which we stand, to the people to whom we speak — but we find ourselves ultimately and unavoidably dependent upon the power of Being itself or the Universe. The method used in the *Glaubenslehre* and a bit more indirectly in *On Religion* is precisely the one that we have seen already in Tillich and Rahner: the interpretation of dogma and practice in terms of this undergirding experience. Schleiermacher shows how hundreds of features of classical Christianity are expressive, in various ways, of this religious feeling. One of the most notorious moves in the *Glaubenslehre* is the relegation of the doctrine of the Trinity to an appendix. Schleiermacher could find no correlation between this teaching, which every theologian from Origen and Augustine to Thomas and Luther recognized as central, and the feeling of absolute dependency and thus felt obliged to marginalize it in his dogmatics.

To be sure, we can trace the Schleiermacher method back even further, to the work of both Martin Luther and René Descartes. As Jacques Maritain pointed out long ago, Luther and Descartes launched together the epistemological revolution that inaugurated modernity when they radically questioned the received tradition on the basis of a subjective experience deemed to be indubitable and foundational, in Descartes' case the *cogito ergo sum*, and in Luther's case the feeling of being justified by grace through faith. And whatever both Luther and Descartes kept from their respective intellectual traditions was reconfigured and reinterpreted in light of the grounding subjective sensibility. At the dawn of the modern period, in short, a crisis of doubt led to a turning inward in order to find justification, religious and intellectual. Both the prompt (a crisis of skepticism) and the method (subjective foundationalism) can be seen in the modern theologians whom I have sketched.

Lest I give the impression that that all of this philosophical and theological reconfiguration remained at the level of academic abstraction, I want to consider the work of one of my own teachers at Mundelein Seminary, the influential practical theologian John Shea. Shea did his doctoral work on the writings of Langdon Gilkey, certainly Paul Tillich's most important American disciple. What Shea did, both in theory and practice, was to adapt the typically modern Schleiermacher/Tillich method to the discipline of theological reflection. In the course of my formation at the seminary I took a variety of Shea's courses and also sat in on any number of his sessions of theological reflection. Invariably, he would commence these latter exercises in the Schleiermacher mode by encouraging the participants to recall a time when they felt "forgiven" or felt "God's presence in their lives" or experienced sin and redemption. Then he would lead the group through a process of co-ordinating those experiences to symbolic and then doctrinal expressions. He was, in short, popularizing and concretely practicing the method of correlation that Gilkey picked up from Tillich and that Tillich, at least implicitly, adapted from Schleiermacher.

This "experiential expressivism" (to give it the monniker provided by George Lindbeck), which I learned from Rahner, Tillich, Shea, and many others, seemed so self-evidently correct that it never occurred to me in those years of formation to question it. Its chief virtue was to have found a ground for Christian claims in an experience that could be immediately verified and that was, at least in principle, universally available. And thus it made those doctrinal assertions seem not so alien, not so abstract, not so incredible to a modern audience naturally skeptical of religious dogma. Following it, I was convinced, would make my teaching and my preaching relevant to life and thus convincing, efficacious.

Then I read Balthasar. Having been immersed for many years in the modern theological thought world, I found the confrontation with Balthasar wrenching, disconcerting, but ultimately bracing. As I perused his texts, I kept waiting for the apologetic or explaining move, the justification for the project on the basis of some self-validating experience, but what I found instead was a stubborn command to "look at the form" of Christ. As I tried to get hold of Christian doctrine, Balthasar kept telling me to relax and let Christian doctrine get hold of me. I was so accustomed to doing "epic" theology — controlling revelation from the standpoint of some higher interpretive vantage point — that the "lyrical" version presented by Balthasar was vertiginous. I wanted to draw revelation into experience, and Balthasar, like Barth, was trying to extricate me from "the musty confines of religious self-consciousness" and draw me into a new world.

It is not the case that Balthasar had no appreciation for the standard modern method. In fact, he had great respect for his Jesuit colleague Rahner, commenting that Rahner far surpassed him in speculative capacity and acknowledging that Rahner's analysis of religious psychology was largely right. But he added that theology becomes really interesting precisely where Rahner tends to stop, at the verge of revelation. Yes, we have a *capax Dei,* but the *capax* should never become the measure of what *Deus* actually says. In the *Theo-Drama,* Balthasar famously compared the human capacity for God to turbines poised at the foot of a great mountain, ready to receive and transform the energy coming from the melting snows above. But when those mighty waters arrive, they so overwhelm the turbines as effectively to render them useless. So it goes with the *capax Dei* in relation to *Deus.* When asked the difference between himself and Rahner, Balthasar responded simply, "Rahner went with Kant; and I went with Goethe." Kant was, along with Descartes, the paradigmatically modern philosopher. His project was the effecting of a Copernican revolution in epistemology, according to which the world of experience is received and structured by the a priori structures of receptive consciousness. And this, according to Balthasar, provided the template for Rahner and his modern theological colleagues: measuring the data of revelation by the structures of religious self-consciousness. But Goethe was playing an entirely different game. Over and against the regnant Enlightenment science of his time, marked by an aggressively analytical technique, he opted for a more contemplative way of knowing, one more respectful of the integrity of the object under study. Thus, Goethe said that the modern scientist would tear a plant out of the ground, severing its roots and extricating it from its natural environment, place it under bright lights, and take it apart, compelling it all the while to answer the scientist's questions. Such a method, he felt, would reveal certain data concerning the plant but would tell the investigator finally very little about the living organism. Goethe proposed that the authentic scientist ought to have the patience to sit next to the plant, observing it over long periods of time, watching how it interacts with its environment and changes with the seasons. He might draw it or chart its developments, but he must allow the plant to ask and answer, so to speak, its own questions.

When he called for a "kneeling" rather than a "sitting" theology, it was this distinction between Goethe and Kant that Balthasar had in mind. The rationalist theologian, sitting at a professor's desk, attempts to master the world of revelation according to familiar receptive categories; the contemplative theologian, kneeling in prayer, allows the Bible, the liturgy, the mystical tradition, Christ himself to be master and to ask questions. Another telling Balthasar image, apposite here, is that of the windows at Chartres. Viewed from the outside, the Chartres stained glass is a rather drab gray, but when seen from inside the church, it becomes radiant and spiritually eloquent. The project of much modern theology, Balthasar felt, was to draw skeptics into the cathedral of Christian truth by showing them the windows from the outside — that is, on their terms — but this finally had little or no compelling power. As Barth first pointed out, the "cultured despisers" have not come streaming back to the faith on the basis of the theological experientialism that was meant to lure them. In point of fact, people will understand the truths of Christian revelation and find them beautiful only from within the church — that is, from the standpoint of worship and contemplation.

So what does the Balthasarian method look like on the ground? It looks like an elaborate, detailed, and patient tour of the biblical universe and the forms that obtain therein. It is a display of the peculiar patterns that emerge from the content of revelation, those matrices of meaning and value out of which Abraham, Isaac, Jacob, Noah, Moses, David, Isaiah, Jeremiah, Ezekiel, Ruth, Peter, Paul, Mary Magdalene, and, above all, Jesus himself operate. If Tillich's and Rahner's biblical theologies are "thin," Balthasar's is "thick." If the approach of the moderns is largely apologetic, Balthasar's is liturgical and iconic. He does not so much justify the biblical world as show it, confident that it has its own convincing and transforming power. It is in this context that we can best understand Balthasar's option for the beautiful as a point of departure for the theological project. Beautiful objects, faces, and lives resist being explained in terms alien to themselves, and they conceal themselves from those who would investigate them too aggressively. Instead, they provide their own interpretations, and they stop (aesthetic arrest), change, and commission those who come into their ambit. For too long, Balthasar felt, the true, especially in its Cartesian and Kantian construal, had come to dominate the theological enterprise, much to the detriment of the very object to be studied. It was well past time for the reign of the beautiful. There is, to be sure, something risky in the Balthasarian method, a sense that, in following it, one is walking a tightrope over an abyss. But one also has the impression that, in this very riskiness, it corresponds more correctly to the radical content of the Christian faith. If modern experientialism has made Christ more credible, it has also domesticated him; if Balthasar's aesthetic and iconic approach is more dangerous, it also honors a Christ worth believing in.

Who Is Jesus Christ?

The methodological shift that I have been describing emerges with special clarity around the question of Jesus Christ. In his three-volume *Systematic Theology*, Tillich developed a rich theological anthropology, a subtle and carefully articulated theology of God, and a detailed theology of the Spirit and the church. But by far the smallest and thinnest of the major sections of his great dogmatics is the second, the part dealing with Christ. Jesus is so thoroughly "positioned" by the anthropology and theology that Tillich lays out that he evanesces into more or less an abstraction, the "bearer of the New Being." We find something very similar in Rahner's *Foundations of Christian Faith*. While Rahner's theological anthropology and the account of God are extremely rich and thorough, his Christology is thin and abstract. As I hinted above, the most remarkable thing about the Christologies of both Tillich and Rahner is how unbiblical they are. Jesus is presented not so much in scriptural terms as in the light of philosophical and psychological categories adapted from the contemporary culture. N. T. Wright has made the observation that much of the Christology of the last two hundred years — say, from Schleiermacher on — is basically Marcionite in form, which is to say, marked by a surprising indifference to the manner in which Jesus should be read against the loamy background of the Old Testament.

Balthasar diagnosed the central difficulty with liberal Christology as a problem of logic. In the measure that Jesus is positioned and explained by a principle of reason or experience outside of himself, he is no longer functioning as the Logos. According to the Johannine prologue, Jesus is the Word who was present with God from the beginning and through whom all finite things were made. And, according to the lyrical language of the first chapter of Colossians, Jesus is the power through which all things were made, in which they hold together, and toward which they tend. He is, accordingly, not one word among many, not one *logos* alongside of competing *logoi;* he *is* the divine reason itself and hence must be that which positions, explains, and grounds everything else. Balthasar was influenced strongly in this regard by Romano Guardini's reflections on the nature of authentic theology over and against various forms of "scientific" theology that were emerging in the twentieth century. Following the apostle Paul, Guardini held that the "spiritual man" is "judged by no one" and in fact judges all. In a word, theologians cannot be positioned by a system of thought outside of what is given through the Holy Spirit, though they can draw those systems into the thought world opened up by the Spirit. In very recent years, Bruce Marshall has been making much the same point when he speaks of the narratives and doctrines dealing with Jesus as an "epistemic trump." This means that in light of the Christian claim about Jesus as Logos, any system of thought — psychological, metaphysical, scientific, or historical — that finally contradicts the fundamental truths revealed in Jesus Christ must certainly be false. Again, this principle by no means precludes the use of systems of secular thought within the ambit of theology, but it insists that there can be no competition in regard to claims of ultimacy. In light of these clarifications, Balthasar identifies the logical difficulty with all forms of correlationalism and experientialism: they presume that the unmeasurable norm is itself capable of measurement. They assume that the *norma normans sed non normata* is in fact normed by a superior or at least coequal epistemic principle.

A key consequence of the liberal approach is an inability adequately to articulate and defend the divinity of Jesus. Indeed, if Jesus is but the means by which a general religious consciousness is awakened (Schleiermacher), or the bearer of a state of affairs that can obtain apart from him (Tillich), or the full expression of the dynamic tendency within the human spirit (Rahner), it is hard to account for his uniqueness or indispensability. He becomes, to use Kierkegaard's language, the teacher who can be left behind once his lesson has been learned, rather than being the savior whose presence and person remain a permanent point of reference. Thus, central to Balthasar's Christology is an affirmation of the uniqueness of Jesus. Whereas the Buddha claimed to have found a way that benefited him and that would, he wagered, offer salvation to others, Jesus said, "I am the way." Whereas Confucius articulated a form of the moral life that would rightly order human affairs, Jesus said, "I am the life." Whereas Muhammad maintained that he had been given the final revelation of religious truth, Jesus said, "I am the truth." Forgiving sinners, claiming authority over the temple and interpretive sovereignty over the Torah, demanding that he himself be loved above all things, Jesus consistently spoke and acted in the person of God, and in doing so, he compelled a decision in a way that none of the other religious founders did. We must either stand utterly with him or we should be against him, for, as C. S. Lewis emphasized, "either he is God or he is a bad man" (*aut Deus aut homo malus*). This is why Balthasar says that although there are superficial similarities between Jesus and the other founders, in point of fact, when we look closely at them, what emerges with increasing clarity is the difference between Jesus and the others.

Another major point of demarcation between the standard liberal Christology and Balthasar's is their differing accounts of the rejection of Jesus. For the modern theologian, skeptical nonbelievers are accorded a sort of pride of place. Their puzzlement over Jesus is seen as understandable, and the theological project is construed as an attempt to make belief in Christ credible to them and on their terms. But this, for Balthasar, is conceding far too much. On biblical terms, he argues, the rejection of Christ is not primarily an intellectual issue but rather a moral one. Those that do not understand Jesus properly are those who, for various reasons, have refused to submit to him, or to state it somewhat more accurately, have failed to fall in love with him. Thus, some have insisted on drawing him into their categories of explanation and expectation; but this is like "trying to record an entire symphony on a few inches of tape." Others saw him as a threat or a rival and thus refused to surrender to him. Concomitantly, those who did "get" him—John the beloved disciple, Mary Magdalene, Mary the mother of God, Peter— were the ones who loved him and allowed him to be the criterion and measure of their lives. In making this methodological move, Balthasar seizes, as it were, the high ground and compels the despisers of Christ to make an account of their opposition, reversing thereby the standard approach of the Schleiermacherians.

Infinite and Finite Freedom

It has been said that the distinctively modern quality in Ignatius of Loyola's spirituality is his stress on freedom. In his famous *Suscipe* prayer, Ignatius employs the classical Augustinian triplet of memory, understanding, and will, inviting God to receive these essential faculties. But prior to the familiar three, he mentions freedom: "Take, O Lord, receive, all my liberty." The puzzle, of course, is that Ignatius, having invoked and specified his freedom, invites God utterly to take it, to claim it as his own. Does this not involve the founder of the Jesuits in a contradiction? Well, only if liberty is construed on modern terms as self-assertion and self-definition. Commencing with Duns Scotus and William of Occam in the late Middle Ages and coming to radical expression in Nietzsche and Sartre, the modern conception of freedom privileges choice, the capacity of the subject to hover above affirmation and denial and to make, on the basis of no internal or external constraint, a sovereign decision.

Balthasar, a Jesuit by training and predeliction, explains the coherence of Ignatius's prayer through an appeal to the Council of Chalcedon's rendering of the relationship between the divine and human natures in Christ. Following the instincts of the Chalcedonian Fathers, even as he improves to some degree on their overly abstract, somewhat static categories, Balthasar sees the natures in Jesus as a play of two freedoms, infinite and finite. In the person of Jesus, divine freedom and human freedom dovetail in an absolutely unique and noncompetitive manner, so that nothing of the human has to give way in the presence of the divine, and nothing of the divine has to be compromised to make way for the human. From this remarkable *Ineinander*, one can read off, as it were, the quality of both authentic human liberty and true

divine liberty. Balthasar holds that finite freedom finds itself precisely in relation to the infinite ground of being, which is God. When the finite subject
emerges into self-consciousness and freedom, it realizes, immediately, that
its liberty is co-involved with and called out by the horizon of Being itself. In
other words, it knows its proper *telos* in the ultimate good, without which
it would lose its orientation. To be sure, this has nothing to do with Occamist freedom of choice but everything to do with what Servais Pinckaers
has called the freedom for excellence. Such freedom is not choice so much
as the disciplining of desire so as to make the achievement of the good first
possible and then effortless. Thus someone gradually becomes free to play
the piano through a long process of discipline and the ordering of the body
and mind toward a very particular good. If on the Occamist reading, the
objective good is a threat to freedom, on the Chalcedonian reading it is the
very ground and matrix of freedom.

And from the relationship of the natures in Christ we can interpret God's
freedom as well. In both classical and modern philosophy there is a tendency to construe the divine freedom as supreme arbitrariness, the Occamist
subjectivity writ large. Thus, the Aristotelian prime mover is blithely indifferent to the world that is so profoundly shaped by its attraction to him;
and the Calvinist double-predestinating God hovers with complete capri-
ciousness over the ultimate choice of salvation or damnation. But there is
nothing, thinks Balthasar, of this voluntarism in the biblical-Chalcedonian
understanding of God's freedom. The God revealed in the incarnation is not
hovering arbitrarily over the world he has made; rather, his freedom is coincident with fidelity to his own being and hence to all things that participate
in his act of to-be. And this is why God's freedom is fully expressed as love,
willing the good of the other as other. What Balthasar sees in the Chalcedonian account of the noncompetitive interplay of the natures in Jesus is just
this ecstatic quality of the divine freedom, God's capacity to let the humanity of Jesus be. Indeed, as Irenaeus pointed out long ago, "The glory of God
is a human being fully alive."

At the heart of Balthasar's deeply biblical anthropology is the conviction,
therefore, that humans are most themselves precisely when they enter into
a kind of loop of grace, accepting life from God (who wants nothing more
than to give it) and promptly returning it as an act of love, thereby receiving
more and more of it. It is into this ecstatic loop that Jesus invites the woman

at the well, luring her out of her cramped and fearful self-regard: "If you knew the gift of God, and who it is who said to you, 'Give me a drink,' you would have asked him, and he would have given you living water... a fountain of water bubbling up to eternal life" (John 4:10, 14). It is into that same circumincession of love that the father in Jesus' best-known parable entices both of his errant sons.

Theologizing in a Balthasarian Context

My confrontation with the Balthasarian thought world coincided with the commencement of my own career as a writer and speaker within the church. Although I have drawn from a wide variety of sources in my work, Balthasar has remained perhaps my most significant influence among contemporary theologians. In a number of articles composed just after I returned from studies, I began to complain about the "beige" quality of the Catholicism that I experienced in the years when I was coming of age. By this I meant a Catholicism drained of its unique and distinctive coloration, designed to be inoffensive, inclusive, and attuned to the secular culture. This was evident, I argued, not only in the theological style of the postconciliar church, but also in its preaching, its pastoral practice, and its art and architecture. The edgy, challenging, and countercultural church of Jesus Christ was in danger of becoming a vague echo of the secular world, one "spirituality" among many. Balthasar's critique of modernity, which I sketched above, allowed me to articulate with greater theological precision not only my unease with the postconciliar scene, but also a vision of a richer, more colorful Catholicism. Much of this came to expression in my book *The Strangest Way: Walking the Christian Path.* To a generation grown accustomed to a toothless, harmless Christianity, I wanted to present the way of Jesus Christ as unsettling, unnerving, and unfamiliar. I began with the story of a gathering of monks — Catholic and Buddhist — at the Trappist Monastery of Gethsemani in Kentucky some years ago. They had come together for fellowship and interreligious dialogue, and for the first couple of days the conversations had unfolded in the accustomed benign manner. But then, one of the Buddhist participants rose to make an observation. He said that throughout the conference he had been offended by the ubiquitous presence of depictions of the suffering Christ, nailed to his cross. His own religion, he argued, was meant to be a path that conduced away from suffering, and yet in this place of Christian prayer and recollection, he was forced constantly to face the image of crucifixion. How, he wondered, could the Christians there explain this to him and his Buddhist colleagues? Those who were in attendance witnessed that this question — blunt, direct, ecumenically incorrect — changed the tenor of the meeting much for the better. The Christians were compelled to grasp the nettle of the gospel: the strange and disturbing Christ, the one who, as Paul said, was a stumbling block to the Greeks and a scandal to the Jews. They were forced, furthermore, to explain how the very peculiarity and scandal of Christ crucified *was* the point. In the course of my book I tried, in the Balthasarian spirit, to bring into sharp relief this very strangeness of Jesus.

I also attempted to lay out a new sort of theological method. Over and against the regnant experientialism, I proposed the model of learning to play a game. To learn basketball, one has to play it, and in order to play it, one must surrender to its rhythms, rules, practices, and basic moves. The person who continues to stand on the sideline, analyzing the game in terms of its analogous relation to similar games or in the light of the generic experience of playing "sports," will never know it. The learner must trust those who have fallen in love with basketball and who have played it with an abandon made possible by certain definite rules that circumscribe and direct their movement. This, I suggest, is similar to the way that one learns the practices and doctrines of Christianity: through apprenticeship, obedience, and embodied imitation. One does Christian things and thereby learns the rules of the game; one plays the game and discovers in one's bones how beautiful it is. The experiential expressivism that was all the rage after the Second Vatican Council in Catholic circles prevented, I argued, just this sort of participation. It allowed people to continue playing a game that they already knew and to give Christian names to its rules and practices. The more Goethean approach grew up out of the rich soil of Balthasar's thought.

In my book *The Priority of Christ: Toward a Postliberal Catholicism,* I explored the implications of a consistent Christocentrism, especially in regard to ethics, epistemology, and the doctrine of God. In the epistemology section, for instance, I squinted through a Balthasarian lens at Thomas Aquinas's understanding of faith and reason. Thomas, I argued, did not conceive of philosophy as either a foundation or necessary propaedeutic for theology;

instead, he saw it as a tool that the theologian can use in his pedagogical task of bringing Christian doctrine to the light of understanding. Theology, in a word, is neither positioned nor conditioned by natural philosophy. Instead, the science of the Logos can utilize the *logos* of philosophy as an *ancilla* (handmaid) in its work of exposition. In point of fact, I maintain, neo-Scholasticism, which held to a much more foundationalist understanding of the relationship between philosophy and theology, was conditioned much more by modernity than by Thomas's own intentions. Here I very much join forces with the Balthasar who, in his youth, rebelled against the rationalism of neo-Scholastic Thomism, and who tried, under de Lubac's tutelage, to recover the scriptural and patristic Aquinas. In the ethics section of *The Priority of Christ* I criticize both deontologism and consequentialism as modernisms and opt for an ethics that takes its point of orientation from the saints — that is, from those who are concretely displaying the Christian form of life. Moral truth cannot, I argued, be arrived at abstractly through deduction from first principles, but rather only through looking at the form of Christ as it is on dramatic display in his faithful followers. In this, quite obviously, I was massively influenced by Balthasar.

In practically everything I have written the theme of God's noncompetitive transcendence emerges. I have come to appreciate this peculiar mode of divine otherness as a sort of master idea of Christianity. In its light, we can come to understand more clearly how God can be universally provident over creation and still allow for the integrity of secondary causes, how God's grace is not repugnant to human freedom but rather its ground, how surrender to God is tantamount to human flourishing, how both heteronomy and autonomy are gathered and overcome in theonomy, and how love (willing the good of the other as other) is the fundamental truth of things. All of these themes, which I have tried in a minor way to develop in my own work, I learned implicitly from Balthasar's reading of the noncompetitive play of infinite and finite freedom within the person of Jesus.

Although I draw back from Hans Urs von Balthasar in certain ways (a subject, perhaps, for another essay), I remain deeply indebted and grateful to him. The boldness and beauty of his theologizing affected in me a sort of *metanoia,* a shift in consciousness and attitude, an entirely new way of looking at the world. In many of the Eastern icons depicting the Last Supper, the apostle John is presented in a peculiar pose. As he rests his head on the breast of Jesus, he twists his face so as to face outward, toward the viewer. He has positioned himself so as to see the world from the standpoint of Christ, through the eyes of the Lord. Balthasar, who was so personally devoted to St. John, attempted to theologize from that very distinctive point of vantage. If I may shift metaphors: as I was about to race my theological car down the Schleiermacher autobahn, Balthasar taught me not only to stop and change direction, but also to set out down an entirely different road.

Chapter Two

How Balthasar
Shaped My Mind

Martin Bieler

First Encounter

It was on an afternoon in the fall of 1974 that a small yellow book on the shelf of a Catholic bookshop in Basel caught my attention. The book had the intriguing title *Only Love Is Believable* (*Glaubhaft ist nur Liebe*), and its author was a certain Hans Urs von Balthasar. Enchanted, I picked up the book, for its title promised exactly what I had been looking for. At that time it had been three years since, in July 1971, I had decided to study theology in Taizé. "If you do something good to another fellow human being, you can die." It was this sentence that had opened up for me everything in an instant. The sentence was uttered on a Wednesday afternoon, July 21, 1971, in Taizé by Milton Carver Davis, of Tuskegee, Alabama, the representative of a Catholic student organization. Today I interpret Milton's reference to death in connection with love (which he illustrated using the example of Jesus of Nazareth) as the indication that there is nothing stronger than love, the source of all being. It was an answer to my question whether there is a God, and the answer was not an abstract theory about God but rather a hint as to where you can find him in this world and who he is: 1 John 4:16.

Coming back from Taizé to Basel, I started reading the whole Bible and was puzzled and shocked by the notion of the wrath of God and the doctrines of judgment and hell. It took me years to come to terms with the tension between these two things: the love of God and the wrath of God. What bothered me was not the question of my own fate but rather the question of who God is: Is he really pure love or is he something else? The ambivalence of our world — beautiful and frightening at the same time — further intensified the problem. I found Karl Barth helpful in dealing with this, but there remained questions. Through Barth's *Epistle to the Romans* I learned that God's "no" can be a function of his "yes." But it was only by reading Balthasar that all the pieces finally fell into place. In retrospect, the problem that startled me then appears to me now almost like a Zen Buddhist koan, which demands that you get involved with your whole being in order to find the solution.

A few days after I bought *Glaubhaft ist nur Liebe,* I came back to the bookstore because I had also seen there a book on Georges Bernanos by Balthasar as well as the first volume of his *Herrlichkeit* (In school I was writing a paper on Bernanos for my French class.) The bookseller, who had noticed my interest in Balthasar, told me that the author lived in town. From then on I read every book by Balthasar that I could get my hands on. For the following years he became my favorite author. I was, so to speak, bred on Balthasar. Therefore, as far as "change" refers to a turn around, Balthasar did not change my mind but rather shaped it. I was awaiting every new title that Balthasar wrote, and I bought it as soon as it was available, especially the volumes of his trilogy.

In July 1975, I looked up Balthasar's address in the local phonebook and wrote him a letter, explaining my interest in Bernanos and asking him about the problem of judgment and hell. He wrote back right away and showed an interest in my plans to study theology.[1] A few days later, I visited him in his house, at Arnold Böcklin Strasse 42, in Basel. He sat at his desk next to a statue of Mary in a study lined with books (in fact, the whole house was full of books). He impressed me as a reserved but friendly man who was aware of his authority. But he could also be astonished like a child. I was struck by his generous willingness to spend time with a "Gymnasiast" — a high school student — and I never left his house without his giving me a book, usually from his own publishing house, but not only.

On the afternoon of our first meeting, we talked about several issues: the Jewish tradition, the cross of Christ, eschatology, Moltmann, Kitamori. I was particularly interested by his appreciation for Epictetus, who understands God as a father. Balthasar's capacity to value this pagan thinker revealed to me something of the breadth of his mental horizon. Balthasar was not pleased by the books that he saw on the desks at the seminary of the Evangelical Theological Faculty in Basel, where I intended to study. He thought that Edinburgh would have been a better place to study theology. He wisely advised me not to get confused by a hypercritical biblical exegesis, but rather to remain faithful to what brought me to theology: Stick with the beginning! Before I left him on this afternoon, he gave me Paul Claudel's *Der seidene Schuh,* Balthasar's own translation of *Le soulier de satin.*

Christ-Trinity-Cross

As I was reading Balthasar, I also read Barth's *Church Dogmatics.* The two authors have much in common. From both I learned the basics of theological thinking. I was especially fond of reading Barth when I was in a depressed mood. The hilarity of faith (*Glaubensheiterkeit*) and the sense of confidence that pervade his writings have a great capacity to "edify" in the Kierkegaardian sense. With Balthasar it was a little bit different. The qualities that I appreciated in reading him were the depth, beauty, and precision of his theology, qualities that often left me feeling awed. Although Barth and Balthasar made different sorts of impressions on me, both impressions were due to their shared christological starting point. Both testified to the joy of being a Christian and a theologian.

From Barth I learned that the person of Christ is in the end the only legitimate measure of this world, for he simply *is* the truth. This gives us a tremendous freedom from all illegitimate attempts to bind our heart to false loyalties. Barth's resistance to Hitler's Germany is a stunning example of such freedom. The members of my mother's family were part of the "Bekennende Kirche" (confessing church) in Germany, which was supported by Barth. Even before the war, they had nothing but contempt for "that criminal," as my grandmother called Hitler, and not just in private (that obviously put her in a very dangerous situation). On my father's side, my grandfather was a career officer in the Swiss army. From both sides of the family I learned that we have to resist tyranny and to defend our freedom as well as the freedom of others. This background gave and gives me a strong sense of identification with the Reformed Church, particularly in the form represented by Barth. In contrast, Catholicism appeared to me in my youth as a sort of obscure secret society that had long since fallen from power. It had lost its ability to oppress, but still one had to be cautious about it. Well, at least it helped to have a Catholic girlfriend and to read G. K. Chesterton's detective stories. I really liked Father Brown, and I enjoyed the way he solved the crimes by "committing" them. And I was very attracted by the way he defended reason against Flambeau in "The Blue Cross."

When I was about ten years old, I happened to read the so-called Stroop Report, which recounts the destruction of the Warsaw ghetto by the Germans.[2] In its coldly bureaucratic yet scornful language, the report was horrible to read. The pictures attached to it forcefully underscored the written content. From then on, I understood intuitively that we can keep our freedom in this world only when we are ready to find the truth by facing reality in all its nameless horror. This also implies the readiness to meet all doubts and problems on the same field where they appear: When psychologists tell us that human beings are such and such, then this claim has to be tested on psychological grounds, and so on. God's truth can be for us if only he comes into our world and speaks to us here and now, in our language, if *his* truth is actually true in *this* world, in the face of all its beauty and all its nitty-gritty reality. God's kingdom is not of this world, which is why Jesus never argues with his critics "on their ground." And yet, God's kingdom comes into our world, which is why Jesus really does face his critics, takes their situation seriously, and, in a specific sense, does meet them on their ground. Therefore reason, aided reason, is an indispensable instrument for us. On this point, the Catholic approach eventually became more compelling for me than the Protestant contempt of philosophy. The deepest reason for the validity of human reason is a Trinitarian one, for the presence of that *a quo homo est id quod est* (Thomas Aquinas) is enabled by God's act of giving us space in his own realm. He does this by letting us participate in his truth, which he finally fully opens up for us in his total self-gift to us in Christ. This is where Balthasar comes into play.

From Balthasar I learned to understand that Christ is the gift of the *whole* Trinity. Balthasar's thinking is always explicitly Trinitarian, even more so than Barth's. Balthasar is thus always unfolding the logic of God's love in his writings. Already in our first conversation, Balthasar emphasized that we have to understand Christ as the gift of the whole Trinity, a gift that enables all human suffering to be contained in God without threatening God's beatitude. God himself is unsurpassable life. Because of that, he can be an exchange, a giving and receiving between the Trinitarian Persons, and can suffer for us without being altered in his nature. For Balthasar, the Trinity, as opened up for us in Christ, is the very essence of Christianity. Looked at from this point of view, the cross of Christ appears as God's unconditional and irreversible absolute "yes" to every human being. This yes is absolute because in and with Christ, God has given us his own Trinitarian being, in order to grant us by grace what he himself is by nature. Balthasar's emphasis on the importance of ontological categories in theology is by no means motivated by a problematic natural theology (in the sense that Barth criticized) but rather is grounded in the gift-character of the cross of Christ. Balthasar, like Bonaventure, held that the Father has the power to "put" his whole being into the Son, to the extent that Father and Son originate together the Spirit: "Origo originans originantem."[3] Thanks to this same power, God is able to give the world his whole being in Christ. Consequently, every creaturely difference is contained in the difference between Father and Son. The nexus of Christ-Trinity-Cross as God's yes for us is the most important thing I have learned from Balthasar. Its meaning is summed up in Balthasar's statement that there is only one dogma: God, who is love, is there for us.[4] All theology must be judged according to this basic insight.

For me, Balthasar's controversial teaching concerning Christ's *descensus ad inferos* is nothing more and nothing less than the description of God's concrete act of love for the world, of what we might call the additional mile that God went with us (Matt. 5:41) in order to put the seal of irrevocability on his commitment to us. Balthasar's teaching is simply the attempt to do justice to the reality of the cross of Christ as it is presented throughout the whole of the New Testament. The core of this presentation is the same in John, who fuses everything into a single point under the heading of "exaltation" (John 12:32–33), as in the Synoptics, who exhibit for us the various aspects of the redemption by unfolding them singly on a time line. What does it mean that God gave his Son for the world (John 3:16–17) by making him to be sin (2 Cor. 5:21)? How are we to understand that one died for all (2 Cor. 5:14)? What does it mean that "Christ redeemed us from the curse of the law by becoming a curse for us" (Gal. 3:13)? These texts obviously are talking about much more than the isolated execution of an innocent man by Roman soldiers. Christ's cross is an eschatological reality transcending the limitations of time and space, because it is a Trinitarian event (Heb. 7:22–28) that changes the situation of every human being and of the cosmos. God's identification with every human being in his or her lostness before God must transcend the limits of an earthly life, for what Christ wants to take from us — by "becoming" it — is the curse of eternal death. This is what the *descensus* stands for. Balthasar puts it succinctly: "Hell is a Christological place."[5] But Balthasar does not confuse Christ's suffering with a being damned or his cross with hell.[6] Precisely because he remains united to the Father as the eternal Son, Christ's experience of the nature and the consequences of sin is immeasurably more severe than that of a damned creature could possibly be. Therefore, Balthasar's language of Christ experiencing "sin as such" is indeed correct after all.[7] By his *descensus* Christ breaks the power of sin and takes possession of hell. Here again Balthasar is very close to Barth![8] This is important because Christ's *descensus* is not just an odd idea of the mystic Adrienne von Speyr, though her theological acumen certainly has been underestimated. (One of the books that Balthasar gave me during a conversation with him was the first volume of *Kreuz und Hölle,* which communicates von Speyr's experiences. Especially helpful for me was her description of the *descensus* as the "experience" of the destruction of the time structure.) I think that failing to take seriously what Balthasar says about the *descensus* of Christ or a fortiori setting it aside altogether brings one to the brink of emptying the cross of Christ (1 Cor. 1:17).

By taking possession of hell through his cross, Christ acquires the power to disturb even the worst sinner in the self-chosen isolation that is the very essence of hell.[9] Nobody has the power to bar God definitively from his or her life. But because God respects, out of love, human freedom, he may possibly accept one's wish to be totally isolated. But what will not happen is that God will stop loving any of his creatures. We humans tend to set limits to our readiness to love, but that is not God's way. "As we forgive those who trespass against us" cannot be supplemented with "to a certain extent" (see Matt. 18:21–35). Nor does forgiving our enemies mean that we forgo avenging ourselves because we hope that, if we forbear, God will wreak vengeance for us instead (Matt. 5:38–48). Yes, vengeance is God's (Rom. 12:19), but his ways are very different from ours (John 3:17–21). As long as we are not ready to accept and live this truth, we will not enter the gates of heaven. I always appreciated Balthasar's emphasis on this genuine "evermore" (*je mehr*) of God's love, whose traces Balthasar also knew how to recognize and praise in creation.

One aspect of Balthasar's Trinitarian thinking that is of particular importance for me is his teaching concerning the "Trinitarian inversion." This idea is directly connected with the "evermoreness" of Trinitarian love. In the Trinitarian inversion, the Holy Spirit takes up a role of active initiative with respect to the Son in the *oikonomia* of salvation: He represents the will of the Father to the Son even in hell. This is an "inversion" because the Spirit is the result of the evermore of the relationship between Father and Son, without which they would not be who they are. As the "endpoint" of the Trinitarian processions, as the "condilectus" of Father and Son (Richard of St. Victor), the Spirit is a beginning, a new initiative that is already present in the Father's generation of the Son. Because the Spirit represents the innermost being of Father and Son, he can represent the Father's will, which is at the same time the Son's own will, vis-à-vis the Son. Thanks to the Spirit, then, even on the cross the relationship between Father and Son remains unbroken and is kept free from any sort of negative heteronomy. It is the Trinitarian inversion that enables the mission of Christ in its unique radicalism. And the mission of Christ brings us to the heart of Balthasar's *Theodramatik* and of the whole trilogy. All of these Balthasarian insights into Trinitarian theology play a decisive role in my 1996 habilitation thesis, "Befreiung der Freiheit: Zur Theologie der stellvertretenden Sühne" ("Liberation of Freedom: On the Theology of Substitutionary Atonement").

Gestalt and Gestalten

My first paper on Balthasar was one that I had to write for my master's degree in theology: "Die Gestalt Jesu bei Hans Urs von Balthasar" (Basel, 1980). Balthasar's notion of *Gestalt* (figure, shape) opened up for me the possibility of theology as a science, and it was an excellent preparation for my study of the metaphysics of Thomas Aquinas. Fortunately, I earlier got access to *Wahrheit der Welt* (1947), which later was reissued as the first volume of Balthasar's *Theologik*. In this book one can see how deeply rooted Balthasar's view of the *Gestalt* is in Aquinas, although the influence of Goethe and others should not be underestimated. The structure of the living *Gestalt* is basically identical with the structure of substance on Aquinas's account of it.

But my first acquaintance with Balthasar's notion of *Gestalt* was the first volume of *Herrlichkeit,* in which Balthasar emphasizes the importance of a holistic approach to reality and warns against getting lost in isolated details. Of course, "holistic" also implies the importance of details, as seen in context. I found Balthasar's insights especially helpful for dealing with biblical exegesis.[10] Balthasar was much more of a biblical theologian than one might think. He knew his Bible very well. And even if one might not follow every aspect of his approach to biblical issues, he certainly was well informed about what was going on in contemporary exegesis. As a student of Reformed theology who had to deal intensely with exegetical questions, I always found Balthasar's contributions to the topic helpful, especially as set out in volumes 1 and 3.2.1–2 of *Herrlichkeit* as well as in volumes 2.2 and 3 of *Theodramatik.* In many ways, Balthasar was ahead of his time on exegetical issues. The main lines of his view of the *Gestalt* of Jesus have been confirmed by contemporary exegesis—for example, by Martin Hengel.[11]

Balthasar's theological understanding of *Gestalt* (something else that he shared with Barth!) enabled him to express three basic facts. First, the *Gestalt* of Jesus is measured by itself. It contains its own evidence. It speaks for itself. We just have to see it. What appears to be at first sight a contradiction actually turns out to be a necessary element of the *Gestalt.* (Balthasar's notion of Gestalt helped me understand Aquinas's notion of *convenientia,* which is something of a key to the nature of theology.[12]) Second, the *Gestalt* of Jesus is beautiful. It has a specific quality that we cannot invent, but only can accept as a surprise. It is not merely the product of human ingenuity; someone else speaks in it. Third, in its beauty this *Gestalt* has a liberating power such as only God's grace can have. The encounter with the *Gestalt* of Christ changes us (Rom. 8:29; 2 Cor. 3:18).

The people changed by this encounter—that is what interests Balthasar most in the history of Christianity; not only the theologians and their works, but first of all the lives of the saints. The saints are the true interpreters of the *Gestalt* of Christ because they are the real experts of love. They are first of all men and women of prayer and of charity. We get access to the *Gestalt* of Christ only through prayer and through doing his will. One of Balthasar's books that I treasure most is his work on contemplative prayer, *Das betrachtende Gebet,* which deals with precisely these issues. I learned from Balthasar that the living act of love is *the* access to divine matters, not just academically, but in a particularly powerful and unforgettable way. As a preacher, I experience time and again that a biblical text opens up in a totally different way when we expose ourselves to it with our whole being rather than merely studying it with the conventional methods of historical-critical exegesis.

Throughout his whole work Balthasar introduces the reader to a tremendous cloud of witnesses. He deals with the *Gestalten* (figures) of Christian tradition, not only in his monographic studies but also in his more personal works such as the trilogy. Balthasar imparted to me respect of our own tradition: Augustine, Maximus the Confessor, Anselm of Canterbury, Bonaventure, Thomas Aquinas, to mention just a few. What giants are the people on whose shoulders we stand! What tremendous wealth they have bequeathed to us! We can be proud of our heritage, and we have a responsibility to treasure it. But Balthasar also made it perfectly clear that it is Christ himself who measures even the greatest of these *Gestalten*. Only in him do they have their truth. It was thrilling to see how the same sort of approach enabled Balthasar to honor less well-known figures such as Johann Georg Hamann or even François Villon. We often discover sainthood where we least expect it. We have to reckon with the work of the Holy Spirit *everywhere* — a very important insight to be learned from Balthasar.

Meta-Anthropology

One of the things that makes Balthasar interesting is that he thought not only as a theologian but also as a philosopher. Whereas Barth was often insufficiently precise in his use of theological or philosophical terms, Balthasar could speak more precisely, or at least he could indicate where to look for a more precise account of the issues. This ability reflected his openness to the importance of philosophy and the arts in their own right.

Balthasar was ready to fight the good fight. He could be rather harsh in his judgment, but at the same time he was quite ready to praise goodness wherever he found it. Balthasar's willingness to deal with all kinds of traditions, as well as the broad spectrum of culture that he included in his thinking, were a tremendous inspiration for me as a young student.

In ascribing to philosophy an important role in theology, I sided with Balthasar against Barth. After all, if we take creation and human freedom as a gift of God seriously, and if philosophy is the science that deals with being as such, then philosophy must have a positive relevance to theology. We have to take human freedom seriously because God does too. (This is also the reason that prevents us from teaching an *apokatastasis panton*.) The Catholic "and" that Balthasar defended (grace *and* nature, theology *and* philosophy, etc.) is based in the person of Christ, who is the "and" par excellence for us: God *and* human. This "and" of the person of Christ is rooted in the Trinitarian status of the Son: since the Son is the total expression of the Father, he expresses the Father, himself, the Spirit, and everything else.[13] Because Father and Son constitute an absolute difference of equals in the unity of the Spirit, it is legitimate to speak of a Trinitarian "and" and ascribe its expression to the Son. This Trinitarian difference grounds the possibility of true creaturely freedom, whose specific nature has to be reflected in an intellectual approach that respects the relative autonomy of the creature: philosophy is indispensable precisely for theological reasons.[14]

This does not mean, of course, that philosophy stands on some neutral ground with respect to faith. Balthasar is quite clear that we do not philosophize in a presuppositionless vacuum. Since humans are fallen creatures, their philosophy is affected by the distortion introduced by sin. But Christ's atonement, made present to us by the Spirit, opens up two things at once: the *Gestalt* of Christ and the possibility for the genuinely philosophical act of understanding our being as a gift of the Creator.

As a student, I was impressed by Balthasar's ability to display the development of Western thinking panoramically in its inherent logic. He made a first trial of that ability in his three-volume *Apokalypse der deutschen Seele*. This initial essay was later superseded by *Im Raum der Metaphysik* (vol. 3.1 of *Herrlichkeit* [1965]), which unfolds the criterion governing Balthasar's account of the Western *Geistesgeschichte:* the "fourfold difference." In this later work, Balthasar develops basic insights of Aquinas's metaphysics with the help of Gustav Siewerth and Ferdinand Ulrich. The special spin that Balthasar puts on the discussion is his idea of "meta-anthropology," which takes the relationship between mother and child as the basic paradigm of how we grasp being. It is another human being who in love opens up for us the meaning of being as such: being (*ens*) is a gift of the loving Creator. Indeed, *esse* commune is a gift of the Creator. I have already dealt with these matters both in my 1991 dissertation "Freiheit als Gabe" ("Freedom as Gift") and in a few articles, so I will not repeat myself here. The key idea is simply that the world, as God's creation, is an imprint of his love. This is the criterion for all sound philosophy. It was this criterion that Balthasar used to measure individual philosophies. Nevertheless, even when a given philosophy failed to live up to this criterion, his attitude was never one of mere opposition but rather always was rooted in the solidarity that stems from the One who is the measure of all being. All this helped me to orient myself in the debates about Horkheimer, Adorno, Freud and others that I participated in at the Evangelical Theological Faculty in Basel.

After my exams, I decided to write a dissertation on Ferdinand Ulrich, whose deep understanding of the philosophy of being impressed me as I read *Homo Abyssus* and other of his works. When I talked with Balthasar about my dissertation plans, he described Ulrich as someone who thinks out of his own plenitude. Whereas Siewerth is a stronger thinker than Ulrich, Ulrich thinks out of his weakness. (But it is a very special weakness, for it is a weakness that *is* plenitude.) It is not the case, Balthasar explained, that Ulrich is an epigone of Siewerth. On the contrary, the late Siewerth was influenced by Ulrich. Balthasar described Ulrich as a thinker who "trenches" every thought: every time Balthasar discovered some new idea, he said, he found that Ulrich not only had discovered it first, but also had already used it as a basis for further explorations. Balthasar could sometimes be rather enthusiastic when he read something that he was able to approve of—perhaps too enthusiastic—but in the case of Ulrich he was not exaggerating. Ulrich is the deepest speculative thinker I know. He clearly is the one who first saw the full importance of Aquinas's understanding of *esse* as *completum et simplex sed non subsistens* (*De potentia* 1.1c). Both Siewerth and Balthasar learned from Ulrich on this point. And Ulrich unfolded the philosophy of being as meta-anthropology as no one else did.

Ulrich and Balthasar were important dialogue partners. Ulrich's influence on Balthasar's development of the *Theodramatik* was considerable. Balthasar, on the other hand, motivated Ulrich to develop and publish his own ideas. The two men were quite different in many ways. Balthasar was the extensive reader, whereas Ulrich was and is someone who dwells in things and "tastes" them from the inside, as Ignatius of Loyola put it in the *Exercises*. In some sense, Balthasar was not a modern man, nor did he want to be one. (He was, for instance, rather skeptical about television, which is not the same in

Europe as in the United States.) This does not mean that Balthasar was not a down-to-earth person in matters of daily life. (He was an excellent publisher, for example.) But there were limitations to his presence in this modern world (which, of course, is not all good), limitations that sometimes prevented him from breaking all the way through to contemporary reality. With Ulrich, on the other hand, one can talk just as easily about the *Sinngestalt* of a punk outfit as about the Trinitarian processions without losing the connection between both themes. Ulrich is able to link the highest with the lowest, as Kierkegaard put it, remarkably well. Ulrich is thus an excellent complement to, and deepening of, what Balthasar intended.

Balthasar told me that if I wanted to write about Ulrich, I would have to read Aquinas. Well, he did not just tell me that; he immediately went to one of his bookshelves and handed me Aquinas's commentary on Aristotle's *De anima*, with Balthasar's own notes in it. Yet another book! Then he answered my question about where to start with Aquinas by recommending that I read *De veritate* 1.1. "But watch out," he said, "because you can meditate on this text your whole life long." I took Balthasar's insistence on reading Aquinas seriously, and I profited very much from it.

Balthasar wrote Ulrich and told him there was a Protestant theology student who was interested in his work. He arranged a meeting between Ulrich and me in the "Rigi-Hüsli," Balthasar's chalet on the Rigi, where Ulrich spent some time every year. So I met Ulrich on the Rigi. The acquaintance with him became very important for me. But that is another story.

Ecclesial Existence

Balthasar also shaped my mind with respect to ecclesial existence. Balthasar vigorously defended the importance of the institutional aspect of the church, but he knew that the institution has to be integrated into the Marian dimension of the church. His sympathies were clearly with John, who lets Peter go first (John 20:5–6), but with whom God goes his own way, beyond Peter's supervision (John 21:20–22). (From this perspective, "Balthasar" and "Cardinal" do not really fit together.) Balthasar's interest in the Johannine led him to study the experience of the mystics, especially their experience of the dark night (John of the Cross). Thanks to Balthasar, I became interested not only in John of the Cross but also in Johannes Tauler, who is particularly dear to me, along with other mystics as well. They helped me understand what is at stake in the trials and tribulations that accompany every Christian life. As Georges Bernanos said, all spiritual adventures are ways of the cross. But cross and resurrection belong together, as Bernanos himself knew so well. Therefore, all spiritual adventures are ways of joy.

Balthasar was familiar with the experience of solitude, even of loneliness, in the church. This experience is not something incidental that might happen along the way; it is something essential that will inevitably happen if one is serious about following Christ. I am grateful to Balthasar for reminding me of the biblical realism of ecclesial existence.

But ecclesial existence is not solipsism. I found Balthasar's description of the constellation around Jesus, represented by Peter, Paul, John, and James, to be illuminating. The church is the living body of Christ, with different organs that are interconnected by their respective missions. And the church is also the bride of Christ. The works of Henri de Lubac (translated and published by Balthasar in German) became important for me precisely because they retrieve these images of the church, which are underappreciated in the Protestant tradition. But I remain a stubborn Swiss Reformed pastor who is skeptical about the hierarchy of the Roman Catholic Church. (If the reader responds that I am creating a problem where there is none, I recommend giving the New Testament another read.) However, I am also all too familiar with the serious downsides of the Reformed churches and their ecclesial structures. Is there a perfect institutional structure for the church? There are better and worse ones, and some are indispensable,[15] yet in all structures what counts are the people who live in them. As for these people, I share Barth's confidence that the Truth is powerful enough to make us listeners of the Word ready to enter into the communion with the body of Christ.

The figure of ecclesial existence par excellence for Balthasar is Mary, the mother of Christ. Even though I do not agree with all of Balthasar's Mariological claims, his effort to retrieve the female aspect of the church is very important. It seems to me that the encounter with Adrienne von Speyr was one of the best things that happened in Balthasar's life, for men need an encounter with "real women" whom we can meet face to face. Mother Mary by herself is not enough; but once we meet "real women," we may come to a new appreciation of the mother of Jesus. When Jesus responds to a woman's

remark "Blessed is the mother who gave you birth and nursed you" by reply-
ing, "Blessed rather are those who hear the word of God and obey it" (Luke
11:27–28), we could turn things around and say, "Blessed is the one who has
such a mother," especially since, according to Luke, Mary actually did keep
Jesus' words in her heart (Luke 2:51). Modern attachment theory has taught
us how indispensable the mother (or another person to whom the child is
attached) is for her child in every respect of the child's development. Christ
received himself from his mother! We should not forget this. Balthasar was
right in putting so much emphasis on the gender issue in theology. We still
have a lot to do in this area.

If I meet Balthasar again some day in another place, it still might be presumptuous of me to give him a hug, but certainly I would want to give him
a smile.[16]

Chapter Three

And the Word Became Text

Materialism, the Culture of Despair, and the Spirit of Childhood

Anthony DiStefano

After reading Aesop's fable of the fox and the grapes to my son one evening, I considered how to adapt it for readers in the age of science. In one rendition, a scientist, working late into the night to develop a new theory of Something Big and Important, examines a large stack of notes containing previous theories. After hours of mounting frustration, he violently pushes his notes away in apparent defeat. Not to be kept from his prize, however, he regathers, reviews, and reworks his notes, tosses most of them away, and states triumphantly, "Finally, a new theory of Something Small and Somewhat Important." In a second rendition the same scientist, again frustrated at his lack of progress, throws all his notes away, walks out of his laboratory, and says, "There's nothing important here, anyway. Time to work on something worthwhile." The scientist is similar to the fox in Aesop's original in that frustration at his inability to attain the desired object leads to the conclusion that he was wasting his time.

It is these responses and how to counter them from within the Christian story that I will address in the following reflections on what Hans Urs von Balthasar has taught me about the nature of modernity and its conflict with Christianity. For the past nine years I have taught theology classes at Xavier College Preparatory, a Catholic school for girls in Phoenix, Arizona, where I have become convinced that the materialistic philosophy endemic to modern Western culture and reflected in the language and vision of my students is in part an attempt to exact a measure of revenge on those mysteries of human life and experience that continue to elude those who embrace a limited form of rationality. Call it the Sour Grapes Theory of materialistic reductionism. The results of this reductionism are not better theories of complex realities but rather poorer and less inclusive ones, along with the skepticism and resignation evident in our society today. Every day I witness signs of the domesticated despair generated by the failures of materialism, as every version of it, from the stark versions found in the writings of Sigmund Freud, Richard Dawkins, and Peter Singer that I assign in different classes, to the more upbeat declarations of independence of the atheists-by-default that fill my classroom, produces a flattened version of reality that leads those afflicted by it to lower their expectations of themselves and their world. As C. S. Lewis said in *The Weight of Glory*, we are far too easily pleased, convincing ourselves that we are satisfied with making mud pies in a slum because we are unable to imagine what is meant by the offer of a holiday at sea. This is hardly surprising, as we have been catechized to believe that the slums are all that exist, and that it is really not so bad there. And what is a "holiday at sea," after all, but a product of wish fulfillment, the will to power, memes, or blind credulity?

Balthasar's insights on modernity's loss of faith in and wonder at the mystery of being, along with his discussion of the spirit of childhood, have helped me better understand these issues. I first read Balthasar after graduate school, and occasional raids into his writings and questions for friends who knew him well convinced me of the need to explore further. The following reflections are therefore the result not of any formal reading or teaching of Balthasar but rather of personal study, nearly a decade of teaching high school girls, and a few years worth of bimonthly meetings of a Communio study circle, in which the joys of fellowship, pints of Guinness, and discussions and arguments have challenged and hopefully sharpened my perspective. And, most importantly, raising three children has been a constant and at times painful learning experience, directly related to what I will say about the characteristics of spiritual childhood in the second part of this essay. My children, along with the students I teach, are both the inspiration for my work and my best guides and teachers.

I

What strikes me about many of my students is their lack of trust in the givenness of the world, which reveals itself in boredom, directionless rebellion, and estrangement from themselves, those around them, and the traditions that have nurtured them. This is apparent every time we read passages from Nietzsche diagnosing the spiritual malaise haunting modernity. In *The Gay Science,* Nietzsche reports that shadows are appearing over Europe, as "a kind of sun seems to have gone down, some old deep trust to have turned into doubt." This process and its consequences remain as opaque to most of us today as they were to Nietzsche's contemporaries, as it is difficult to convince people that the floor on which they are standing is being removed. Likewise, the indictments of his madman concerning the murder of God make little sense to my students, as Nietzsche demands a radical reimagining of our central convictions about ourselves and the world in which we live, including the accepted moral order. Bewilderment and indifference continue to greet his demand. What I find fascinating about class discussions on this material is the moral schizophrenia that frames them, as many students hold an untroubled allegiance to the permanence of what they take to be the good while at the same time maintaining a skepticism about the good and our ability to articulate it. After virtue, indeed. The English blockheads whom Nietzsche lampoons in *Twilight of the Idols* for celebrating God's absence while insisting on an ethic that presupposes his presence have plenty of American cousins, as students will protest that they have a friend or relative who not only is an atheist but also a really good person. In their assessment, only the most sectarian bigot would question this, as they are convinced that God has little to say that they did not already know, especially about morality. To suggest that the issue is neither moral performance nor the number of ethical injunctions that Christians share with atheists but rather the very concept of the good is to be met with silence. Any ensuing discussion will usually veer in the direction of "Well, this is all a matter of opinion, anyway" — an invitation for me to move on to something else. The predictability of the very same students who moments earlier were defending the moral goodness of their atheist acquaintances now arguing for a moral relativism fails to make such a move any less striking, no matter how often it occurs.

In the third volume of *The Glory of the Lord,* Balthasar claims that the *monde moderne* includes "a view of man as a mere calculating intellect, . . . the loss of relationship with God, the loss of all real nourishing roots, the quantifying of all value, the triumph of mathematics and technology all along the line, the shallow optimistic ideology of progress." Those "nourishing roots" include that which enables us to experience what Nietzsche called a deep trust in our world. When those roots are poisoned and dug up, much is lost, as my students demonstrate that what is at stake is the ability to speak a language that reflects a proper stance toward mystery, being, and the absolute. A discussion that I had with a student after class one day illustrates the absence of such a language.

B. was a bright and motivated student whom I taught both semesters her senior year. In the fall she took a course called Love and the Human Vocation, in which we examine different views of human personhood and the contrasting approaches to relationships, marriage, and sexuality that follow. In the spring she took Introduction to Philosophy, where one of our units covers arguments for and against the existence of God. An atheist or agnostic (she was not sure which), B. routinely expressed her discomfort with religious belief of every kind. Like many of her fellow students, she often wanted "the other side" of the story, by which they usually mean the "non-Catholic side," regardless of what topic we were considering. I finally learned to respond to this request with a variation of "This *is* the other side," for B.'s view of herself and her world, like that of most of my students, is expressed in the language of a secular modernity, which, though peppered throughout with the standard Catholic school jargon of "religious values," is materialistic to the core. Of course, most of my students recoil from the materialistic philosophy that they see in assigned readings, for they cannot bear the thought that the universe has, in the words of Richard Dawkins in his popular *River Out of Eden: A Darwinian View of Life,* "precisely the properties we should expect if there is, at bottom, no design, no purpose, no evil and no good, nothing but blind, pitiless indifference." This precludes few, however, from adopting a nihilistic stance, even if it must be cheerful enough to allow them a bright future. That many are uneasy with the contradictions inherent in their juggling act is evident, and one day B. admitted her doubts as she described her excitement about her upcoming graduation and her gratitude for all that she had been given. She then said, "I just want to thank *some-body*, but I don't know who. Can't I just thank my parents and teachers? Isn't that enough?" When I suggested that she knew what I would say, she mentioned Luigi Giussani, whose reflections on the religious sense we covered first semester. "Is he saying that I'm religious without even knowing it?" she asked. "Can't I leave God out of this?"

"In a world that no longer has enough confidence to affirm the beautiful," Balthasar wrote at the beginning of the first volume of *The Glory of the Lord*, "the proofs of the truth have lost their cogency." So too has the language of thanksgiving, which comes naturally to those who trust their deepest instincts and the world that they experience, but which becomes strange once they surrender their trust. In the rest of part 1, I will address as examples of this surrender what Allan Bloom called the fall of *eros* in the West and the personhood theory of Peter Singer. Common to both is what Gabriel Marcel saw as the degrading of a mystery by turning it into a problem, something we can solve or overcome by technique. The elusive and enigmatic character of mystery, which characterizes all personal and interpersonal realities and which can be grasped only imperfectly through words and requires the committed involvement of the subject, is denied by those who claim that improved methods of impersonal scientific analysis will lay siege to mystery and finally break open its secrets. This is the methodological sin of modernity, and its fruits are evident not only in the confusion of students like B. By claiming that we can "solve" the mysteries of ourselves and all our interactions with the world that we inhabit, we turn our old, deep trust into the skepticism and despair apparent today. Freud may have only jested about his homage to "our god *logos*," the type of scientific reason to which he granted exclusive rights to guide our thinking, but this commitment is hardly a joking matter, especially when we consider the price that we pay for it.

Modern attempts to disguise the nature and power of *eros* by reducing it to brute sexual desire or an itch in need of a pleasant scratch are reminders of the vapid character of reductionistic interpretations of human longings. From the clinical language of Freud's treatises on sexuality to the debaucheries celebrated in the media, *eros* has been so trivialized that it now runs the risk of becoming boring. Once respected as a dangerous, unpredictable force over which humans had no control, it has lost its potency and charm due to a century's worth of attempts to render it rationally intelligible and thus safe. Whereas the Greek poets and their successors produced poetry, drama, and tragedy of the first order to honor this dangerous god, we have renounced not only their reverence but also their forms of discourse. It is the sexologist and the psychologist, not the poet and the priest, who teach us about love and sex today. Christians will rightly point to the deepening of our understanding of love resulting from the Christ event, but we will always share with the ancient pagans, even in their celebration of ecstatic rites, a sensibility that refuses to treat *eros* as just another physical impulse. The cultic prostitution of antiquity deserves censure for many violations, but banality is not one of them. Today people speak the language of "It's only sex," as if the qualifier can erase from our memory the recognition that there is no such thing.

Some might reply that there is plenty of dangerous sex mysticism out there, but true disciples of D. H. Lawrence are hard to find now. It is the nature of our common language regarding sex that betrays us, as we speak of sexual orientations and expressions, highlighting our commitment to sacrificing the moral and spiritual content of sexuality at the altar of personal choice, the god we are most anxious to please these days. Unless you are a religious zealot, "immoral" has become a legal category, except in our condemnation of rape, pedophilia, and "unsafe" sex, which are morally repugnant because personal rights are violated and pregnancy or disease may result. My students always respond predictably to the more metaphysical claim of Leon and Amy Kass that "safe sex" is the delusion of shallow souls. "How judgmental!" they protest. In one class a student wondered aloud if the Kasses were young Catholics (!) who taught Natural Family Planning. "What about AIDS?" "What about overpopulation?" "Do they want *more* abortions?"

Similar skepticism greets John Paul II's theology of the body. Yet I see a barely concealed sadness behind the bewilderment that anyone believes this stuff, detected in the frequently heard claim "That would be nice if it were true." In our culture of raunch it is much safer to lower one's expectations and accept the assumptions that not only is everything sex, but sex is not worth fussing about. Growing up in the aftermath of Freud, Kinsey, the Cosmo girl, and the contraceptive revolution encourages a cynicism about seeing *eros* as anything interesting or important, much less transcendent.

What chance will a Diotima or John Paul II have in speaking to a society that treats pornography as kitsch and the human body as a playground on which to perform the rituals of polymorphous pleasure? From teenaged girls sporting tee-shirts with "Porn Star" emblazoned across their chests, to television physicians warning of four-hour erections as they peddle pharmaceutical intercourse, we are assaulted daily with reminders of how far we have fallen. And our modern version of *eros* is impossible either to celebrate or lament, as it can generate nothing dramatically compelling. The narrative possibilities of an *eros* who torments and slays are endless, and from the Greeks through Ovid, Shakespeare, and their modern heirs, writers have capitalized on these possibilities by creating characters who, in their willingness to die and kill for love, witness its awesome power. When Freud reduces *eros* to sex and writes that the aim of sexual desire is "union of the genitals in the act known as copulation, which leads to the release of the sexual tension and a temporary extinction of the sexual instinct—a satisfaction analagous to the sating of hunger," what possibilities remain for art of any kind?

It is neither Plato nor fundamentalist Christians who have driven the poets out of the city but rather the insipid orations of social scientists and the entrepreneurs following in their wake who, in their attempts to modernize and commodify *eros,* have reduced it to petty slogans. The poets have always known that the arrows of the god of love wound deeply, leaving scars and stirring a desire that no earthly comfort or pleasure can match, and Christian writers have eloquently witnessed longings for what eludes our grasp during our pilgrimage here on earth. We are restless creatures, doomed to frustration by the world's inability to fulfill our strongest desires. This tempts us to arm ourselves and fight back, which we do with our theories. Like the scientist in my renditions of Aesop, we respond to the frustration produced by *eros* either by shrinking its scope and grandeur to manageable proportions or by denying its power, all in an effort to gain absolution from that which must always escape our control. Perhaps we need a chastened Nietzschean madman in our public square announcing our murder of *eros* and demanding that we get, at the very least, a little imagination. Much is at stake here, for, as Balthasar noted, we are dealing with a "perversion of Being" which manifests itself in the formula "A is nothing other than. . . ." We must acknowledge with him that A is always still "something other than . . ." and follow C. S. Lewis in suggesting that if Freud can say that "It" is sublimated sex, we can say that sex is undeveloped "It." That this is truer to human experience is something that the poetic, dramatic, and artistic traditions of the West corroborate.

Our modern responses become possible, according to Balthasar, when we lose the "flair for the central mystery of being." We "unlearn" reverence, wonder, and adoration, and begin to overlook the "wondrousness of every single created entity," including and especially human beings. How better to understand the work of Peter Singer on personhood than as an illustration of Balthasar's point here? Singer strikes me as a combination of the scientist in my renditions of Aesop, someone who wants both to simplify at the expense of his subject matter and to ignore altogether the complexities that rise up in protest of his ideas. A theory that neatly specifies which human being counts as a person may contribute to Singer's goal to construct an ethics on entirely "rational" grounds, but what kind of rationality and at what price? A student this year discussed her assigned Singer reading with her mother, who thought that he had good points to make. Humans are, she noted, the only species that does not kill its retarded young. (I noted that humans are also the only species to honor their parents by taking care of them when they are no longer able to care for themselves.) This god *logos* is certainly demanding, but in rather grotesque ways — something that my students instinctively understand but struggle to articulate. Sometimes they are right on target. I will never forget when a student, silent all semester until we reached Singer, told the class that she had been diagnosed prenatally as a Down Syndrome child. Her mother refused the advice of her doctor to have an abortion, making it possible to for her to be at Xavier, listening to a noted philosopher describing how kindness will sometimes kill people like her. Another student asked if Singer really believes that a chimpanzee is more of a "person" than her severely retarded little brother, whom she reads to every night, while another asked if the preference of a thousand Nazis to kill outweighs the preference of three Jews to live. Singer answered a similar question, with a different ratio (ten to one), in a 1999 interview in *Psychology Today:* "Numbers matter, but I'd assume the preference of that one being not to die is much more intense than the preferences of the other ten to kill it. You'd have to live all eleven of those lives to know for certain." It is hard for us to know *for certain* that the hunted has a stronger preference not to be murdered than the hunters have to murder. This has to make someone's list of the most ridiculous and reckless things a philosopher has ever said. That his interviewer let him off the hook is almost as troubling as what he said.

C. S. Lewis once said that he did not believe that you could study people, but you could get to know them. But since getting to know people requires believing in the "wondrousness" of the person before you, what happens when we embrace the cynicism that appears in Singer? His inability to claim certainty in the example that he gives is not only absurd but also an indictment of the very thing that he is trying to achieve as an ethicist, for how can you say anything ethically meaningful about persons while treating them as mere abstractions who must measure up to an arbitrary standard of "personhood"? We are wise to recall that it is always those who say they "love humanity" in the abstract who proceed to murder real humans, always in the name of some greater good, and Singer plays along, regardless of his repeated dismissals of talk of any slippery slope. His preference utilitarianism is another variation on an old theme: the sacrifice of those incapable of defending themselves must be made for the good of those who can. I have tried to show up to this point some of the other sacrifices required when Freud's god *logos* demands that rationality be narrowly defined, believing that we are left at the whim of an abstract, textualized version of love, sexuality, persons, and reality that claims revenge upon mystery for its intractable refusal to bend before our intellects and our language. That this rage for explanation often produces accounts that increase the distance between the truth and its would-be conquerors should not be surprising, for treating human beings as objects defined by their biology and social functions is guaranteed to produce confusion.

In his reflections on Dostoyevsky's The Grand Inquisitor, Nicholas Berdyaev noted the fear that social reformers have of human freedom, which is always unwilling to keep in step with any utilitarian calculus. These reformers seldom believe that human beings are called to any kind of higher life, and cultivate a "euclidian mind, full of revolt and self-limitation at the same time," seeking to improve upon God's work, a task made necessary by the presence of evil and suffering that results from the burden of freedom placed upon weak humanity. The Inquisitor speaks for all those dissatisfied with the order of creation when he scolds Christ for his greatest failure: "And then, instead of giving clear-cut rules that would have set man's conscience at rest once and for all, you put forward things that are unfamiliar, puzzling, and uncertain.... By so doing you acted as if you did not love mankind." Revolt against this policy is required to overcome the evil of uncertainty regarding not only the moral order but also all the pressing questions of life. The cure is a "rationalized organization of life" that eliminates freedom but promises contentment, though it predictably leaves considerable debris in its wake, as is seen when we examine the best interpreters of their thought, the lives of the people who, like my students, illustrate the logical outcome of their proposals. In the remainder of this essay, I will draw attention to those features of spiritual childhood discussed by Balthasar that are a sort of antidote to the poisons of modernity discussed above.

II

It is helpful to remind ourselves that everything that we encounter is unnecessary and undeserved, that the cosmos and life within in it are gifts that have their source and meaning in the God who freely spoke them into being and sustains them by his word. The human freedom that is part of this gift is, as the Grand Inquisitor understood, the bane of any philosophy that seeks predictability, which is something that Kierkegaard recognized: "That God could create beings free over against himself is the cross that philosophy could not bear but upon which it has remained hanged." This highlights the disparity between Christianity and the Euclidean mind of the modern age, as against the *logos* celebrated by Freud. Christianity professes that the principle of intelligibility by which we understand anything presents itself in the frail guise of a human being. The word became flesh, not text, and the incarnational logic of Christianity exposes the pretense of every attempt to choose abstraction over the real. The incarnation of Christ is thus not an arcane dogma that theologians quibble over but rather an interpretive key that enables us to receive light and life. "Receive" is the salient point here, as it is in receptivity to God and his creation, and in giving thanks to him, that we are most human. Balthasar emphasizes this point in his reflections on spiritual childhood, a topic open to misunderstanding, especially by sentimentalists wishing to contrast the sweetness and light of an untroubled childhood with the stale and unexciting present that we muddle through as adults. Balthasar was aware of the need to avoid mere nostalgia and to refrain from romanticizing childhood as a state of lost paradise, and warned against attributing to the child virtues possible only for adults. Yet he draws the theme of childhood into fruitful conversation with the Christ event and shows, especially in his brief *Unless You Become Like This Child,* how the childhood of Jesus, and, by extension, the childhood of every person, is of continuing importance for all believers. This book is far more than its length suggests, as I discovered when I first sat down with it, anticipating a quick, unproblematic read. "Perhaps this will be devotional Balthasar," I thought, looking at the cover. "*Easy* Balthasar," I hoped, having recently been rebuffed in my attempt to speed through *Love Alone.* Instead I ran into a dense series of reflections on the unity of the Christian life, how childlikeness and mature discipleship flow from the same source. Our model in prayer, faith, and thanksgiving is Christ at the highest point of his maturity and responsibility, and taking seriously his and our childhood enables us to see the key element of our obedience as a "repetition of the eternal Son's loving readiness to obey the command of the Father." It is in childhood that we see for the first time, and often most clearly, the specific qualities that we are called to develop throughout our lives as disciples, as the end form toward which God calls us is nothing other than the original form out of which we live. And it is here, I believe, that we can find some of the resources to counter the despair produced by the habits of thought discussed in part 1.

One of those qualities is the capacity for wonder and amazement. Christ had an "eternal childlike amazement" over everything, which comes naturally to those who are, in Balthasar's words, open to the absolute. In our modern societies we have developed the skill of sliding down the surface of things in new and frightening ways, and it is not surprising to hear college teachers complain about their students' lack of critical thinking skills, as a sense of wonder is the beginning not just of philosophy but of all learning. While we should avoid apocalyptic rants about the shallowness of the modern student and what this means for the future of Western society, I cannot deny a surprising crudeness in some of the things that my students say, which seems related to an unwillingness or inability to experience wonder at anything outside their immediate frame of reference. I have had students say that Plato's *Republic* is stupid, that Wendell Berry is a judgmental idiot who lacks the brains to make it in a world of computer technology, and that asking even the most elementary philosophical questions is a waste of time. One should expect students, especially the younger ones, to say things like this from time to time, but what concerns me is how quickly dismissive so many students weeks away from graduation are when dealing with texts and issues, and how they display few signs of the capacity to be unsettled by the questions raised by writers such as Plato and Berry. Balthasar was correct to note that wonder and amazement are difficult to preserve today in light of a pedagogy that stresses mastering tasks and grasping automatic functions, as our increasingly technical approach to education often equates the acquisition and display of technical skills with a good education. While many students may not be able or even wish to read foundational texts with a modicum of interest, some have learned to text message without looking at their cell phones. Technology adds a new dimension to our delight in "mastering things" that can reduce our capacity for wonder by dulling our sensibilities to anything outside the boundaries of moment-to-moment life. The world of information that students have at their fingertips encourages habits which ironically keep the most important information from them, and they often lose themselves in trivial activities and come to see education as reducible to "the facts," those bits of information that educators decide are important for them to store in their short-term memory, regurgitate on demand, and then forget. The world in which our children live appears to be shrinking, not growing larger, and Luther's *incurvatus in se* takes on a new technological meaning as our young are finding little outside themselves to be amazed by. Balthasar makes an interesting comment about *eros* that connects with this loss of wonder, saying how it "can keep alive an awed amazement at one's partner's self-surrender within all the routine of the common life, even after the first sensual stimulus has evaporated." The dullness of spirit apparent in so much of our modern chatter about sex is of a piece with students' attitudes toward learning and the world that they inhabit.

Fundamental to the sense of wonder and amazement Balthasar describes is the receptivity seen in children. The virtues of docility and trust are not achieved by children, according to Balthasar, as they are the most unreflectedly natural things for them. In the childhood Jesus calls us to, there is always a confident hope that becomes our present reality, as we live in trust that we already possess everything we ask for. This trains us to see ourselves as dependent creatures, with all the vulnerability that this entails. For Balthasar, this dependence is associated not with fear, but rather with thanksgiving. Plea and thanks are indistinguishably one in the child, and the parent has an obligation to teach the deeper meaning of thanks, as Balthasar notes: "[The child] should not be taught to be thankful only for specific things received, but his original awareness that he himself—his 'I'—is something given and that he must give thanks for it, should also be transposed into the sphere of the maturing consciousness." In this way we never outgrow childhood. There is no initiatory rite or graduation ceremony that places us outside the realm of dependence where we are to be thankful for our very being. Thus it is not enough, as my student B. wished, to thank only one's parents and teachers who helped her during her high school years. She intuitively understood the need to give a different kind of thanks, even if she could not express it. This goes beyond the religious sense to a definite form of revelation, as Balthasar explained: "Only the Christian religion, which in its essence is communicated by the eternal child of God, keeps alive in its believers the lifelong awareness of their being children, and therefore of having to ask and give thanks for things."

Passages such as this are counterintuitive to my students, and not just because of their concerns to avoid any sense of religious exclusivism. We tell our students in myriad ways that they are becoming independent young women who are ready to make their own futures. Childhood is a phase they passed through on their way to autonomy. And, apparently, they are getting through it earlier than ever. The death of seven-year-old Jessica Dubroff in April of 1996 is a chilling example of the cult of autonomy currently celebrated in American society. Jessica, wearing a hat that said "Women Fly," was attempting to become the youngest pilot to complete a cross-country plane flight when she, her father, and her flight instructor crashed and were killed while trying to take off on the second leg of their flight. Her mother, who taught Jessica to avoid words like "danger" or "risk" and told the press, "I beg people to let children fly if they want to fly," celebrated her daughter's freedom in the midst of this tragedy, while television journalist Jane Pauley opined, "She may have lost her life, but she'd had her freedom." As the father of a seven-year-old daughter, I have to wonder what kind of thing this "freedom" is. Yet this mind-set is so common today that we instinctively react against anyone who dares to challenge it, as is seen in some of the responses to C. S. Lewis since the cinematic version of *The Lion, the Witch and the Wardrobe* came out a few years back and brought new attention to Lewis and his Narnia stories. In "The Passion of C. S. Lewis," published in the

New York Review of Books in February, 2006, Alison Lurie expressed a concern shared by other critics over Lewis's portrayal of the Pevensie children and their relationship with Aslan, challenging how his guidance is so essential to their well-being. According to Lurie, to accept authority, to love and follow Aslan instinctively, and to believe that by ourselves we are weak, ignorant, and helpless may work in the fictional realm of Narnia, but it does not make sense in our real world. Unless, of course, we are conservative Christians who "will admire and fear and obey whatever impressive looking and powerful male authority figures we come in contact with." This is a deluded mind-set, cultivated among those taught to vote against their economic and social interests and to bow at the feet of rich and powerful figures such as Donald Trump, or worse.

There you have it: submission to Aslan, the creator and redeemer of Narnia, finally uncovered as the virtue of patriarchy-loving Republicans. Who knew? Well, those for whom *dependence* is a dirty word and who think that the bumper-sticker philosophy expressed by the phrase "Question Authority" runs deep. Lurie's reading leads her to miss most of what Lewis actually does suggest in his Narnia books about authority, including the important question of how we are to determine which authorities to trust. Elsewhere Lewis addressed more formally these questions, and in the second book of *Mere Christianity* he noted that *authority* is not the scary word that those like Lurie wish to make it. In fact, believing things on authority simply means believing them because you have been told them by someone you trust. Most of what we believe is on the basis of authority, which is true not only for theocrats who believe that God is a wealthy Republican, but also for the more enlightened folks who vote knowingly, distrust the rich, and read the *New York Review of Books*. Rather than pretending that children are little adults in temporary disguise who are best served by bigger adults allowing them their "freedom," is it not more sensible to help children gradually learn how to discriminate between conflicting authorities and to develop their abilities to make wise choices? And does this not include parental oversight and direction? Lurie's article reveals the common fear that such direction is little more than an indoctrination that cancels out the freedom and responsibility of the child, and reflects the common prejudice that parents, especially fathers, are very much like the dim-witted oafs of TV sitcoms who cannot be trusted to make dinner, much less guide their children into young adulthood. Parents and teachers today are increasingly expected to uncritically affirm the opinions and feelings of children, regardless of their content. Imagine the master carpenter asking the apprentice, "How do *you* feel that the table should be made?" and you get the picture. The impulse to shape and govern everything on our own apart from the care and experience of our elders, no matter our age, is a central feature of "technical man," and it has, according to Balthasar, more than any other factor helped to empty the mystery of childhood of its value.

George Orwell once said that the essence of being human is that one is prepared to be defeated and broken up by life, which is the inevitable price of loving other people. Apart from the "defeated" in this statement, this is consistent with what we know about the human condition as Christians. To be human is to be vulnerable, something that people such as Peter Singer who are trying to redefine personhood for our brave new world implicitly deny, which leads them to miss what is most important about being human. In my Love and the Human Vocation class students read Henri Nouwen's *Adam: God's Beloved* following our survey of Singer and personhood theory, an account of how Adam Arnett, a severely disabled epileptic who lacked the capacity to speak or to do much of anything on his own, became Nouwen's teacher by leading him to a deeper understanding of what it means to be a human beloved by God. In his brokenness, Adam became for Nouwen an icon of the brokenness of Jesus and thus a true representative of the human condition. By watching Adam and above all caring for him every day — or, by "getting to know" him in Lewis's terms — Nouwen passed through a difficult and painful process of self-discovery. Over time he came to see Adam's "passion" and death as a reminder of a truth about ourselves that we often neglect:

> The truth is that a large, if not the largest, part of our lives is passion. Although we all want to act on our own, to be independent and self-sufficient, we are for long periods of time dependent on other people's decisions. Not only when we are young and inexperienced or when we are old and needy but also when we are strong and self-reliant. Substantial parts of our success, wealth, health, and relationships are influenced by events and circumstances over which we have little or no control. We like to keep up the illusion of action as long as we can, but the fact is that passion is what finally determines the course of

our life. We need people, loving and caring people, to sustain us during the times of our passion and thus support us to accomplish our mission.

"He who does the truth comes into the light" (John 3:21). Nouwen illustrates this through the story of his work with Adam and what he learned from him. Having struggled all his life to be independent and self-secure, in need of no one but himself, Nouwen realized his mistaken notions through loving one of the least of his brothers, and his book highlights the contrast between Christian and materialistic understandings of knowledge of human things and how we attain it. André Gide wrote that in Dostoyevsky what is opposed to love is not hate but rather "rumination of the brain." The nihilist in his novels is a "lackey of the brain," committed to rationalistic schemes that make love unnecessary and finally incomprehensible. As Nouwen shows, it is only love that reveals the truths about human persons, and love requires us to treat persons as mysteries whom we can only gradually get to know through commitment and risk, not as problems to be solved at a critical distance. This is hardly a new theory of personhood discovered by Nouwen as he did research in a home for the severely disabled; it is another illustration of a truth found throughout the history of salvation. In the silent passion of Adam Arnett something of what it means to be human is spoken to those who embrace the logic of the *logos* made flesh. The form of reason pursued by modernity is deaf to such things, as its *logos* dictates that subjective engagement distorts and demands a clarity that leaves little room for uncertainty. Any teacher of theology or philosophy will regularly hear this demand, along with the agnosticism and cynicism that flow from it. Why does God, if he exists, not make things more clear to us? Why should we bother with questions that cannot be answered in a definitive manner? In our demand for a disinterested certainty, we moderns adopt a judicial pose before God, placing him "in the dock" and waiting for a well-argued brief before we issue our favorable verdict. This is also true of any question regarding values, which we now perceive in terms of personal choices made in the marketplace of ideas.

I do not know if Balthasar read any of the writings of Charles Dickens, but the English novelist believed that inherent in the human heart is the quality of Fancy, the inclination to respond with wonder and imagination to the world. We must nurture Fancy, and we can bludgeon it by miseducation, something that routinely occurs in Dickens's novels. In *Hard Times* the schoolmaster Thomas Gradgrind, a "man of facts and calculations," chastises his daughter for beginning a sentence with the words "I wonder." "Louisa, never wonder!" he interrupts. "Herein lay the spring," the narrator says, "of the mechanical art and mystery of educating the reason without stooping to the cultivation of the sentiments and affections. Never wonder. By means of addition, subtraction, multiplication, and division, settle everything somehow, and never wonder." Behind this sentiment is the belief that humans are weak, selfish brutes prone to ignorance, a belief common to those who resent the desire of the unwashed masses to raise their eyes above the confines of a purely naturalistic world and imagine there is anything or anyone out there. Rumors of mystery and magic, of realities that transcend the capacities of the Euclidean mind, of a holiday at sea that takes us out of the slums cannot be tolerated. Never wonder. There is a reasonable explanation for our delusions.

I have suggested that much of this tendency of thought is the result of frustration at the inability to understand and control that which eludes our critical abilities. This frustration can easily turn to anger, as can be seen in some of the writings of Richard Dawkins, the latest village atheist to defend the honor of Lady Reason against her villainous detractors. I briefly survey Dawkins on religious belief in my philosophy course, and reading him is great fun, as his ejaculations on religion, morality, and meaninglessness remind me of the comic books that I read as a youth, filled as they were with an overheated rhetoric of large capital letters and triple exclamation points. "Haven't you fools been listening?" is the sneer running through Dawkins's writings on society and religion, and I am almost beginning to feel sorry for him, as it is increasingly painful to watch his intellectual gymnastics bear him so little fruit. Almost. For this frustration is more visible, because less skillfully concealed, in so many of my students, who are paying the price for being raised in a society badly confused about first things. They are closer to childhood than their teachers and parents, and they are impatient to distance themselves from much of what they and others associate with it. It will not be long now when my own children, the oldest of whom is seven, will become visibly embarrassed by the many reminders of their dependence on others, especially their mother and father. This is natural, a necessary part of growing up. But how do I help them, and my students, to resist the temptation to go further and declare a complete independence that helps them to miss what is essential to being fully human? The first impulse of the teacher in me is to lecture, to assign readings, to target their intellects with the clear draughts of sound doctrine, but this is a mistake. The correct "answer" is love, and not just the saccharine niceness that merely affirms but rather the kind of commitment that leads Henri Nouwen to share himself with Adam Arnett, that leads my student to read to her retarded brother every night, that led the Son of God to pour himself out for the world. For as Balthasar and many others within the Christian tradition have written, love alone enables us to grasp the mystery of other persons, and to give ourselves to them. This is not the solution of an abstract problem that exists outside us; it is the entering into a mystery that we are caught up in. This is one reason why Balthasar could write so compellingly about St. Thérèse of Lisieux as a theological witness, pointing out the need for a tempered hagiography to vitalize and rejuvenate theology. Of course, we must test and hone our ideas as a necessary part of our witness to Christ, and parents and teachers will always teach. Part of my witness will be to teach my children and students about Jesus' call to become like the child they once were and, in the most important things, still are. As Balthasar teaches, in childhood there are natural guards against our false sophistication, and in neglecting these guards we fall prey to modes of thought that leave us incapable of understanding who and what we are as human persons: weak, vulnerable creatures beloved by a God who gives us so many gifts that our natural response should always be an amazed word of thanks.

Chapter Four

The Message in a Bottle

How Hans Urs von Balthasar
Changed My Mind

Raymond Gawronski, SJ

A literate friend of mine from our high school in the New York area used to quip, "The onward march of Western civilization ground to a halt in Jersey." Some would say that it ground to a halt a long way east of there, in the centuries while something new but not unrelated was being created on our shores. No matter: it was the "message in a bottle," as Hans Urs von Balthasar described his opus in his *Epilog,* that I discovered as a Jesuit scholastic. Henri de Lubac called him the "most learned man of the twentieth century," and although that century was a dark time for Western civilization, Balthasar knew and treasured the patrimony of millennia better, perhaps, than did any other living human being, and I believe that he understood it all through the lens of Jesus Christ. It was his message that has changed my life and has, in fact, given birth to the Jesuit priest I have become.

It is not too much to say that were it not for Hans Urs von Balthasar, I never would have attempted a doctorate in theology. I would have seen no reason for it. I never wanted to be a theologian. The ones whom I had met as an undergraduate seemed arrogant and too full of themselves to have much room for God, and although subsequent acquaintance has revealed exceptions, first impressions stick. My roommate in college gave himself completely to a most influential German theologian who dominated the field from the 1960s onwards. He was introduced to this theologian's thought by a very appealing ex-priest on our campus who had come back from Germany full of this theologian and accompanied by a very attractive

German wife. This "new theology" seemed to him to be far more appealing, far more real, than the neo-Scholastic theology that filled textbooks of our colleges. But although it claimed to be very "relevant," it actually continued the intellectual tradition of Germany of the past few centuries, and therein lay a difficulty for me.

I have been asked to describe how "Balthasar changed my mind," and I will attempt to do that. But before I can go into how my mind was changed, I must relate how Balthasar helped me to see how my mind could, or should, be used at all. I have also been asked to be autobiographical, and that is what I must be. For a son of a Polish concentration camp survivor to give his life to the work of a man whose academic major was *Germanistik* takes some explanation. For Balthasar had no terminal degree in either philosophy or theology; it was the study of German culture and literature that was his academic field. His work, and the message in his bottle, were profoundly European, but it was even more profoundly Christian.

I picked up that bottle in the wilds of America, but my own roots here are fairly shallow. My family is deeply rooted in Catholic Poland, but, not untypically, with strong connections of blood and culture with Poland's neighbors on either side. Although Balthasar's beloved (and lamented) Nietzsche was so taken by the passion for freedom of the Polish nation that he proudly boasted of Polish origins, his presumptive intellectual heirs in the German intellectual world shared none of his admiration for the nation of my family. Indeed, the science and philosophy of that language were for a considerable stretch given to its utter destruction. So there were good reasons why I have not been drawn to a theological tradition that seemed to have ignored the doings of Nazi Germany, at least looking east.

For a number of reasons, Balthasar gave me hope that a Western theologian might be brother to Slavic Christians. Given recent history, there was much need for healing, but that need often was ignored. The one time I met him and was able to ask him a question, Karl Rahner seemed uninterested in the east of Europe except insofar as it dealt with the West's agendas.[1] Others with whom I spoke viewed the East with contempt as a failure in the Marxist utopias that they dreamed of creating in Central America; at the heart of that was contempt for the "piety of the lower middle class." In stark contrast, Balthasar was pious, interested in the east of Europe, well aware of the horrors of communism.

By the time of Vatican II, the Rhine seemed to be flowing into the Tiber. Incredibly, to me, the countries of western Europe most implicated either by outright aggression or by cowardice and collaboration in the nightmares of the twentieth century became the very ones to set about transforming a thousand years of Catholic experience, while ignoring the "suffering church" to the east, a church that they had been ignoring for a very long time. Perhaps because of his Hungarian grandfather, more likely because of his deeper commitment to the tradition, Balthasar managed to do an utterly remarkable thing: he was able to fully represent the best of his German tradition (and along with it, the best of Western Catholicism) and yet be so fully grounded in Christ that he was able to use his cultural specificity as a way to make contact with others, with full respect. That means the religions, cultures, literatures of other lands — India, China, as well as the "forgotten Europe" — were always part of his purview. When he wrote, "If any book deserves to survive the twentieth century it is *The Gulag Archipelago*," he revealed a sensitivity directly at odds with his contemporaries in the German-speaking world (and their American disciples), who, far from fully understanding and repenting of the fatal errors of their Idealistic tradition, were triumphantly exporting a version of it to the Third World in the form of liberation theology. The fact is that tens of millions of people enslaved in the communist world were suffering extermination and hell on earth while theologians in the west of Europe, ignoring their suffering, spun a vision of their own, fundamentally related to the worldview that was creating this hell on earth. Balthasar seems a lone exception.

Viewed from a different angle, and prior to these considerations, there was the Jansenist-flavored neo-Scholasticism of my American Catholic boyhood. The pre-Vatican II church balanced a dreadfully desiccated intellectual world with a very rich devotional life: whatever one might experience (or not) in the manuals was amply made up for by the riches of the devotional life. After the Council, the devotional life was systematically leveled. Seeing the arrogance and seeming sterility of the "new theology," I came to see that the hyperdevelopment of the *ratio* that I had come to identify as a characteristic of the modern church was not unrelated to the horrors of the modern world. It is possible that, as a Slav, I was especially led to worship God in beauty. Liturgy, song, poetry, the beauty of nature; feelings, intuitions, dreams, visions — these were the stuff of religion. Some of my religion teachers in early life kept trying to limit religion to the driest of catechism material; and the modern theologians who succeeded them (the children of Lonergan and Rahner) only seemed to want to update the whole thing and to do this, again, without benefit of a devotional life (in spite of the examples of their teachers), while being very "technical" in their whole method. In short, an approach entirely different from that was necessary if religion were to speak to me.

By the end of college, in 1971, I had "checked out" not only from the Western theological tradition but also from the intellectual tradition. For the reasons mentioned, I felt excluded from it; I felt that I and those who shared my people's history had no place there. There also seemed to be no place for an intuitive intellect, no place for beauty. Eventually, I sought refuge in the Eastern church, especially the Russian, for, apart from the nineteenth and early twentieth centuries, it was so uncerebral, but rather mystical, experiential, ascetical, holy. The modern theologians of my own Catholic tradition barred the way from my entering into the holy wilderness of God. Everything had to become as controlled, as rationalized, as completely figured out as the countries of the Common Market, this new dream world of the Benelux and the German *Wirtschaftswunder.* That was about the only *Wunder* around in the 1960s, and it had a legion of devotees. The Rhine was overflowing the Tiber, and no other rivers were allowed.

But the problem was even bigger than the East-West divide, and that further division between Russia and everyone else. The roots of this were ancient, and they transcended subsequent divisions. The spirit that drove Luther away from Catholicism was a spirit that could crave a freedom, and a truth, beyond that contained in the syllogisms of St. Thomas and his smug-seeming heirs. And although in a profound way it was clear that Luther had "gotten it wrong," there was also a sense in which his insistence on the heart, and on a passionate, biblical relation with the God of blood and guts resonated profoundly with me. It also profoundly resonated with Balthasar, who keeps looking over his shoulder to Luther.[2] Even as Luther as pivotal figure in German national consciousness was problematic for me, as another child of the northern forests, radically skeptical of the often cynical wisdom of more ancient peoples, Latin or Greek — or even Hebrew — he drew me as well. But like Balthasar, I had known the sweetness of God in the sacraments, in the liturgies, in the faith and holiness of what he liked to call "the Catholica," and although I longed to see her liberated from her neo-Scholastic and, frankly, Latin captivity, I also knew that the various cultural responses, whether the Germanic one of Lutheranism or the Slavic one of Russian Orthodoxy, were inadequate to the universality of the Catholica.

In this, Balthasar offers a vision of the church that takes into account Reformation concerns while remaining fully faithful to the Catholica. His love of the church is breathtaking, surpassed only by his love for her bridegroom. He has no patience with a morbid traditionalism. And, although he is fully in communion with the successor of St. Peter, he insists as well that the center of the church is the Real Presence, the Eucharist, wherever it is celebrated and adored in the world, not in any relics in the Vatican.

As time went by, I came to see that because of my family's history I could not "do theology" as my peers did. I do theology from the other side of Europe, and, to turn a phrase, from yet another side of Auschwitz: from the losing side of history many times over, one that kept losing in the prisons of the Soviet world for many decades after the Nazi camps were emptied. It is a different way to see things. Balthasar took the crisis in Western civilization seriously, and he emerged as the one voice that was able to help redeem his native German — and European — civilization in my eyes. Ratzinger continues that project. Other theologians, building heavily on German Idealism, never dealt with the profound evil that emerged from their tradition. Or else, like Hans Küng (exempted from any need for rethinking as a Swiss), they just kept on moving into the modern world, as if they were not part of the problem. So a certain feel of arrogance and blindness to spiritual realities and whole worlds of injustice attached to the theological establishment that seemed oblivious to the fact that millions of the faithful suffered unspeakable tortures — and heaven kept appearing, and speaking to, the likes of shepherds, whether in Judea, Portugal, or Bosnia.

As I noted earlier, Balthasar did not so much change my mind as show me that I could use my mind to come to God and not just to some highly articulated mental edifice. The other theologians, lost in *ratio,* had nothing of *intellectus* to them to commend them to me. Balthasar prayed, led me to Scripture, led me to beauty. More, he was clearly obedient to the church, and his spirit of humble obedience was like balm after some decades of the often sophomoric theologians that the modern world has produced. He showed the way to have the spirit of obedience: the presumption of obedience, trying to place oneself heart and soul in union with the magisterium and the tradition, while thinking critically "in full communion" with the best of the world and other Christians, and living the tension of the dialogue — but always, always, in full communion with the Catholic faith. And underneath this obedience was the simple spirit of reverence, which, when encountered, always witnesses that one is in the presence of the One who is always greater, and of a soul that is perceiving that.

But how did I discover him? After my own realization of the inadequacy of the neo-Scholasticism of my boyhood Catholicism, and the gradual articulation of my own hunger for mysticism — that is, for God — I searched for, and eventually found, much sustenance in the world of comparative religions, or, more accurately, comparative mysticism. Starting in a college year spent traveling around the world with him, Huston Smith became both mentor and friend. I trusted him, for he knew the Western intellectual tradition and yet believed in an intellectuality rooted in the mystical vision — that is, in intellect rather than *ratio.* By the 1970s, he had begun to discover Islam and one of its great teachers, in its Sufi interpretation, Seyyed Hossein Nasr. The group around him — the Perennialists — were speaking of sacred tradition as bearing something lost to the technocratic mind, which was exactly the mind that was barring the way to the Catholic tradition.

So when, in graduate school years, Smith suggested to me that a man named Hans Urs von Balthasar was the only contemporary Christian who could speak to my concerns and gave me a copy of Balthasar's book *Prayer,* I was eager to read it. At the time, and for years afterwards, I found it impenetrable. The book utterly lacked the language of natural mysticism to which I was accustomed and the human control of things mystical that seems present throughout the nonbiblical world. And so my one desultory attempt to read Balthasar, as a graduate student in a bus on the New York Thruway, led me nowhere, and I did not approach him again for a half dozen years.

Later, in Berkeley, where I was beginning theology studies as a religious, I found myself turning to him. There was an epiphanic moment during that first year when I had gone to a non-Jesuit, seemingly conservative Catholic theology faculty to begin my first course in theology. The professor was a sophomoric modern recently doctored at the University of Chicago (at the end of the year, in a pattern now familiar to me, he left the priesthood and got married). We were to read an anthology of theologians — the usual liberal theologians whom I had been exposed to for twenty years and against whom I had developed strong antibodies: they simply struck me as spiritually superficial, technicians with no eye, or heart, for the deeper life-giving currents. In the collection, however, there was one Seyyed Hossein Nasr, the Sufi intellectual. I had heard him lecture in Teheran fifteen years before in one of Smith's classes. His writings on sacred tradition were the only writings in the "Christian" collection that struck a resonant chord within me.

There was one other student who clearly felt the same way. His story is illustrative of the times and the need that Balthasar filled. Tom Case had been a published poet and long-term bohemian resident of San Francisco, Boulder, Mendocino County. He had picked up the thread of Catholicism through a chance reading of Belloc and Chesterton. Desirous of being received into the "One True Church," he went to local parishes in San Francisco, either to be told that there was no reason for him not to simply stick with his native Episcopalianism, or, elsewhere, to be enthusiastically presented with Latin American liberation theology. As we spoke, I realized that we had two pieces that needed to be connected. Through the counterculture, we had experienced the rediscovery of the supernatural, of the mystical, especially in Asian traditions. But we had also retained a particular attachment to the person of Jesus and also a sense that in the papacy of John Paul II the church was miraculously glowing through the dark night of modernity, emerging from its ruins. And there seemed to be no one in the theological establishment who was making this connection between the Catholic tradition and where the Spirit seemed to be leading the church today.

And then there appeared Balthasar, in whom at long last I found a voice big and strong enough to bear the song of the Catholic faith in the halls of academe. In him I found a Catholicism that was unquestionably faithful, reverent, wise, and loving, and also tremendously erudite and critically intelligent without giving criticism the last word. That goes to "love alone": a wisdom that was broad and totally open to all that is good, true, and beautiful in the world, including its mystical traditions (*logoi spermatikoi*); and a total commitment to Christ, his cross, and his church, in communion with the saints and mystics, of all simple, holy believers of all times and places.

As I began to read Balthasar, I was always led to prayer and to a prayerful reading of Scripture. This was something that other theologies had never done for me, and it served to confirm my discernment that in this thinker I had found someone to whom I could entrust my mind, my *Geist*. And then, in my first year of theology, I was asked to review *Seeing the Form*, the first volume of *The Glory of the Lord*, for a Catholic journal. I found myself reading the book several times and seeing that I had found the theological master in whose work I would find that for which I was hungering.

Still, in the 1980s, Balthasar was not yet being taught at many of our major institutions (a situation that still obtains to a considerable extent even now, over twenty years later). A theology that insists on mysticism as an essential source is quite alien to much of modern academic theology. When I began my own studies in theology, I felt that I had to opt for the mystical at the price of the intellectual. I moved into the world of the Russian spiritual tradition and completed a master's thesis on the life and work of Russo-Canadian mystic Catherine de Hueck Doherty. Her central teaching—"Fold the wings of the intellect and enter the heart"—certainly spoke to the *ratio/intellectus* divide, in altered words. She had deep roots in a Russian Romantic tradition that was really Slavophile, and she had attempted to be a missionary of the best of that tradition to the West. She was Catholic, but she "breathed with both lungs" and caustically criticized what she saw as the hyperrationality of the technologized West.

Catholicism in America, at least in its post-Vatican II version, was simply unable to speak to something in me—perhaps it was the "Slavic soul."[3] I had found the "chattering classes" disconnected from their hearts, and for all the "God-talk," God seemed nowhere in evidence. So I too was tempted to opt for the spirit of the Slavophiles, cursing the darkness of the West, finding refuge in a romantic vision of the mystical East, whether in the forests of Russia (and Canada) or even further east.

And yet I was a Jesuit now, with years of philosophical formation behind me,[4] and an intellectual hunger that the heart alone could not satisfy. If I had to choose between the two, heart would win over head every time; I was only too aware of what a head-centered world would look like, having seen the lived fruits of modern philosophy in modern Europe. And yet, having spent much time in some villages of the Soviet Union, I was also mindful that a world that was all heart and no head would be very undesirable indeed. To put it in very different terms: I had a strong sense for the nothingness of all that is not God, and for the folly of all that is not of God. This could lead me to a total silence; and yet as a man in the world, I had to speak. What could I say? Who could help me say it?

As I pondered this dilemma, about to continue my work on Catherine de Hueck Doherty to the doctoral level (I ambitioned a biography), Balthasar emerged as the one figure who had taken with full seriousness the gap between the emptiness of all that is not God and the God revealed to us in the God-man Jesus. Balthasar alone, it seemed to me, had seen that "only love is credible," and that the only word that could bridge the gap was the Word of God, Jesus. The Scripture — "words about the Word" — and the witness of tradition centered on the form of Christ, like filings around a magnet, as he noted. I instinctively felt that I could and would trust him as my teacher in the things of God. I have not regretted it.

In a way, it is not so much any idea or ideas of Balthasar — though his essay "Theology and Holiness" certainly is programmatic — that have been as powerful an influence on my life as the example of his own life. He himself valued his work with students far above all the other intellectual work — the ideas — that he presented. Anyone who has read his own description of his life's work will recall the importance of names such as "Robert Rast" in his sense of personal mission, conveyed personally. In this he was radically personal, writing that "in Heaven, everything is personal, nothing is private." His personalism, both in theory and practice, is made known to me from his writings, for I never had the opportunity to meet him (the one letter that I did write to him was most graciously answered just before his death — that letter arrived posthumously).

He was an aristocrat, and so a man who loved the peasantry as well, a natural ally in the common faith of millennia; he was not really a man of the urban middle class, and he did not share the contempt for the piety of the common person that has come to dominate modern theology.

He loved literature and art. In philosophy, he had a great sympathy for Nietzsche's suffering, and he greatly disliked Hegel, whose passion for system was, for him, anathema. This profound rejection of Hegel and all that he represents might explain part of the difficulty of his finding acceptance in America, for Hegel had the highest praise for America.[5]

He was an outsider all around: an aristocrat in a nonaristocratic age, a Renaissance man in an age of academic specializations, a genius with no chair

in the academy. In a heavily politicized church, he steadfastly rejected a political approach, always mindful of the Third Reich and the communist hells.
Taking his cue from Adrienne von Speyr, he would often repeat, "There is
no system in the things of God." And that explains his radical rejection of
Hegel and modern Idealist systems as radically anti-God in the end.

His relation with Adrienne von Speyr is rather illustrative of his relation
with the contemporary world. Anyone familiar with the literature on Balthasar will have to observe how many very serious scholars of Balthasar reject
his explicit assertion that his work and Adrienne's works were two parts of a
whole, of which hers is the more important part. I have often suspected an
unadmitted misogyny behind this rejection, but a misogyny cloaked with
a very respectable feminism. Von Speyr is often unacceptable to academics
precisely because her approach so embodies the classically feminine: she is a
visionary — intuitive, nonsystematic, nonconceptual — and this half of all
reality has never found a home in the academy. *Der Begriff* is simply lacking
in her writing; it is amply supplied by Balthasar's work that is rooted in hers.
Their works are complementary. Balthasar was a passionate defender of *das
Weibliche,* bemoaning the loss of the feminine as one of the greatest tragedies
of the contemporary world. Herself a physician and leading citizen of her
city, Adrienne yet had a soul radically feminine in its relation to God. It is
no wonder that John Paul II, with his sense for a Christian feminism, was so
obviously drawn to von Speyr, sending his blessing to a Roman conference
on her work. He was also much drawn to the work of Balthasar, whom he
finally made a cardinal.

In a prophetic word, Karl Rahner had said that Christians of the twenty-
first century would be mystics or they would not be. It belonged to Balthasar
to insist that essential as mysticism was, not all mysticism was Christian.
If many modern theologians developed a tradition going out from the
Scholastic tradition onto the branches of modern German thought, Balthasar worked his way back to the Fathers of the church, but not in the way
of a patrologist; rather, he himself has been called a "church Father living in
Switzerland." That is, he came to know the Fathers intimately, and then he
did what they did, and, some would say, became what they were.

That mysticism in fact belonged at the heart of theology was liberating
"beyond words." His central essay "Theology and Holiness" pointed the way
to the revolution that he would effect in theology, and in my life. Although

my boyhood in the pre-Vatican II church was hardly the profound "languishing in the wasteland of neo-Scholasticism" that Balthasar lamented in his formation, there was enough of this around in the Catholicism of the 1950s and early 1960s to make its presence felt, even in my young mind; and it was not appealing. The certitudes seemingly spun out of thin air, the atmosphere of a triumphalist omniscience combined with a dismal lack of human compassion, of heart, and the absence of the Word of God made me sympathize profoundly with his desire to bring down the whole edifice, like Samson chained in the Canaanite temple. The taboo against reading mystical literature was so forcefully impressed upon me as a child ("It is only for saints"; "It is only for Carthusians") that it was not until I was a professor of theology, having written on the mystics, that I was able to begin seriously reading the mystics. Although this might have been a salutary caution against the facile popularization of what must by its nature be somewhat esoteric, that which seems esoteric really is the birthright of the properly initiated Christian, as Balthasar insisted.

Further liberations followed. In the spirit of his writing it is pellucid that for Balthasar, Scripture is in fact inspired, holy writ, and he shows a way to be liberated from the tyranny of exegetes. When Balthasar wrote of "the little ones" and lambasted Scripture scholars for creating a new class of scribes and Pharisees who, while not entering the kingdom of heaven themselves, keep others from entering, my heart rejoiced. This is truly "liberation theology," for it is rooted and grounded in God.

And there is much more. The church that emerged from the Vatican Council was one in which the personal was much in abeyance. As I have noted, the devotional life that had sustained the faith of Catholics for centuries was dismantled in favor of ever more abstract approaches to God. To be sure, the new theology spoke much of transcendence and mystery, but precisely here, where the hunger of the human heart is the greatest, the forms that had sustained the Catholic heart from the beginning were being dissolved. Devotion to Christ in the Eucharist, devotion to the hearts of Jesus and Mary, devotion to the saints virtually disappeared. Eucharistic adoration ceased; the concrete images of the saints of heaven, whether in statues or stained glass, were removed, largely replaced by banners proclaiming programmatic ecclesial statements similar to advertisements (West) and propaganda (East).

A return to Scripture, which was to have replaced Catholic devotionals in a new, Word-oriented faith, was rendered ever more difficult both by the emergence of a class of scriptural experts/exegetes who increasingly blocked access to the Word of God by a growing thicket of sophisticated critique. Perhaps especially in the English-speaking world, a seemingly endless proliferation of translations removed the concrete, and beautiful, articulation of the Word of God that could speak to, and take root in, the heart. All of these changes were destructive of form — that is, iconoclastic; all of them tacitly presumed that all forms were strictly relative, and even unimportant, in the face of the abstract concept that the changing forms were seeking to convey.

Along with this destruction of traditional Catholic forms there grew an interest in "spirituality" that spread out from this world of shattered forms, seeking satisfaction beyond or without form. In the Christian tradition, this meant a turn from a traditional presentation such as the *Spiritual Exercises* of St. Ignatius, focusing on the person of Jesus and the details of his life and passion and death, to an often formless mysticism in which the Godhead of Meister Eckhart, or *The Cloud of Unknowing*, seemed both liberating and satisfying as well as adequate. In an age in which the depths of non-Christian mystical traditions were being discovered, this meant a discovery of the formless, and faceless, meditation offered by various Asian traditions, most notably Zen[6] and certain schools of Hinduism. The perhaps too highly articulated Christianity of the Baroque era, endlessly kept alive before the Council, was leveled and was replaced by what Balthasar called "A little seancing, a little Zen, a little liberation theology."[7]

Into this ever more formless Christianity Balthasar centered his entire project on form: the form of Christ. He has written, "In light of the Resurrection of the flesh, the poets have the last word" — that is, over the philosophers. The body — its particularity, its form — does not evanesce in the face of "the transcendent"; rather, the body is transformed and assumes its place "at the right hand of the Father." Elsewhere he wrote,

> The whole mystery of Christianity, that which distinguishes it radically from every other religious project, is that the form does not stand in opposition to infinite light, for the reason that God has himself instituted and confirmed such form. And although, being finite and worldly, this form must die just as every other beautiful thing on earth must die, nevertheless it does not go down into the realm of formlessness, leaving behind an infinite tragic longing,

but, rather, it rises up to God *as form,* as the form which now, in God himself, has definitively become one with the divine Word and Light which God
has intended for and bestowed upon the world. The form itself must participate in the process of death and resurrection, and thus it becomes coextensive
with God's Light-Word. This makes the Christian principle the superabundant and unsurpassable principle of every aesthetics; Christianity becomes *the*
aesthetic religion *par excellence.*[8]

Deeply aware of other religious traditions, at least in a scholarly way —
he had early studied Sanskrit and was surrounded by the flood of Buddhism
inundating the Germanic countries — he was also aware of the weariness of
the human soul with all words, and with the fact that the dogmas of word-
centered Christianity must seem like "a barbed wire fence" for the soul eager
for a wordless flight of mysticism.

So, on the one hand, there is a recognition of the inadequacy of all earthly
forms to fully articulate "the mystery," and on the other hand, there is the
statement of faith that in Christ Jesus God has created a human form that
is in fact capable of expressing, and has in fact expressed, who God is. As he
boldly states, "Jesus is the exegesis of God." The Christ-form emerges, for
Balthasar, at the center of all reality, in harmony with the words of Colossians, which Balthasar took very seriously indeed. Christ is the center of all
reality: all has been made for him, through him (Col. 1:16). In this, Balthasar created a "radical Christocentrism" that perceived Christ as the magnet
drawing all the *logoi spermatikoi* of creation to their *telos* in his form.

Child of the 1960s, I was naturally being formed in the world of "anonymous Christianity." It seemed, at the time at least, a benign way of both
respecting the uniqueness and the claims of Christ and the goodness and
truth found elsewhere. And yet, during all those years, as the church and its
unique claims seemed to sink beneath the waves of contemporary issues, the
person of Jesus remained present for me, a unique presence, even if I was not
finding a way to articulate this presence. It was by focusing his light clearly
on the person of Jesus, whom I had long encountered as the one opening
to the living God in this dark world, that Balthasar helped me integrate the
thirst for the mystical, which was already being slaked by exploring Asian
mystical traditions. And all this stood in the context of his conviction that
the encounter with the world religions so characteristic of our day is parallel
historically to the gospel encounter with the philosophy and mysticism of

pagan antiquity — yet perhaps even more important, as the mysticism of Asia is of a unique depth.

Balthasar's respect for the integrity of other religious traditions and his respect for the uniqueness and integrity of the gospel have led me to what I describe as "radical Christocentrism." Over the years, I have come to challenge my students on what they mean when they use the word *God.* In the face of all our irenicisms, I make bold to proclaim to them: God is the One whom Jesus calls "Father." With at least as much conviction as a Muslim proclaims there is no God but Allah, the God of Muhammad, I make bold to proclaim that there is no God but the one whom Jesus calls "Father." To say less is to betray the gospel, and Balthasar was very clear about this.

To Balthasar's credit, even as he is celebrating the "cosmic Christ" of Colossians and the mystical Christ of his favored Johannine tradition, Christ, for him, is always the Suffering Servant, the man bloodied and crowned with thorns. He is the Man of Sorrows, the one considered a fool in this world. One of the most beautiful characteristics of his writing is that at any point one can pause and poke through the material and touch the wounds of Christ. Anyone who is connected to the twentieth century in the east of Europe, at least, can recognize no other Christ. No matter how sophisticated, Balthasar is always looking for the crucified Christ in everything that he writes, and, as has been often acknowledged, his range is vast. Everything is *AMDG:* to the greater glory of God.

When, in my twenties, I gradually returned to the Catholicism in which I had been confirmed, and I came to see the reality of life in the world in the light of Christ, the reality of hell opened up for me as well. Balthasar's writings on hell made me nervous for a long time, as they seemed to be a weakening of the church's teaching, and so at the very least, pastorally unsound. As I have meditated on his writings in this area over the years, I have learned to savor this invitation to hope for a universal compassion, which will not allow me to project my own fears and "damn" others and presume their destruction (and my salvation). In the light of God, in the light of the *Spiritual Exercises* of St. Ignatius, I am invited to come to know the reality of hell and the very real possibility that it is for me, a sinner. And then, as I come to know ever more deeply God's saving will and love for me in Christ, I am also reminded that I must hope that the miracle that God has effected, and hopefully will keep effecting, in my own story is a miracle that can take place in the life of others. But no claims must be made beyond that, for only God is God, and all must reverence his sovereign freedom and inscrutable judgments, even as all must adore his loving mercy.

Balthasar wrote that he had suffered in the desert of neo-Scholasticism, and he wanted to tear down the pillars of the pagan temple, like Samson did. He also knew and loved the glory of the true Scholasticism, but he was hardly interested in moving back there. Rather, the atmosphere in which he lived and worked was more in the spirit of the Fathers, which then flowed through a profound identification with Jesus from the *Spiritual Exercises* of St. Ignatius, and was articulated in the words of Scripture, and engaged with the best of human thought. In this deepest sense, Balthasar showed me that one could use one's mind to great profit in the things of God, and in this as well he proved himself a true son of St. Ignatius.

Balthasar changed my mind by showing me that the mind is marvelous, and yet that the mind is not the last word: to be fruitful (and faithful), the mind must be grounded in the heart. For him, always averse to psychology, it was not a sentimental heart but rather the heart of Christ. He wrote that although there is a devotion to the Sacred Heart, there is no devotion to the Sacred Head in Catholicism, unless it is a head bloodied and crowned with thorns. He has also written that in the light of Calvary, no human horror is too great for the Christian. By taking history and its horrors seriously, by leading his vast vision through the narrow gate of the cross, Balthasar leads us to the light of the resurrection beyond. Like the poet Czeslaw Milosz, tempted to Manichaeism because of his long meditation and insertion in the horrors of the twentieth century, or the gentle despair in the voice of T. S. Eliot, Balthasar was profoundly mindful of that hell on earth that had emerged in the modern world for humankind, and planting himself on Calvary, he dared to make *beauty* the first word of his theological opus.

Preaching at Balthasar's funeral was a German cardinal who had also come to represent the best of that tradition, which in its perverted form and in twisted offspring had been the nightmare of Europe and then, through Marxism and its progeny, of the world. *Corruptio optimi pessima est* was being stood on its head. With the election of John Paul II, the "heart of Europe" was put back in place. The artificial division of East and West, in place for fifty years, began to dissolve. The injustices of imperialism and colonialism that parts of Europe had extended over the world and other parts of Europe were being righted as the colonized began to make their voices heard and the "cry of the poor" was being echoed by one who had been poor. When the German cardinal, who is a reader of Balthasar's works, became pope, it became clear beyond the shadow of a doubt that Hans Urs von Balthasar, himself long excluded and marginalized, had come home to the place where he had always been: to the heart, the center of the Catholica. And all of us could see it "as for the first time."

Chapter Five

A Few Words on
Balthasar's First Word

Michael Hanby

I had begun fumbling toward the problem that has come to preoccupy my
meager theological reflections long before I would discover what a crucial
role the work of Hans Urs von Balthasar would play in my attempts to re-
solve it, though I must hasten to add, at the outset of this essay, that I remain
more an admirer than a true scholar of Balthasar. I was in the midst of my
doctoral work on Augustine and Descartes when, partly as the result of that
work, I came to believe that one of the greatest troubles besetting Christian
theology and the church was their failure to make the world's status and inner
meaning as *creation* compelling to the modern world, from whose vantage
point the doctrine of creation *ex nihilo* can add nothing to our knowledge of
the natural world that is not fideistic, moralistic, and thus ultimately arbitrary.[1] I believed then and I believe now that the consequences of this failure
are catastrophic, for if it is true, as the Second Vatican Council states in
its reiteration of a traditional Christian commonplace, that Christ "reveals
man to himself" (Vatican II, *Gaudium et Spes,* no. 22), then a failure to heed
that revelation is tantamount to a crisis of intelligibility over the meaning of
created, and specifically human, being and dignity.

Indeed to call the present situation a "crisis of meaning" may be to trivi-
alize it. If there is anything to the Augustinian notion of illumination as we
find it in a figure such as Bonaventure, and if indeed the splendor of being's
truth — like light — is hidden mainly by virtue of being the thing most
evident, then blindness to this splendor can never be simply inadvertent. It
must be *willed,* and this in turn always includes a measure of dehumanizing

self-deception and self-forgetfulness bordering on self-loathing. John 3:19 states, "And this is the condemnation, that light is come into the world, and men loved darkness rather than light, because their deeds were evil." So in an age of hyperbolic atheism so unthinking as to be hardly worthy of the name, when even much of Christianity is so manifestly determined by its parameters, we attempt to erase the memory of God the only way we can: by eradicating the traces of his image within ourselves. Thus we revel in humanity's technological conquest of nature in the very instant that we deny, with at least equal vehemence, the reality of "natures" altogether, most of all anything approaching a distinctly human nature with its own intrinsic form, ends, and dignity. While it is therefore certainly true and surely dangerous enough that the intelligibility of created and specifically human being has become clouded — and not accidentally — at the very moment of their submission to our technological dominance, this increasing unintelligibility should not be regarded as a matter of simple ignorance. Entailed in it, and indeed in the very logic of modern technological abstraction that perpetuates it, is rather a profound *pathos* of self-hatred, a kind of exuberance for self-mutilation now on display in every sector of society. The posthuman future that is already upon us is not simply a fact; in many quarters it is a matter of celebration carrying all the force of a cultural imperative.

I had become acquainted with the themes of self-forgetting and debasement through my work on Augustine and the Augustinian tradition. Also through Augustine I had come to appreciate the significance of the patristic reckoning of beauty among the transcendental attributes of being, and the contrast between his understanding and the mechanistic reductionism of Descartes was clear enough, as were the deep and ultimately anti-Trinitarian implications for divine and human voluntarism. Still, I had failed to recognize the deep logical connection between Augustine's "humanistic" and aesthetic preoccupations. Moreover, due partly I think to what in Balthasarian terms we might regard as certain "undramatic" features of Augustine's theology and of the Trinitarian theology of the Fathers more generally, or, perhaps more accurately, due to my failure to perceive the dramatic quality of patristic thought, I failed to appreciate how deeply linked are the modern crisis of intelligibility and the eclipse not just of the transcendental attributes of being, but of this transcendental in particular. Nor could I see how much promise the recovery of this forgotten transcendental might hold for reclaiming the intrinsic importance of the doctrine of creation in the face of a material and intellectual culture that are tyrannically reductive.

Through Augustine and also Thomas, I had begun to think about what I would call, with some hesitation, the metaphysics of creation and causality more generally. And quite independently of this I had also begun to think through the implications of the traditional notion that the "powers of the soul" have the transcendentals as their formal object, though my thinking on this matter was largely determined by my crudely Thomistic sense that the first object of the intellect is being, understood in terms of the Scholastic formula *verum est ens*. But it was only when Balthasar, contending that the truth of being first reveals itself *as* beauty in the "primal phenomenon" that is the dramatic encounter with form, that I began to see how integral beauty might be to an explication of the doctrine of creation that was comprehensive in the sense that encompasses both the objective being of the world and our subjective apprehension of it through the various branches of knowledge.

In order to see what promise Balthasar holds for this endeavor, it is first necessary to rehearse briefly the familiar features of the ontology governing modern science and arguably modern society's self-understanding more generally. The first move, which is common to Descartes, Galileo, Bacon, Newton, and probably all the major protagonists of early modern natural philosophy, is to collapse the question of being wholesale into that of substance evacuated of all formalizing and finalizing activity, thereby erasing the act-potency distinction, the manifold forms of Aristotelian causality, and the real distinction of *esse* and *essentia* upon which Aquinas's notion of creation as an intrinsic, asymmetrical relation had depended. With *esse* collapsed into an essentially empty *essentia,* there is no longer a need for a science of being as such to explicate the way for and the hidden implications in the sciences dealing with particular beings. Thus the path is open for natural science to ascend to the position of first philosophy (the Cartesian epistemological interlude notwithstanding), relegating philosophy to an increasingly marginal cultural position. The second move is to identify substance, and thus nature, with a revolutionary new conception of matter dependent upon these developments. This is a point that tends to be occluded in the commonplace complaints against "materialism," whose chief problem is not its insistence upon the exclusivity of material existence but rather its positivist conception of matter.[2] In the movement from medieval Aristotelianism to early modern natural philosophy, matter ceases to be seen as a potency whose actuality depends upon acts of form and finality determining it in this or that kind of thing. Instead, it becomes positive in its own right — in spite of the fact that it never does exist save in this or that sort of thing — and identified by such "essential" characteristics as extension or mass (or later, energy transfers) that are formally identical in every existent thing and differ only in dimensions or quantity.

The effects of this sudden, and I would argue ultimately arbitrary, transvaluation are at once deep and far-reaching and affect virtually every aspect of modern life, initiating not only a new conception of nature in which, ironically, there will be no room for "natures," but also a new regime of what could count as truth or the knowledge of it as the Scholastic formula *verum est ens* gives way to the notion that of *verum quia factum*. Indeed, philosophical and cultural developments of the past century reveal how deeply the collapse of *episteme* into a debased form of *techne* has called into question the very notion of truth, now pragmatically reduced to function.[3] As a consequence, "we have given up seeking the hidden 'in-itselfness' of things and sounding the nature of being itself" for the quite simple reason that it is the very nature of modern technological abstraction to obliterate the "hidden 'in-itselfness'" of unrepeatable beings, and even being itself is regarded within much of what passes for philosophy as a redundant semantic trick.[4] With the whole meaning of nature now collapsed into a matter regarded as fully positive in its own right, all formalizing and finalizing activity, whether that of God or mind, must now be thought of as essentially extrinsic to a nature whose most fundamental characteristic is self-identical inertia or meaninglessness. Or in what amounts to the same thing, the meaning entailed in formal and final causality is regarded as an epiphenomenon ultimately reducible to interactions between more basic material components that are "essentially" identical. This extrinsicism profoundly distorts the relationship between God and world, incoherently depicting God as another item in or quite literally beyond the universe in violation of a real conception of transcendence and ontological difference, and this deformation carries in its train a profound distortion of the concept of nature. With causality reduced to extrinsic force and substance to positive inert matter that is the ontologically and historically prior basis for form rather than actualized by it, the way is now clear to imagining the unity and identity of each actual existent thing as merely the sum of its interacting parts and the antecedent historical causes which produced it. And since the evacuation of essence from nature carries within it a displacement of the good, freedom comes to be understood not as a realization of the form at once determined and spontaneous but rather in opposition to order. Hence the very givens and necessities of nature come to be felt as alien intrusion upon the indeterminacy of sheer freedom, something to be conquered and overcome. With biological wholes reduced to the sum of their parts, the temptation to manipulate these parts to a design of our own inchoate imagining becomes irresistible.

"Beauty is the word that shall be our first."[5] With this announcement, Balthasar advances a stark alternative both to the "subjective" reduction of knowledge to a truth that can always and everywhere be resolved into mathematical expression and the "objective" reduction of the objects of knowledge to the precise sum of so many measurable interactive component parts and antecedent causes. Indeed, he goes so far as to suggest that the recovery of a proper theological aesthetics penetrating the cosmos to its very depths is finally the only protection afforded to the world and ourselves against the tyranny of these reductions, for the dual reason that only a proper acknowledgment of beauty can safeguard the objective being of creation and the subjective condition of soul that fully and finally keeps us human.

Balthasar detects in the manifestation of the beautiful two elements common to every traditional aesthetic. The first is form, though in a sense neither exactly Aristotelian nor Platonic inasmuch as "form is determined by many antecedent conditions," including the historical conditions under which it unfolds and is apprehended dramatically.[6] As such, form for Balthasar is not simply "individuated" by matter, but form *qua* form is both concrete and universal at once. Indeed, it is in this manner that form manifests itself and is grasped as beautiful. This second feature, entailed in the first, is splendor, by virtue of which the form is compelling as an object of attention and a subject of wonder. The coincidence of these two aspects means

> The beautiful is above all a form, and the light does not fall on this form from above and from outside, rather it breaks forth from the form's interior. Species and lumen in beauty are one.... Visible form not only "points" to an

invisible, unfathomable mystery; form is the apparition of this mystery, and reveals it while, naturally, at the same time protecting and veiling it. Both natural and artistic form has an exterior which appears and an interior depth, both of which, however, are not separable in the form itself. The content (*Gehalt*) does not lie behind the form (*Gestalt*), but within it. Whoever is not capable of seeing and "reading" the form will, by the same token, fail to perceive the content.[7]

Form, in other words, is at once both a principle of identity and a principle of mystery. These aspects are neither identical nor opposed, as is evidenced both by the reciprocal dependence of Being and beings in the actuality of every concrete thing and by science's need to get beyond initial phenomenal appearances. Rather, they are mutually constitutive polarities of a unity.[8] This is to say that the mystery of a thing's being consists partly in an ecstasis that is self-donation always pressing toward visibility.[9] Crucial here, then, is the fact that for Balthasar, mystery is neither the opposite of truth and knowledge nor the unknown that lies just beyond their boundaries waiting to be discovered but an immanent feature of them. Indeed, mystery makes real knowledge possible (in the old sense that knowledge concerns "what is") inasmuch as it protects the actuality of the world from the homogenizing violence of technological abstraction. Not that abstraction as such is the enemy, since every particular thing is also formal and thus universal. Yet it is the very essence of modern technological abstraction to destroy the coincidence of universality and concreteness in the identity of this particular thing or person for the sake of a plastic and malleable formality. To see this form of abstraction in action, one need only think of the pervasive tendency in modern thought to regard systems of whatever kind, be they biological, thermonuclear, organic, or economic, as simply the aggregation of interchangeable variables and functions.

Because of the coincidence of mystery and identity, Balthasar insists that form, a unity that is phenomenologically first and that transcends its components, is irreducible to those components or its antecedent causes. "Our first principle," Balthasar adamantly states, "must always be the indissolubility of form.... If form is broken down into subdivisions and auxiliary parts for the sake of explanation, this is unfortunately a sign that the true form has not been perceived as such at all. What man is in his totality cannot be 'explained' in terms of the process by which he has become what he is."[10]

The implications of this assertion of aesthetic form for scientific reductionism, and particularly biological reductionism, should be immediately
evident. However, we would fall well short of the full profundity of Balthasar's claims, and the full force of their implications for developing an
orthodox theology of creation capable of engaging the hegemony of modern
science, were we merely to rest content with the realization that reduction-
ist biology is destined to get humanity wrong. The richer implications and
the promise of his thought as a hedge against the dominance of a perverted *techne* become apparent as Balthasar moves into his consideration
of revelatory freedom as a condition of possibility for the world's truth.

> If each and every thing were nothing more than an "instance of..." or a kind
> of algebraic "x" that could be exchanged for other entities without loss, then
> things would possess absolutely no intrinsic value of their own as individu-
> als. By the same token, they would have no claim whatsoever to any sphere
> that might be their own by right or reserved to them alone. Any knower who
> grasped the essence of the species of which they are exemplars would imme-
> diately comprehend at the same time every individual entity that fell under it:
> no individual could present him with any further mystery. Knowing the in-
> dividual would accordingly be a matter of an endlessly repeatable application
> of knowledge of the universal, in the same way that a mathematical theorem
> can be applied to any number of objects or a cookie cutter can be used to
> make as many cookies as one wants. The object's whole essence would then
> consist in being an object for a subject; there could be no more question of a
> free self-revelation on its part.[11]

What Balthasar helps us see in such passages, and what I could not see
before though it was right in front of me, is how self-revealing beauty must
necessarily be a transcendental attribute of being if we are finally to save
truth, not to mention goodness. This is because

> only the apprehension of the expressive form in the thing can give it that
> depth-dimension between its ground and its manifestation which, as the real
> locus of beauty, now also opens up the ontological locus of the truth of being,
> and frees the striver, allowing him to achieve the spiritual distance that makes
> a beauty rich in form desirable in its being-in-itself (and not only in its being-
> for-me), and only thus worth striving after.... In the luminous form of the
> beautiful the being of the existent becomes perceivable as nowhere else, and
> this is why an aesthetic element must be associated with all spiritual striving.
> The quality of "being-in-itself" which belongs to the beautiful, the demand

the beautiful makes to be allowed to be what it is, the demand, therefore, that we renounce our attempts to control and manipulate it, in order to be able to be happy by enjoying it: all of this is, in the natural realm, the foundation and foreshadowing of what in the realm of revelation and grace will be the attitude of faith.[12]

Beauty, insofar as it is regarded as such, has within it a kind of "whyless" disinterestedness, a kind of superfluous gratuity with no point or justification beyond itself.[13] Balthasar interprets this as the beautiful object's freedom to conceal its surplus depths in the very act of its self-revelation. Thus the objectivity of beauty is rooted in a kind of ecstatic freedom that is the mark of "being-in-itselfness" and the hedge against reduction of the object's truth to pragmatic or sheerly formal categories. It so happens, then, that the freedom and objectivity manifest in the "whylessness" of beauty are the very conditions upon which there can be a truth of the world.[14] For this reason, Balthasar insists that "without aesthetic knowledge, neither theoretical nor practical reason can attain their total completion," and why, more starkly still, "[Beauty] will not allow herself to be separated and banned from her two sisters without taking them along with herself in an act of mysterious vengeance."[15]

Balthasar's recovery of the primacy of beauty has deeply reshaped my thinking about creation in a manner corresponding roughly to his distinction between the subjective evidence and the objective form of revelation, though I by no means wish to claim that all my thoughts in this regard are strictly Balthasarian. Corresponding to the first, subjective dimension, I mean the *doctrine* of creation as a form of knowledge or explanation with its own content and logical form. In the second instance, I mean creation as a "fact" intrinsic to the internal constitution of the world as world. With respect to the first, he has helped me see what sort of "explanation" the doctrine of creation is and hopefully to acquire a truer and more sophisticated sense of its relation to the claims of the sciences.

For one thing, the priority of beauty in the apprehension of truth would suggest a feature about the doctrine of creation that I take to be entailed positively in the "fact" of creation: it has a deeply *apophatic* dimension, though this should not be misunderstood. Balthasar consistently stresses that "negative theology" has its foundation in the positive, unfathomable difference internal to God as "ever-greater." So once again, this *apophatic* dimension of the doctrine of creation should not be regarded as merely the negative point where our knowledge leaves off, a point always subject to repair by further knowledge, but rather as the depth inherent in the radiance of beauty's *cataphatic* manifestation that makes truth "possible." "Mystery is, not transcendent, but immanent in relation to truth. On this supposition, the knowledge of a truth, far from annulling its mysteriousness, actually brings it to light."[16]

In thinking about the relation between the doctrine of creation and the claims of a science that often erroneously takes itself to have refuted it, I initially thought it sufficient simply to oppose this mystery to scientific reductionism and the category mistake of supposing "creation" to be the same sort of explanation as modern science.[17] In my earlier reflections I took care to distinguish between the doctrine of creation and natural science as modes of explanation, and I recognized that science instantiates numerous judgments of a metaphysical and theological nature that are the starting point and not the conclusions of scientific inquiry and that then determine how "God" will be allowed to appear to thought. Among these are determinations as to the nature of nature, matter, causation, truth, knowledge, the goods that their inquiry serves in the light of broader human goods, and the role, if any, of metaphysics in their deliberation. I recognized that this is particularly true of Darwinian biology, which is constituted in part by its relationship to the presuppositions of eighteenth-century natural theology, whose view of God it continues, ironically, to perpetuate. Yet in spite of all this, I failed to appreciate how crucial were the metaphysics of a proper theological aesthetics to science's own integrity and autonomy *as science*.

If it is indeed only the beauty of form, coterminous with mystery and identity at once, which secures the truth of things, then only by acknowledging this mystery as something positive and immanent and not simply an unknown to be overcome can science hope to preserve its own truth *as* science. This means, ironically enough, that in order to insure its scientific status, science must acknowledge its dependence upon metaphysics. It must acknowledge its own constitutive insufficiency as a form of knowledge and the insufficiency of the conception of truth that it projects for itself. As (then) Cardinal Ratzinger put it, "Calculable practical knowledge is limited by its very nature to the apparent, to what functions, and does not represent the way in which to find truth itself, which by its very method it has renounced."[18] This is certainly true, though Balthasar helps us to see that even what is "apparent" — what is phenomenologically first in all in all its wholeness, radiance, intelligibility, and irreducible singularity — eventually becomes a casualty under a regime in which "calculable, practical knowledge" is thought to suffice for knowledge as such.

What I wish to suggest, in other words, is that Balthasar gives us grounds for reimagining something like the subalternation of the sciences on the distinctly aesthetic terms that specifically mark the doctrine of creation; and that, moreover, the recovery of just such a notion is necessary if we are to save either "the phenomena" or the scientific truth as something more than Baconian power or function. I harbor no illusions, of course, about the hope of installing such an understanding in practice. There is little appetite for philosophy in our barbarously pragmatic culture, and there is a great deal of money to be made in remaining barbarous and pragmatic. I would nevertheless maintain that it is only by acknowledging its need for the metaphysics upon which it always depends in fact that science can enjoy its legitimate autonomy and avoid falsifying itself and its objects by taking recourse to a deficient form of the metaphysics that it ostensibly denies and by exercising a reductive tyranny over the things that it purports to explain. If this is true, then a good theological aesthetics, rather than simply opposing the sciences or remaining indifferent them, in fact liberates science to *be* science and helps to constitute its genuine autonomy, partly by freeing it of the burden of being theology.

I am, of course, aware that a great deal more technical specification than I can supply here is required to make good on this claim, which is at once a claim as to the limits and disorder of scientific reason and the intrinsic possibilities of the metaphysics of creation understood in aesthetic terms. But this much should be clear. Only a metaphysics that takes seriously the primacy of beauty can hope to be truly comprehensive while remaining nonreductive in its determinations, because only such a vantage can avoid absolutizing itself, behold the mystery of its objects as a positive, constitutive facet of their being and essence, and grant a legitimate autonomy to the approach taken by other sciences to the same object. As we have already seen, by insisting on the priority of beauty and its necessity for truth, Balthasar is insisting upon just such a comprehensive and nonreductive vantage, one that grants to both the sciences and their objects their "being-in-itselfness" because of the very manner in which it encompasses them.

In opening up the mystery "of depth-dimension between ground and its manifestation," worldly beauty opens by the inner necessity of its own worldliness onto the real distinction between beings and Being. And because of the "dependence of Being on its explication in the existent," this distinction opens yet again into the mystery of creation just as metaphysics opens of its own accord into theology, thus preserving and fulfilling at one and the same time the wonder that constitutes the genuinely metaphysical *eros,* the distinction between divine glory and worldly beauty, and the genuine "autonomy" and integrity of each.[19] Of course, this is to suggest neither that this internal tendency of worldly being can be apprehended without the eyes of faith — after all, it is always possible *not* to see — nor that the need for faith compromises the objectivity of this demonstration, but only that the eyes of faith are eventually necessary for a proper grasp of worldly being as worldly and that philosophy and science find their consummation in their opening to theology. Indeed, perhaps now more than ever, that truth which we cannot in some sense help *but* see, that truth which is phenomenologically and ontologically first and last, Alpha and Omega, without which all lesser truths are but shadows and all advances toward it never commence, is apprehended only by the higher gaze of a faith that possesses its object only by relinquishing it to what is both in and beyond it. Thus in allowing that the immanent "truth of the world" is constituted in relation to one who is wholly other to it, the doctrine of creation preserves the wonder and ambition of secular science, the mystery and integrity of its objects, and its own comprehensive scope by relinquishing its own claims to ultimacy to the mysterious Truth upon which they all depend.[20]

By contrast, any science that fails to acknowledge the mystery of Being and the *ordo rationis* that follows from it is destined to regard itself, at least implicitly, as the highest science and thereby to fall prey to a threefold illusion. It will mistakenly assume, by virtue of its pragmatic success, that it accounts for its own condition of possibility. It will thus exceed its competence and stray into the metaphysics that it has foresworn but that it requires in any event. It will thereby determine in advance, through its own assumptions about being, causality, truth, and nature, the conditions under which

"God" may be considered, invariably compromising a coherent understanding of God as "wholly other" and thus fully immanent. And denying that the mystery of the world's being constitutes a real question, it will reduce by technological abstraction the "real" world to what appears through its presuppositions and is adduced by its methods, thereby occluding the world of meaningful wholes that is both ontologically and phenomenologically first. It should be clear from all I have said thus far that these "objective" illusions are not without their subjective counterpart. Inasmuch as they constitute a closure or blindness to the mystery of being — and deafness to the summons of God — they impose a kind of death by slow suffocation on the souls over whom they hold sway, extinguishing the very *eros* that makes the human soul human.

Of course, it is fashionable within much of contemporary science to eschew "reductionism," but science in its current self-understanding is incapable of giving a principled answer of what the "more" exceeding the sum of a thing's parts might consist in, requiring, as it does, the admission of other conceptions of causality besides debased forms of the efficient and other legitimate forms of knowledge besides its own. Consequently, even scientific paradigms such as so-called emergence theory that attempt to account for this "more" cannot attain to the question of essences that ontologically precede their component parts even as they depend upon their historical unfolding. Much less do they attain to the question of being.

If a theological aesthetics is subjectively obliged to regard existent things as mysteriously and irreducibly "more" than their antecedent causes and interactive component parts, this is ultimately because the novelty and excess entailed in this regard are objectively implied by the understanding of creation that is part and parcel of what makes such aesthetics theological. But here we run up against a bedeviling question: "In what sense novel?" To say that wholes are irreducible to their parts or that effects are irreducible to the sum of their antecedent causes is to say that the generation of being *ex nihilo* is the precondition for and intrinsic to every causal transaction, that there intervenes between cause and effect a genuine novelty or surplus of being and that it is on the basis of this very difference that a genuinely causal transaction can be said to have occurred. But is this novelty real or merely apparent? Does it make real "additions" to being, or does such inexplicable and irreducible excess merely appear novel to us? Lurking barely beneath such questions is one still more mysterious and fundamental: "Where can there be a place for the world if God is, after all, 'the entire ocean of being?' (John Damascene)?"[21]

If, on the one hand, we simply accept the traditional conception of divine *esse* as first, eternal, most simple, most actual, most perfect, and supremely one such that nothing can be either subtracted from or added to it,[22] then it is difficult to regard the difference inherent in apparent novelty as other than a diminution of a more basic unity, and it seems that we must resign ourselves to the conclusion that "caused things are deficient [*deficiunt*] in their imitation of their causes."[23] Now that Thomas had paradoxically invoked this Platonic principle to accord a certain emphasis to the existence of the creature, "it may possess a *nobilius esse* in God, yet it is truer 'in itself' where it is 'real' and 'possesses its own activity,'" and like Augustine before him and Dante after him, he saw the creature's capacity for self-movement (actuality) as positively correlated to its movement into God.[24] And yet this conclusion stands in a degree of tension with what is undeniably a tendency in the opposite direction — as Balthasar puts it, "wherever God's absoluteness and nonnecessitous totality are taken seriously; it seems that the conclusion must be drawn that, to the extent creatures are, were or will be in God, they participate more in being and are more true there than in themselves."[25] Inasmuch as this fails to give due credence to the genuine "in-itselfness" of the world, it risks relegating the "real" novelty of creation to the mere appearance of novelty "for us." This has far-reaching implications for how we regard the truth of faith, from whose perspective alone the meaning of this novelty may be adequately grasped, in relation to the explanations of science. If all effects are really just the sum of prior causes, and if all that is "really there" is thus exhaustively susceptible to scientific methodologies, then faith will have to make do with truths belonging to some world other than this one or with a moralistic realm of values having little to do with truth at all and little claim on the meaning of human being and life. Conversely, it may even risk compromising the ontological difference in the name of protecting it, requiring, in something of an alternative view, that we regard God as the being of the world. Yet if, on the other hand, we admit that the advent of the world marks a real increase in being, if the world that is manifestly not God somehow "adds" to God, then it would imply that God has a "real relation" to the world after all and thus would run afoul of this very difference that the tradition has so rightly safeguarded.

By no means do I wish to exaggerate Balthasar's originality by mischaracterizing the antecedent mainstream tradition and claiming that it ever fell into either extreme of this tension. Indeed, it is intrinsic to the very notion of creation to maintain simultaneously God's absolute transcendence of and "indifference" to the world *and* the integrity of worldly being, both of which are lost when either is compromised. Aquinas's distinction between *ipsum esse subsistens* and *esse creatum non subsistens* is arguably unparalleled in securing God's difference from the world, establishing the integrity of created *esse* (reflected in the order of the sciences) and constituting that integrity on the basis of its intrinsic relation to and dependence upon God (reflected in the role of *sacra doctrina* in grounding and ordering lower forms of knowledge). And for the tradition as a whole, in Denys or Bonaventure, for example, the notions of divine unity and simplicity that potentially give rise to this problem were always complicated by a triunity understood in terms of "self-exteriorizing" love.

What I do wish to suggest, however, is that Balthasar's treatment of this tension, developed partly on the basis of his profound reading of Thomas, provides peculiar resources for bringing this positive, objective dimension to light in the face of the modern technological oblivion of the mystery of being.[26] Indeed, as his aesthetics moves by its own internal compulsion to the dramatics, this tension moves into the foreground. For Balthasar insists with the tradition, perhaps even more radically than the tradition, on God as the Wholly Other, who is for that very reason non-other. And yet there is an analogy, perhaps more than an analogy, between the need to give a positive account of the irreducibility of the world's mystery as something "more" than a deficient reflection of God and the need for a "personal 'I'" that does not "surrender itself to some all-embracing life or essence" to be engaged by the dramatic question of his existence.[27] For "if we had not discovered this unique 'name' (Rosenzweig) of the individual addressed by God and endowed with the personal name, the irreplaceable human being, the 'absolute unique instance,' we would hot have been attempting a theory of theo-drama, for the unique God would have lacked a partner."[28] Hence, in *Love Alone Is Credible,* Balthasar "universalizes" this dramatic question, extending it to the creation in particular and as a whole and bringing its constitutive mystery to light.

> Why in fact is there something rather than nothing? The question remains open regardless of whether one affirms or denies the existence of an absolute being. If there is not absolute being, what reason could there be that these finite ephemeral things exist in the middle of nothing, things that could never add up to the absolute as a whole or evolve into it? But, on the other hand, if there is an absolute being, and if this being is sufficient unto itself, it is almost more mysterious why there should exist something else. Only a philosophy of freedom and love can account for our existence, though not unless it also interprets the essence of finite being in terms of love.[29]

It is precisely Balthasar's "philosophy of freedom and love" that allows us, in what at first seems like a paradox, to imagine the world as somehow "more" than God without compromising, but rather underscoring, God's transcendence and otherness vis-à-vis the world. This same philosophy turns out to be at the root of the aesthetics.

In short, the "philosophy of freedom and love" has its ontological basis in the radical difference at the heart of the divine life itself. Consequently, this philosophy is completed from beyond its own resources as this difference is manifest in Christ's kenotic descent into human form, the cross, and the hell of Holy Saturday.[30] This difference in Balthasar's estimation is not the antithesis to the unity of being but rather *is* this unity understood as love. In Balthasar's reckoning, the very possibility of understanding the divine being as love depends upon a mutual "letting be" coincident with infinite freedom. This is the Father's eternal self-giving, the Son's eternal act of "being begotten," and the Spirit's own expropriation as the "we" of the Father and Son. This "letting be" is the basis of the intra-Trinitarian circumincession, but it is dependent on the real irreducibility of the Trinitarian *Personae* to each other, even the "transcendence" of each Person with respect to the others consistent with being possessed as free dispossession. As a consequence, "there is no end to being surprised and overwhelmed by what is essentially immeasurable."[31] This is because "God is always greater than himself on the basis of his triune freedom," though this does not imply that he is ever less than himself. Balthasar thus takes the classic Trinitarian stipulation that the Son is all things that the Father is save that he is *not* the Father and gives the "not... an infinitely positive sense."[32] We must say at once that the Persons of the Trinity "are perfectly transparent to one another, and they possess a kind of impenetrable personal mystery."[33] And it is precisely because "the hypostatic modes of being constitute the greatest imaginable opposition to one another" that "they can mutually interpenetrate one another in the most intimate manner conceivable."[34]

Because this difference internal to God, by which he is always greater than himself, constitutes by definition "the greatest imaginable opposition," it encompasses the lesser difference between God and the world. It is for this reason that we can regard creation *ex nihilo* as generating a real addition in being, a difference that is even somehow "more" than God, without for all that compromising God's transcendent otherness. (It is also how, in Christ, God, who needs nothing, can really receive creation's offering.) Creation in the Son is creation in him by whom God is greater than himself. Hence, "the transition from infinite freedom to the creation of finite freedoms (with all this implies) need not constitute the 'ultimate paradox' of thought."[35] "For the infinite distance between the world and God is grounded in the other, prototypical distance between God and God."[36] It is this positive difference entailed in love and inherent in God as ever-greater that makes it possible for God to establish and abide a world not-God replete with its own being and even to accompany that world to its "wit's end" in his kenotic descent into the dereliction and hell of Holy Saturday.[37] Neither ceasing to be himself nor needing to find himself, God in his freedom of self-abandonment is able to encompass and embrace, and in a sense even constitute, what is not God.[38]

Such conclusions, Balthasar thinks, are implied in the axiom of the Fourth Lateran Council, which he is quite fond of citing, to the effect that whatever similarity creation bears to God is encompassed by an ever-greater dissimilarity. Note here, however, how it is the very dissimilarity of God to creation, manifest in God's freedom to embrace all that is radically not God, that is the basis for the positive analogy of creature whom he simply lets be as something other, and not simply less, than God. For as we have seen, it is just this irreducible something more, this "being-in-itselfness" always kenotically pressing toward visibility that is for Balthasar the mark of worldly beauty and therefore truth. In simply being, for no other reason than its gratuitous splendor, creation both mimics and manifests the self-abandoning love of its Creator.

There, is of course, much to question in all of this, and I, like many of Balthasar's mere admirers, find the darker aspects of his theology of Holy Saturday profoundly unsettling.[39] This is probably as it should be, if for no other reason than that the scandal of Good Friday is profoundly unsettling, and the moment that it ceases to be so is the moment when we should fear that God's dramatic summons has ceased to lay claim to our attention and affections. Be that as it may, let it suffice for my purposes here to indicate how Balthasar's "philosophy of freedom and love" thus stands at the root of his aesthetics and is indeed responsible for it, as love itself is at the root of the beauty that we find there. Because the meaning of being is love, we can regard the beauty that mimics the self-donation of love as something genuinely real. And thus in the highest of worldly sciences we can give a principled account of the inexhaustible "more" at the basis of all other sciences, a surplus on which science invariably depends but to which it seems permanently at risk of remaining blind.

Although Balthasar's recovery of beauty as a transcendental attribute of being is profoundly important in helping us to restore, at least in theory, something approaching an order of objective truth, his greater profundity may consist in the way his aesthetics, in maintaining the unity of the subjective and objective dimensions, binds the recovery of this order to the recovery of our humanity and our failure to perceive it with the spiritual abyss at the heart of the modern soul. Of beauty's apprehension he writes, "We can be sure that whoever sneers at her name as if she were the ornament of a bourgeois past—whether he admits it or not—can no longer pray and soon will no longer be able to love."[40]

In seeking to recover beauty and in pleading for the urgency of this recovery, Balthasar thus seeks to preserve the love that foregrounds a drama of even greater existential urgency, a faith that alone can forestall our *pathos* for self-mutilation, and a hope that God abides even in our attempt to eradicate his image. "Anyone who penetrates into the mysteries of God recognizes more and more that the world as a whole is created 'for nothing,' that is, out of a love that is free and has no other reason behind it; that is precisely what gives it its only plausible meaning. Recognizing or failing to recognize this relationship will constitute the core action in theo-drama."[41]

Helping me to recognize this relationship and to glimpse what it implies and all that is at stake—this is how Balthasar changed my mind.

Chapter Six

Being Lost

Hans Urs von Balthasar
on Love and Hope

Nicholas J. Healy

I first heard the name "Hans Urs von Balthasar" in a conversation between my father and Alice von Hildebrand in which the latter expressed strong reservations about Balthasar's hope for universal salvation. I do not remember taking a position, but most likely I deferred to my esteemed teacher Dr. von Hildebrand. In any case, my interests lay elsewhere. I was beginning graduate studies in philosophy, and my attention was focused on the question of "Christian philosophy" and on the dispute between Thomists and phenomenologists regarding the convertibility of being and the good. Balthasar was neither read nor discussed in my philosophy classes.

A few months into my studies I had the good fortune of attending a lecture by David L. Schindler titled "Sanctity and the Intellectual Life." Interpreting what he called Hans Urs von Balthasar's theology of mission, Schindler made the following claim:

> The relation of love that Jesus shares with the Father is not exclusive but opens on to the cosmos the Father has created in and through Jesus ("That they all may be one, Father, even as you and I are one" [John 17:21]). That is, all of creation is dynamically ordered from and toward the love revealed by God in Jesus Christ.... All created entities are thus understood most truly when and insofar as they are brought into this relation of prayer, obedience, and service to God in Christ: when and insofar as they are thereby taken up into a cosmic liturgy.[1]

Of course, I had heard before that all things were created in and for Jesus Christ; this is stated plainly in the opening chapter of Paul's letter to the Colossians. The novelty here was the idea that the love revealed in Christ is relevant to the structure and inner intelligibility of being; that is, love has something to do with the nature of reality as understood by philosophy and the sciences. In Christ's freely giving himself away out of love for the Father and love for the world, God reveals both his innermost secret and the final meaning of created being: "Being itself here unveils its final countenance, which for us receives the name of trinitarian love; only with this final mystery does light fall at last on that other mystery: why there is being at all and why it enters our horizon as light and truth and goodness and beauty."[2] Everything that followed in my studies was an attempt to understand and remain faithful to the initial promise that love is the meaning of being.

It is characteristic of Balthasar as an author and publisher that he allows others to speak whenever possible. Anyone who tries to draw near to him is brought necessarily into a relation with the entire tradition. When asked which of his own books was dearest to him, Balthasar pointed to his translations of Origen and Paul Claudel. Or, within the trilogy, it is the second volume of *The Glory of the Lord,* "the one in which I tried to expound twelve great theologians,... in their integrity they let the sound of what I wanted to make heard ring out."[3] The concluding monograph of this volume is on the French poet Charles Péguy (1873–1914). Reading Balthasar's account of Péguy's life and concerns, and then reading the writings of Péguy, was an unsurpassed introduction to the meaning of catholicity understood first in terms of the unity of creation and redemption, the unity of the old and new covenants, and ultimately as a hope that excludes no one: "We must arrive together before the good Lord. What would he say if we arrived before him alone, if we came home to him without the others?"[4]

Rather than recall the narrative of my own itinerary, the following reflection considers some aspects of Balthasar's teaching on the relation between love and being and then suggests the relevance of this teaching for the question of damnation. It should become clear that the convergence of being, love, and hope is found in the mystery of the Eucharist, the sacrament of Christ's patient love. Balthasar changed and continues to change my mind because he shows us that thinking is a matter of attunement to the Eucharist.[5]

Love as the Light of Being

As Pope Benedict suggests, the difficulty today is not that there is too little talk of love, but rather too much: "Today the word 'love' is so tarnished, so spoiled and so abused, that one is almost afraid to pronounce it with one's lips."[6] The word is like a coin whose image has been worn away from being passed unthinkingly from hand to hand. "And yet," Benedict continues, "it is a primordial word, expression of the primordial reality; we cannot simply abandon it, we must take it up again, purify it and give back to it its original splendor so that it might illuminate our life and lead it on the right path."[7]

One attempt to purify and safeguard love is to affirm interpersonal love as perhaps the last remaining source of warmth and light in an indifferent cosmos. As more and more of the natural world and human culture fall under the domain of modern science (knowledge as power over nature), "there remains," Balthasar suggests, "like the last of his emergency rations, only love among men."[8] The concluding stanza of Matthew Arnold's poem "Dover Beach" is a particularly striking example of this appeal to love when all else seems lost:

> Ah, love, let us be true
> To one another! for the world, which seems
> To lie before us like a land of dreams,
> So various, so beautiful, so new,
> Hath really neither joy, nor love, nor light,
> Nor certitude, nor peace, nor help for pain;
> And we are here as on a darkling plain
> Swept with confused alarms of struggle and flight,
> Where ignorant armies clash by night.

Unfortunately, the attempt to hold fast to interpersonal love as the last remaining treasure in a dead cosmos inevitably leads to a reduction and loss of love itself. Why? At the heart of love is gratitude — a receiving of the other as gift. A relation to another person that fails to receive the other as a sign and promise of something "more" has nothing profound to receive or give, and hence is undeserving of the name love: "This means that there is no gleam of glory surrounding personal love any more, or at most the deceptive illusion of one, which lovers are always supposed to see through in a melancholy or cynical way — for the glory of love can flourish only within the context of

an at least intuited glory of being."⁹ Part of this "more" is a light that begins to radiate from literally all things. The poets are not wrong when they
describe lovers as seeing the world anew. At a deeper level, the mysterious
"more" at the heart of love suggests a generosity or grace that transcends the
self and the other, both of whom have been permitted to be and allowed to
participate in a giving and receiving that does not originate with them. This
is why Balthasar makes fruitfulness the touchstone of interpersonal love. In
giving themselves to each other, the lovers give "more" than they are able to
give. "The sudden appearance of a child," Balthasar writes, "is an incomprehensible wonder that fills them with unexpected delight."¹⁰ In opening their
love to the gift of children, the lovers implicitly acknowledge the Creator as
the origin and end of their love for each other.

In the wake of the evident failure of a melancholic clinging to human
love — "Let us be true to one another" — Balthasar suggests a different
path for recovering the "original splendor" of the word *love:* a renewed
understanding of creation as gift. As the centerpiece of his doctrine of
creation, Balthasar adopts Thomas Aquinas's unique account of the act
of being: "Being [*esse*] signifies something complete and simple but nonsubsistent."¹¹ According to Thomas, every created thing bears within itself
an inexhaustible fullness, a fullness that is pregnant with the very mystery of
God. And yet this fullness is nonsubsistent; it stands in need of an essence
to attain subsistence. The fact that *esse* is both source of all the perfections
of a being and nonsubsistent suggests that the complexity of the essence in
its nonidentity with *esse* is not simply a limit that is foreign to *esse* itself,
but rather is a difference that is generously allowed by *esse* itself. Balthasar
characterizes the mysterious interplay between *esse* and essence as a reciprocal, asymmetrical generosity that is analogous to the giving and receiving
proper to love. Being, which Thomas calls a likeness of the divine goodness,
is transparent to the divine generosity of the Creator. Thomas writes,

> Divine love did not allow him to "remain in himself without fruit," that is,
> without the production of creatures, but love "moved him to operate" accord-
> ing to a most excellent mode of operation according as he produced all things
> in being [*esse*]. For from love of his goodness it proceeded that he willed to
> pour out and to communicate his goodness to others, insofar as it is possible,
> namely by way of similitude, and thus his goodness did not remain in him,
> but flowed out into others.¹²

Why is there something rather than nothing? "How is it possible," asks Balthasar, "that creation can come from God, who is everything, in such a way that God remains everything in creation and yet creation is not God?"[13] An initial answer is given in the nonsubsistent fullness of being, which is thus a sign both of God's abiding presence in creation and of God's graciously having brought into being something other than God. "This is how things resemble God," Aquinas argues, "for precisely as beings [*entia*] they resemble the primary and universal source of all *esse*."[14] A second and related answer, suggested by both Aquinas and Balthasar, is that the possibility of creation resides in God's Trinitarian nature. The positive otherness of Father, Son, and Holy Spirit opens a space for the creaturely otherness of the world in relation to God. "The temporal procession of creatures," argues Aquinas, "comes from the eternal procession of the Persons . . . the first procession is the cause and ground of all subsequent processions."[15] This teaching by Aquinas provides a warrant for returning to the meaning of *esse*'s nonsubsistent fullness in light of the Trinitarian love revealed in Christ's mission. Christ's gift of himself in love is both the revelation of the mystery of the Father, who gives himself away eternally in generating the Son, and the final justification of the goodness of the world's being other than God.

Balthasar is aware of a basic objection to the idea that love is the meaning of being: "Is such a supposition not contradicted a thousand times each day by the shrillness of all that is ugly, that is warped, that is hopelessly mediocre and vulgar?"[16] The objection cannot be pushed lightly aside as though the destitution of one's neighbor were a matter of indifference to the question of being or as though the instrumentalism and poverty of spirit in an age dominated by technology were matters of indifference to the philosopher who is called to wonder over being. Balthasar describes the Christian as the guardian of metaphysical wonder: "The Christian will be the responsible guardian of glory as a whole, just as once the Jew was, as he sang the psalms of creation to God and so was the responsible guardian of the glory of covenant *and* creation."[17] Acknowledging being as gift means assuming a particular responsibility for areas of loneliness and darkness:

> The Christians of today, living in a night which is deeper than that of the later Middle Ages, are given the task of performing the act of affirming being, unperturbed by the darkness and the distortion, in a way that is vicarious and

representative for all humanity.... Those who are directed in this way to pray continually, to find God in all things... are entrusted with the task of bring light to those areas of being which are in darkness so that its primal light may shine anew not only upon them but also upon the whole world.[18]

The responsibility for keeping wonder alive is at once a matter of thinking and deeds on behalf of love. Perhaps the most characteristic feature of Balthasar's metaphysics is the refusal to separate these two dimensions of receiving being as gift. Responsible thinking takes on a special urgency in a positivistic age that reduces being to a neutral concept. When being is no longer understood as a gift, everything in creation, including human love, loses its true meaning in relation to God and becomes vulnerable to being instrumentalized. By the same token, acts of personal love, such as Mother Teresa's gracious care for the abandoned children of Calcutta or Jean Vanier's hospitality for the most severely disabled, provide a light that guides and sustains thinking.

Being Lost

In the monograph that concludes the third volume of *The Glory of the Lord,* Balthasar assigns to Charles Péguy the task of "providing a valid representation of twentieth-century Catholicism."[19] He is "the representative of the Church in dialogue with the world."[20] As a young man, Péguy had left the church because he found the idea of eternal damnation intolerable: "La damnation est mon seul problème."[21] Balthasar explains, "A religion that has resigned itself to eternally losing its brethren without eternally regretting this has a fundamentally egotistic view of salvation and thus is at bottom utterly bourgeois and capitalistic."[22] Why, then, did the idea of damnation remain the central concern of the non-Christian Péguy? Why did the socialist Péguy compose a drama titled *Jeanne d'Arc* (1887), in which the heroine revolts against the idea of damnation and offers to suffer eternally in place of others? Because even after the dogma is dispensed with there remains a kind of hell on earth: destitution, exile, the absence of love. How better to express the consequences of indifference to the exile and suffering of one's neighbor on earth than the utter absence of solidarity that is damnation. "Am I my brother's keeper?" For Péguy, there is a strict parallel between abandoning one's neighbor to suffer on earth and abandoning one's neighbor to suffer eternal punishment. Hence, the second movement of Péguy's work *Marcel, premier dialogue de la cité harmonieuse* (1898), which calls for a city ruled by love, a city without exile. The only adequate response to the exile and destitution of others is absolute solidarity or communion:

> Our solidarity is with those who are eternally damned. We cannot bear that human beings should be treated inhumanly. We cannot bear that human beings should be turned away from the gate of the *polis*. That is the grand passion that animates us. We will tolerate no exception in Heaven or on earth.[23]

Around 1908, Péguy found his way back to the Catholic Church. The same idea that drove him out of the church led him back inexorably to the ecclesial body of Christ as the deepest source and form of absolute solidarity in love. Communion among people can be striven for (i.e., the founding of a just city) only because it has first been graciously bestowed by God in Christ:

> Innumerable connections bind all beings to Jesus, bind every soul and every body to Jesus — through this community, this communion. What an inextricable mesh, my children! Everything is linked with everything. You are linked together and linked to all. Everything is linked with everything and everyone, and at the same time all of this is linked with the body of Jesus.[24]

The first fruit of Péguy's return to the church was a reworking of his prose drama *Jeanne d'Arc* (1887) as *Le mystère de la charité de Jeanne d'Arc* (1910). Nothing is deleted from the first work; he simply added a meditation on Christ's passion that gives a new depth and horizon to Joan's revolt against the idea that fellow humans are eternally lost. The difference now is that Joan's refusal to resign herself strikes a nerve in God's own heart. God himself is not resigned to the possibility of damnation.

Péguy's next poem opens with the image of Hope as a little girl who holds the hands of her two older sisters, Faith and Charity; she is scarcely noticed, yet secretly, it is she who leads and carries them all. This meditation on the little girl Hope leads seamlessly to the image of a father working in the forest in winter who remembers having placed in prayer his sick children in the arms of Mary. The tenderness of the heart of a father who prays and hopes for his children opens a new perspective on the parable of the lost sheep. Why is there such rejoicing over the sheep that was lost and found? "Why," Péguy asks, "is it precisely the one that was lost, that had perished, that's worth precisely the ninety-nine others, the ninety-nine that were not lost.... It's unfair. Here is one (and it's precisely the one that was lost), who is worth as much, who counts as much, who causes as much joy as these poor ninety-nine others that had remained constant.... Secretly you have the impression that it weighs more, when you read the parable."[25] The possibility of loss brings to light one of the deepest mysteries of love: "He who loves places himself, by loving, by that very act, from then on, into dependence."[26] In the freedom of his love, God has initiated a covenant of reciprocal hope: "We must place our hope in God since he has so placed his in us.... God took the first step.... He has put his eternal hope in our hands, in our weak hands."[27]

> I think I said this (in my *Mystères*): that the lover enters a state of dependence upon the beloved, and that therefore God himself arrives at a state of dependence upon the lost sheep, and you could say that, to find the sheep again, he takes his bearings from it and from its wanderings.[28]

At this point, the poet returns to the theme of fatherhood in light of the parable of the prodigal son:

> It has been told to innumerable men,
> Unless one had a heart of stone... who could hear it without crying.
> It has touched a unique place in man's heart, a secret place....
> Like a nail of tenderness.
> *Then he said: A man had two sons.*[29]

Nothing more from the parable is recounted; these words are enough: "A man had two sons." These words that touch on the tenderness of a father's heart follow and accompany humankind in all of its follies and estrangement from God.

The poem had opened with the words "The faith that I love the best, says God, is hope."[30] God himself is speaking to his creation. The full significance of this remarkable shift of perspective becomes clear only in the concluding words of the poem, when God the Father speaks about the consummation of his Son's mission:

> Everything was finished. Let's not talk about it anymore. It hurts me to think about it.
> My Son's incredible descent among men.

Into their midst.

When you think of what they made of him.

Those thirty years that he was a carpenter among men.

Those three years that he was a sort of preacher among men....

Those three nights when he was dead in the midst of men.

Dead among the dead.

Through the centuries that he has been a host among men....

Now every man has the right to bury his own son.

Every man on earth, if the great misfortune befalls him

Not to have died before his son. And I alone, God,

My hands tied by this adventure,

I alone, father at that moment like so many fathers,

I alone was unable to bury my son.[31]

The image of the Father who has handed over his Son without reserve — "what the Father has given he will never take back" — is brought together with the image of a father who patiently awaits the return of his prodigal son. Balthasar sees in the poetry of Charles Péguy something unprecedented in the history of Christian thought: "a breakthrough into a comprehensive theology of hope ... [that] makes its presence felt today, gently but irresistibly, by a structural shift in the whole theological edifice."[32]

> The whole of Péguy's art and theology flow more and more towards prayer.... It is a dialogue with God ... which is constantly developing into a monologue of God the Father, addressed without distinction to his Son, to the men he has created and to himself. It is a form of "theology as Trinitarian conversation."[33]

At this point, the poetry of Charles Péguy is at one with the Trinitarian theology of Adrienne von Speyr.[34] The question of the loss of a fellow human being can be addressed adequately only within the dialogue that unfolds between the Father and the Son. Balthasar received from both Péguy and von Speyr a new way of thinking about solidarity and the possibility of damnation. I suggested in the introduction that this new path for thinking about hope is guided and measured by the mystery of the Eucharist. Let me try to explain. The key insight that Balthasar takes over from Odo Casel and von Speyr, among others, is the idea that Christ's entire life from the first moment of the incarnation is one of obedient thanksgiving or Eucharist to the Father. The incarnate Son gives thanks to the Father both for his divine existence received eternally from the Father and for the gift of the Father's creation. The unity here is crucial. The Son's eucharistic gift of himself in the paschal mystery is simultaneously a revelation of the Father's love and a revelation of the original purpose of creation. The mission of the Son is to receive the whole of creation, including every last human being and ultimately the entire material cosmos, as a gift from the Father and to bring creation back to the Father in his life, death, resurrection, ascension, and Eucharist. It is not surprising that one of the clearest statements of the universal mission of the Son is found in the discourse on the bread of life in the Gospel of John: "This is the will of him who sent me, that I should lose nothing of all that he has given me, but raise it up on the last day" (John 6:39). Because the entire life of Christ is eucharistic, the gift of the Eucharist includes a participation in the saving mysteries of the incarnate Son's life and mission:

> Christ, in surrendering his sacrificed flesh and shed blood for his disciples, was communicating, not merely the material side of his bodily substance, but the saving events wrought by it.... The fundamental presupposition is that the Person of Jesus is really present; but along with the Person comes his entire temporal history and, in particular, its climax in Cross and Resurrection.[35]

The Eucharist is a divine and a human gift. It is divine because Christ communicates the very substance of his being (transubstantiation), which means that he communicates in the Eucharist what is best and most intimate in the life of God: the Holy Spirit, who is the reciprocal love of the Father and Son. In the words of St. Ephrem the Syrian, "He called the bread his living body and he filled it with himself and his Spirit.... He who eats it with faith, eats Fire and Spirit.... Take and eat this, all of you, and eat with it the Holy Spirit. For it is truly my body and whoever eats it will have eternal life."[36] The Eucharist is also a human gift, which means that the best fruits of creation and human work (bread and wine) are gathered into the body of the Son and brought back to the Father in praise and thanksgiving.

Balthasar's friend and teacher Henri de Lubac helped to recover the patristic and medieval understanding of the causal relation between the Eucharist and the church: "Each has been entrusted to the other, so to speak, by Christ; the Church produces the Eucharist, but the Eucharist also produces the Church."[37] In receiving the sacrament of the Eucharist, we receive the gift of communion with all of Christ's members on heaven and earth. The final encyclical letter of John Paul II confirmed this insight: "Our union with

Christ, which is a gift and grace for each of us, makes it possible for us, in him, to share in the unity of his body which is the Church" (*Ecclesia de Eucharistia* 23). John Paul II further emphasized the missionary implications of the Eucharist:

> By its union with Christ, ... [the Church] becomes a "sacrament" for humanity, a sign and instrument of the salvation achieved by Christ, the light of the world and the salt of the earth (cf. Matt. 5:13–16), for the redemption of all. ... From the perpetuation of the sacrifice of the Cross and her communion with the body and blood of Christ in the Eucharist, the Church draws the spiritual power needed to carry out her mission. (*Ecclesia de Eucharistia* 22)

The communion that we receive in Eucharist draws us into Christ's own love for the world, especially for those who seem lost. In his own way, Origen brings to light the missionary implications of the Eucharist when he speaks of the apostles and the disciples of the apostles becoming food for the life of the world:

> Our Lord and Savior says, "If you do not eat my flesh and drink my blood, you will not have life in you. For my flesh is food indeed and my blood is drink indeed. ... " For with the flesh and blood of his word he feeds and refreshes the whole human race, as with pure food and pure drink. In second place, after his flesh is the "pure food" of Peter and Paul and all the apostles, and, in third place, their disciples. In the same way everyone can be "pure food" for his neighbor.[38]

What is meant by sharing in Christ's having become food and drink is clarified by something that Origen writes earlier in his commentary:

> "The Son of Love," who humbled himself for the love that he had for us, and though he was equal to God sought not his own but our advantage, and to that end emptied himself. Do you think that having gone so far in seeking our good; he now ceases to seek it? ... He stands at the altar making propitiation for us to the Father. It was for this very reason that on the eve of his sacrifice he uttered the words, "I shall not drink of this fruit of the vine until the day when I drink it new with you."
>
> But your full joy will only come when not one of your members is lacking. Wherefore you must wait for the others, just as others have waited for you. Surely, too if you who are a member have not perfect joy as long as a member is missing, how much more will he, our Lord and Savior, consider his joy incomplete while any member of his body is missing.[39]

By virtue of receiving the Eucharist, we are invited to bring to our neighbor and even to our enemy an unimagined gift; we are asked to receive them in Christ as an image of the Father's unfathomable love. In humility and patience we are called to receive our neighbor and our enemy so thoroughly that we could not conceive of a happiness or joy that would exclude them. In solidarity and hope we are willing to wait for them as long as necessary. Balthasar writes, "Christian community is established in the Eucharist, which presupposes the descent into hell (mine and yours)."[40]

Balthasar is known, of course, as a theologian who never ceased to mediate and marvel at the depth of Christ's suffering *pro nobis*. It is significant, then, that the first and last word of his thought is not the suffering of the cross but rather the simple joy of a child. "To be a Child of the Father," he writes, "holds primacy over the whole drama of salvation."[41] Balthasar's work in service to the church, including the community that he founded with Adrienne von Speyr and the astonishing breadth of books that he translated, published, and authored, will continue to bear fruit because his work radiates something of the simple joy of a child for whom all is gift.

Chapter Seven

Not Peace, but a Sword

How Balthasar Changed My Mind

Rodney A. Howsare

There are two themes in particular in Flannery O'Connor's short novel *The Violent Bear It Away* that I would like to use as lenses through which to explain how Balthasar has changed my mind. The first concerns the status of reason in the modern world and the relationship between that reason and religious faith. The second theme flows from the first and concerns the violent conflict that is bound to arise between genuine Christian faith and modern reason, or concerns, to put it differently, what I will call the nonneutrality of modern reason. The first could be considered a more humanistic or catholic sort of concern and the second a more crisis-oriented or evangelical sort of concern. O'Connor was, after all, something of a walking oxymoron: a Southern Catholic. And it is just this strange mix — call it Bible Belt Thomism if you will — that makes her uniquely suited to help me explain how Balthasar has come to influence my theological development.

The short novel contains four main and very well developed characters: old Tarwater, a living, breathing twentieth-century prophet; his estranged nephew, Rayber, a citified, modernized school teacher who has decidedly turned his back on his uncle's religion; Rayber's own nephew, young Tarwater, a figure caught somewhere between these former two, born into Rayber's house, reared in the old man's, only to return to Rayber's; and Rayber's dimwitted son, Bishop, a symbol to Rayber of God's nonexistence and to Tarwater of God's judgment on Rayber. The novel charters, in typically brilliant fashion, not only the violent clash between reason and faith in the modern world, but also the apotheosis of modern reason and its inability either to grasp or explain the reality of the world placed before it. Such reason, we are shown, refuses to see beyond the surface of things, refuses, namely, to press to what it is that makes things what they are in the first place or to what it is that enables us to name them. And, as such, it balks in the face of anything that cannot be reduced to the level of the quantifiable or scientifically categorizable.

What makes O'Connor's novel provocative is that she sees rejection of God — whether Rayber's explicit rejection under the guise of enlightened reason or young Tarwater's struggle against the faith of his uncle under the guise of adolescent rebellion — as a concomitant rejection of all that makes life beautiful and meaningful. In this sense, the novel is not merely an incisive depiction of the modern struggle against faith; it is also a reflection on the nature of truth and beauty. O'Connor, in what can only be called good Nietzschean fashion, refuses to allow modernity to have it both ways, refuses, namely, to allow modernity to have a meaningful world without God, and in this she is, in the final analysis, a twentieth-century heir to Dostoyevsky. To put it differently, O'Connor understands that the modern rejection of God — which need not, incidentally, amount to an explicit atheism — cannot but have *this-worldly* sorts of consequences, and so she will not stand for what the late Allan Bloom called America's "happy nihilism." In the novel this is presented with great perception in terms of Rayber's struggle to come to terms with the love that he has for his mentally handicapped son, Bishop. This must be quoted at length:

> His [Rayber's] normal way of looking on Bishop was as an *x* signifying the general hideousness of fate. He did not believe that he himself was formed in the image and likeness of God but that Bishop was he had no doubt. The little boy was part of a simple equation that required no further solution, except at the moments when with little or no warning he would feel himself overwhelmed by the horrifying love. Anything he looked at too long could bring it on. Bishop did not have to be around. It could be a stick or a stone, the line of a shadow, the absurd old man's walk of a starling crossing the sidewalk. If, without thinking, he lent himself to it, he would feel suddenly a morbid surge of the love that terrified him — powerful enough to throw him to the ground in an act of idiot praise. It was completely irrational and abnormal.
>
> He was not afraid of love in general. He knew the value of it and how it could be used. He had seen it transform in cases where nothing else had worked, much as with his poor sister. None of this had the least bearing on his

situation. The love that would overcome him was of a different order entirely. It was not the kind that could be used for the child's improvement or his own. It was love without reason, love from something futureless, love that appeared to exist only to be itself, imperious and all demanding, the kind that would cause him to make a fool of himself in an instant. And it only began with Bishop. It began with Bishop and then like an avalanche covered everything his reason hated. He always felt with it a rush of longing to have the old man's eyes — insane, fish-coloured, violent with their impossible vision of a world transfigured — turned on him once again. The longing was like an undertow in his blood dragging him backwards to what he knew to be madness.[1]

Notice that Rayber wants to treat Bishop in the manner of the scientist, whether it is the hard scientist who wants to analyze Bishop as a case of this or that disorder, or of the social scientist who *knows* that *love* can have a positive influence on cases such as these. O'Connor points out two things in particular about modern reason that correspond nicely to Balthasar's analysis of the same. First, in a world without God, the world can have only the meaning that we give it; it can have no inherent meaning or order. Here, then, Bishop's retardation stands as a sign that the world has no meaning and points to what O'Connor calls "the hideousness of fate." But, second, and this follows from the first, if the world has no inherent meaning, then reason is absolute master over all that is: insofar as it has given (indeed, made) the only meaning that the world has, there is nothing that reason cannot, at least potentially, grasp. The basic irrationality of the world leads to a hyper-rationalism in which reason is understood as mastery or power over that which is given. Indeed, "that which is given" is no longer distinguished from that which is made. As Wendell Berry has pointed out in his critique of E. O. Wilson's *Consilience,* to Wilson a mystery is not that which intrinsically transcends reason, but rather is that which reason has yet to solve.[2] And this accounts for the fear that Rayber feels in the face of his inexplicable love for Bishop: love points to the fact that there is something worthy of love, something that is not simply to be mastered by the lover. If the struggle against belief exists in Rayber, in young Tarwater it becomes palpable, and it amounts, in many ways, to the same thing,

He [young Tarwater] tried when possible to pass over these thoughts, to keep his vision located on an even level, to see no more than what was in front of his face and to let his eyes stop at the surface of that. It was as if he were

afraid that if he let his eye rest for an instant longer than was needed to place
something — a spade, a hoe, the mule's hind quarters before his plow, the red
furrow under him — that the thing would suddenly stand before him, strange
and terrifying, demanding that he name it and name it justly and be judged
for the name he gave it. He did all he could to avoid this threatened intimacy
of creation. When the Lord's call came, he wished it to be a voice from out of
a clear and empty sky, the trumpet of the Lord God Almighty, untouched by
any fleshly hand or breath.[3]

It is interesting that the initial battle here is not between religious faith and
unbelief, but rather between two different ways of perceiving the world, and
it is here I think that O'Connor's thought is closest to Balthasar's, especially
in *The Glory of the Lord: Seeing the Form.* Here Balthasar understands, as
does O'Connor, that religious faith cannot just be added onto any old form
of reason, in what could only be, at any rate, a heteronomous fashion. As
Balthasar puts it, the eyes that are unable to see this-worldly beauty are the
last that will be able to see the actual glory of the Lord. The connection
implied between faith and reason in this passage is an intimate and intrinsic
one: if young Tarwater allows himself genuinely to see what is in front of
him, all the way to the point of discerning what it is that enables him to
"name" it, and name it "justly," he will be on the verge of something that he
is trying to escape — the old man's faith. And if it is the case that even *this
world* is a sign of what is more than this world, then it will not be as easy
to escape his calling as young Tarwater thinks. Indeed, Tarwater is perfectly
happy to wait until God calls him from some heavenly heights — "from
out of a clear and empty sky" — what he cannot bear is a God who comes
to him from within this world, from what O'Connor calls "this threatened
intimacy of creation." In such a view, creation itself, right down to a "mule's
hind quarters" and "the red furrow under him," takes on the character of
signs, signs that signify something more than just hind quarters and red
furrow. Or, as Balthasar states it, *x* is never merely *x*.

We come finally to old Tarwater, a prophetic figure right out of the Old
Testament. Old Tarwater is not the philosopher that O'Connor is, and he
himself could not explain what she does in the story. Yet, as a simple religious
believer, Tarwater knows that something is wrong with the modern world
and its truncated view reason, knowing, furthermore, that he must fight
against it with the whole of his life. It is at this point that the "violence" of the

novel comes into view. What makes modern reason particularly dangerous, O'Connor seems to be telling us, is precisely its peaceful and humanitarian exterior. In many ways, Rayber is a much better person than is Tarwater. He certainly seems to care more about humanity and has an enormous desire to improve it. Furthermore, Rayber is not hostile, at least in theory, to the old man's faith. There is no clash here as there was between, say, Christianity and ancient paganism or between Christianity and atheistic communism. Rather, Liberal reason wishes to make room for faith, wishes to give it its proper sphere of operation and render it its proper domain and use. At one point in the story, in fact, old Tarwater decides to move in with Rayber, in secret hope that he will have a chance to baptize (a very physical thing, baptism) little Bishop. But Rayber has secret designs of his own. While he has the old man there, he keeps asking him questions about his faith. The old man, for a while, is taken in with this and sees it as an opportunity to restore his estranged nephew's faith. But as the investigation proceeds, the old man begins to notice that Rayber is taking notes on their conversations. Intuitively, Tarwater understands what is happening: Rayber is trying to contain the old man's religious faith and calling into a larger "system," in order to make a place for it, categorize it, and grant it its proper role; he is attempting to *explain* it, thereby explaining it away. And the old man realizes that, as such, as something explained and allotted a place, it can no longer be what it, in fact, is. *Si comprehendis non est Deus!* When the old man recalls this to young Tarwater, the "violence" of the struggle becomes clear:

> "That's where he [Rayber] wanted me," the old man said, "and he thought once he had me in that schoolteacher magazine, I would be as good as in his head."... "Where he wanted me was inside that schoolteacher magazine. He thought once he got me in there, I'd be as good as inside his head and done for and that would be that, that would be the end of it. Well, that wasn't the end of it! Here I sit. And there you sit. In freedom. Not inside anybody's head!"[4]

With the character of Tarwater we meet with what I understand as the "Southern" aspect of O'Connor's work. Rowan Williams has pointed out recently the influence of Jacques Maritain's aesthetic theory on O'Connor and has shown it to be at work in the critique of scientific reason outlined above.[5] But beside this Maritainian-Thomistic critique of modern reason lies an equally incisive critique of any religion that makes its peace with "the

world." And, indeed, the second critique flows from the first: if modern reason is not construed in terms of neutral space within which one can practice
any religion one wants, if there is something in it that constitutes in fact
a contrary metaphysic, then there simply cannot be peaceful coexistence.
What O'Connor seems to admire — in the midst of all the ridicule — about
the evangelical Protestantism of the South with which she was surrounded,
was its vivid sense that the world was still *world* in some Johannine sense of
that word. She had a strong sense that no matter how polished Christianity became, as long as it preached the singularity of Christ and the central
role of the cross (and here we would have to look at her brilliant short story
"The Artificial Nigger"), it would appear as foolishness to the wise. And this
explains why all of her religious figures have something about them of the
fanatic, something about them that Kierkegaard would identify with the difference between an apostle and a genius. In short, O'Connor has, along with
a strong Thomistic sense of the insufficiency of modern reason, a strong Lu-
theran sense of the scandal of the cross. And these two coincide in her in a
way that, as I stated before, makes her uniquely suited to help me talk about
the two aspects of Balthasar's theology that have most changed my mind.

Grappling with Modernity

There is an old saying about Pennsylvania that it is Pittsburgh on one end,
Philadelphia on the other, and Kentucky in between, and the fact that I grew
up in that "in between" might help to account for my attraction to the southern aspect of O'Connor's fiction. And I grew up not only in southwestern
Pennsylvania, but also in the Pentecostal holiness version of American evangelicalism. In fact, I attended an Assemblies of God undergraduate college,
where I at least had a number of very thoughtful young professors, took six
semesters of biblical Greek, and received some excellent advice about graduate school. Upon graduation, however, I took a year off to do pastoral work,
get married, and do a significant amount of reading. It was 1987, and Allen
Bloom's *Closing of the American Mind* had just come out. I had not heard
of Bloom, but the endorsement by Saul Bellow on the cover was enough to
convince me to buy it and read it. During my last couple of years in college, I had become increasingly interested in philosophy and, in particular,
in apologetics and the question of the place of faith in the modern world. Of

course, the college that I attended did not have a developed philosophy of modernity; it was simply understood that we rejected it. Being a branch of American evangelicalism meant that we had, in fact, basically defined ourselves in our differences from Liberal Protestantism, most of this difference boiling down to what we called a high view of Scripture and its authority.

And yet already at this age, something about our reaction to modernity did not seem right to me: it seemed reactive and superficial. It seemed as if the "Liberals" had determined the playing field and the rules of the game, that we were playing that game, and that we were reaching more "conservative" conclusions in the process. And there was a strange combination of rationalism and fideism in the manner in which we did this. Our apologetics was not significantly more sophisticated than that of Josh MacDowell, who was still making the old arguments from the prophets — that what, say, Daniel had predicted came to pass, and therefore the Bible was indisputably true. What was interesting about arguments of this nature, however, is that the logic that they used was in some strange and even obvious ways rationalistic. The proof that the McDowells of the world sought was, in fact, of the "smoking gun" variety. And, if I remember correctly, he had scientific proof of the resurrection, although I cannot for the life of me remember what it was.

At any rate, this rationalism was coupled with an equally baffling fideism, insofar as theology was basically reduced to biblical studies (biblicism, fideism), even as our biblical studies were undertaken in a highly scientific fashion (rationalism, historical criticism). My professors had nothing but scorn, for instance, for the "allegorical" reading of Scripture, which they referred to as "isogesis." Furthermore, our biblicism led to a rather strange disengagement from the surrounding culture, insofar as there was no attempt to engage any of the key thinkers who paved the way to modernity, and yet we were engaged in certain sorts of intellectual practices and habits that were thoroughly modern. We had ignored modernity, refused to engage it, indeed, did not even see the need to engage it, and so we had unknowingly bought into some of its deepest presuppositions about the nature of reason, reality, and knowing.

It was under these conditions that I first read Allan Bloom. I had never read an author who had placed modernity under such close scrutiny before, and it was clear to me that his critique went much deeper and was much more profound than the one I had been trained in. I also knew, the moment I had finished this book, that I must enter graduate school to study philosophy rather than theology. So, I went to a relatively typical state school in order to study philosophy. The department had no real identity: there were analytic philosophers, a Presbyterian Thomist (!), a few Continental types, and an expert in American philosophy who had studied at the University of Chicago with Leo Strauss. Make no mistake, he was no Straussian, but he did agree to direct my thesis on Strauss's political philosophy. It is from Strauss that I learned something that I mentioned above with regard to Flannery O'Connor, something that would greatly prepare me for my eventual encounter with Hans Urs von Balthasar: modern, Liberal thought is not merely neutral space within which one is free to develop one's own views concerning ultimate ends and truths; rather, modernity has its own logic, which is just so far an alternative to that of either classical political philosophy or with the development of that philosophy as undertaken by the great Christian, Muslim, and Jewish thinkers of the Middle Ages. Much later I heard Alasdair MacIntyre say something similar: "Liberalism is the only metanarrative which has convinced the world that it is not a metanarrative."

More precisely, I learned from Strauss to be suspicious of the Kantian move that lay at the bottom of just about all modern thought. This move begins by making a strong separation between what can be known empirically and what can only be posited or believed, and it is the basis of Weber's famous fact/value distinction. As Michael Polanyi puts it, Kant spends a great deal of time dismissing the possibility of metaphysical knowledge (noumenal), contrasting such non-knowledge with the more sure-footed empirical knowledge (phenomenal), only then to build his entire system on a series of postulates from the noumenal that alone make what he does in the phenomenal worthwhile. As Polanyi states it,

> Instead we meet with the typical device of modern intellectual prevarication, first systematized by Kant in his regulative principles. Knowledge that we hold to be true and also vital to us, is made light of, because we cannot account for its acceptance in terms of a critical philosophy. We then feel entitled to continue using that knowledge, even while flattering our sense of intellectual superiority by disparaging it. And we actually go on, firmly relying on this despised knowledge to guide and lend meaning to our more

exact enquiries, while pretending that these alone come up to our standards of scientific stringency.[6]

For Strauss, the issue was modern social science and its tendency to make numerous prescientific assumptions even as it went about its allegedly "value free" and scientific work. As Strauss once quipped, "Even a social scientist who goes out to interview people for his latest scientific study knows to interview people rather than chimpanzees."

By the time I went to work on my Ph.D. in theology, this time at a Catholic university, I had been well prepared to see this trick of modern thought. And it was this that helped me to see, once I began, that the real debate in the modern Catholic university was not between liberal Catholics and conservative Catholics; rather, it was between those who saw this modern move as a problem and those who did not, for in many ways the "conservatives" had accepted the move just as thoroughly as had their liberal counterparts. In other words, their critique of progressive Catholicism was, much like the one that I had gotten as an undergraduate, entirely too superficial. As David Schindler has been known to say, "Being a conservative Liberal is like rearranging the furniture on the Titanic."

The school that I attended was predominantly Transcendental Thomist in outlook, and I was introduced in a rigorous and fairly sustained manner to the thought of Karl Rahner and Bernard Lonergan. Many of my conservative friends thought that Rahner and Lonergan were theological progressives, but I did not see it that way. Rather, both men were making use of Kantian categories of thought, not to sustain a secularist stance but rather to undermine it. Rahner, not unlike Balthasar in this regard, wished to reassert the intrinsic connection between nature and grace that modernity had severed. The problem stems from the fact that the cure does not get to the root of the illness, which, finally, is a problem not of epistemology but rather of metaphysics. In other words, Kant is astute enough to see that if there is simply no connection between the world as it actually is and the subject's knowledge of that world, then even scientific knowledge is doomed. The problem is that he tries to bridge this gulf entirely by appeals to the transcendental subject. Notice that in such an approach, knowledge of God, and even goodness, sits squarely on the subjective side of the subject/object divide. If the issue, then, is not addressed at the level of being, theology tends — and in the case of the school that I attended did more than just tend — in one of two directions. In one direction, theology will proceed in an inordinately "from below" fashion that inevitably leads to tailoring the faith to subjective experience. This happens because anything that is from above — insofar as it has lost its intrinsic connection to the subject, insofar as the subject has been alienated from either the object in particular or being in general — is now seen as heteronomous and as therefore a threat to autonomy.[7] In the other direction, theology will rest content to do its work on the fact side of the fact/value distinction, resulting in a fixation on theological methodology. Here, since there is now no possibility of knowing the whole, theology is reduced to the study of parts, without the recognition that, even if unwittingly, there has already been a decision about the relationship between the whole and the part that does not itself stem from the study of the parts. For example, the entire historical-critical approach to Scripture has already (at least implicitly) made a decision about the whole that allows it to think that it can prescind from that whole in its investigation of the part. When Balthasar makes the comment, in the first volume of *The Glory of the Lord,* that autopsies are done only on dead people, he is not just being funny — although he is also being that — he is pointing out something simply true. The reason that I do not, under normal circumstances, begin to disassemble living bodies, the way I would, say, a lawnmower, is that I already have a prescientific (metaphysical) understanding about the whole of that living body that determines the manner in which I treat the part. Even if, for medical reasons, for instance, I have to sometimes treat the human body as if it is a machine, I can do so only under the prior recognition that it is never merely that. It seems to me that if this insight were taken more seriously, it would alter the way in which Scripture is studied in the modern university. Or, it would at least force the modern university to admit that its approach to Scripture is not theologically neutral.

But to return to Balthasar, it was not until my second-to-last semester that I took a course in which I was required to read Henri de Lubac's *Catholicism* and the first volume of Balthasar's *Glory of the Lord.* I must admit that I did not fully appreciate the revolutionary nature of de Lubac's work at the time, but Balthasar's work came like a revelation. At the risk of sounding overly dramatic, it was as if everything that I had learned up to that point was simply preparation for the reading of that book. First, Balthasar fully understood the nature of modern reason and the "intellectual prevarication" that lay at its foundation:

> Modern rationalism, attempting to narrow the range of truth to a supposedly isolable core of pure theory, has exiled the good and the beautiful from the domain of the rationally verifiable, relegating them to arbitrary subjectivity or to a world of private belief and personal taste.[8]

Since he recognized this, Balthasar knew that the response to such thought must involve a renewed discussion of the transcendental properties of Being, a renewed discussion, in short, of metaphysics. Any critique of modern epistemology must begin, in Balthasar's view, with an investigation of Being. The first thing that had to be healed — and the reason that Balthasar begins his trilogy with "the Beautiful" — was the severed connection between the things that appear and that which appears in the things that appear that enables us to know them and name them, and this means a reconnection between the phenomenal and noumenal realms, which Kant had severed. This is why I think that it was fitting to begin this essay with Flannery O'Connor. O'Connor, like Balthasar, understood that modern human beings had lost their ability to see things for what they are, and that the crisis of faith in the modern world could not be healed without attending, first, to this blindness. In the first volume of *Theo-Logic*, for instance, Balthasar, with some help from Josef Pieper, points out that at some point in the late Middle Ages it no longer made sense to say that "all that exists is true." Truth had become reduced to statements of fact and had lost its intrinsic connection to the nature of things in themselves. Metaphysics had given way to epistemology, and the latter had been divorced from the former. The more classical approach, on the other hand, pointed to the fact that in order to be known, things must not only be knowable, but they must first have been known in some preeminent way. Notice that in this approach there is an intimate connection, first, between knowing and what it is that the thing known gives of itself, and, second, between the nature of things and the Origin and End of things. It was on this basis that Aquinas could argue that when one knows anything, one implicitly knows God. This must be what O'Connor has in mind when she refers to "the threatened intimacy of creation." It should also be noted that this older approach had a paradoxical effect on knowing that preserved it from that tendency in modern thought to be at once too rationalistic and too subjectivistic at one and the same time. In claiming to know nothing, we in fact have an explanation for everything.

Yet Balthasar's thought cannot be reduced to the simple reassertion of a realist metaphysic. Balthasar is not, in the final analysis, an uncritical romantic. He appreciates that modernity is a response to something in late medieval thought that had underappreciated the "rightful autonomy" of the created order. Nominalism did not come out of nowhere; it was a sign of the fact that the relationship between God and the world and the relationship between divine and human freedom had not yet been sufficiently worked out. As such, nominalism can be seen, in a positive light, as trying to reestablish, on the one hand, a proper notion of the transcendence of God and, on the other, the proper autonomy of the created order. Unfortunately, it did so by beginning with a series of false dichotomies that doomed it to failure from the beginning. For instance, since it abandoned the participatory framework of classical Thomistic metaphysics, it had either to rob divine freedom to pay human freedom or vice versa. Still, Balthasar sees nominalism as a symptom of the confusion of late medieval thought as much as a cause.[9]

The important point for the purpose of the present essay is this: besides clarifying the above — the need to return to the metaphysical — Balthasar taught me that that return cannot be a simple return insofar as modernity was really attending to things that were the proper progeny of Christianity. It would not be too much to say that Balthasar taught me to view modernity as a heresy, but — and this is important — to see it as a *Christian* heresy. This means that at least some of its central concerns are Christian, and that, furthermore, they need to be resituated in their proper Christian context. I do not have sufficient space here to go into the details of this, but let us note that Balthasar sought to address modernity, then, not simply by rejecting it (insofar as what would remain after the rejection might be Christian, but it would be less than fully Christian), but rather by situating its positive insights into a Christian context. In order to do this, Balthasar turned to the insights of philosophical personalism. This was not just an arbitrary preference in his view insofar as it could easily be argued that the concept of personhood is Christianity's single most important contribution to Western philosophical thought. In other words, the personalist philosophies that were growing up around thinkers such as Martin Buber, Franz Rosenzweig, and Gabriel Marcel were not without Christian influence, and yet they were not simply Christian theology either.

This makes Balthasar's relationship to past Christian thought a rather complicated one. On the one hand, he is thoroughly and unapologetically traditional when it comes to the Nicene and Chalcedonian definitions. Balthasar will make no compromising concessions with modernity in order to mitigate Christianity's scandal of particularity. On the other hand, Balthasar will excoriate the tradition when he feels that it is not allowing its Trinitarian breakthrough to permeate its entire way of thinking. He worries, for instance, that too often the great theologians of the tradition *begin* with Plotinus's One until they are done doing their "theologia" (what we might today call "natural theology" or "negative theology"), only then to tack on, sometimes in an extrinsic manner, their insights concerning the "economia" (positive theology). Balthasar will often point out that both the philosophy and the spirituality of the Fathers is not sufficiently influenced by their thoroughly Trinitarian theologies. He also sees a similar tendency in Aquinas's overly neat separation of *de Deo uno* from *de Deo trino*. But Balthasar's solution to this oversight is never simply to abandon the tradition; rather, he engages in an act of retrieval that allows that which is most authentically Christian in the tradition to correct that which is insufficiently so.

Balthasar, then, turns to just those things that are most distinctively Christian — the doctrine of the Trinity, the notion of personhood, the notion of creation as a deliberate act of love — in order to find the key to the proper relationship between all of the things that modernity falsely separated: nature and grace, God and the world, divine and human freedom, faith and reason, and the like. Of course, this may make it seem as if Balthasar has artificially forced a theological and heteronomous solution onto a philosophical and human set of problems, but he insists that this is not the case, for even at the level of the creaturely, antinomies arise that are best dealt with in the context of "love alone." As Balthasar is constantly pointing out, I only come to know myself in the smile of my mother. In other words, I am constituted — to borrow language from David Schindler — at my very core not *apart from,* but rather precisely *in,* my relationship to others. And this goes for beings all the way down to the level of the inanimate. This insight enables Balthasar to avoid the mutually exclusive sort of thinking that has dominated and crippled modern thought: either me or the other guy, either freedom or tyranny, either reason or faith, either freedom or equality, either the individual or the group, and so forth. Rather, even at the level of this-worldly being, things are not what they are *in opposition to,* but rather *on account of,* their relations with the things that they are not.

So, in addition to the Thomistic insight mentioned above in the framework of O'Connor's work, Balthasar also taught me about the centrality of relationality to all things. This attention to the relational allows Balthasar to give sufficient weight to modernity's concern for freedom and individuality without having to buy into the fateful fragmentation that still plagues modern thought. To conclude this section with one example: modern thought seems unable to overcome a fateful separation between freedom and responsibility, and it makes almost no difference, in this regard, whether one is a liberal or a conservative. Indeed, conservatives are wont to limit freedom in the area of culture while liberals are inclined to limit freedom in the area of economics. I often tell my students that a conservative is one who believes that you are free to do whatever you want with your wallet, while a liberal is one who believes that you are free to do whatever you want with your genitals. The lack of consistency here, however, stems from the fact that neither side of the political spectrum has yet dug deep enough to deal with the modern opposition between freedom and duty in the first place, so that they simply pick and choose the areas, seemingly arbitrarily, upon which they are willing to place limits.

But what if freedom and duty are mutually conditioned from the ground up? What if, to go back to Balthasar, I really do only come into my own identity *within* the context of my prior relation to my mother? Is it not now the case that my freedom can hardly be pitted against the freedom of my mother without undermining that very freedom, that my prior indebtedness *to her* is the very thing that grounds my freedom *from her* in the first place? And is it not furthermore the case that my mother's freedom is also similarly grounded? And so on. We are now at Balthasar's famous fourfold distinction, which achieves two things at the same time. First, it shows that identity is rooted in relationality insofar as it reveals the gift nature of all that is, and a gift cannot help but refer, naturally and *as a distinct thing with its own proper identity,* to a giver. Second, it provides a transition from natural to revealed wisdom that seems less forced and less fraught with danger than the sometimes standard one that still fails to make an intrinsic connection between Plotinus's One (or Aristotle's unmoved mover) and the God of Jesus Christ. If Plotinus's One is not a Trinity of loving Persons, it only stands to reason that the relationship between it and the world would be different than that of a God who is a Trinity of Persons in one Being. Only a Trinitarian God would create, Balthasar reminds us.

This latter point is crucial because it allows Balthasar to make a renewed claim for the centrality of theology to the human predicament without in any way wanting to replace thinking (philosophy) with believing (theology). For Balthasar, philosophy leads, naturally and of its own accord (providing that it does not artificially short-circuit its quest) to the theological; just as the theological provides answers that, even if always and, given the limits and sinfulness of human reason, even necessarily surprising and disconcerting, are, in hindsight and with the eyes of faith, always fitting to the questions that they address. There is a great deal that would still need to be discussed if this were to be an even remotely adequate treatment of Balthasar's Christian metaphysics — for instance, the real distinction between *esse* and *essentia,* the relationship between God, nonsubsistent being, and beings in the world, and so forth — but hopefully this will suffice to account for the first way in which Balthasar changed my mind. Before proceeding to the second way in which Balthasar changed my mind, a brief summary should prove helpful.

First, Balthasar taught me that the modern crisis of faith is, at bottom, a crisis of reason. By reducing reason to the factual and no longer asking the question as to what it is that makes things knowable in the first place, or what it is that enables us to name things and name them justly, modernity had severed the natural link between knowing and metaphysics or between knowing this or that thing and knowing God. The world had lost its sign character and had ceased to be interesting even as world. Next, drawing on the work of philosophical personalism, Balthasar was able to refine my understanding of the relationship between God and the world in a way that, on the one hand, did justice to the modern concern over creaturely autonomy and, on the other, established an intrinsic connection between our natural knowing and the God of Jesus Christ. It is not that one can now know on the basis of reason alone that God is triune; it is that even our earthly knowing points to the relationality of all things in a way that makes sense in the light of the fact that God happens to be triune. Here, Balthasar follows Romano Guardini in his notion that besides the areas of philosophy (truths known on the basis of reason) and theology (truths known on the basis of revelation) lies is a third area where natural wisdom takes on a new light in the context of what is known through revelation (cf. Étienne Gilson's "Christian philosophy").

The Violent Bear It Away

If there is one thing that I learned to appreciate while growing up in a Southern version of evangelical Protestantism, it is that there is a violent conflict between Christianity and "the world." It was a constant theme in the sermons that I heard (at the rate of three a week, at about an hour each): "we" were not "of the world," even if we had to live in the world. Of course, many of the ways in which we distinguished ourselves from the world now seem a little silly and superficial compared to the ways in which we did not. For instance, we did not play cards or dance or go to movies, but we did buy big cars and own large televisions, and we practically had a corner on the markets of gluttony and gossip. Nonetheless, and in spite of the superficiality of our critique, I grew up with a deep appreciation for all of those passages in the Bible that speak of the violent conflict that will inevitably exist between the followers of Christ and "the world."

When I left that world in order to go to graduate school, first at a secular state school and then at a fairly Rahnerian Catholic school, this apocalyptic approach to things began to look a little quaint. With regard to the secularist stance, it appears judgmental and intolerant; with regard to a Rahnerian Catholic stance, it seems to have an underdeveloped doctrine of creation or seems to fail to realize that we live in a "world of grace." By the time I got to a Catholic university, American Catholicism had long since made its peace with the world. Windows had long since been thrown open and a great deal of air had come in, making any distinction at all between the church and the world seem a bit strained and certainly old-fashioned. And I have to admit that I had become quite confused and even somewhat schizophrenic on these matters. The Christianity that I had grown up in certainly seemed to lack an adequate theology of creation, making it impossible to appreciate any human work that was not explicitly about Jesus Christ. Everything that was not explicitly Christian was "secular," and we did not use "secular" as a compliment. Philosophy, literature, the arts, politics, economics, psychology — these were "secular" pursuits, and we were perfectly happy to let "the world" have them. Anything that we did borrow from the world had to be Christianized, even if such Christianization was almost always embarrassingly superficial. Our "literature" was Christian, our music was Christian, our psychology was Christian; even the cruises that our church members took were Christian.

Of course, there are many ways to get away from this sort of narrowness. I had long since put this version of Christianity behind me, but the problem that stood before me seemed to fall under two possible solutions. There was the solution of "old school" Thomism, which clearly delineated between the realms of nature and grace, relegating the former to the purview of reason and the latter to the purview of the supernatural. God was the God of both, but they were clearly and distinctly divided so that no intrinsic connection appeared to exist between the two of them. Reason and this world go together; revelation and the next world go together. Natural virtues provide the means to goodness in this world; supernatural virtues provide the means to life everlasting in heaven. Nothing that is natural or "secular" needs to be disparaged, provided that it is good and reasonable and is not in clear contradiction to what we know through revelation. This approach also had the advantage of making it very easy to live in a place such as the United States, with its radical separation of church and state, insofar as state procedures come clearly under the auspices of natural reason and thus are separate from church issues. Of course, the state should do nothing to undermine religion insofar as the common people's values are informed by faith, and such faith-filled subjects invariably will be better citizens than their atheistic counterparts; but when it comes to matters of public policy, debates should proceed on the basis of natural reason alone.

Needless to say, this is not the Rahnerian solution. For Rahner, such an approach undermines the actual connection that exists between nature and grace. Building on the philosophy of Joseph Maréchal, Rahner reasserted the Thomistic insight that in every act of knowing, the subject implicitly knows God. Rahner also seems to have accepted de Lubac's rediscovery of the fact that for Thomas Aquinas there are not two ends for the human person, one natural and the other supernatural, but rather one supernatural end. (Rahner refers to the concept of "pure nature" as a *Restbegriff*.) Human beings, in short, are created in and for Christ Jesus. Nobody is created merely for this-worldly beatitude. However, Rahner diverges from de Lubac at one crucial point: while de Lubac insists that our desire for the beatific vision is a natural one, Rahner uses the language of "supernatural existential." And this seemingly minor difference leads to two rather significantly different approaches to "the world." Insofar as de Lubac insists on the naturalness of the natural desire of God, he can have a much clearer sense, paradoxically, of the distinction between nature and grace. Since for Rahner it is all grace from the ground up, he cannot avoid a kind of gradualism — everything is gradually becoming Christ and is implicitly already Christ — that seems to undermine the radical nature of biblical conversion and the radical division in the New Testament between Christ and "the world." "The world hated me, and it will hate you," Jesus says to his disciples. And yet it does not seem that Rahner's theology can account for this. If everything is already grace, then why did the world react so violently when it met grace incarnate? In short, Rahner's approach cannot seem to account for the New Testament's theology of the cross. Interestingly enough, neither does the older, tradition-alist Thomistic approach, insofar as nature is deemed to be neutral. If people can be naturally happy in this life through the use of natural reason and nat-ural virtue, why should Jesus bother them so much? Why did Jesus' message appear as foolishness to the Greeks (the most philosophically astute) if it did not touch their natural existence or philosophy? Why should a decision for Christ involve such a violent and radical break with one's past life and thought system? "I have not come to bring peace, but a sword," Jesus says at another point.

To go back to Balthasar, again, with a little help from O'Connor, any theology adequate to the nature of the Christian message must be able to account for the cross. The cross is not simply an afterthought to the Chris-tian message, nor is it adequate to say that it is the sign that God is always already reconciled to the world. "Strange sign," Balthasar retorts. Because Balthasar follows de Lubac with regard to the above discussion regarding nature and grace, he can do two things. First, he can make drama central to his thought. If nature is naturally oriented to grace, then nature is not "just fine" outside of Christ. Human nature is made for Christ, and it will not find peace apart from Christ. But, far from leading to the sort of inevitab-lism that Rahner's thought seems to, such an approach actually accounts for the dramatic nature of Christ's message. Sin is nothing more and nothing less than nature demanding to remain pure nature. That is, it is nature's attempt to have itself without having to refer to what made it. As Alexander Schmemann puts it in *For the Life of the World,* the fruit in the garden represents Adam and Eve's desire to make this world an end in itself. This was the one fruit in the garden that was not blessed as a gift from God to humankind, so that eating it was their way of saying that they wanted the world with no strings attached. It was at this point that nature became, for Adam and Eve, pure nature, theirs but not God's. "You shall be like God" means something like "Since you are God, you do not need God." And here comes the paradox: nature cannot remain pure nature without becoming something far less than nature, indeed, something demonic! As C. S. Lewis puts it, "An egg cannot very well go on being an egg, it must either hatch or go bad." If sin, then, is our inordinate attachment to our created nature, if, that is, it marks our desire to have something that is purely ours and not God's, then it only stands to reason that our reaction to Christ must necessarily be a violent and dramatic one, one way or the other.

Second, Balthasar's approach to nature and grace allows him to affirm two things at once, things that I used to think were mutually exclusive. Balthasar can affirm the goodness and autonomy of the natural order without in any way undermining the centrality of Christ. On the one hand, as stated above, if the natural order is naturally ordered to Christ, then it stands to reason that it cannot go on being natural without ceasing even to be natural. On the other hand, insofar as God created the natural order and called it "very good," and insofar as Christ took on human nature without in any way having to destroy that nature, then it follows that the integrity and proper autonomy of human nature is preserved precisely only in this radically christocentric, dramatic, and cross-centered approach to theology. As such, I came to see that, like O'Connor, Balthasar can preserve all that rings true in that Southern evangelical version of Christianity without forfeiting the proper Catholic concern for the integrity of the created order *as created order.* Recall that in O'Connor's view it is the "violent" who "bear away" the kingdom of God. This violent conflict is only exacerbated when it is between Christ and a version of goodness and knowledge that insists that it can be good and true without Christ. Rayber is both good and smart. But that is precisely the problem. By refusing to acknowledge the source of all true goodness and knowledge, it is precisely his goodness and knowledge that lead him astray. It is Balthasar who has most enabled me to give a theological account of this. I guess that I could conclude by saying that on account of Balthasar, the little Luther in me sat down with the little Aquinas in me, and they became friends. And that has made it much easier for me to live with myself.

Chapter Eight

Truth Grounded in Love

Han Urs von Balthasar's *Theo-Logic* and Christian Pedagogy

Francesca Murphy

As a Christian, I have always had a difficulty about being truthful, or about being "charitable," or, more precisely, about being both at the same time. Charity seemed to be just a kind of Christian political correctness or self-censorship. When I was truthful about others, this sometimes met the humorously deprecating comment that my observations were uncharitable; and when others were charitable, they frequently seemed to me to be deliberately skirting around the whole truth. Oftentimes, being "charitable" about others seemed synonymous with being less than perfectly honest. And it seemed, and still seems, morally wrong not to be truthful about a person or a situation. I do not necessarily mean being mean-minded or reductionistic about other people's motives or one's own. Our contemporary culture often seems to be governed by a spirit of ridicule, regarding the truth of a person as that person's lowest and meanest elements. I do not mean this satirical spirit, but rather attempting to describe the whole situation, as one sees it. A scholar must have a strong sense of the importance of trying to get at the truth about things. You cannot do the job of a scholar and teacher without giving accurate reports. A professional educator must be able to convey fairly and accurately what happened in history, or what people said or wrote, or, most importantly, what actually is the case. Curiously enough, the same culture that pushes "truth" to the point of ridicule frequently undermines the educational task by denying that we can know what actually is the case. Everything a scholar and teacher does, from marking essays to assessing a text, requires homing in on, or at least noting, their minus points as well as their pluses. And yet, it is undeniable that Christianity poses a command of charity. I have never had any positive wish to deny this, but I could not see how it fit with my need to know and tell the truth. My dilemma was that, on the one hand, it does not seem possible to hold that Christianity is true unless there is such a thing as knowable truth, such as can be passed on in conversation or writing, but, on the other hand, telling the truth seems to run counter to the Christian command of charity. Jesus taught, "Judge not that ye be not judged" (Matt. 7:1). How, on that basis, is one supposed to write an academic reference or a book review? How is one supposed to tell students that *X* is right and *Y* is wrong about what actually is the case? Are truth and charity in inverse proportion?

I have been reading Hans Urs von Balthasar since 1984, when Michael von Waldstein suggested that *The Glory of the Lord* would be some help with my projected Ph.D. on christological aesthetics. I spent the second half of the 1980s reading one volume after another of *The Glory of the Lord* as the translators slowly achieved their awesome task. One of the six chapters in the book that emerged from that Ph.D., *Christ the Form of Beauty*, is about Balthasar's aesthetics. My second book, *The Comedy of Revelation*, tries to put biblical criticism in the framework of his dramatics, and my third one, *Art and Intellect in the Thought of Étienne Gilson*, ends by trying to show that Balthasar is Gilson's authentic heir, reconciling the artistic, Bonaventurian strands in Gilson's thought with his existential Thomism. It was only after writing that third book that *Theo-Logic* appeared in English and I read it. No book will ever be so beautiful to me as the seven volumes of *The Glory of the Lord*, with its lovely, Gothic symmetry of clerical styles and lay styles, ancient and modern metaphysics, old and new covenants, laid out in their solemn splendor like a cathedral. And yet, *Theo-Logic* changed me more than studying *The Glory of the Lord* in my twenties had done. I have wracked my brains over *Theo-Drama*'s finite and infinite freedom and am still pondering how to make sense of it; however, it was the in some ways less intellectually perplexing *Theo-Logic* that turned me around. This is what Balthasar calls "apostrophe," turning around to hear the voice or conversion.

One reason why Balthasar's *Theo-Logic* had the most impact is that it gives a simple solution to an insistent conundrum. His answer to my dilemma is that *truth is grounded in love*. The measure or criterion of truth is therefore love; love is the measuring jar of truth, the scale in which truth is created, measured, and dealt out. To see another, or oneself, *in truth,* then, is to see with the eyes of love. Some people who imagine they are being "charitable" may just be avoiding saying what they honestly think, but authentic charity is love, and it sees the whole person as God sees and creates that person — in love.

The first volume of Balthasar's *Theo-Logic* is "Platonic." It presents the truth of an object as its archetype, its pattern within the mind of God: "The archetypes present in the divine mind contain the measure of the things that God has brought into existence, the measure, then, of their truth."[1] The creative power that generates the archetypal truth of a thing or person is the love of God. The archetypal form of a person is not just their absolute truth, but their best, that person in the shining light of perfection in which God makes them. And thus, God sees people as they "ought" to be — that is, as God intends them to be. Thus, the more truthful one is about a person, the closer one arrives at knowing their personal truth, the more one sees them in their archetypal perfection. Balthasar explains this:

In the creative mirror of the subject, the object sees the image of what is and of what it can and is meant to be. This creative act of the subject is no longer a mere attitude of justice but much rather an act of *love*. . . . The rigorous objectivity that is required in truth would be impossible without this natural love that from the beginning rises beyond justice, tempers it, and, in various degrees and modes, elevates it and integrates it into a higher sphere. The creative side of human knowledge is therefore the creature's analogical participation in the act by which God's archetypal, productive knowledge creatively metes out truth. By a kind of grace, knowledge draws the other into the properly spiritual sphere, thus giving it the opportunity to unfold therein by the power, and in the light, of the subject — *before* it has to become, in its objectivity, the object of knowledge. Indeed, the full knowledge of the object unexpectedly completes . . . this objectivity, . . . raising it to the true measure and image that only love can inventively behold. Only the creative image of love is able to measure the object with the measure, and hold before it the mirror, that contains its definitive and . . . objective truth. This is because even the gaze with which God looks upon his creatures is not only the judging gaze of justice but also the loving gaze of mercy. . . .

Because God sees things thus [archetypally], they should be as he sees them. It is to this idea of things held in God's safekeeping that all of man's creative

knowledge has to look. Only in God can one man see another as he is supposed to be. Only in the light of God can he place before the other the ideal
image. Only in reference to God can he encourage the other to correspond
to this image. If he did all of these things without God, his fancied assistance
would be nothing but arrogance and vanity; he would presume to be better
and smarter than his neighbor; he would require his neighbor to be bound to
an ideal and would force him into total servitude to this image.[2]

The "archetype" language runs through the first volume of *Theo-Logic,*
but it does not do full justice to the book's intentions. We find here the
old, familiar Christian-Platonic argument that from our human point of
view truth is always "truth from a perspective," or as one person sees it, and
yet, since "perspectival truth" is, effectively, not much better than subjective opinion, truth must be grounded in an absolute perspective, that of the
"archetype" within God. But God's perspective is not a view from nowhere.
It is not a nonperspective, but rather is a supraperspective, the entire realization of what "perspective" means. In other words, although the easiest way
to criticize relativism might seem to be to hammer perspectivism, Balthasar
does not take that route. Taken statically, the fact that people have perspectives is a dead end as far as the search for truth goes; taken actively, as the
sharing of perspectives, it is creative. Balthasar reframes "perspectivism" by
conceiving it as dialogue, a genre with which Plato was not unfamiliar. Because he is thinking *theo-* logically, he can say, sure, truth is perspectival, but
the Trinitarian God, absolute truth, is the absolute meeting of perspectives.

When two or three people compare their different perspectives, they gain
a deeper insight by listening to one another's take on the situation. We will
not grow in our knowledge of the truth of any event or person, then, unless
we not only think very hard about it for ourselves but also cultivate the art
of listening to others and hearing what they have to say. Truth emerges from
dialogue, from a genuine intermeshing of perspectives. *Theo-Logic* does not
argue that truth is nonperspectival, but rather that truth is this interweav-
ing of different points of view. Truth is always situated, always seen and
understood, from a multiplicity of perspectives because truth is not just the
correspondence between one person's take and an object, but rather is a synthesis of perspectives upon the object. The truth of a situation is the truth
of a dialogue about it, not of a monologue.

But in that case, there is something higher than truth, something that judges and creates it: the *event* of dialogue about it. The truth that God sees in the archetypes is dialogical truth, truth as grasped within that intra-Trinitarian "dialogue" that is the love of God, the love of the Persons of the Trinity. This is what it means to say that God creates and sees the truth in love: God creates and sees the truth in the unity of the Trinitarian love. Truth really is grounded in love.

One reason why it took me nearly twenty years to recognize the centrality of love in Balthasar's trilogy is that I saw it in terms of the transcendentals, beauty in *The Glory of the Lord,* goodness in *Theo-Drama,* and, as I was led to expect, truth in *Theo-Logic.* I have never had a problem about the reality of truth, beauty, and goodness. I had read the first book of Plato's *Republic* in my last years at school, and I appreciated, in my judgmental way, that Thrasymachus was a bad egg. In 1977, at the age of seventeen, I was talking about beauty with a man in New York, and he pointed at the light switch and said, "If I think a light switch is beautiful, it is." Since I knew only the first book of the *Republic,* I did not hit this Manhattanite Thrasymachus with the theory of the forms. I went to college determined to find the argument that would demolish this aesthetic relativism. Because I was a great reader of novels, I was particularly interested in what constituted the possibility of the truth of a text, what makes it possible for a reader to have more than an opinion or a subjective viewpoint on a book. From reading Thomas Aquinas, and the modern neo-Thomists, and realistic phenomenologists such as Roman Ingarden, I came to consider that truth is attained through the grasp of the meaning of a concept or a book or a situation. This seems to require that meaning is somehow formally latent in a text, for instance.

Since most students come to college having read little, and will read little after they graduate, I saw my pedagogical task as helping them to read a few good theology books for once in their lives. And what I wanted them to do was understand the texts. As I saw it for twenty years, taking the question of how we know the truth (or beauty) of a book back to the author is a disastrous and unnecessary move because, on the one hand, the author's personal motivations are unknowable or obscure, whereas, on the other hand, the author's intentions are publicly exhibited in the concepts within their published writing. In the Scholastic sense, an intention is a *ratio,* a thought, and intentions are just a mind turned outward. So the last thing one wants to do in seeking to understand a text is to go back behind the already outwardly expressed thought to the opaque, concealed, and unexpressed motivations for writing. To do so is the genetic fallacy, which, as an antirelativist, I saw as the trap through which modern hermeneutics fell into despair about the truth of texts: since we cannot know what the author "intended to mean," they seemed to say, we cannot know at all. How much better, I thought, to avoid the author trap altogether. Understanding a text is then a matter of actualizing or realizing the meaning of the concepts lying potential within it or of actualizing the formal structure that informs it. One has to keep the personality of the author out of it if one wants to preserve the objectivity of the author's meaning. That is how it seemed to me.

Theo-Logic shows that this is not the whole story. The formal, conceptual structure of a text, or even the meaning of a conversation, is also, and more importantly, something that somebody puts into it, with all the force of their personality. One can keep the author out of understanding a book, out of "hermeneutics," only if one extracts the event of writing from it or eliminates the personal, determinative act of putting across the meaning. This act is, in a sense, prior to the conceptual intentions of the author that find their expression in the book that the author produces. It is not impossible or illogical to think of a text like a message in a bottle, and of the act behind the writing of it like the movement of throwing the bottle into the sea. All that seems to be left of the act is the message, which gets washed up on another shore. At best, the idea that someone threw this message into the sea seems to be an inference behind the text.

However, the text is actually an expression of the author's situation, holed up on some lost island. The truth of the text is the link that suddenly emerges between the faraway author and the reader, who is addressed with a cry for help and recognizes it: the truth is the bonding of the two perspectives, the sender and the recipient coming into dialogue, a meeting of minds. Hence, understanding a text involves coming into confrontation with the person behind it. Although this meeting of minds is not possible without the author's words and the concepts that the words combine to produce, neither is it actual, an event, unless an act of self-expression pours through it. This power to express oneself, in truth, with moral rectitude and in beauty, is love, a generous self-giving that hits the mark. This act of love could be compared to the "fact" behind conceptual truth and formal beauty, in the sense of the more solid thing without which they would just be lifeless abstractions. It could also be compared to what we understand as a "person" in the sense that it is people, not ideas, who make everything happen. It is love, with all the facticity of an acting person, that underlies truth, goodness, and beauty; this is the basic thesis of Balthasar's trilogy.

A bad listener is a bad writer and speaker. Self-expression requires putting oneself in a perspective or a register in which one can be seen or heard, situating oneself in relation to one's audience. For scholars, the best way to learn to do this is to teach. I have known this for a long time, for I have been inestimably fortunate in that my teachers, such as Dallas Willard and Louise Cowan, were just that, teachers, before they were writers. It is hardly surprising that students in today's research universities are relativists or little Thrasymachuses; it is exactly what one would expect, since their teachers are larger ones. I remember a terribly sad meeting with a dear friend, a philosopher who was dying of AIDS. He wanted to give me a bundle of photocopies of his articles, never realizing that *he* mattered so much more than his writing. He was the pearl, and the writing was just the shell grown to guard that more precious thing (I appreciate that this is anatomically inaccurate). That was a long time ago, and it was many years before I realized why the person, this act of personal being that is "love," is the heart of the world and of the university. I came to understand it from *Theo-Logic,* but I would never have recognized the value of Balthasar's insight without having known teachers who put being a giving personality above dedication to research or even to knowledge. I am not disparaging erudition. Of course my teachers had something good, beautiful, and true to say. But if one has known a teacher who listened to an adolescent's questions patiently, who did not overpower one with a stream of words, but rather brought one to understanding by drawing out one's better self, one's better questions, then one has known practical love. I have seen myself as the person I ought to become, because that is how I have been treated.

By discussing truth in relation to dialogue in *Theo-Logic,* Balthasar explains this pedagogical experience. He shows that one cannot have truthful dialogue without love. Hearing another's truth and giving back one's own is not just an exchange of information; it is taking the other person into one's confidence. It is interesting that Balthasar wrote the first volume of *Theo-Logic,* titled *The Truth of the World,* and then laid "truth" aside for a couple of

decades, writing *The Glory of the Lord* and *Theo-Drama* before completing
his odyssey in *The Truth of God* and the *The Spirit of Truth,* the conclusion to
the trilogy. Joseph Ratzinger wrote that the importance of aesthetics is that
beautiful things have an evidential power that pure demonstrative argument
(about truth) can never attain:

> Being overcome by the beauty of Christ is a more real, more profound knowl-
> edge than mere rational deduction.... Taking this insight as his point of
> departure, Hans Urs von Balthasar built his *magnum opus* of theological
> aesthetics.... His fundamental approach, which is actually the essential theme
> of the whole work, has not been widely accepted. Of course, this is not only
> and not even principally a problem for theology; rather, it is also a problem
> for pastoral ministry, which must arrange for people to encounter the beauty
> of faith. Arguments so often have no effect, because too many contradictory
> arguments compete with one another in our world, so that one cannot help
> thinking of the remark of the medieval theologians that reason has a wax
> nose: in other words, it can be turned around in any direction, if one is clever
> enough. It is all so clever, so evident — whom should we trust?[3]

It may be that what Balthasar began by calling "truth" in the first volume
of *Theo-Logic* is really a synthesis of truth, beauty, and goodness. What syn-
thesizes the three proud transcendentals and sets them in a context in which
they can be properly appreciated is some "superfluity," something more than
accurate correspondence or pure goodness or even the evidential force of har-
monious beauty. Love is even more "prerational" than beauty, a sharper and
more accurate *co*-respondence than truth, and more "moral" than the greatest heroism because it is the personal event that begets and breathes them:
"*Whom* should we trust?" is the basic hermeneutical question. Our cultural
relativism, our abrogation of truth, originates from an abrogation of trust,
of love. Love is a self-expression that humbly defers to its recipient and thus
enjoys the recipient's "confidence."

The *perfect* power of self-expression would exist, then, in a Being who *is*
an act of love, of responsive dialogue — that is, the Persons of the Trinity
in their reciprocal generation. The act or event that makes the triune God
one God in three Persons is the act or event of love, where love is simultaneously diffusive and unitive. Above all, perhaps, love as thus conceived is
creative. One tends to avoid describing intra-Trinitarian love as "creative."
"Fertile" seems to be admissible, and "fecundity" is allowable, but "creative"

and "creativity" are out. It is acceptable to speak of the "fertility of the intra-Trinitarian relations," but not of the creativity of the love of the three Persons one for another, because subordinationism first arose in connection with the idea that the Father in some sense "creates" the Son; it was thus crucial to say that the Son is "uncreated," that he lies, along with Father and Spirit, "above the line" that distinguishes the Creator and created beings.

It is a shame that the adjective *creative* seems to be unacceptable with respect to the intra-Trinitarian relations, because it ties up so many threads and is theologically fertile. One could apply the adjective *creative* to Bonaventure's God as one might say of a human being, "She is very creative," meaning, "She is full of ideas." Every reader of Thomas Aquinas's *Summa contra Gentiles* comes spontaneously to think of God as the Creator because the idea of God's causality is so important to Aquinas. Perhaps this is because it is easy to think of the one as a supernatural Idea, the Idea of ideas, and of the other as a supernatural first Cause, the Cause of causes. There is something true in both notions of God, but both are incomplete. If we combine them, as perhaps Balthasar did in order to arrive at his conception of divine love, we get a synthesis of expressiveness and causality, which seems to be love conceived as *creative*. For instance, as he says in the first volume of *Theo-Logic,* it is creative for me to see and respond to the other as he or she *ought* to be, because only doing so will permit her to become this archetypal reality and not to be imprisoned in my narrow perception of what she merely *is.* In an analogous way, the Persons of the Trinity "permit" one another to be Father, Son, and Spirit by recognizing and acknowledging one another as Father, Son, and Spirit. This reciprocal and creative acknowledgment of the character of the beloved is what the Trinity is.

As a student and in my early years of teaching, I always heard the complaint, from people who wanted to reconstruct Christianity from the ground up and rebuild it in their own image — process theologians, ecofeminists, and so on — that the early church had "Hellenized" the gospel. I warned students against it with the usual stock of intelligent rebuttals of this claim: the Fathers at Nicea had to go beyond anything conceivable within Hellenistic philosophy in order to achieve the *homoousios,* and so on. In coming to appreciate the depth at which Balthasar roots "creative" or fecundacious love within the Trinity, I have rethought this reactive orientation. Long study of Balthasar's works enables one to let up on defensiveness about the patristics and medievals precisely because everything that he writes is steeped in them. A Balthasarian can trust the tradition, as I constantly admonish my students to do, contextualize its strong and its weak points, and make some advance upon it in order to speak to our own age. The positive gains of the church Fathers' thinking about God and the Trinity were creative and new in relation to earlier, secular thought, but some of their preventive mechanisms were influenced by and indebted to Hellenism. There is a way in which the Creator/created divide is conceived by them, negatively, in terms of absolute power over creation rather than absolute love for creation. In other words, for instance, while Arius's belief that the Son is not wholly God because the Son is "passible" is rejected, Arius's idea of what the impassibility of God means is, to a certain extent, conceded. The result is that certain scriptural affirmations have to be filtered through a philosophical mechanism conceived with the purpose of eliminating heresy — heresy as it looks to a somewhat Hellenized Christian, perhaps. I am all for avoiding heresy, but slurs against an Aristotelian or Platonic God are not such. As far as I can recall, Balthasar does not explicitly say that, in their negative deployment, as a filter against heresy, the patristic doctrines of God conceive God somewhat more in terms of power than love. The first thing that any reader of Balthasar learns about the patristics and medievals is that they are jolly interesting. One sees them as they ought to be, reading them reverentially, as the medievals read the Fathers. But place Balthasar's trilogy alongside Augustine and Basil and Dionysius the Areopagite, and one can see what Balthasar has left out, what he has incorporated, and what he has done that is new, such as admitting an inflection of vulnerability into his overall conception of the loving Trinity. He has begun and ended his reflection on the Trinity with the thought that truth is love, for

> God is love. This does not mean ... that his essence is substantial love, while his other infinite properties are dissolved into this love. There is an order here: love presupposes knowledge, while knowledge presupposes being. But the love that stands at the end of the sequence as the goal of its unfolding stands, in another perspective, at its beginning as the basic impulse underlying it. Eternity is a circulation in which beginning and end join in unity. By the same token, everything that has a ground, every truth claim that needs grounding, occurs within this order, but the order itself is sustained by the ultimate ground, which is love. To be sure, God is eternal truth.... But the

very existence of truth, of eternal truth, is grounded in love. If the truth were ultimate in God, we could look into its abysses with open eyes. Our eyes might be blinded by so much light, but our yearning for truth would have free rein. But because love is ultimate, the seraphim cover their faces with their wings, for the mystery of eternal love is one whose superluminous night may be glorified only through adoration.[4]

These days, Balthasar's admirers and detractors have become so fixated with the daring passages in his writings that I am somewhat glad that it took me so long to see what is new in him in relation to the Fathers and the medievals; at least I did not read him as teenagers used to read *Lady Chatterley's Lover* for page 111. I have slowly come to realize that Balthasar has made an upbeat contribution to the debate about the "feminine within God." This consists in providing, within a conception of the Trinity as dialogical love, a sense of the creativity of passivity, or listening. I am not sorry that I began by seeing Balthasar as a "continuator" rather than an innovator. For it is not difficult to observe the damage that has been done, for instance, to his friend Henri de Lubac by those who plunder his works for innovations, not realizing that, like Balthasar, this great Jesuit wanted to make a contribution to ecclesial tradition that was wider than his own private genius because he loved the church.

Through his friendship with de Lubac, Balthasar got caught up in the excitement and the travails of the French proponents of a *nouvelle théologie*. On the one side of the battlefield were those who spoke of faith and symbolism and the Fathers, and on the other side were their opponents, who saw their project as a renewed fideism, historicism, and thus modernism. *Modernism* is the theological word for *relativism*. Which comes first, faith or reason? The neo-Thomists put reason first because they rightly saw the dangers of relativism. But perhaps the neo-Thomists were wrong to assume that what reason can autonomously deduce ought to be the foundation for faith. This was a mistake because it simultaneously disabled faith from making a creative contribution to what reason can know and snuck belief in through the back door, so that what the reasoner takes pride in as a rational argument, a support to the truth of faith, actually looks good only to a believer. But, at the same time, the antimodernists were right to appreciate the real danger of fideism: the self-reflexive turn to "*my* faith," which ends up making having faith in God more important than either God himself or the evidence for God that God provides. Balthasar's poetic and thus systematic project of bringing everything back to love was developed in response to this problem of theological modernism, which cast a shadow over the question of faith and reason from the modernist crisis of the early twentieth century, in the wake of which conservative reason won out over faith, to the modernist crisis of the post-Vatican II era, in the wake of which liberal reason won out over faith. His essay "Theology and Sanctity," about reconnecting theology with prayer, is a contribution to this debate.[5]

These questions are not merely a matter of theory for me. I am a teacher, and I have a very practical, experimental interest in what works in teaching theology. I am, in practice, rather more interested in *how* to teach theology than in the deep and — to a "bear of slow brain" — unresolvable problems of antifoundationalism versus antifideism. I taught about Balthasar for years and years, but I was unsure whether or how to take his method on board in teaching. I tried getting as many great books into the students' intellectual digestive systems as I could, and I tried teaching them the history of Christianity with thousands of slides of Gothic cathedrals. I did it successfully, but I felt that I was just transmitting information. I teach theology, albeit in a secular university (we have no Catholic university in the United Kingdom). And in any case, is not the best way to get theology students to think for themselves to challenge their faith? Since students learn from their teachers, would I not be teaching them bad academic manners if I renounced a neutral position with more than a nudge and a wink? The answer to the first question is, I am now pretty sure, no. I became convinced that students could learn to think within faith only if they were explicitly taught within faith.

In the first volume of *Theo-Logic,* published in 1947, Balthasar's polemics against those who wanted a rational foundation for Christian faith are quite fierce; he effectively equates such rationalizing neo-Thomism with Hegelianism. But Balthasar was not simply a fideist either. Rather, he changes the axis: not "faith first" or "reason first," but love first. This, I have learned to see, is the basic Christian attitude, with respect to persons, theories, ancient and modern texts, theologies — everything. I am not a reformed character, but you never know what might happen next.

Chapter Nine

How Receptivity Opens the Mind for Creative Collaboration

Danielle Nussberger

I first paid special attention to Balthasar's theology because I was captivated by this theologian who was wholly enraptured by the beauty and grandeur of God. Like Balthasar, I readily entered the theological profession to utilize the tradition for the sake of training my eyes to see God in revelation and in Christian communal experience. My own predisposition to a rapprochement between theology and spirituality made it natural to assume Balthasar's view that enhancing theological sight requires a heightening of both the physical and the spiritual senses.[1] The physical senses are undoubtedly fundamental in witnessing to God's beauty in the dynamic events unfolding in the liturgy and in the spoken and written revelatory word on the scriptural page. In addition, the spiritual senses are equally vital so that we might look and see ever more deeply by penetrating the inner meaning of devotional actions, words, and events and thereby come closer to the unseen, unspeakable, unknowable mystery who is God.[2] When the marriage between the physical and spiritual senses has been consummated, the devotional realities of the Christian community's worship extend beyond their ritual settings into the world of human social interaction with a mandate for responsible, morally driven engagement between the religious and the secular realms.

Exploring the nexus between theology and spirituality in the thought of a kindred spirit, I have given my fullest attention to the significance of the saint in Balthasar's theological project. I have concluded that the saint is

Balthasar's fully matured theological person within whom the physical and spiritual senses are wedded as she is looking to God at all times and allowing this contemplative, worshipful posture toward her Creator to consciously mold her actions on behalf of a world in jeopardy. Balthasar's theology exhorts all Christians to look to their God just as the saint does, with the saint serving as an icon of Christ through whom the Christian can look and see the beauty and grandeur of God. I have studied Balthasar carefully in order to explain how the Balthasarian saint as icon is a flesh-and-blood interpretation of Balthasar's *The Glory of the Lord* and his *Theo-Drama*, and how the saint makes these highly elaborate theological works more accessible to a wider audience.

Describing my introduction to Balthasar as a meeting of two sympathetic minds is telling only one side of the story. Interest in another's theology may quite often begin with an immediate attraction that is supplied by the commonalities in each other's judgments. However, if our entire exposure to other thinkers consisted of "mutual admiration," a genuine encounter would never take place. Productive dialogue is intensified when we reassess both the beliefs of the other and our own theories for the sake of mutual growth. Sheer contentedness with another's thinking cannot generate the dynamic exchange of ideas that presses theological inquiry forward; we need to be willing to feel uncomfortable and to have our assertions tried and tested to the point of possibly revising them. Openness to a "changing of the mind" does not mean that we relinquish our cherished convictions, but rather that we sharpen them in light of the constructive features of another's viewpoint.

I have stretched beyond an unquestioning acquiescence with Balthasar's proposals to an ever-deepening conversation with him that raises unavoidably difficult questions regarding the Balthasarian saint's relevance in today's theological environment. How can the prototypical self-sacrificial, receptive Balthasarian saints such as Thérèse of Lisieux and Elizabeth of the Trinity have something to say to women whose voices have been silenced? Can such contemplative examples of sainthood contribute to a world in need that cries out for prophetic saints such as Oscar Romero who actively combat suffering and injustice? These questions expose a contrast between what kinds of Christian exemplars I might feel are necessary in a world where affliction and abuse already abound and what kinds of saintly examples Balthasar recommends. In order to avoid a hasty reversal of my earlier agreement with Balthasar, I reject an either/or mentality and apply a nuanced approach that accurately indicates the complexity of both the saintly persona and the world that she inhabits. When we circumvent the temptation to polarize differing perspectives, we recognize that the qualities of self-sacrifice and receptivity are not the opposites of other traits such as strong-willed dedication to equality and stout resistance against the dishonoring of human dignity.

In order to dismantle unprofitable dichotomies between our worldviews and Balthasar's, we need to be ready to see what Balthasar is seeing. This entails receptivity to whatever ideas are not the same as our own. Openness gives rise to numerous possibilities, including that we and Balthasar have the same objective to sustain theology by continually returning to its source in God's revelation. We can walk toward this goal with Balthasar by bringing him into contact with the issues that we are currently facing. In this way, Balthasar is contributing to contemporary circumstances that he was not taking into account, and these new contexts can help us to rethink Balthasar's import for theology today. Now is the time for our minds to meet, as Balthasar converses with a voicing of present feminist and liberationist concerns.

The changing of minds takes place when we clear a space for another's ideas alongside ours and make room for a more panoramic vision. These pages are a step in that direction. First, we will enter Balthasar's worldview and watch how a theologian such as Jean-Luc Marion has been influenced by it. He and Balthasar will offer us the saint as icon, setting the stage for our opportunity to bring together what we cannot separate any longer: the mutual value of kenotic Christic imitation and feminist concerns, and the dual worth of the contemplative vocation and the active charism of liberation theology. Rather than being irreconcilable opponents, both sides of the "and" can be partners working together — if only we have the eyes to see that this is so. This is what Balthasar's theology is auspiciously all about, opening our eyes to see what is most important: the God who wants us to cooperatively advance toward a justice and a freedom that are God's will for us.

Entering Balthasar's Vision of the Saint in *The Glory of the Lord*

Balthasar's *The Glory of the Lord,* his theological aesthetics, is where he illuminates how the nuptials between the physical and spiritual senses are realized during contemplation of God's glory in its supreme manifestation of the beautiful, crucified, and risen Christ.[3] With beauty as his theological starting point, Balthasar educates the human subject on how to prayerfully apply her inextricably linked physical sense perception and mental comprehension that are shaped by God's own hand in order to come back to God. God's beauty, then, becomes a suitable site for Christian conversion. We are the human subjects whom Balthasar addresses, and we can experience his theological vision by being open to our own metamorphosis.

In his validation of the transformative efficacy of a divine beauty that is appropriately conceived, Balthasar distinguishes his project of a theological aesthetics from other aesthetic ventures. The first distinction between a theological aesthetic and its generic counterpart is the referent, the one to which or whom the aesthetic discourse refers. The second contrary aspect is the role of the subject, the one who is observing, contemplating, and changed by the beauty of the object. In the first instance, that of the location of the referent, a theological aesthetic is obviously referring to God who as the object of the contemplator's gaze is a subject in God's own right. Second, the subject's role to see and express such beauty is solely based upon the extraordinary unveiling of the God who is being viewed.[4] God governs how God is being seen; the deciding factor of the theological aesthetic is not the subject's God-given appetite for divine beauty. Rather than conforming to personal taste and social custom, as beauty is wont to do in a more general aesthetic discourse, the Word of God in the cross of Christ astonishingly topples and reconstructs individual, cultural, and societal paradigms of beauty's definition and purpose.

In the first volume of *The Glory of the Lord,* Balthasar intently contrasts subjective and objective evidence for God's glory in order to give the objective evidence more weight than the subjective.[5] This is essential to the formation of his theological aesthetics because it establishes how revelation's validation of divine beauty is superior to that of the subject, since God is responsible for the contemplative subject's perception and acceptance of divine self-disclosure. The beauty of revelation impels the subject to move outside of herself in ecstasy as she comes face-to-face with the grandeur of God. God's magnificence is what drives the subject and what allows her to see in the first place; revelation's objective evidence produces the subjective evidence or the subject's personal experience of God's transcendent beauty. As Balthasar states, "The subjective unity of faith and vision in the Christian life would perforce remain incomprehensible if it could not be elucidated in terms of a unity in the objective revelation which demands and conditions it."[6]

In the seventh volume of *The Glory of the Lord,* he vehemently asserts,

> It is God himself who illuminates us, who indeed marks us with his word and places his image in us, and it is only in this grammatical reversal (in which the object becomes the active subject) that Christian seeing is attained. What is finally perceived depends on the initiative of the object.[7]

To contemplate God, then, we are obliged to turn ourselves over to the relationship between God and creature, which Balthasar's theological aesthetics clarifies. We are to be subjects who are grateful for God's motivation, for our awareness of God and of God's created reality comes not from us but rather from the Artist-God who paints the intimate bond between God and the human creature. The saint, as she is first introduced in detail in the fifth volume of *The Glory of the Lord,* is the practiced contemplative subject of the first volume who knows and acts upon the truth that she is dependent upon God for her vision of God and for her very existence in the sight of God.[8] For Balthasar, the theological aesthetics of the first volume is physically embodied by the saint of the fifth volume who is the spiritual teacher of a Christian metaphysics and epistemology where the order of being and the order of knowing coincide, both orders beginning with God and ending with the human creature. God is the sculptor of our being, and God is the author of our knowing so that our existence and knowledge are oriented toward and fulfilled in the divine artist.

Balthasar's saintly metaphysic in the fifth volume of *The Glory of the Lord,* wherein created being is understood to be nonreciprocally dependent upon divine Being, is his response to any philosophical system that makes being and Being indistinguishable, making the human person the artist of her own existence.[9] As human inventions, some philosophical systems precariously suppose that Being can be humanly structured, that a grand metanarrative can be written to take God's place in controlling the shape and role of individual being. Like the Hegelian relation between master and slave, any totalitarian blueprint is drawn by the oligarchy promoting the self-sacrificial yielding of others. However, despite its imagined self-rule, this leading faction consists of human beings who have been written into the divine Author's drama as docile servants.[10] According to all philosophies that oppose anything resembling the divine drama's saintly metaphysic, there are those who decide for themselves what their being entails, and there are those who are furnished with their being by the oppressive other. Not capitulating to the single saintly esteemed hierarchy of divine Being to creaturely being, the self-proclaimed masters instate the counterfeit ranking of greater over lesser human beings. The false deities, who set up their fabricated Being, ignore and deform the valid determination of Being that is the grandeur of God and God's relationship to creation as its artist and sustainer throughout all of time and eternity. I confess that I too am guilty at one time or another of thinking that I am the source of my own existence and sustenance, of snatching the feigned prerogative to create my own being, and of demarcating what is good, bad, and beautiful all by myself. Balthasar begins the first volume of *The Glory of the Lord* with the priority of objective above subjective evidence for this reason, to put all human subjects like ourselves in our rightful place as receivers of our being from God rather than the givers of it.

Marion and Balthasar Together
Envisioning the Saint as Icon

Jean-Luc Marion incorporates Balthasar's vision in his phenomenological and theological investigations when he confronts metaphysical questions with a Balthasarian allegiance to revelation as the gift in excess that is prior to the subject's experience of it.[11] Like Balthasar, Marion appraises the contentious association between theology and metaphysics, now within a postmodern context that accuses theology of the ontotheological sin that secular philosophers have also been charged with. In answer to the onto-theological indictment — the allegation that anyone has elevated her own Being that stratifies reality into segments of who is within and who is outside of a humanly concocted schema — Marion argues that revelation does not fall within this category because it is completely outside of humanity's experience. There is no way in which revelation could be construed as coming from human beings. Marion appeals to Pseudo-Dionysius and his mystical apophasis in this regard, because Denys was well aware of revelation's freedom from the constrictions and prejudices of created existence.[12] Although Pseudo-Dionysius can come perilously close to the ontotheological proclivities that Marion is trying to distance him from, Marion still argues that his God of darkness and unknowing cannot be controlled by human metaphysical and epistemological accomplishments. Moreover, it is this ungraspable God who endows humans with their metaphysical heritage as beings utterly dependent upon God and with their epistemological capability to receive knowledge that they cannot acquire by their own ingenuity.

In *God without Being,* Marion provides a phenomenological portrayal of the relationship between the idol and the icon that elucidates the absolute difference between a Being of human making and the revelation of non-human origin.[13] The idol is exactly like the biblical golden calf that the people of Israel chose to represent their Savior God, who led them out of Egypt, but that instead stood for a god of their own contrivance. Whenever it appears, the idol is always formed out of misguided human aspirations for abusive power and a privileged *gnosis* that feeds corrupt authority over others. Through the icon, however, our gaze is directed beyond ourselves to a view of Being and existence that is impossible for us to grab hold of or to manipulate.[14] The artistic genius of the icon is that it forces human beings to see what they are not able to perceive on their own, so that when they look at themselves again in the icon's light, they discover who they really are as contemplators of Being instead of the artists of it. Transferred from its original phenomenological program to an explicitly theological one, Marion's comparison of idol and icon aptly illustrates the inferiority of human gods to the one God, who is glimpsed through icons of God's choosing and fashioning. In the final analysis, though divine revelation is necessarily bestowed through mediums such as the scriptural word in which human beings cooperate, these intermediaries are God's instruments.

Since Marion is inspired by Balthasar, it is not surprising that his phenomenological description of the icon in its denouncing of the idol bears a resemblance to the status of the Balthasarian saint who is transparent to God with her christologically patterned obedience to the Father that disapproves of any self-sufficient metaphysics. Balthasar's theology of the saint is especially fruitful when we understand her to be an icon through whom Christ is seen again. We can then look through her to find the Artist-God who has painted her and us. The iconic character of the saint is developed in the fifth volume of *The Glory of the Lord,* where Balthasar presents her as the living, metaphysical alternative to the ontotheological option that is Marion's idol. She puts her metaphysic that stands against any human inclination to be her own artist into practice when she kneels before the Creator God with humility, obedience, and self-sacrifice and stretches out her arms to heaven in imitation of the crucified Christ. The three trademark qualities of the saint — humility, obedience, and self-sacrifice — will be forever scorned by the prevailing idols, which are desperately trying to become their own gods.[15] The saint as icon does not fight her enemy idols by adopting opposing battlements of human rule; instead, she remains transparent to Christ and replicates his transparency to the Father on the cross. Balthasar recovers a redefinition of beauty in the saintly icon's invocation of the crucified one, just as Paul discovers a divine wisdom in the cross that confounds all human logic.

Balthasar meditates upon the cross with a humility and reverence that resembles the saint's contemplation of God, and there he discerns something about both God and humanity.[16] Nailed to the cross is humanity's disobedience and utter refusal to meet God; the ugliness of human sin is displayed for all to behold. Looking to the cross and penetrating through it, Balthasar sees the God whom humanity does not see when it abandons itself to its narcissistic predisposition. He knows that where there is God, there is beauty, there in the Savior's bloody, abandoned, humiliated, and dying body. This is the Christ, who sacrifices his life by casting it into the fiery furnace of suffering so that in him the human person is purified of her sin and emerges anew with Christ in the resurrection.[17] The beautiful God is the God who is servant and who in Trinitarian community is the everlasting movement of self-sacrificial gift.

The saint has taught Balthasar about the cross; before him, she was the one who saw cruciform beauty and who was reformed by it when she accepted the role of servant that corresponded with her life's God-given mission. When Balthasar advocates the saintly embodiment of cruciform beauty, he is not extolling suffering or the annihilation of the saint's personhood. Instead, he shows how the saint as icon of the crucified Christ continues the revelation of the cross's metaphysical paradox: servanthood in obedience to God is the place where real human existence and individuality is to be found.[18] The saint now transitions from her primary theo-aesthetic position of icon in *The Glory of the Lord* to her secondary theo-dramatic role as interpreter of *Theo-Drama*'s God-human play.[19] In *Theo-Drama*, Balthasar's saint acts out her part in God's drama by becoming the living, acting icon of a genuine human freedom that comes from Christ, whose perfectly aligned human and divine wills revealed that human beings are most themselves when their wills are also uncompromisingly united with God's plan for their lives.[20]

The Coming Together of Balthasar's Vision with a Feminist Point of View

Up to now, we have seen the saint as icon painted in broad theological strokes. It is amply instructive to hear each saintly voice of the fifth volume of *The Glory of the Lord* one by one. These are men and women who share the principal saintly attributes of humility, obedience, and self-sacrifice but vary widely in their saintly modes of transparency to Christ.[21] Out of the array of saintly models, two women stand out as exemplary Balthasarian saints (though Balthasar wrote about them before his more explicit dealings with the saint and her metaphysical and epistemological allegiances in the fifth volume of *The Glory of the Lord*): Thérèse of Lisieux and Elizabeth of the Trinity.[22] These two women are hyperbolic representations of the contemplative ideal that Balthasar expands in his later theological aesthetics. At first glance, they appear to be a challenge to the ability of Balthasar's saintly standard to operate successfully within either a feminist or a liberationist point of view.

Our worldview separated from Balthasar's might suggest that Thérèse and Elizabeth are not the type of saint we need. After all, their Carmelite cloisters and their early deaths sheltered them from what was going on outside their walls and made them unable to concretely interact with and visibly refashion the world in which they lived. What does Balthasar's favoring of such contemplative examples of sainthood say about the embodiment of Christ in a world where tangible, steadfast commitment to its betterment is compulsory? Furthermore, what can these two ostensibly voiceless women say to affirm women's potential as icons of Christ? Once again we have an unfortunate clash between two perspectives and an interrogation as to what Balthasar can offer to an alternate agenda that has another set of priorities. Instead, we can raise a different set of questions. What would we see if we were to collaborate with the other point of view? How would Balthasar's vision when joined together with the feminist viewpoint make the Truth we are seeking more evident than it would be without his contribution?

Thérèse and Elizabeth may not be physicians for the social ills of their time, but for Balthasar they achieve a refocusing of modern self-advancement to contemplative receptivity to God's advances toward the human person. These women have prepared themselves for contemplation's art of seeing God and knowing who one is as God's masterpiece by zealously absorbing Scripture and dutifully accepting their apprenticeship to its Jesus in simplicity and obscurity.[23] As a result, they are the novice Christian's précis to the exceedingly learned project of *The Glory of the Lord* that begins with the first volume's explanation of a contemplative theological aesthetics and continues in subsequent volumes by showcasing the masters of the contemplative art within the Christian theological and literary traditions, including, for example, Pseudo-Dionysius, Bonaventure, John of the Cross, Gerard Manley Hopkins, and Charles Péguy.[24] On the one hand, Balthasar points expertly to the contemplative masters of *The Glory of the Lord,* whose erudite expressions of the union with God are philosophically influenced, and, on the other hand, he casually gestures toward Thérèse and Elizabeth, who simply offer a childlike rendition of Christianity's centuries-old contemplative theory. They are, ironically, a much more effective blow to the modern age's Enlightenment values because they are not participants in the common intellectual foundation that both an Aquinas and a Descartes share. Analogous to the beautiful, crucified Christ, of whom they are icons, these two women's contemplative experience is outside of the boundaries of human epistemological conquests. In their innocence, they have known the dark night without being able to express it either poetically or philosophically; their contemplation makes them feel their nothingness.[25] However, they are able to go further than this because they know intuitively through the grace of God that they are only nothing without God, only dead without Christ's death and resurrection. Their dark night has cleared everything away, leaving room for them to see the grandeur of God and to be graced with the dazzling beauty that God's human artwork possesses.

Thérèse and Elizabeth illustrate the disparity between the contemplative art and the modern preeminence of rationality even more radically than the men and women of the saintly metaphysic in the fifth volume of *The Glory of the Lord*. For Balthasar, the philosophical, rationalistic discourse counts on itself for knowledge, while contemplation is intuitive as an art in the truest sense and relies on the Spirit for a wisdom that cannot be gained by reckless, human pursuits. The contemplative epistemology of the saint makes way for God to overtake the saint and to creatively bring about Christ's presence again through the saint's embodiment of the suitable relationship between human and divine being. Balthasar is repeatedly compelling his reader to notice Thérèse and Elizabeth's startling invisibility to the point of near nothingness. We can either injudiciously interpret that he is doing this because he erroneously presumes that women are by nature out of sight and insignificant, or, we can entertain his crucial opinion that their transparency makes it possible to see the Spirit's inspiration in holding up Thérèse and Elizabeth as God's antinomy to the idolatrous rule of modern autonomy and self-aggrandizement.

Choosing the second option opens the door for a collaboration of Balthasar's worldview with the feminist standpoint. Balthasar's vision of the saintly icon with her receptivity and obedience and the feminist vision for the dignity and equality of all human beings can illumine one another. We can rethink the saint's self-emptying capacity as liberation of the self and others from destructive behaviors. This is what our shared vision would be able to see: the kenotic, contemplative art mastered by these women is the means by which the saintly icon is a "re-presencing" of Christ himself. Likewise, it is the way to knowledge and truth that trumps a solely rationalistic approach that relies on individual human initiative. This affirms that God desires both women and men (without a humanly instituted hierarchy between the two) to re-present Christ by taking up the same Christlike attitudes of humility, obedience, and self-sacrifice; both women and men are meant to be servants in the christological sense of the word.

We can look together with Balthasar at Thérèse and Elizabeth and see what all Christians are called to be: transparent icons of Christ. Furthermore, with receptivity and liberating strength in one, these women saints are not standing still. They are rebuilding society from the ground up with their uncompromising embrace of the christological existence of self-sacrifice and obedience before the Father. Their proper understanding and performance of a contemplative relationship with their God, reflecting the contemplative intimacy that Christ himself maintained with the Father, is the ground-work needed to re-create the world at its innermost core. A second look at Thérèse and Elizabeth would reveal that human action continues the work that Christ began in bringing the world back to its Creator only when it is full of contemplative acknowledgment of the grace-filled power of God.

The Coming Together of Balthasar's Vision with a Liberationist Point of View

If we were asked to name an icon of Christ in today's society — someone who knew that his or her freedom meant reliance upon God even if the consequences of such radical dependence were uncharacteristic of his or her time and place — we would probably not immediately suggest two inconspicuous contemplative women such as Thérèse and Elizabeth. This is not only because of their seemingly inactive roles as receptive and obedient women, but also because they did not leave a noticeable mark on the earth. Does not our ravaged and war-torn world dictate that the saint's reincarnation of Christ should be one that boldly ministers to suffering peoples in his stead? Balthasar is well aware of our tendency to seek out the most courageous actors in our world's drama and to identify them as saints, and this is why he sets two nonheroic women before his readers as saintly embodiments of Christ. He raises Thérèse and Elizabeth to iconic heights in order to restore contemplation to its rightful place as action's constant companion and as its inner compulsion.[26]

We are reminded of the negative tone that Balthasar employs elsewhere to write specifically about liberation theology, when he critically refers to the hubris of those who perform revolutionary, world-changing action in his foreword to *Two Sisters in the Spirit*.[27] His central critique of liberation theology in his 1977 essay "Liberation Theology in the Light of Salvation History" is that it can unwittingly slip into a risky trust in linear human progress that is a product of modernity and the philosophical systems that espouse it rather than relying solely on the vertical disturbance of God's groundbreaking grace.[28] Balthasar is concerned about liberation theology if it does not realize that when it fights against the idols of governmental and monetary tyranny by swearing allegiance to an opposing, presumably upright political and economic idol, it is waging war in the same manner as the enemy rather than holding fast to the Creator-Savior God. Balthasar believes that he has reason to be alarmed if liberation theologians were to reverse the order of knowing that begins in God and ends in the human person by upholding secular epistemological archetypes such as Marxist socialism. The same principle is at stake here that was indispensable earlier: the resolute proviso for something like the saint as icon to symbolize the one fitting account of the creature's relationship to her God, who alone can justly bequeath being and its meaning.

If we were to remain solely within the scope of Balthasar's critical observations about liberation theology, there would be objections to selecting someone such as Oscar Romero as our saintly icon of Christ. Romero did speak out against the tyrannical government of his time, and he did support popular workers' organizations that fought hard to safeguard the poor at a time in El Salvadoran history when they were in danger of becoming extinct. He rallied behind the people with his heartrending homilies that exhorted both the poor and their oppressors to reclaim their Christian identity by living justly and ending the unthinkable, catastrophic suffering and death. However, if we were to bring both theological visions together — Balthasar's view with that of liberation theology — we could see Oscar Romero, the saintly icon. Romero shows us how liberation theology can speak persuasively to a Balthasarian theology of the saint that is signified in Marion's ciphers of idol and icon.

By ardently desiring the oppressors to hear his words of compassion as the call of Christ's love to them, Romero proves that he was not erecting a counter-idol against the menacing god of the Salvadoran government. Instead, he was being Christ for the oppressors and the oppressed by speaking out to both of them and ministering to both of them in their need. Romero stood up against a violent dictator who wanted a vast gulf to remain between master and slave, a chasm that Balthasar would also like to eliminate when he proffers the saintly alternative that admits only one hierarchy between God and creation. Archbishop Romero's liberating actions are just as hyperbolically iconic as the lives of two contemplative women, for he joined the poor in solidarity in the same way that Christ did, and he died a martyr

at the eucharistic table just as the Lord did before him. The church's liturgy and devotions that are so important to Balthasar in their promotion of
the union between the physical and spiritual senses are brought to poignant
depths here. To see Romero gunned down during Mass, with his sacrificial
blood spewing forth from his mouth, nose, and ears, is to look upon an icon
of Christ who gave his lifeblood for his people. The suffering one who sees
through this saintly icon gazes upon the Christ who is saving her; the ruler
who looks through Romero's iconic transparency sees Christ's servanthood
ending his reign of worldly power.

In this light, Oscar Romero is one of the most translucent icons of Christ.
He not only makes Christ present again by sight but also changes the world
in which he lives so that Christ's salvific action on the cross is perpetuated
and bears fruit in Romero's historical time and circumstance. Looking at
Romero as saintly icon, we can echo Balthasar's words:

> The closer a man comes to this identity [between role and person], the more
> perfectly does he play his part. In other words, the saints are the authentic
> interpreters of the theo-drama. Their knowledge, lived out in dramatic exis-
> tence, must be regarded as setting a standard of interpretation not only for
> the life-dramas of individuals but ultimately for the "history of freedom" of
> all the nations and of all humankind.[29]

Romero's liberating action prompts a further implication of saint as icon
that broadens Balthasar's theological vision: different historical moments ne-
cessitate varied actions on the part of the saint, providing multifaceted views
of Christ from every angle, like a diamond being refracted in the sunlight.
Balthasar's rhetorical elevation of the contemplative mode of *imitatio Christi*
that a Thérèse or Elizabeth embodies can be brought into conversation with
a contemplatively infused action like Romero's that was also shaped by his
distinct historical situation.

We can look at both styles of saintly mission side by side, allowing each
to illuminate the other. On one side, we have two contemplative saints engaging in the only divine-human dialogue that can foster truly life-altering
action in the world. For intuitively experiencing our absolute dependence
upon God as Thérèse and Elizabeth have enables us to work passionately
for the world that the Artist-God dreams of. The contemplative saint is an
icon of Christ because she sees Christ in order to see the world as it was

meant to be and behaves accordingly despite not changing the world in an earth-shattering way. On the other side, we have a saint of action who takes his contemplative art and re-creates the world with it. The active saint is an icon of Christ because he envisions the world from God's perspective and actively implements the divine-human hierarchy in order to overcome this-worldly hierarchies that perpetuate injustice and oppression. Contemplation and active determination for the improvement of our society are not incommensurable. They are part of an integrated whole that we can glimpse by using Balthasar's theology of the saint to look at Romero's life as an icon of Christ.

When two or more perspectives earnestly come together in the same place, we find ourselves reflecting on our separate standpoints with a more objective sight. Dissolving false antitheses makes it easier to see the forest for the trees. It should be apparent to us now that Balthasar is not advocating a contemplation that is disconnected from action in the world. This is why his theological aesthetics and dramatics are inseparable halves of a single vision. Similarly, proponents of liberation theology such as Gutiérrez, Segundo, and Sobrino would never champion action in the world that was not being cultivated by prayer and contemplation.[30] The dialogue between a theologian such as Balthasar and liberation theologians such as these is ours to encourage and ours to carry out.

Conclusions

My mind is made up. We are to have generously open minds. It is our task to pioneer ways to appropriate Balthasar's saintly icon as a beneficial method for seeing the beauty of God's Word anew in the world. Balthasar's role in contemporary theology is far too valuable to eschew because of all the possible barriers that we can put up to obstruct an appreciative view of the heart of Balthasar's intention. If we do in fact agree with him that Christianity is a wellspring of a plurality of voices worth hearing, we would be remiss in effortlessly listening solely to our own voices. Christ calls all of his followers to listen to the voices that are goading them to go beyond their opinions and hear something that has the potential to strikingly alter their positions. Our joint quest is to reexamine today's urgent dilemmas by turning to Christianity's storehouse of resources for answers.

We can mine Balthasar's saint as icon for a profound appreciation of God and of humanity, since the essence of the icon is to stimulate us to go to Christ and to experience Christ's reciprocal gaze, which will recreate us. The saintly icon is an authentic work of art that cannot be controlled or manipulated by its human interpreters. Therefore, it is the perfect site to broaden our outlook, for there can be no leveling of one perspective against another in a place where God's vision of us is the most imperative view that we can defend. Look at Thérèse and Elizabeth as icons of Christ and see the contemplative life from which the church cannot stray in its rightful enthusiasm for world-renewing action that still requires the firm ground of God's grace to stand on. See two women who contest the fear of obedience and self-sacrifice as destructive possibilities. Witness Romero as saintly icon and be honest about his self-sacrifice that led him to die in obedience to the will of God. The beautiful gaze of the submissive and obedient crucified Christ is so piercing that it cannot be evaded.

I continue to pay special attention to Balthasar's theology because he has directed me back to the suffering Savior. I have used my spiritual senses to look at Christ and my physical senses to see Christ in those who are suffering in order to help tear down the false human hierarchies devised to suppress a people that Christ's obedience has already set free. Seeing God from Balthasar's point of view, I agree that God's grandeur in Trinitarian mutual deference and self-giving is not the world's version of servanthood. Therefore, God's glorious sacrificial nature cannot be ignored as if being raptured by it would lead to an acceptance of the way the world has always been. Balthasar's saint as icon can prime our Christian imaginations to actualize godly obedience in a multitude of saintly incarnations that prosecute the ruling class's subjugation of all who are impoverished for its vilification of bona fide christological kenosis. True to Balthasarian form, receptivity is a must in order to look out upon the theological landscape with Balthasar and to resourcefully speak to contemporary theological concerns together.

Chapter Ten

I Am Not What I Am
Because of...

Cyril O'Regan

It would be misleading to suggest with respect to my encounter with Balthasar that there was something like a declarative epiphany that forced itself on me and manifestly effected a change in how I viewed the nature of theology and its task. It would be equally misleading to propose a Proustian madeleine moment that permits itself to be subsequently mined for the future of a theological sensibility that comes into being slowly through recollection. The temptations to go in one or other of these directions are obviously not the same. In the case of the former, this fiction of epiphany has the aesthetic value of miming Balthasar's own emphasis on the "sudden" (*exaiphnes*) as a mark of transformation. In the case of the latter, it has to do with complicating, but also importantly raising the stakes about, what constitutes memory and its purpose and suggesting the need of a conversation between Balthasar and Proust, if only to mark the difference. Try as I might, there simply does not appear to be a singular experience that would not risk falling within the brackets of T. S. Eliot's dismissal of our pretensions in "The Love Song of J. Alfred Prufrock." Nor does letting memory be, allowing it to move toward the involuntary, produce a savor that brings the self back only to shoot forward to being more than itself. I am left with the inelegant truth that my habit of attending to Balthasar was acquired in bits and drabs, fits and starts, and completely without fuss or announcement.

In my case, in the middle 1980s it began with some dipping into *Apokalypse der deutschen Seele* (1937–1939), which later reading has persuaded me is a crucial text for the interpretation of Balthasar. This was followed by my

151

reading of *Kosmische Liturgie* (1942), and in order again Balthasar's books on Gregory of Nyssa and on truth, both of which date from the mid-1940s. Following close on their heels was the English translations of Balthasar's annotated anthology of selected writings of Origen, *Spirit and Fire* (1984), and Balthasar's brilliant Barth book. After these came the *Balthasar Anthology* and selected essays of Balthasar in *Explorations*. In almost all of these cases my express interest was not Balthasar himself but rather in the figures about whom he wrote and the topics with which he concerned himself. When I read parts of *Apokalypse der deutschen Seele*, I had a specific interest in Balthasar's treatment of German Romanticism and Idealism and how it related to other accounts and other kinds of accounts. When I read Balthasar on Origen, Nyssa, and Maximus, I was centrally interested in these figures themselves, although I understood that Balthasar was in the business of critically retrieving these thinkers for the contemporary period and not simply in providing a neutral historical account, if that indeed were possible. Similarly in the case of Balthasar's Barth book, although the motive here was complicated by the status of this book as representative of a Catholic encounter with the Reformed tradition, and more specifically of Catholic appropriation of a theologian who had harsh things to say about Catholic propensities to engage culture and Catholic openness to other discourses, especially the discourse of philosophy. I read Balthasar's book on truth as an example of a phenomenological adaptation, or possibly correction, of Aquinas's view of truth, thus a text to be placed alongside Karl Rahner's *Spirit in the World* (1939) and read against the backdrop of mid-twentieth-century Catholic appropriations of the thought of Heidegger.

Only with the *Balthasar Anthology*, however, did Balthasar become a figure in his own right, acquire the definition of a particular voice, and come to be recognized by me as having a determinate theological perspective. However dated it seems twenty years later, this text telescoped defining Balthasarian themes such as Holy Saturday, Trinitarian inversion, sainthood as constituted by obedience, and the foundation of church in Mary's amen. Around the same time, I did manage a quick perusal of the English translation of the first volume of *The Glory of the Lord* (*Herrlichkeit*). It grabbed my attention, in fact all of my attention. With all due respect to his superb interpretations of Maximus and Barth, and even his book on truth, which is by far the most philosophically adroit of all of Balthasar's texts, the first volume of *The Glory of the Lord* seemed to be on a different level than anything of Balthasar's that I had read before. Now while a number of essays in *Explorations* provided clear hints as to its basic thesis, and especially the essay on "Beauty and Theology," I judged that the thesis was given the kind of articulation that it deserved. This was due in significant part to the way Balthasar marshaled all the resources of the Christian tradition toward an end with which I was intuitively sympathetic: that the best of Christianity endorses explicitly or implicitly Beauty as a transcendental, and furthermore that Beauty essentially has a christological center and a Trinitarian horizon. I had time, or only gave myself time, for a taste, since work that I was doing on the intersections of theology and philosophy in the nineteenth century was at a critical point. But the taste was a promise, specifically the promise that Balthasar was worth reading in his own right and in detail. This necessarily would involve reading the whole of *Herrlichkeit,* which was in the process of being translated, and possibly the entire trilogy. Required also, I thought, would be intense study of the first volume, which had proved so persuasive precisely because it performed the theological program that it laid down. Further study has not lessened my enthusiasm for the first volume, which I judge to be Balthasar's most accomplished text, even as I recognize that Balthasar's achievement can be measured only by the trilogy as a whole.

Here I could sense the difference between Balthasar's procedure and that of other contemporary theologians. I understood how Balthasar could be placed by appeal to Protestant and Catholic templates concerning the niceties or necessities of preliminaries: formally the relation of Balthasar to Rahner bore at least a family resemblance to the relation of Barth to Schleiermacher. Being a student of, among other things, Hegel, I could not but recall the famous passage in the preface of *Phenomenology* where Hegel inveighs against methodological preliminaries and advocates simply jumping in. Balthasar, then, seemed to be saying that the best way of preparing for theology is simply to do it, and either not consider at all, or at the very least postpone until later, worries about warrants, whether those of intelligibility and truth or meaning and meaningfulness. Perhaps it might be best, for example, to attempt to understand the person of Christ through biblical witness and the various interpretations supplied by the theological tradition rather than to exhaust an immense amount of intellectual capital on establishing the conditions of the possibility of theological analysis. Similarly with regard to the

Trinity, grace, Mary, and the church. It would make a world of difference, however, whether the providing of reasons was avoided or postponed. Wherever Barth can or should be placed on this issue, it certainly was the case that Balthasar was involved in postponement rather than avoidance. Still, despite much more than favorable impression, definite interest, and the brewing of questions, it was true that by the end of the 1980s, I knew Balthasar less well than I knew other representatives of *nouvelle théologie* such as Henri de Lubac and Jean Daniélou. And, it is probably true to say, I knew him less well than Rahner and possibly even Bernard Lonergan, whose central texts I had studied with some measure of concentration and discipline. I had begun my career, after all, as a philosophically inclined theologian, and while Balthasar was, I realized, both favorably disposed toward philosophy and profoundly philosophically literate, in general he does not demonstrate the philosophical talent of either Rahner or Lonergan, nor even that of his mentor Erich Przywara. Certainly, he falls well short of Aquinas. *Wahrheit der Welt,* the first volume of *Theologik,* is best understood as the exception that proves the rule.

Truth be told, in my own case ecclesial politics played no role in my serious turning to Balthasar at the beginning of the 1990s. I had read some of Balthasar's more trenchant essays on the negative fallout of Vatican II and essentially took his view under advisement. *The Office of Peter* had a considerably deeper effect, since Balthasar did persuade that a Catholic ethos was being generated that was constitutively antimagisterial and thus fundamentally "protestant" in complexion. Interestingly, however, Balthasar's defense of the magisterium was bounded by what I have subsequently taken to be an identifying note of Balthasar: the too-little is not to be compensated for by the too-much. The office of Peter is inviolable, but there are other offices, as well as other forms of life, other spiritualities, and in the end any and all offices are normed by the passion, death, and resurrection of Christ. The lesson of *The Office of Peter* is that all authority is finally the authority of service, for responsiveness and gratitude to the mystery of salvation enacted in Christ is constitutive of the very nature of Christianity. This essentially Ignatian view of Christianity offered not only a specifically theological view of the church that he found lacking in contemporary ecclesiology, but also offered a principle of internal critique that trumped the external critiques of the church couched largely in sociological, psychological, and political terms. While it would require discernment, it should be the case that the conscience of the church is such that it will notice when service has been replaced by power and the preservation of power. Still, what most interested me was the project of the trilogy, and more specifically how Balthasar was going to be able to fashion a comprehensive theology, biblical in general orientation and faithful to the common tradition, while determined to play it in the key that most suited his gifts and more nearly corresponded to the needs of the contemporary world. The trilogy has not disappointed: it provides an incredibly rich feast of theological wisdom, spiritual insight, and discernment of what is living and dead in the theological tradition. It also demonstrates the ability to see the interaction between theological and nontheological discourses, and how the latter can be construed as complements rather than rivals of the former. This is especially true of artistic and philosophical discourses.

The trilogy deserves all the accolades that have come its way. Besides the exemplary first volume of *The Glory of the Lord*, Balthasar's performance is distinguished in the two biblical volumes. This is true especially of the sixth volume, *Theology: The Old Covenant*, despite the controversial nature of Balthasar's periodization in which the intertestamental period is understood to represent the eclipse of divine glory and thus divine presence. In addition, the second volume, *Studies in Theological Styles: Clerical Styles*, is hardly without its virtues. Although his essays on Augustine and even Bonaventure are disappointing, the former insofar as it presents only the early Neoplatonic Augustine, the latter because of a certain flatness in presentation, they are more than compensated for by the superb profiles of Anselm and Irenaeus. Of the five volumes of *Theo-Drama*, the fourth and fifth particularly recommend themselves, the former for laying the apocalyptic foundation of the drama of salvation history, the latter for being, arguably, Balthasar's most sustained reflection on the Trinity and its relation to the kingdom.

The latter text is crucial also for its testimony to the importance of the charismatic Adrienne von Speyr for Balthasar. From the point of view of modern theological method, Balthasar's blending of his own voice with Adrienne's in *Theo-Drama* is a scandal and tends to force Balthasar's most staunch supporters on the defensive. It is one thing for Balthasar to praise and applaud, another thing altogether for Balthasar to behave as if von Speyr is already something like a doctor of the church and for him — the professional man of letters, if not a theologian by training — to play or to move toward playing the role of amanuensis. For Balthasar, however, the embarrassment is simply misplaced, indeed, doubly misplaced: there is plenty of evidence throughout history of relationships of these kinds; many of the medieval women mystical writers enjoyed the kind of support that Balthasar provided and behaved in an even more self-effacing fashion than Balthasar. Second, and perhaps even more importantly, Balthasar would consider that the embarrassed implicitly subscribe to a profoundly modern and secular view of authorship as personal property. In this regime the authority of a text is invested in authorship's being single and thus univocal, and undermined in the case of its being plural in some fundamental respects and thus equivocal. Here Balthasar seems to find common cause with postmoderns such as Jacques Derrida, although his reasoning is both different in kind and considerably more local. His is not the postmodern conspectus on the semiosis of language; rather, it is the conviction that the self-erasure is required so that the persona of reflection is always, in the end, the church. Throughout the entire trilogy, as indeed throughout his entire career, Balthasar practices the ascesis that is the condition of the possibility of the ecclesial persona: he cedes his voice to an array of voices in the Christian tradition. The blending of voices with a living other is just another and unique form in what one might call the vocabulary of ascesis.

Of the three parts of the trilogy, arguably, *Theo-Logic* is the most even in terms of quality and is most consistently rewarding. This cannot be regarded as a foregone conclusion, given that the first volume simply recycles *Wahrheit der Welt* (1947) with the addition of a second introduction. The second and third volumes offer rich accounts of the economies of the Son and the Spirit, respectively, in terms of both the biblical text and the theological traditions across the centuries, Protestant and Eastern Orthodox as well as Catholic. Individually, each of these volumes represents a serious rival to the fifth volume of *Theo-Drama* as representing the richest account of Balthasar's Trinitarian theology; together, they certainly are a match at least in terms of theological substance. If these volumes do not issue in a grand Trinitarian synthesis, at the very least they point toward the congruence of different points of view, all of which have relative validity, the Augustinian as well as the Cappodocian, the Thomistic as well as the Bonaventurian, theologies that support the *Filioque* and theologies that do not. For Balthasar, Trinitarian synthesis is asymptotic and is possible, because actual, only in the triune life itself; to assume otherwise is to be influenced by the Hegelian dream of the absolute knowledge.

Massive accomplishment notwithstanding, not all of the volumes of the trilogy are equal in terms of composition, insight, or point. This criticism is justified even if one has forsworn the view that theology approximates to *rein oder strenge Wissenschaft.* It is not unreasonable for the reader to expect some express rationale in *The Glory of the Lord* for Balthasar's selection of figures who figure or configure Christian witness in such a determinate way as to constitute a style. The need for rationale becomes acute especially in the third volume, in which Balthasar deals with "Lay Styles," by which he means forms of Christian thought fashioned after the thirteenth century outside the guild of theology as such. One understands that Balthasar is only providing representative samples; Georges Bernanos, about whose work Balthasar wrote a marvelous book, and Paul Claudel, whom he translated, could conceivably have joined or replaced Gerard Manley Hopkins and Charles Péguy as representatives of modern theological styles of a literary bent. But why Vladimir Soloviev, whose apocalyptic and sophiological discourse seems so out of kilter with the tradition, when Balthasar shows such sustained animosity toward Nilokai Berdyaev? Balthasar's external and peremptory treatment of Aquinas in the fourth volume is also disappointing, even if Balthasar compensates somewhat for this in his interesting confrontation of Aquinas and Heidegger at the end of the fifth volume. It simply has to be conceded that throughout the trilogy that there are pages of professorial wandering and padding. The programmatic first volume of *Theo-Drama* is especially egregious in this respect. Although, the survey of the history of Western drama is entirely legitimate, especially so since the survey is intended to refute two influential theses of Hegel: the one, the impossibility of Christian drama, in effect the view that Christianity displaces rather than qualifies or subsumes drama; and the other, the death of drama in the modern age, a Hegelian view popularized in the contemporary world by George Steiner. Of all of the volumes of the trilogy, this is the one that most obviously suffers from Teutonic encyclopedism. Note that the complaint here is not that the book is simply too long; arguably, Balthasar could, and possibly should, have said even more about Stoic drama and the drama of the Baroque — perhaps given special attention to Lope de Vega, who so influences Claudel's *Le soulier de satin*, which is an absolutely indispensable text for Balthasar. The pages gained here would, arguably, have more than made up for what ought to have been cut. But that those pages should have been cut goes without saying. At points the first volume degenerates into an exercise in the presentation of drama-critic bona fides devoid of express theological point. And a number of the later volumes could do with a severe editing with a view to making the underlying argument more clear.

None of this is to deny that the theological or nontheological erudition on display even throughout the weaker volumes of the trilogy is impressive. But, perhaps, it does suggest that Balthasar's being "the most educated man in Europe," to cite de Lubac's judgment, can never be the ultimate point. As with any theologian, indeed any thinker, Balthasar is always under the obligation to show the point of a reference and to demonstrate how discussion or evocation of a particular thinker adds a note to a theological or nontheological discourse that we would do well not to dismiss. The sheer dimensions of the task that he has set for himself — the presentation or representation of the glory of the Christian tradition in its variety and proliferation — definitely invite us to give him a free pass. Given its herculean nature, is it not appropriate, even necessary, to relent some of our expectations? Surely, standards can and ought to be relaxed, given the vastness of the coverage that takes account of many of the more historically important spiritual and theological discourses of the church, the forms and varieties of scriptural interpretation, and the lives of the saints as witness to the truth of Christ and the possibility of an impossible form of life. I admit the apparent self-evidence of the apology, and I understand the plea that Balthasar is a victim of heightened expectations that his very excellence provokes. Still, it is not simply punitive to hold a theologian to his own very highest of standards. It is an act of respect. More, it is an act of avoiding idolatry. For what is important to the theologians, religious thinkers, and religious believers who come after is the thinking, not the thinker, and the essential Balthasarian vision of the polyphony of the theological and nontheological traditions that can, nonetheless, be resolved into a symphony.

As always, God is in the details. On my reading, Balthasar would not have it any other way. He interprets his charism as that of the conductor of the orchestra of the tradition, which is pure gift made possible by the sending of the Son and is enlivened and shaped by the Spirit. In general, Balthasar superlatively enacts what it is to be an ecclesial theologian by pointing away from himself not only to the phenomenon of revelation that has provoked all this fuss, the silence of the cross that has engendered all this speech, but also to biblical witness and the uniquely calibrated responses of all who in word and act pledge themselves to the impossibly beautiful truth of Christianity. Yet sometimes throughout the trilogy, as, for example, in the first volume of *Theo-Drama,* the emptying of self is insufficiently radical, and thus Balthasar insufficiently ecclesial. Balthasar's inordinate display of awareness of the history of drama bespeaks not so much arrogance as the anxiety to persuade that he knows what he is talking about as he counters Hegel's theses and their various modern and contemporary inflections. But this only goes to show that anxiety as much as professional or professorial hubris can get in the way of that ascesis that allows one to forget oneself, to give testimony to the phenomenon, and to speak with Christian confidence and boldness. At his best, Balthasar is a wonderful rememberer because he remembers not simply the fact but the meaning of a particular discourse of Christian witness, not just the individual form of its language, its actions, and prescribed forms of life but their ecstatic pointing to a linguistically uncontainable referent. Balthasar understands, as all proponents of *nouvelle théologie* do, the difference between ecclesial memory and the memory of the antiquarian. In the first volume of *The Glory of the Lord,* in his own appropriation of Nietzsche's distinction between living memory and antiquarianism, Balthasar distinguishes his enterprise from the nostalgia of François-René de Chateaubriand, which represents in his view the mummification of tradition. To remember well is to have memory laced by, maybe even lanced by, forgetting. Forgetting too is a power of the spirit that gives life. Sometimes Balthasar forgets, however, his own point about the necessity of forgetting.

This interpretive dilemma concerning Balthasar, whether to alibi or hold him to the most exacting standard, relates closely to the experience of paradox that I had when I first encountered the trilogy. This experience has not gone away, and it has deepened over time. Balthasar, to use the word that W. H. Auden put back into circulation, is the most "replete" of all modern

Catholic theologians, and yet, arguably, also the most underdetermined. The repletion or abundance cannot be dismissed simply as a personality trait, although it would seem pointless to deny the relative truth of this ascription. At the very least, two other factors can be adduced, the one more nearly rhetorical, the other more nearly theological. For Balthasar, as for Augustine in *De doctrina christiana,* theology is intrinsically connected with persuasion. This involves more than a change in particular opinions, in fact nothing less than a fundamental change in the compass of the self that is defined by what plays the role of magnetic north. Balthasar is much more anxious than even Augustine as to whether the triune God of Christian confession will in fact play this role, given the status of science and the authority of a basically propositional discourse characterized by clarity and reserve. Balthasar agrees with the Romantics and Heidegger in judging that conceding the authority of this model represents the death knell of any discourse that would pretend existential transformation. But he also agrees with a more Augustinianly inclined figure such as Giambattista Vico, who suggested in the eighteenth century that the only way to overcome the debilitating linguistic diet issued and regulated by a rationalist modernity is a recovery of the classical rhetorical tradition of Cicero and Quintillian. In their regimes the emphasis falls on copiousness. That is, one could think of Balthasar as a rhetorical theologian to the second degree; he is rhetorical in the first instance by Christian conviction, and in the second by a consideration that in the modern context rhetorical strategies have self-consciously to be preferred to the demands of scientific rigor. Reasons for copiousness, however, are not reductively humanistic. The inexhaustibility of the mystery of Christ as the mystery of salvation offers a theological reason. No single angle is adequate to this task; thus a variety of passes in the singularity that is the Swiss theologian Hans Urs von Balthasar. But again, as in the case of rhetoric, this more nearly theological commitment functions at two different levels. On one level, the theological commitment is resolutely first-order, and for this reason constitutively practical and performative. Christian mystery is such that in his own person Balthasar tries to offer a view that is not reductively one-sided. At another level, however, Balthasar is aware that true copiousness is the prerogative of the entire Christian tradition that braids together the different, even plural, viewpoints of the singularities that are its major thinkers and major saints. This self-consciousness in turn is not without influence on his own writerly performance.

Yet, as already indicated, Balthasar's work not only evinces repletion; it also is underdetermined. Of course, one can couch this in such a way that it counts as a criticism. It is certainly true that in comparison with Aquinas, for example, Balthasar is not the kind of theologian who sticks to *die Sache* and with extraordinary deftness summarizes and critically weighs varying opinions on an important theological matter, with an eye to ordering which involves suppositions about the global Christian narrative and instincts about what topic conceptually presupposes what. If the benchmark for Balthasar is set by the quality of argument evinced by Aquinas, then "underdetermination" can only be a negative. Similarly, it is perfectly fair to suggest that, unlike a much more methodologically focused theologian such as Rahner, Balthasar generally neither explores a single line of reflection nor finishes off single lines. The lines are multiple, and suggestion is often in excess of performance along a single line. The point about underdetermination, however, not only admits of a positive inflection, but also is much more satisfactorily translated by highlighting its connection with fertility, or with what Balthasar calls "fruitfulness." His texts invite completion, indeed multiple completions, but at the same time give direction.

A couple of examples help to bring out both the positive and negative sides of the phenomenon of underdetermination. My first example is from Balthasar's theological aesthetics. Given the depiction of Christ in the first volume of *The Glory of the Lord* both under the rubric of form and formless and their impossible synthesis in a "superform," Balthasar's treatment of theological aesthetics cries out for a serious engagement with Romantic reflection on the relation of the aesthetic and the sublime. This is not simply postponed until his treatment of the Romantics in the fifth volume of *The Glory of the Lord;* it never really gets off the ground, despite hints in this direction in his treatment of Kant. He encourages the good reader to follow this line of implication. In so doing, one would see how Balthasar's conjugation challenges modern and postmodern divagations in that the sublime as well as the aesthetic have an ontological tenor. In his seeing them together in Christ — for Christ is both beautiful and sublime at once — Balthasar also challenges a totally contrastive understanding of their relation, as well as responding to modern and postmodern exclusion of the religious domain from being a proper subject of these categories. Of course, imagining completion involves evaluation. It would be impossible to talk about completion unless one was convinced beforehand that the categories of the "aesthetic" and the "sublime" matter in their conjugation as well as their application. But if one is persuaded thus, one is grateful to Balthasar twice over: once for pointing the way, and again for allowing his reader the dignity of actually doing intellectual work that Balthasar handed off. But the gratitude also involves the burden of inquiring more fully into the prerogatives of the sublime, both in the realm of art and in Christology. Does Balthasar too blithely ignore the agitations of the sublime in avant garde art and literature and thereby deprive himself of opportunities for reimagining Christ that his view of analogy encourages? Does Balthasar too quickly smooth out Markan rough edges in his essentially Johannine Christology?

My second example comes from *Theo-Drama*. Within the very wide brackets of this part of the trilogy Balthasar associates a fully adequate form of apocalyptic (volume 4 of *Theo-Drama*) with a fully adequate form of theo-drama, which finds a particular compelling model, Balthasar believes, in the drama of the Spanish Baroque (volume 1 of *Theo-Drama*). Although it might seem at first simply meretricious, it is obvious that not only should the lines of connection be further developed, but also that Balthasar's conjugation should be put into conversation with Walter Benjamin, with whose work Bathasar shows significant familiarity. In *Trauerspiel,* on the basis of a very different selection of Baroque drama (German rather than Spanish, Protestant rather than Catholic), Benjamin articulates a very different form of apocalyptic, an apocalyptic indeed of pure interruption just the opposite of the visionary apocalypse of Revelation that Balthasar sees as central to the articulation of the dramatic prospectus of Christianity. This is a conversation or confrontation that needs to be faced straight up, since Benjamin is at the root of some of the more influential postmodern revisionings of Christianity.

At a time when outbreaks of apocalyptic fervor shame Christianity, and in which the biblical genre of apocalyptic is commercially exploited in popular fiction and cult, it is interesting that Balthasar can be regarded as the foremost Catholic defender of apocalyptic. Balthasar could certainly have made clearer how an apocalyptic frame of reference is required for the kind of Trinitarianism that he recommends and what he believes to be its most successful articulations. In the trilogy Balthasar tells us much more about the species he dislikes than the ones he likes, although we can infer that he thinks positively, for example, about the apocalyptic theology of Sergei Bulgakov. At the same time, *Theo-Drama* and *Theo-Logic* remain remarkably consistent with avowals made in *Apokalypse der deutschen Seele* in their shared opposition to forms of eschatology that have a Hegelian, and ultimately Joachimite, bent. Balthasar has a special dislike for those forms of apocalyptic that avail of Christian Trinitarian language to unmoor individuals and communities from the authority of Christ and his paradigmatic obediential relation to the Father. In this respect, Balthasar is not unlike de Lubac, whose own reflections on the apocalyptic tradition owe much to Balthasar's early work, but on whom Balthasar relies heavily in the trilogy in his chastising of eschatological forms of Trinitarianism. Here, as in the previous example, much work needs to be done to articulate the positive and not simply negative relations between apocalyptic and Trinitarian theology. At the very least, however, Balthasar had provided a rough sketch of what this apocalyptic Trinitarianism would look like, and how it can be distinguished from its Trinitarian apocalyptic counterfeits.

The two examples that I have selected are, admittedly, nonstandard and obviously reflect some of my own interests. Other interpreters might point to the need for greater clarity concerning the role that philosophy is permitted to play in theology when it is denied the kind of role assigned to it by Rahner or even Aquinas. Others again might cavil at Balthasar's Trinitarian thought, which, although quite detailed, leaves much of the debate between East and West unresolved and indeed complicates matters considerably by introducing into the discussion of the relations between Persons notions such as "superspace" and "supertime" (volumes 2 and 4 of *Theo-Drama*), which are symbols that themselves require interpretation. Finally, one can understand the frustration of some who seek for a political theology that might rival those that are currently regnant, even if there has been good work done on Balthasar that shows how Balthasar's thought can be considered to fund such an enterprise. I agree that these issues are more central than the ones to which I have referred, but only in the last of these do I think that we are talking about the need for completion. Balthasar's articulation of the relationship between philosophy and theology and of the Trinity is complete and coherent. With respect to the vital question of the relation between philosophy and theology, the issue is not completeness, but rather whether Balthasar has understood analogy well enough and calibrated it finely enough. Very roughly, Balthasar's position is one of a number that articulate a *tertium quid* between the dismissal of philosophy (Barth) and the assertion that philosophy functions as a foundation for theology (neo-Scholasticism and, arguably, Rahner in some moods). Again, while it is partly true that, as with the Hermetic conjugation of God, the theme of the Trinity is everywhere and nowhere in the trilogy, happily there are critical foci — for example, volume 5 of *Theo-Drama,* volumes 2 and 3 of *Theo-Logic,* and even volume 1 of *The Glory of the Lord.* Although Balthasar does not arrive at a synthesis of Western and Eastern reflection on the Trinity in *Theo-Logic* or elsewhere, he exploits the failure in order to make the positive theological point that the mystery of the triune God admits of a variety of forms of scrupulous Trinitarian speech and thus a variety of spiritualities. In addition, Balthasar's use of symbols as if they are concepts invites analysis more than dismissal. What need does he think symbols serve? What conceptual value do they have? And what relation do the specific symbols that I mentioned have to biblical apocalyptic?

Given that I have philosophical, literary, and theological interests in excess of Balthasar, I cannot say that I have devoted the last decade and a half to the study of the trilogy. But I have attended to it without a huge degree of interruption, and I have taught various parts of it as doctoral seminars. I have found it impossible not be stirred by its conviction of the absolute worth of the Catholic tradition in all of its aspects, and difficult not to be impressed by the level of organization in a multivolume work that, eschewing the Hegelian model of systematicity, suggests the musical metaphor of fugue as well as the architectural metaphor of the cathedral. In either case, one is dealing with a copious space in which to think, live, and — dare one say it? — pray. For, like a great literary work, the trilogy succeeds in rendering, or at the very least inculcating, the prayerfulness that it recommends. In an important sense, the trilogy does articulate a "kneeling theology." At the very least, the trilogy shows what this kind of theology would look like and argues how the absence of the doxological dimension from theology evacuates it. Still, while Balthasar can be edifying, as is shown in his many essays and in his minor work, the trilogy cannot be classed as an edifying discourse, any more than Kierkegaard's great texts can. In important respects the discourse of the trilogy is second level: essentially, it represents an extended argument as to why "kneeling" is essential to theology; it is not literally a discourse "from the knees." As such, then, while Balthasar exploits, he also subverts, the distinction between a "kneeling" and a "scientific" theology.

To have read Balthasar is to know that one will continue to read him, and read him with profit. Of course, all our reading—the same is true of our teaching—involves in some way judgment of adequacy with respect to parts and wholes. But writing involves it even more directly. Judgment is displayed in the very choice of what we write on in Balthasar, and when we interpret rather than report what he says. I take it that these are burdens that the theologian should bear for the sake of the church, about which and for which Balthasar wrote. I have spent too long with Hegel not to understand that judgment (*Urteil*) has embedded in it a sense of separation. This connotation helpfully reminds that we do not do thinkers justice by reproducing them, literally or otherwise. We enter at a different angle, or we enter multiple times in different places, trying to increase our critical advantage with respect to a part or a whole, or the whole through the part. As I try to make sense of what I have written and what I am currently preparing for publication, I am reminded not only of the fact of, but also of the need for, nonidentical repetition. Balthasar's theology of tradition demands that this be so; the way in which his own theological work is both overdetermined and underdetermined encourages it.

For a few years now I have been working on Balthasar as a theologian who finds it necessary to respond to modernity characterized by forgetting. Obviously, the primary mode of response for Balthasar, as for any exponent of *nouvelle théologie,* is to remember, and remember well. Memory is response as redress, and it would be difficult to think of any modern theologian as more engaged in remembering the tradition than Balthasar. But as Balthasar does so, inevitably he raises the question of the very nature of tradition. Obviously, the points that I have already made about plurality and integration—in Balthasar's preferred idiom, about polyphony and symphony—and the contrast between tradition and mummification are relevant here. The latter contrast brings to the fore the difference between mechanical reproduction and the art of memory, just as the former suggests that the tradition is an intricate web rather than a set of discrete propositions, a conversation and argument rather than something that proceeds more *geometrico.* The kind of

memory exhibited by Balthasar in his own work, and recommended as ecclesial, depends upon the instinct that the past of response to the mystery of
salvation and the articulation of that response are not simply past but rather
are a moment of concentration pregnant with possible futures. That the past
is pregnant precisely as response to mystery is crucial, for time essentially is
the time of response. This does not mean that the mystery that is responded
to does not affect time; for, as Balthasar points out in *Theo-Drama,* with respect to the incarnation, passion, and death of Christ, one is talking always
about more than affect, because on his view, this mystery actually effects and
thus constitutes time.

Particularly interesting is the fact that Balthasar allows two different
theological scopings of time. Time and history can be conceived equally
meaningfully as framed by the brackets of creation and apocalypse, with the
incarnation, passion, and death of Christ serving as the hinge moment, or as
an enactment within the christological parenthesis of Christ's having come
and the expectation of the second coming. The christological parenthesis,
however, is flexible and inclusive enough to stretch or distend backwards
to creation. Throughout each part of the trilogy, albeit in different ways,
Balthasar points beyond the exhaustible fecundity of Christ to provoke tradition to the role of the Spirit in effecting it. The first volume of *The Glory of
the Lord* very much sets the table in this regard. Moreover, in *Theo-Drama*
and *Theo-Logic* in particular, authorizing a move that some contemporary
Trinitarian theologians might find objectionable, Balthasar suggests that in
the final instance the triune life itself is responsible for the dynamic of tradition. For while without responsiveness there is no tradition, ultimately
tradition or *traditio* means gift. By regressive analysis from the gift of the
church, through the gift of Christ as the compelling aesthetic object that
provokes response that constitutes the church and the gift of the Spirit that
enables and formats the response, one arrives at the font of gift itself—that
is, the triune life in which the church participates.

The book on tradition focuses on those elements of Christian faith and
practice that Balthasar thinks essential to recover, especially the christological
center of faith and the Trinitarian horizon and the call to holiness. It also
concerns itself with Balthasar's treatment of such key figures as Maximus,
Bonaventure, and Aquinas. It is at the same time a book that deals with

issues such as catholicity and the construction of heterodoxy and its distinction from heresy, while examining the relationship between Balthasar's view of tradition and the more influential Catholic accounts in the last two centuries, including those of Johann Möhler and Johann Drey from the Tübingen school, and John Henry Newman and Yves Congar. Although resolutely theological, the analogies between Balthasar's view of tradition and the more philosophically inflected views of Hans-Georg Gadamer and Mikhail Bakhtin also come in for discussion. Similarly with Nietzsche, who after an extraordinary degree of prominence in *Apokalypse der deutschen Seele* seems in the trilogy to have faded completely from view. An especially important feature of this comparison with Nietzsche is the fact that "forgetting" serves in Balthasar as a constructive, if not constitutive complement, to memory. While Nietzsche has been interpreted as advocating forgetting *tout court* and thus encouraging a new barbarism, perhaps he, rightly understood, is a proponent of the view that unless forgetting (de)regulates memory in some respect, then effectively there is no memory at all, for nothing is selected for our attention. I would suggest that Balthasar translates the more moderate Nietzsche into a theological idiom and construes Spirit as the agent of productive forgetting precisely as the agent of memory.

What makes Balthasar especially fascinating as a theological figure, profoundly interested in the contemporary cultural crisis, is that he presumes that he cannot attend simply to the forgetting that is constitutive of modernity and the Enlightenment in particular. From *Apokalypse der deutschen Seele* on, Balthasar shows awareness that modernity is extraordinarily complicated; it is defined just as much by the history of the attempts to overcome forgetting as it is by forgetting itself. Thus, out of necessity theology has to engage modernity's most recent history of memory, inadequate as well as adequate. There are numerous forms and variations of inadequate memory, and throughout the trilogy Balthasar covers widely different specimens. What I have increasingly come to see is that beyond the bands of inadequate memory, the trilogy is engaged in critically vetting and overcoming two powerful discourses of memory that counter Enlightenment forgetting and hold out the prospect for a rehabilitation of Christianity. These discourses are associated with the names of Hegel and Heidegger. In the manuscript that I have just finished, I make the case that the dialogue/confrontation with these thinkers operates at a deeper level than with any other pair of modern thinkers — indeed, to the point that it provides one of the keys to the unity of the trilogy itself. What makes the conversation/argument so necessary is that Balthasar judges that these discourses inscribe significant aspects of Enlightenment forgetting; they represent monumental discourses of misremembering of the Western tradition of philosophy, and of Christian discourse and practice, and also the relation of one to the other. Hence the title for my book: *An Anatomy of Misremembering: Balthasar against Hegel and Heidegger.*

It is important for me in this book not to neglect the ways in which Hegel and Heidegger are, for Balthasar, constructive influences in the trilogy. If in the end Hegel's systematic allure must be resisted, since it annihilates rather than preserves Christian faith, nonetheless, Hegel is, for Balthasar, a productive theological resource in his drawing attention to the centrality of the cross, in his acceptance that reality's ultimate horizon is Trinitarian, and in his emphasis on and elaboration of the participation of the human in the divine. In Balthasar's view, these are necessary features of Christian thought often neglected by more mainline forms of Christianity in general, and Catholicism in particular. Similarly in the case of Heidegger. If, for Balthasar — and here he agrees with a critic such as Karl Löwith — Heidegger effectively offers a pagan substitute for Christian faith, he is also of the opinion that no modern thinker so productively criticizes the philosophical and theological traditions as forms of false memory and upsets the primacy of the propositional model of truth while at the same time recovering the importance of mystical, apocalyptic, and literary forms of discourse. I have found it important to underscore differences in the level of intensity of *Aussein-andersetzung.* Here Hegel is privileged in that, as rendered in *Theo-Drama* and *Theo-Logic,* the intensity of battle with Hegel borders on that exhibited by such diverse nineteenth-century figures as Kierkegaard and the Tübingen theologian Franz Anton Staudenmaier. Balthasar's resistance to Heidegger necessarily demands more subtlety and indirection because of Heidegger's drawing of a clear line of demarcation between the domains of belief and inquiry that Hegel does not observe.

Nonetheless, however different the discourses of Hegel and Heidegger are, and however much Balthasar actually repeats Heideggerian criticisms of Hegel, in the final analysis Balthasar thinks that both discourses represent seductive forms of misremembering that need to be outed. The unveiling of misremembering or "false memory" is the complementary to theology's primary obligation, which is to remember well. To remember well is not necessarily to remember everything. Balthasar would likely agree with Heraclitus's distinction between knowing deeply and knowing much, but he is of the opinion that suspicion might be cast on a church that remembers little; such a church likely moves toward a condition of weightlessness. Although the issues between Balthasar and the two great modern German philosophers are ineluctably substantive, as well as being motivated by theological concerns, there are formal concerns also. Hegelian recollection (*Erinnerung*) is a form of memory that refuses the slightest semantic gap, with dialectic being the means to overcome the appearance of such gaps and the forgetting that they threaten. By contrast, memory in Heidegger, and thus the constitution of tradition, is profoundly episodic; tradition is the tradition of the moments of mindfulness, which by definition cannot form a pattern. Tradition in Heidegger, then, is not simply the overcoming of forgetting; in a sense, it is the enactment of another and deeper kind of forgetting, whose nihilistic consequences Balthasar sees Heidegger coming more and more to accept. Balthasar is persuaded that his specifically Christian model of tradition represents the alternative to both: it remains irreducible to a Hegelian dialectical-developmental unity and the merely productive forgetting of Heidegger, which picks up on the more radical side of Nietzsche. The Spirit remembers well but also productively forgets, and somehow or other the responsibility of the theologian is in some unique way to illustrate this mysterious unity that the Spirit enacts in multiple centers. Balthasar provides an instructive example as well as offering a powerful reflection on the entire process.

The lesson that Balthasar teaches about memory plausibly applies also to a theologian's reading of him. The sheer prosaicness of how Balthasar came to be read does not matter; real effect is not disqualified by the banality of its occasions. I cannot but believe that because of him I hold different views on a host of theological matters. But I also suspect that the influence that Balthasar now exerts reaches down beyond the theological positions that I hold and defend to the kind of theological thinking that I perform. In ways not fully measurable, theologically I think differently than I once did. I think. Because of Balthasar, theologically I am not what I once was. But being changed by Balthasar means some quite determinate things and not others.

Balthasar did not make me unrecognizable to myself: in a sense, his influence was of that most benign sort that may have made me more rather than less myself; indeed, in a way, he was the conduit of a giving of my theological identity. Balthasar's books and essays are ever proven invitations; if *any* theologian creates space for the other, it is he. At his best, Balthasar mimics that "letting be" that is ingredient in any doctrine of creation, and thus he participates in it and exemplifies the dialogical principle that he so self-consciously supports in the trilogy and especially in *Theo-Drama*. It helps that however determinate a style Balthasar enacts as a theologian, fueled by his conviction about the tradition and his sense of responsibility to it, he does tend to move toward the condition of impersonality. To imitate Balthasar cannot in the slightest mean to reproduce him. It means, rather, that instructed by his ascesis, as a theologian one lives, moves, and has one's being in the wide and ever expanding space of tradition — which is not as wide as the triune love — to which it attempts to be adequate, and enters its dynamic flow — which mirrors only distantly the *dunamis* that characterizes the triune life. Balthasar's texts provide no impediment with respect to what the culture of literary production calls originality, for he has always pointed away from himself to multiple others whom he remembers as having remembered the God who is never past but rather is the "absolute future" that turns back all anticipation. A theologian who takes Balthasar seriously will supplement him, and it is only by such supplementation that one does him justice.

When I bring to mind Balthasar as an example and a teacher of the tradition, I cannot help but recall the scene at the end of James Joyce's "The Dead." As the tenor in the drawing room upstairs runs through a love song in keeping with the Christmas celebration, at the bottom of the stairs the woman of the house is riven by its loneliness, or *uaigneas*. Loneliness echoes the disappointment of love, attends scrupulously and mindfully to its wounds, even on the day that celebrates new life. But as the reader of this most famous of short stories knows, and now because of John Huston's gorgeous movie knows even better, the loneliness and sadness of the woman that marks the day that is too quickly passing is the end of the action but not the meaning of the story. For this sadness, itself an aspect of celebration, provides a connection with the dead, who were simply the objects of our all-too-human conversation over dinner. At that moment in the story, or out of the story, Joyce seems to have folded Christmas into All Saints Day, and he seems to reach toward a sense of community that cuts across not only the brokenness illustrated by the fracturing of argument but also the chasm between the living and the dead, whom we presume to be out of communion. Joyce does not consistently rise to Rainer Maria Rilke's level in his pondering of the mysterious unity of the dead and the living, which Balthasar looks so favorably on in *Apokalypse der deutschen Seele* and later on in the fifth volume of *The Glory of the Lord.* And Joyce does not make it into Balthasar's literary canon. But in this short story at least, Joyce does manage to rise to the level achieved by Rilke in *Duino Elegies,* and moreover, he manages to speak of this relation in a truly Catholic key that suspends some of the more egregious Romantic notes of one of Balthasar's favorite poets. Despite, or perhaps because of, its understatement, there is, perhaps, no more beautiful rendition of the *communio sanctorum* in all of English literature.

To have been instructed by Balthasar, to have mused with him, is in effect to have entered a conversation not simply with him, but with the many dead to whom he gives a proper name. The tradition is the dynamic flow in which new voices are added, precisely as a process of revoicing. It is only apparently that the living theologian is alone the questioner and the speaker. As Balthasar would see it, the dead have an agency and an interrogative ability peculiar to them. This can easily be laundered in a Gadamerian way, but Balthasar wishes to suggest more theologically that this is a result of what Christ has effected on the dead — moreover, not only the dead for whom we have proper names, but rather even more mysteriously those who have not left us with any textual remains. They too witness to the most relentless love. When one thinks of Balthasar's own rendition of the *communio sanctorum,* one feels that the invitation to any of us to speak is from the dead, who precisely constitute the community that is irreducible to being a mass. One understands that one is invited to be a different note — itself one might say indissolubly tied up with one's theological mission — precisely as an invitee. I said above that I am not who I was because of Balthasar. Now with this understanding, maybe I can say that I am not who I am because of him, for Balthasar reminds that identity is granted not by repeating or reproducing, but rather by that reaching out in ecstasy to what is only eschatologically available. I am only by not being; I am only who I will be.

Chapter Eleven

The Paradox of
Hans Urs von Balthasar

Russell Reno

It was a sign of the times, and it caused me to recollect my own complicated relationship with the thought of Hans Urs von Balthasar. In a 2006 article in *First Things*,[1] Alyssa Lyra Pitstick and Edward Oakes tussled over Balthasar's legacy. The main focus was Balthasar's theology of Christ's descent to the dead. However, Pitstick has a larger agenda. "It is undeniable," she writes, that Balthasar's "theology of Christ's descent entails a *de facto,* and sometimes even conscious, rejection of Catholic tradition. Thus, Balthasar's work fails to adhere to an essential element of Catholic ecclesial theology and its standard of truth." Still further, insofar as "the mysteries of Christ's life, death, and resurrection are all knit together," failure on one point implies a deeper problem: a heretical Christology and distorted account of the Trinity. By Pitstick's reckoning, the evidence clearly indicates "that something went gravely awry in Balthasar's execution of the task of ecclesial theologian," and contemporary Catholics ought to look elsewhere for guidance in the renewal of the church's theological life.

Pitstick's suggestion that this renowned Swiss theologian made no trustworthy or healthy contribution to Catholic theology is striking. It would be difficult to find a Catholic figure from the twentieth century more widely admired for his literary élan, theological imagination, and often lyrically expressed devotion to the Catholic tradition. Moreover, the kinds of people who write appreciatively of Balthasar are almost always from the so-called *Communio* wing of the church, a term derived from a journal founded (by Balthasar, among others) after the Second Vatican Council to resist the irresponsible and destructive theological liberalism that came to dominate most theological faculties in Europe and North America.

My own story provides further evidence on behalf of Balthasar's positive role in the renewal of theology. As a young graduate student I greedily read the first volumes of Balthasar's *Herrlichkeit,* and as a young professor I found his little book on the church, *Razing the Bastions,* explosive. More importantly, to a theological writer trying to find his voice, Balthasar was and remains for me an example and inspiration. He wrote with passion and immediacy. His mind ranged across the Western tradition with synthetic insight. Literature, music, and philosophy (and *not* that blinding postmodern preoccupation, politics!) animated his theological imagination. Both Christian to the core and unapologetically intellectual, Balthasar's vast literary output strengthened my own faith and helped me persevere as a writer, and he stiffened my resistance to the narrow careerism and perverse intellectual pragmatism of American academic culture.

In short, along with a youthful debt to Karl Barth and a longer, more mature engagement with John Henry Newman, Hans Urs von Balthasar has been one of my touchstones. I have long thought of him as one of the greatest, most creative, and most enduring theological figures of his generation. How could anyone question his Catholic bona fides? How could anyone throw into doubt his contribution to Catholic theology?

But time went by, and Robert Miller, an intellect not to be trifled with, asked me what I made of Pitstick's quite cogent argument. Did I not agree with the key premise that Catholic theology should take its bearings from the teachings of the church, and in view of the evidence, did her conclusion not follow rather forcefully?

Slowly, my mind worked its way into a dilemma. On the one hand, I was not at all shaken in opinion (backed up by some of the great minds of the church) that Balthasar is a theological hero, someone to be read and reread. On the other hand, Pitstick had made a very strong case that Balthasar should not be considered an ecclesial theologian — an argument that I could not simply dismiss. My mind turned the puzzle over and over again. John Paul II wanted to make Balthasar a cardinal specifically to honor his intellectual service to the church, and yet, if Pitstick's logic holds, he failed to contribute to Catholic theology. It may not have been precisely what Pascal meant, but, in my thoughts, Balthasar was beginning bear out the truth that a man is a paradox to himself.

What, then, was I to think? Is Balthasar helpful or unhelpful? Does his theology contribute to a robustly faithful future, or is it a distraction, all the more dangerous because dressed up in the appearances of orthodoxy? Furthermore, the paradox of Hans Urs von Balthasar casts long shadows. If Balthasar was something of a heretic, then what am I to make of John Paul II's enthusiastic endorsements? Was his long pontificate itself a failure, at least from the standpoint of renewing Catholic theology? And what of Benedict XVI, who seems to share a similar high regard for Balthasar? The question of the future of faithful Catholic theology and Balthasar's role in that future was forcing me to think in fresh ways. My touchstone not only inspired, but also presented problems.

When I teach on Thomas Aquinas, I emphasize to students that the great master of the Scholastic method did not treat objections as simple impediments to be overcome. The pressure of reasons against helps clarify the deeper springs of reasons for. In many cases insight and precision come from seemingly plausible objections that capture an important dimension of truth. In these cases, Aquinas formulated distinctions that not only show contradictions to be apparent rather than real, but also shed a fuller light that incorporates rather than rejects the partial truths contained in the objections. The more I thought about Pitstick's charge against Balthasar, the more I realized that I should adopt a similar approach. For her objection to standard celebrations of Balthasar's theological genius contains an important partial truth, not only for my assessment of Balthasar, but also for my understanding of how theology serves the church. I needed to see not only how Balthasar influenced my theological development; I also needed to know more fully how Balthasar failed to shape and guide my thought.

To start, I turned to a distinction between doctrine and theology. Doctrine serves as official and authoritative teaching. Throughout the modern period, the Catholic Church has developed precise principles regarding the conditions for and authority of various types of doctrine. Thus, doctrine is a body of clearly defined teachings, and the principles of doctrine are well defined in official definitions of the role and competence of the magisterium, the teaching office of the church. In contrast, theology is a much more fluid and ill-defined reality. Biblical interpretation is a type of theology. Philosophical arguments for the existence of God play a role in another type. Historical analysis of the ancient creeds counts as still another. We possess few authoritative definitions of theology, which is fitting, for theology is made up of a diverse set of disciplines that set about to study the sources, implications, logic, and rationales for doctrines.

Amidst all this diversity, theology has one important and consistent role. The magisterium of the church never sat down one day and decided to work out an overall account of Christian truth. Quite the contrary, doctrines develop out of and in response to the already existing (and always internally complex) theological culture of the church. As a result, the relationships between doctrines and of doctrine to Scripture and liturgy, as well as the relations of doctrine to any number of theological questions, are rarely clear and apparent. Doctrine, in short, needs to be applied, analyzed, and explained. By doing this sort of work, theology gives doctrine a coherent form that can be integrated into the cognitive lives of believers. This work is one of the main vocations of theology.

With the systematizing and expository role of theology in mind, a further distinction needs to be made that bears on Pitstick's argument and Balthasar's role in my own theological development. There is a broad sense of Catholic theology that presumes subjective assent and material conformity to church teaching. But subjective assent and material conformity are entirely consistent with the development of very creative theological explorations. What the church teaches admits of a wide range of interpretive and systematic treatments, most of which require conceptual innovations and dramatic revisions of standard readings of the history of theology and doctrine. Few will dispute that Balthasar, however loyal to the church, was just this sort of creative, exploratory theologian.

In nearly all cases, the church trusts in the faithfulness of those committed to its service, and in many, many cases, questions of material conformity are very complex and difficult to determine, so much so that reliable judgments often require the divinely assisted role of the magisterium itself. But the church must have more than loyal theologians, more than theologies consistent with church doctrine in the minimal sense of not being precluded by magisterial teaching. The church is not a community of independent scholars, each pursuing individualized syntheses, however important and enriching these projects may be. Instead, the church teaches and minis-ters in order to build up the faithful. To do so effectively, the church needs theologians committed to developing and sustaining a standard theology, a common pattern of thought or framework for integrating and explaining doctrine.

Any historian of Christian theology — ancient, medieval, Protestant, Catholic, Orthodox — will recognize the distinction between exploratory and standard theologies. The first type is creative, personal, and lacks widespread communal acceptance. It is ecclesially loyal but not ecclesially normative. It serves in ways that leaven, extend, and enrich the church's in-tellectual life, often by criticizing and questioning the adequacy of standard views. Saint Bernard was of this type, and so was Saint Francis de Sales. So were Erasmus, François-René de Chateaubriand, and John Henry Newman. Each has made remarkable and lasting contributions to Catholic theology, but none provided a pattern or mode of theology that can serve as a widely taught baseline for communal understanding of doctrine.

The second, more pedagogically suitable form of theology necessarily ap-pears to be more pedestrian. It accepts the vocation of explaining, sustaining, and teaching a standard theology, not innovating so much as improving, not rejecting and beginning afresh but rather refining and renewing through carefully articulated additions, adjustments, and adumbrations. No patron saint of standard church theology begins at the center. Thomas Aquinas waxed and waned in popularity in the late Middle Ages. Instead, standard theologies are invariably "isms" — Thomism, neo-Scholasticism, Calvinism, Augustinianism, and so forth. The point is not that every Thomist agrees or thinks along the same lines. Rather, what makes a standard theology stan-dard is the broad agreement to accept the general framework of a theological system. The effect is to create a school of thought that tends toward internal reinforcement through ongoing research and gives rise to a tradition of good textbooks that introduce new students into an ongoing mode of framing and answering theological questions.

With a distinction between exploratory and standard theologies in mind, I am now able to return to Hans Urs von Balthasar with a more precise sense of his contribution to the church and to my own thought. I find that he exemplifies the first, experimental type of Catholic theology, one that flour-ished in his generation of influential Catholic figures. It was this type of theology that I was trained to prize, and as a modern American who fancies himself creative and unique, I did not need much encouragement. Smitten by Balthasar's virtuosity — who remains untouched and unmoved by his ability to load the Christian faith with kinetic energy? — I was keenly aware of the enriching potential of his properly loyal theological culture of exploration. What I tended to ignore, however, was the role of a widely known standard theology, a mode of theology that Balthasar did little to encourage me to pursue.

My quick rush to enjoy Balthasar's faithful creativity had made me blind. The church can no more function like a debating society that happens to meet on Sunday mornings, forever entertaining various analyses and assessments of its doctrines, than a physics professor can give the classroom over to eager students who want to make progress by way of freewheeling discussions. Believers are unable to develop an intellectually sophisticated faith without a baseline, communally recognized theology. As Leo XIII recognized in his commendation of Thomas Aquinas to the nineteenth-century church in the encyclical *Aeterni Patris,* in order to have a coherent, ongoing grasp of the truth of the faith, the church must have a standard ecclesial theology. Indeed, without this kind of ecclesial theology, the church will lack the internally coherent and sophisticated theological culture that is necessary for understanding bold new experiments and fruitful recoveries of past traditions. This is a problem that most teachers of theology sense today: students do not know enough to be able to appreciate how striking, innovative, and fruitful are Balthasar's musical variations on traditional Catholic themes. Without a standard theology, exploratory theology, no matter how loyal to the tradition, will remain eccentric and indigestible.

As I look back, I can see that the one-sided nature of Balthasar's theology had long characterized my relationship to his work. I read and continue to read him for inspiration and encouragement. He was and is always compelling. I remember being unable to put down the final volume of *Theo-Drama.* His ability to tense theological concepts with scriptural energy and give God's sovereignty, judgment, and love such vivid immediacy gave me goose bumps. But at the same time, he has always been for me largely unusable. For the most part, I have not been able to employ the concepts, formulations, or pieces of his technical analysis in my own theological work. When I wrote something on the doctrine of atonement a few years ago, I tried to work with Balthasar, but his motifs and images and allusions and amazing ability to give lyrical content to concepts were simply unmanageable. I gave up. For a good, cogent, logical account of Christ's saving work, the now out-of-print manuals by Matthias Scheeben (superb excursus on historical theology) and Adolphe Tanquerey (succinct and rigorous) were much more useful.

I was experiencing a distinction between Balthasar's distinctive, remarkable, and penetrating spiritual imagination and his relative lack of contribution to the existing forms of standard Catholic theology. Balthasar could deepen my apprehension of key Christian teachings. Reading *Mysterium Paschale* as a graduate student gave me my first and most powerful experience of the doctrine of the Trinity as the *sine qua non* of saving truth. He could excite me with bold thrusts through the history of theology. His little book *Love Alone Is Credible* opens with two short chapters that provide an extraordinarily simple and profound framework for understanding the history of Western theology from Irenaeus to the present.

Balthasar's hyper-Cyrillian Christology and his whirlwind synopses of history, literature, and theology were very heady stuff, but at the end of the day they did little to orient me with respect to the main lines of pre- and post-Vatican II theology. For example, in the years leading up to Vatican II Balthasar made common cause with Karl Rahner and others against the supposedly soulless manual theology of the seminaries and the "fortress mentality" of the hierarchy. Yet, soon after Vatican II Balthasar published *Cordula oder Ernstfall,* a harsh attack upon what he saw (presciently) as tendencies toward anthropocentrism and secularization in contemporary Catholic theology, tendencies encouraged by Rahner's transcendental theology. When I was studying Rahner, I read the book and felt the spiritual intensity and truth of Balthasar's objections, but I could not identify the precise nature of his disagreement. The book provided me with no technical help in understanding the logic of Rahner's theology. *Cordula oder Ernstfall* was a powerful and timely thrust against the emergence of Rahner as the dominant figure in post-Vatican II theology, but, like so much that Balthasar wrote, it lacked the patient engagements with standard modes of theological analysis that are necessary for any work of scholarship to have a precise and lasting ecclesial effect.

One exception helps to prove the rule of Balthasar's ecclesial eccentricity. Balthasar's exposition of Karl Barth in his early book *The Theology of Karl Barth* has been justly praised. More important and lasting, however, is part 3 of the book, "The Form and Structure of Catholic Thought." There, Balthasar lays out and defends the underlying logic of Tridentine theology against Barth's relentless reduction of Catholicism to the double-headed monster of Pelagianism and idolatry. It is a tour de force in which Balthasar shows how the central categories of neo-Scholastic theology — nature, grace, and the *analogia entis* — can be deployed to do the greatest possible justice to the *sola gratia, sola fide,* and *solus Christus* commitments of Barth's own Protestantism.

Whether or not they are interested in Karl Barth, students of Catholic theology should read *The Theology of Karl Barth* in order to gain a more complete understanding of the relentlessly soteriological structure and latent Christocentrism of Catholic theology in the nineteenth and early twentieth centuries. I have read it a number of times, and I often recommend it to others. Any yet, even with this enthusiastic recommendation, the paradox of Hans Urs von Balthasar reemerges. Balthasar never followed up this profound defense of the Christian genius of Tridentine theological categories with a disciplined and detailed engagement with neo-Scholasticism. Quite the contrary, he was one of the Young Turks in the decade prior to Vatican II who offered only criticism of the neo-Scholastic tradition, much of it bitter, dismissive. Yet, if his exposition of the genius of the crucial neo-Scholastic distinction between nature and grace is taken seriously, then these harsh criticisms were at least partially misguided and counterproductive.

In this instance, Balthasar was true to his usual form. Instead of a sustained engagement with previous patterns of Catholic theology, Balthasar's habit was to launch out in new directions with little regard for the official, mainstream theologies. He made his counterthrusts against Rahnerian theology, but he never offered a patient diagnosis of what went wrong in this influential form of post-Vatican II theology. He defended and then departed from the concepts of the subtle neo-Scholasticism of one of his teachers, Erich Przywara, but he never clarified the senses in which his monumental meditation on beauty, goodness, and truth continued (or rejected) that legacy. In these and many other instances, his brilliant essays and massive volumes were eccentric to the main lines of Catholic theology both before and after Vatican II.

Because Balthasar never slowed down long enough to suggest how his thought fit (or did not fit) with standard ecclesial theologies, with the exception of *The Theology of Karl Barth,* it would never occur to me to assign one of his books to a student who wanted to understand why the church teaches this or that doctrine. He is not, as they used to say, reliable. This need not imply that Balthasar is broadly mistaken or at odds with magisterial doctrine, as Pitstick suggests. Given a better memory, a more thorough knowledge of the tradition, and time, I am willing to wager that I could produce a cogent argument showing that the main elements of Balthasar's theology of Christ's descent, while not entailed in the authoritative doctrines, can be shown not to contradict them. But I take Pitstick's point. Even as Balthasar opens up remarkable new vistas, a student will have a very difficult time understanding how he relates to the past theological consensus in the church.

Balthasar's impatience with the standard theologies of his day may or may not be accounted a failure on his part. Times were different for the theologians trained in the early twentieth century, when the exploratory mode of theology was undervalued, discouraged, and sometimes prohibited. Nonetheless, his neglect, even hostility, to standard modes of theology was one-sided and counterproductive. Balthasar neither explains how his thought rightly modifies the neo-Scholasticism that was normative for his theological training, which apparently he found boring, lifeless, and uninteresting, nor provides a basis for developing a new, widely accepted synthesis. Indeed, in *Love Alone Is Credible* the rhetoric of reduction into the form of Christ is so powerful that one has the impression that Balthasar felt that any stable systematic theology would intrinsically corrupt and falsify the singular form of love. Thus, in a very precise sense, it needs to be said that Balthasar was not an ecclesial theologian, at least not in the sense of working within standard conceptual categories and accepting normal frameworks. To no small degree, he contributed to an atmosphere of neglect of, and even antipathy toward, an important aspect of the vocation of theology: to sustain a functional, communally accepted and widely taught mode of analyzing, explaining, and defending doctrine.

To a great extent, the one-sidedness of Balthasar and his generation is exacerbated by historians of the Second Vatican Council who tend to lionize the innovators. But even though I now see the dangers of an overly exclusive tilt in the direction of creative, exploratory theological innovation, I remain no less enthusiastic about Balthasar's lasting achievements (and, I would add, the larger achievement of his theological allies). Balthasar did not renew Catholic theology in the narrow sense of contributing to a standard theology, but in his many books he provided the twentieth century with one of the most compelling expressions of a Catholic *sensibilité,* and his theological voice remains vitally important.

First, he gave lyrical expression to the truth that theological wisdom is born in prayer and purified in spiritual discipline. Second, his extraordinary literary and cultural breadth of interest bore testimony to the truth that all that is human belongs to Christ. Third and finally, he reminded the Catholic world that the words of Scripture provide theology with its deepest source of intellectual and spiritual power. In my own work as a Catholic theologian, I hope never to lose sight of these fundamental imperatives.

Pray always. Balthasar insisted again and again that theology must be formed in and through a purifying participation in the nuptial holiness of the church. Against mere learnedness and intellectual training, he wrote that the true end of theology is adoration. He never tired of pointing out that the early and medieval church treated sanctity and wisdom as interlocking theological realities, and he bemoaned on many occasions their separation over the last five hundred years, wondering why our theologians are no longer saints. Thus, in the message for the centenary of Balthasar's birth, Benedict XVI summed up Bathasar's achievement: "In a word, von Balthasar deeply understood that theology can only develop in prayer that accepts God's presence and entrusts itself to him in obedience."

By my reading of our present situation, this contribution to the future of Catholic theology is of incalculable significance. Intellectuals are trained to develop and extend the explanatory and interpretive power of conceptual systems. Modern science has shown the tremendous potential in this endeavor, as have the critical tools of social and historical analysis. However, it is easy to become bewitched by systems and to confuse the cognitive power of our modes of analysis with the deeper and fundamental *ratio* of reality. To know the world is to participate in its truth, and systematic analysis serves that end; it is not an end in itself. This is all the more true of theology, whose goal is to deepen, through understanding, our participation in the truths of faith. It is a terrible temptation for theologians to think a theological system provides a more direct and reliable route into the mystery of God than sanctity. Balthasar, one of the most intellectually gifted men of his times, provided a powerful witness by warning us against this temptation.

Today, his warning takes on a further and more pointed significance. From where I sit, I see theology shifting from clerical to lay practitioners — like me. For two millennia, the church could cultivate methods and systems of intellectual rigor in an educational system that presupposed a ready supply of talented men already formed in religious orders. Now, faculties of theology train large numbers of men and women from extremely diverse backgrounds and with highly variable degrees of spiritual formation. Balthasar's continual emphasis upon prayer and sanctity as the animating center of any true theological vocation is a direct challenge to this state of affairs. If we take his insight seriously, we cannot continue with the old modes of theological training that divide responsibilities: intellectual rigor in the lecture hall, spiritual discipline in the priory. Contemporary theology must recognize that the methods and systems that it has inherited are not merely intellectual, nor can they function on their own. Spiritual discipline needs to accompany theological training; otherwise, theology loses touch with its divine *ratio.* As Balthasar writes in one of his characteristically vivid passages, "The flame of worship and obedience must burn through the dispassionateness of speculation."[2]

In my own theological work I have repeatedly come to the humiliating realization that the deepest, most lasting, more debilitating problems facing modern Christians are spiritual and not intellectual. It is a self-congratulating fantasy to imagine that a critique of nominalism or a new metaphysical vision will somehow revive the fortunes of Christianity in the West. No methodological masterstroke will restore theology. A clever appropriation of postmodern hermeneutics will not free us to read the Bible as the Word of God. Intellectual work is necessary, and there are many advantages to be gained by clear thinking and effective syntheses. However, as Balthasar has taught me (reinforced repeatedly by the very different theological projects of George Lindbeck and Ephraim Radner), it is our spiritual corruption that hollows out and mutes the power of the gospel in our age. Grace alone, sought and received in prayer and obedience, can cure our corruption and bring to fruitful exercise the intellectual gifts of men and women called to theological vocations in the service of the church.

All things belong to Christ. Our standard histories tell a simplistic story. Once upon a time, they say, the Catholic Church was closed to the modern world. Spanish priests wrote books with titles such as *Liberalism Is a Sin.* The Syllabus of Errors rejected the Enlightenment. So pervasive was the impression that the essence of Catholicism rests in its antithesis to modernity that Thomas Mann, in *The Magic Mountain,* portrayed the future of the European soul as torn between the ineffectual humanism of the voluble Italian Settembrini and the ultimately nihilistic dogmatism of Naphta, a Jew turned Jesuit, who is willing to say that black is white if the church so commands. Then, so the standard history continues, the church repented of its antimodern ways. At the Second Vatican Council the church opened itself to the world. The church was suddenly preaching a kinder, gentler faith, a liberalism ready for dialogue.

This simplistic story had a good run, but John Paul II refused to play according to the script. He led the church into an unanticipated, renewed, and articulate rejection of liberalism, and at the same time into an unprecedented engagement with threats to human dignity that liberalism had slowly come to accommodate: first the communist tyranny and then the Western culture of death. He turned out to be a zealot of a confusing sort. He was zealous on behalf of submission to the truths of the faith, and he was zealous on behalf of reason, freedom, and human rights. Under his leadership, the Catholic Church became simultaneously more robustly and confidently christocentric, and at the same time more politically and culturally relevant.

It is no accident that John Paul II wished to make Balthasar a cardinal to honor his contribution to the church, for Balthasar mirrored intellectually what John Paul II enacted ecclesially: intensified commitment to Christ prepares us for ever greater service to the world. In Christ, the truth of love goes out to the all the world, and it does not return empty, for in Christ all things find their fulfillment. Insofar as we allow our minds, our theologies, our literary judgments and philosophical concepts to be formed by Christ, our intellectual work will bear the fruit of love, no matter how far it ranges out into the world.

Balthasar drew two different but mutually reinforcing conclusions from the breadth of the light of Christ. The first is a counsel of confidence. All of us feel at sea in a vast and diverse world. We have no desire to cram reality into simplistic molds; we want to do justice to the particularity of the human spirit. In his exquisitely detailed and nuanced treatments of European literature, Balthasar manifested his own confidence that Christ guides us to all truth by bringing us to a deeper and fuller understanding of our shared humanity. The second is a counsel of responsibility. "A Christian commitment," Balthasar observes, "can humanize whatever is threatening to slide into the inhuman."[3] Thus, when reading Friedrich Nietzsche or Charles Péguy or any other figure beyond or on the borders of Christian faith, Balthasar's analysis consistently pressed toward integration and fulfillment. He did not lack judgment. He was quite willing to point out failures. Yet, all judgment and censure was oriented toward incorporation. What is human belongs to Christ, and he rescues our humanity and our culture from its self-incurred debasement.

Balthasar's counsel of confidence is important for contemporary Catholicism. Karl Rahner often observed that the day had passed when a scholar could take responsibility for the great diversity of knowledge in modern culture. I have always thought that Rahner's protests were self-serving, reflecting more the anxieties of a German university professor worried about being caught making a mistake than any sound theological principle. For if Jesus Christ is the Alpha and Omega, then it seems to follow that knowledge and love of him will provide genuine insight into all things. As Thomas Aquinas put the matter, theology, rightly understood, is the queen of the sciences. The eyes of faith are not infallible, but they are expansive. On this point Balthasar urged Catholic intellectuals to have the courage of universality promised in Christ.

John Paul II often expressed the second implication of Balthasar's Christocentrism, the counsel of responsibility, and it continues to be emphasized by Benedict XVI. We live in a postmodern age in which the intellectual and moral confidence of Western culture erodes as rapidly as its technological, military, and economic dominance increases. A false and nihilistic kenosis seems to predominate, evacuating reason of its spiritual power by cynically assuming that truth is nothing but worldly power dressed up in arguments. In this environment, Balthasar's work outside the confines of traditional theology and beyond the range of reliable Catholic authors illustrates the redemptive, incorporative power of truth. He does not police the boundaries of discourse, as postmodern professors claim truth requires. Instead, Balthasar's mind moved with a confidence that the breath of the Holy Spirit brings even the coldest embers of truth to burn brightly. In our despairing postmodern era, with its culture of historical forgetfulness and self-willed myopia, all forms of truth now need the caring, encouraging spirit of Balthasar's Christocentrism.

I possess immeasurably less knowledge of Western culture than did Balthasar, but I have long found his witness to the true vocation of the Christian intellectual a lasting challenge to my own ignorance and lack of courage. It is tempting to follow Karl Rahner's advice, burrowing ever more deeply into areas of specialization. But as academics recede into their jargon-filled sanctuaries to offer holocausts of technical prose to the gods of professional journals, our public culture spirals down into a subliterary spectacle of celebrity sound bites. Intellectuals migrate to think tanks where they must respond to the news cycle, and the life of the mind begins to narrow into the categories of the moment. The old questions that gave life to culture — Bathasar's beloved transcendentals: beauty, goodness, truth — devolve into a mix of politics and entertainment. Against these trends I have tried to follow Balthasar and add my voice to a church culture of books and ideas. He has encouraged me to ask big, fundamental questions. And his example has helped me come to see the Western literary, artistic, and philosophical traditions as living voices. A theologian need not — should not — be a narrow specialist.

By scripture alone is the voice of truth made full. In his return to Scripture, Balthasar was truly a Catholic revolutionary, and perhaps here he has affected me most deeply. A late nineteenth-century theological textbook, itself an abbreviated translation of a multivolume work by the estimable Matthais Scheeben, expressed a typical judgment of its times. Doctrine is described as "materially complete," and "formally perfect," as well as capable of universal application. In contrast, Scripture lacks "systematic arrangement," is "often obscure," and remains ever susceptible to "many false interpretations." In other words, because doctrine uses theoretical categories, it enjoys a kind of clarity and definitiveness that one does not find in the muddy, multifaceted, and often maddeningly complex language of Scripture. As a result, this textbook concludes, Scripture is largely "unfit for the general use of people."[4] If preachers or theologians want to preserve and deepen the people of God in the truth, then the clear outlines of doctrine guide the way. The strange, unwieldy world of Scripture only confuses and hinders, and therefore the Bible should be put to the side.

More than any other theologian of his generation, Balthasar saw the absurdity of any theology that allows doctrine to supersede Scripture. Moreover, he understood that it is a spiritual fear of the incarnate form of God's love rather than an intellectual or methodological mistake that causes us to turn away from Scripture. "God's love renders itself concrete," he wrote, "with an almost terrifying exclusivity in the person and work of Christ."[5] As intellectuals and theoreticians, we feel an almost irresistible pull away from the immediacy of scriptural language, away from its blinding particularity, and toward cooler and more manageable and more cognitively useful concepts. Instead of "the personal *concretissimum* of the God-man," we take refuge in "such abstract notions as 'redemption,' 'justification' and so forth."[6]

I certainly have attempted to wriggle free from the brutal particularity of Scripture more than once. But in the move from concrete biblical word to abstract theological concept a danger emerges that parallels a theological neglect of prayer and holiness of life. Theology rightfully abstracts and deploys concepts, for a faith that seeks understanding must use the proper tools for systematic analysis and synthesis. However, a clear theological formulation can bewitch with its precision, and we can confuse what is easily understood with the real object of our faith: Christ crucified and risen. His death and resurrection have metaphysical meaning. Indeed, Christ is the Alpha and Omega, and knowledge and love of Christ must inform all our metaphysical judgments. But the Lord cannot be reduced to a metaphysical conceptuality. Incarnationalism, sacramentality, kenosis, sanctifying grace—these and countless other concepts, many drawn from Scripture itself, are true only insofar as they serve to more fully and completely draw us into the scriptural witness to Christ.

Hegel raised particularity up to the dignity of the concept. Balthasar's theological practice was consistently anti-Hegelian, and I hope that my own theological work follows this aspect of Balthasar's work without any deviation. Across the seemingly endless pages of his vast theological output, he consistently renewed concepts by drawing them ever downward, drenching them in the power of Scripture. I regard this movement of theology, this headlong dive deep into the primal ocean of the Bible, as the single greatest imperative of our time, the imperative of every age of the church. Pray always, and may our prayers be that we recite God's words as we go in and as we go out, as we rise and as we lie down. All things belong to Christ, and Scripture is their story, the code that maps the figure of Christ, the DNA of reality. To think in the idioms and figures of Scripture prepares us to enter into the truth of our humanity. Scripture is not alone; the church, the body of Christ, provides the Word of God with its proper context and guards and promotes our ever fuller entry into the truth of Scripture. But Scripture alone gives full, verbal form to Jesus Christ, and in him everything, including the church itself, finds its fulfillment.

Even if I am able to construct a plausible defense of its orthodoxy, I am willing to concede that Balthasar's theology of Christ's descent may be judged misguided or unhelpful. I can entertain the thought that his vast triptych of dogmatic theology — *Herrlichkeit, Theodramatik,* and *Theologik* — may end up unread on library shelves, a grand witness to one man's personal vision and intellectual creativity. The secular institutes such as the *Johannes Gemeinschaft,* to which Balthasar devoted so many decades of his ministry and in which he invested his hopes for the future of Catholicism, may find their way back into more traditional patterns of religious life. Everything that materially defined and influenced the theology of Balthasar may lose its relevance and influence. All this may come to pass. Who can know the future? But of this I am certain: Balthasar's fundamental and lasting and renewing contribution to Catholic theology will be his uncompromising commitment to the explosive power of Scripture.

In one of his self-reflective moments, Balthasar wrote, "Is it not better for me to come right out and confess that I am impatient?" He was a brilliant man whose mind seemed to operate with sudden insights and through bold syntheses. Is it surprising that he found the Scholastic manuals that were so prevalent in his theological training painfully constricting and uninspiring? He was like a brilliant young mathematician, frustrated by long and drawn-out explanations of matters that seem to him pedestrian. I imagine him sighing inwardly, "Why can't we get on to the really exciting stuff?" The sentiment is understandable, but a zeal for and love of deeper truths can also give rise to a self-centered blindness. What the genius does not need, or needs only for a brief moment, others require. A Pascal or a Fourier may best flourish in an atmosphere free from textbooks and problem sets, but these sorts of tools are crucial for building a mathematically literate culture. The same is true for theology and the church.

By my reading, in the English-speaking world contemporary Catholic theology is an aimless affair. The post-Vatican II professors have perpetuated the myth, first given currency by Balthasar's generation of Young Turks, that Catholic theology of the nineteenth and early twentieth centuries is a vast desert of dry and dusty theology empty of spiritual life. Those Young Turks destroyed the old Scholastic consensus that allowed the church to use the textbooks that are always necessary for a widespread theological culture, but they failed to produce a lasting theological synthesis to take its place. In this way, Balthasar differs not at all from other great Catholic theologians of mid-century whom we rightly celebrate: Henri de Lubac, Yves Congar, Jean Daniélou, and other major figures from the period just before and after Vatican II. They were men of brilliant insights, and they were masterful critics of the shortcomings of their predecessors, but they could not provide a workable, teachable alternative. They did not formulate a theology that could be standardized, taught, and assimilated by the wider church.

The effect of the eccentricity and experimentation of Balthasar and his generation of leading theologians was to create a vacuum. Karl Rahner was not the most brilliant thinker of his generation, and he certainly was not the most innovative. Instead, he emerged as the dominant figure because, in his own way, he retained the idioms and techniques of the earlier Scholastic theology. In that sense, Rahner was patient. He worked hard to show how his transcendental theology could be molded into a teachable textbook system, preserving the scaffolding of Heinrich Denzinger while hollowing out the force and import of traditional doctrine. Balthasar and others might warn against and criticize the emergent Rahnerian consensus, but the vacuum that they created ensured its triumph. Thus, however sharply they may have criticized the easy anthropocentrism and loss of Christian confidence after the Second Vatican Council, they bear some responsibility for its ill effects.

Today the failure of Rahner's misbegotten post-Kantian Scholasticism is plain to see. What is needed now is not another experimental theology of Christ's descent, or for that matter, an exploratory or creative account of any other doctrine. A college freshman in physics needs a good introductory course that presents modern physics in a direct, accessible, and systematized fashion. The same is true for today's theology student. Our current situation is absurd. Unlike training in other disciples, theological faculties these days offer almost no basic orientation to the logic of the faith. Instead, we socialize students into all the innovations, complexities, and difficulties of mid-to-late twentieth-century theology. We teach the extraordinary insights of figures such as Balthasar, Congar, Rahner, and de Lubac without giving our students the slightest exposure to a normal, comprehensive, and well-argued systematic theology. Fearing the narrowness derided by Balthasar and his generation, we end up with shallowness that they would have despised.

As I have contemplated my own ambiguous relationship with the theology of Hans Urs von Balthasar, I have come to recognize that his indispensable Catholic *sensibilité* is now forcing me to grapple with and learn from what he *did not* give or teach me. Instead of reinventing the Catholic tradition, I see that I need to contribute to a genuine, fuller form of *Ressourcement*. We need a cogent account of how the Tridentine categories and convictions of Catholic theology gave rise to and were enriched by the two great councils of the modern era, Vatican I and Vatican II. We need to recover the systematic clarity and comprehensiveness of the neo-Scholastic synthesis. We need a textbook theology, an approach that may not satisfy a literary genius such as Balthasar, but that most of us must rely upon in our endeavors to develop an intellectually sophisticated faith. After a period of creativity, exploration, and discontinuity, much of it fruitful and necessary, we need a period of consolidation that demonstrates how the innovative vision of the great Catholic figures of the twentieth century such as Balthasar contribute to a continuous Catholic tradition. In short, we need what Balthasar and his generation failed to give us: a renewed theology capable of being standardized and widely taught. Only then can the true genius of Balthasar and his generation be appreciated and integrated into the life of the church.

Here the paradox of Hans Urs von Balthasar remerges yet again. I have not found that Balthasar gives me very much in meeting the systematic needs of our day. Perhaps I lack sufficient plasticity of mind, or perhaps I am crimped by insufficient theological imagination. But by his own account, Balthasar was impatient with systems and idiosyncratic in his use of traditional theological categories and concepts. The more I have read him, the more I have become aware that he embodied the genius of Catholicism of the nineteenth and early twentieth centuries so thoroughly that he could explore without leaving home, criticize its failure without departing from its achievements, exercise his imagination confident of his inner obedience to the Catholic tradition. This led him to be silent where I need to be vocal, implicit where I need to be explicit, unique where I need to be conventional. After all, barely Christian when I was twenty-one, and only received into the Catholic Church after I turned forty, I lack what Balthasar and his generation could take for granted: a life formed by the rich coherence and sanctity of a church that knew its own mind.

Balthasar is not reliable, but he is inspirational in the best and fullest sense. I have many books mapped out in my head and stacks of folders jammed with notes and drafts on my desk. Daydreams often provide visions of writing a textbook that combines the best of the nineteenth century with the best of the twentieth. I picture Scheeben translated, revised, and corrected by the insights of *la nouvelle théologie.* I imagine a plain-Jane systematic theology that draws on the Scholastic potential of Robert Sokolowski's phenomenology. But all these projects, struggles, and dreams are for naught if I lose sight of Balthasar's lasting contributions. I am convinced that his Catholic *sensibilité* offers a great deal to my generation. Our task is not his. We need to recover and renew the achievement of the textbook tradition that formed Balthasar (and the other great theologians of his generation), the venerable and useful tradition that he (and they) often shortsightedly maligned. But in so doing, we must work toward a more standard, more Scholastic theology that will, God willing, benefit from his faithful service to the church that he loved.

Chapter Twelve

A Catholic Appropriation of Romantic Themes

Tracey Rowland

My earliest memory of the Catholic Church is attending the baptism of my cousin who was converting to Catholicism from Anglicanism. He was around twelve years old, and I was about three years old. We lived in outback Australia in a town called Barcaldine with a population of around two thousand. The town serviced the local sheep stations. My uncle and aunt and grandmother ran two of the small businesses. In the town there was a convent school run by the Sisters of Mercy. It was regarded as the better option by some of the Protestant families who wanted their children to receive a good musical education. After seven years of sitting through catechism classes, my cousin badgered his parents into letting him "turn." A few years later I too was sent to a convent school and converted.

I have a memory of visiting St. Brigid's Convent in Rockhampton just before I started school. My grandmother took me to meet the mother superior and asked her for a book of Catholic prayers. She did not want me to suffer the humiliation of being a Protestant child at a Catholic school who did not know the drill. I was given a beautiful little book with a guardian angel on the cover, and a brooch in the shape of a flower. I was invited to choose the latter from a box of treasures that was sitting on Mother de Chantal's desk.

Her convent was built in the Spanish mission style that suited the tropical climate. It had magnificent high ceilings, oil paintings of saints hanging over the entrance to rooms, and a chapel that was hidden off a cloister; and there were two cats, both Persians, one called Thomas Aquinas and the other Juliette Marie. It was not as grand as the monasteries in Balthasar's Switzerland, but in a country that only two centuries before had not a single permanent building, it was still something of real beauty that stood out from the rest of the neighborhood.

All the above may seem like a rather long and irrelevant preamble to an essay about Balthasar, but it may provide some background to the fact that discovering Balthasar confirmed a lot of childhood impressions and intuitions about the importance of beauty, of memory, and of cultural practices and placed these within a richer theological framework. Unlike those of so many of the great English converts, my conversion to Catholicism was not intellectual in the usual sense. I was far too young to sift through all the issues that divided Christendom in the sixteenth century and decide that I wanted to be on the side of the Catholics. However, I did have a sense for things that are beautiful, and the most beautiful things that I had ever encountered were Catholic liturgies and convent gardens.

By the time I went to university, much of this world of Australian colonial Catholic culture was dying. Nuns left in despair, Thomas Aquinas was run over, and Juliette Marie died of natural causes and was never replaced. St. Brigid's was sold to the government as office space for public servants, and the local bishop traded in the episcopal Mercedes for a Mazda. (Anyone who does not understand the cultural significance of this should read Betjeman's poem about the young executive who drives the firm's Cortina.) It was an era of retreat from sacramentality and its replacement by a lot of "infantile claptrap" (to quote Joseph Ratzinger). Bob Dylan sang "Blowin' in the Wind," and New Age nuns strummed "Kum-ba-ya."

Soon after I arrived at university, I read *Brideshead Revisited.* In one of the earlier chapters Charles says to Sebastian, "You can't seriously *believe* it all.... I mean about Christmas and the star and the three kings and the ox and the ass." Sebastian replies, "Oh yes, I believe that. It's a lovely idea." Charles then says, "But you can't *believe* things because they're a lovely idea." Sebastian replies, "But I *do.* That's how I believe." I now often quote this passage to students to illustrate the difference between the Protestant Enlightenment mind (represented by Charles before his conversion) and the Catholic disposition (represented by Sebastian). Reading *Brideshead Revisited* and other works by Evelyn Waugh confirmed my conviction that the conciliar generation had somehow developed the sensibilities of neo-Protestant puritans. The *Brideshead Revisited* character that they are most like is Hooper, the chap who could not see any point to Castle Howard as a family home.

Although at this time I was an arts/law student, I spent very little time studying law. When I did read cases, it was mostly for their literary quality, not for their legal principles. I can still remember whole paragraphs of Lord Denning's judgments, and I particularly liked all the Latin maxims in equity and property law. I had no interest whatsoever in mergers and acquisitions and the duties of company directors. I would sit in the library reading Waugh's novels and James V. Schall's political philosophy. Neither Waugh nor Schall were on any reading list in any subject in the university. Through reading Schall I came to Christopher Dawson. I became quite interested in Dawson's observation that Protestant cultures are "bourgeois" and Catholic cultures are "erotic." I think he took the terms from the Swiss sociologist Werner Sombart. In any event, anyone who has ever attended a low-church Protestant service and then attended Mass somewhere like the Brompton Oratory in London or the Church of St. Eugene in Paris will instantly know the difference between a bourgeois culture and an erotic culture. At the same time I was reading lots of writings by Jacques Maritain. This was because Tony Abbott, who at the time was the Minister for Health and Ageing in Australia, had written an article in the *Catholic Weekly* in which he listed a number of books that he thought helpful for Catholic students trying to defend the faith in a secular university. On his recommendation, I read all the Maritain classics, and these led me into Thomism proper.

By the time I finished my B.A., I had already been to Mass at the Brompton Oratory, read John Henry Newman, Christopher Dawson, and Evelyn Waugh, and taken in large doses of James V. Schall, Jacques Maritain, and Étienne Gilson. I had also majored in political philosophy with a special focus on the Marxist tradition, since I was privileged to be taught by one of those Czech exiles who spoke seven languages, had two doctorates, and a music degree. This led me to write a master's dissertation on the attitude toward the Liberal tradition of leading members of the central European anticommunist intelligentsia. Most of the authors whom I covered were Thomists of some stripe or other, though some of the Czechs were Hussites. While compiling the research, I lived in Cracow. One of the things that attracted me to the central Europeans was their interdisciplinary character. I liked the way they explained philosophical principles by reference to literary characters and historical events. I remember coming across an essay by Zdzislaw Krasnodebski titled "Waiting for Supermarkets." The theme of the article was that Poles who long for a return to mainstream western European culture need to be prepared for the banality of postmodernity. He concluded, "there is no archaic Ithaca to which one can return, Penelope did not wait faithfully, but submitted to her suitors."

When I returned to Australia, one of my colleagues was quizzing me about my beliefs and diagnosed me as a "MacIntyrean type." I had not read Alasdair MacIntyre, but I decided that I should at least read *After Virtue*. I read the trilogy of *After Virtue, Whose Justice? Which Rationality?* and *Three Rival Versions of Moral Enquiry*, and I ended up going to Cambridge to write a doctoral dissertation on the topic of "Tradition-Dependent Rationality in the work of Alasdair MacIntyre." By this stage I had worked out that I was a MacIntyrean type of Thomist — that is, one who believed that concepts can never be understood outside of the cultural context in which they are formulated. I tend to believe that one cannot be a good philosopher or a good theologian without first being a person who knows and loves history. MacIntyre explains the principle when he says that when studying any philosopher, one must always ask, "Against whom is he or she writing here? Within what controversy is this or that particular contention to be situated?" Scholars characteristically invite us not simply to assert *p*, but rather to assert *p* rather than *q* or *r*, and thus we can understand the point of asserting *p* if we know what *q* and *r* are.[1] Thus if one wants to understand the mind of Thomas Aquinas, one needs to know something about the ideas of his contemporaries at the Universities of Naples, Cologne, and Paris, and about the jurisdictional conflicts between the powers of the emperor and the pope during the period in which he was writing, and even about the stance that Aquinas took on the behavior of jongleurs hanging about the entrance to the Sorbonne singing anti-Dominican songs.

Such an approach to philosophy (and by logical extension theology) that addresses the historical and cultural dimensions of problems is often described in British academic circles as the "Cambridge School of Ideas," for it contrasts rather sharply with the analytical tradition of philosophy, strong in places such as Edinburgh and Oxford, which take a more ahistorical approach. The interesting point is that while MacIntyre is in some ways an example of an analytical Thomist, he is nonetheless a brand of Thomist who emphasizes the importance of history and culture; and in this sense there is a strong affinity between MacIntyre's philosophical works and the approach to theology of Hans Urs von Balthasar. For both, history and culture are key elements.

It was at around the time that I began reading MacIntyre that I first heard of Balthasar through my friend Anna Krohn, who is a *Communio* reader. I also have a postcard sent to me by my husband soon after we met on which he had copied a couple of sentences from Balthasar about the relationship between *philokalia* and *philosophia*. What I remember about this time is that it was precisely Balthasar's idea that there exists an inextricable nexus between a love of beauty and a love of truth that prompted me to dive into the *The Glory of the Lord* series. Having done so, I discovered, for the first time, a theologian who used the concrete stuff of history and poetry and even music around which to present his theological reflections.

When I arrived in Cambridge, I had a meeting with my supervisor, who asked me what type of Catholic I was, and before I had time to answer the general question, he asked specifically whether I preferred Rahner or Balthasar. This was the first time anyone had suggested to me that this really is the key question of postconciliar Catholicism. During my first few weeks in Cambridge I was also introduced to Aidan Nichols, and eventually I made my way through his extensive series of essays and books on the thought of Balthasar. Although in his typically English understated style he described his guides to the thought of Balthasar to me as "Balthasar for idiots," these are more than nutshell guides for lazy undergraduates.[2] In a MacIntyrean manner, they place Balthasar's thought within the context of its own history and culture, and they are presented in an elegant prose style worthy of *The Spectator* and Balthasar himself. Without these introductions, many young scholars would find themselves drowning and would give up.

My dissertation on MacIntyre's notion of tradition-dependent rationality led me into the territory of theories of the relationships between traditions, culture, and language and eventually to the relationship between nature, grace, and culture and their treatment at Vatican II; and ultimately all roads on nature, grace, and culture lead to Lucerne and Einsiedeln. In getting to that point, I spent several months studying the German Romantics, particularly Johann Gottfried von Herder and Wilhelm von Humboldt, and a collection of essays in Erich Przywara's *Humanitas* that really deserve to be translated into English. Although that was something of a detour, it was great preparation for ultimately reading Balthasar more closely. Indeed, one shorthand way of understanding his oeuvre is to think of it as a Catholic appropriation of Romantic themes. In *The Mind of the European Romantics,* H. G. Schenk made the point that the Romantic movement is a halfway house between Catholicism and nihilism. Catholics and Nietzscheans share an interest in the themes of individuality and the uniqueness of the human person, the movements of the human heart, the place of art in culture, and the significance of history and memory (even if Nietzscheans want to destroy both, they think them sufficiently important to warrant destruction). More generally, the Catholic and Romantic traditions share a dramatic sensibility and a synthetic temperament.

What Balthasar does is take the Romantic themes and demonstrate that the deepest longings of the soul can be fulfilled only by participation in the mysteries of the life of the Trinity. Catholicism, unlike anything that the Romantics found attractive in the inheritance of classical Greece, is "No Bloodless Myth."[3] For precisely this reason he argued that the real battle between religions begins only after the incarnation. Moreover, this participation in the life of the Trinity is mediated through a church, and this church has a culture that informs other cultures. In a sense, the church is the mother of culture. This seems obvious to anyone who has thought about the Benedictine influence on the history of Europe, and it was one of Christopher Dawson's favorite themes. For me, it was always rather clear that nuns teaching music and foreign languages in outback Australia were in an analogous position to the sixth-century Benedictine monks. Fortunately for Europe, no one ever told the monks that they needed to be more relevant by adopting the cultural practices of Gothic tribesmen. Perhaps because he was, in Henri de Lubac's judgment, the most cultured man in Europe of his generation, Balthasar never fell for the "infantile claptrap" embraced by so many of his generation. As John Milbank has noted, Balthasar understood that "without Christian culture there is only a nominal, not a mediated grace, which must remain uncomprehended and without real effect."[4]

It seemed to me that precisely this understanding (of the need for a Christian high culture through which grace might be mediated) was sadly missing from much postconciliar thought. Aidan Nichols, in *Christendom Awake,* summed up the problem when he wrote, "To hand down authentic tradition while manifesting *insouciance* towards the forms in which Tradition is embodied . . . has been, in recent decades, the somewhat contradictory policy of numerous representatives, some highly placed, of the Latin church."[5] In the 1960s and 1970s form did not seem to matter: to care about tradition was to render oneself a member of a very unfashionable club of social dinosaurs. The conciliar peritus Albert Dondeyne spoke enthusiastically about the "democratization of culture" and described "mass culture" (from which the postmoderns are now all trying to liberate us) as a "genuine contemporary cultural creation." It was as if Rousseau had suddenly become a doctor of the church. Meanwhile the real avant-garde, the Frankfurt school of social theorists, were busy explaining to the generation of 1968 how mass culture was turning the human person into a mere one-dimensional being. When Marxists are against something marketed as "democratic," one should realize that it has problems, but Catholics were being exhorted to move with the spirit of the times, and it suited the upward social mobility prospects of those in Western countries to do so. As E. Michael Jones has observed, the generation of 1968 Catholics were "lusting after Modernity."[6]

The more theological impetus behind many of the pastoral programs of the 1960s and 1970s seems to have come from interpretations of Karl Rahner's work and from John XXIII's opening address to the Council Fathers. In this the Holy Father suggested that Catholic doctrine is one thing, and the language in which it is presented another. The first, the content, is in some way above history, while the form can change with historical fashion. It is said that both Rahner and John XXIII were operating on an instrumentalist theory of language according to which concepts are easily translated from one set of idioms to another. This is now regarded as naïve. The expressivist theory of language by which concepts take their meaning from the cultural environment in which they are enunciated is the more incisive and now commonly accepted school of thought. One of my academic interests at the time of writing my doctoral dissertation became the way that these issues were never really addressed by leading Catholic scholars and prelates in the immediate postconciliar era and the pastoral consequences of this oversight.

One of the saddest illustrations of this lack of attention to issues in linguistic philosophy and to the broader questions of the relationship between language, tradition, and evangelization is found in an address by Paul VI in

1968 on the subject of the introduction of the new rite of the Mass. The form of the address was that of a eulogy. In line after line Paul VI listed arguments against the new liturgical project. He used emotive language acknowledging that we were "parting with the speech of Christian centuries: becoming like profane intruders in the literary precincts of sacred utterance." He suggested that we might have "reason for regret, reason almost for bewilderment," and that we were "giving up something of priceless worth." Nonetheless, he concluded that the new rite was necessary because "participation by the people is worth more — particularly by modern people, so fond of plain language that is easily converted into everyday speech."[7] Deconstructed, that particular address sounds like "I know that some of you think that we are behaving like philistines, but if modern man is a philistine, we need a liturgy for philistines."

The idea that the Catholic faith can be hooked up to any culture and expressed in any idiom, and that it might be too high, too transcendent, for certain sociological types like "modern man," could only have arisen in an intellectual context where people naturally thought in extrinsicist terms, with separate boxes for grace and nature, the sacred and the secular, history and ontology, faith and reason, liturgy and ethos. The entire 1960s approach of attempting a distillation of form from content and then repackaging the content runs counter to insights expressed by Balthasar even before the Council about the impossibility of separating the interior principle of form from its concrete manifestation. Moreover, both Balthasar and de Lubac were alert to the problems inherent in this kind of dualism, and they had attributed a certain amount of it to developments in Baroque theology. In trying to understand the reasons behind the pastoral errors of the 1960s and 1970s, I therefore became interested in what happened to the Catholic theological tradition during the Tridentine period. I found myself accepting the genealogies of the culture of modernity that one finds in the works of *Communio* scholars such as Peter Henrici (Balthasar's cousin) and David L. Schindler, and in the works of Radical Orthodoxy scholars John Milbank and Catherine Pickstock. Both the Radical Orthodoxy and *Communio* scholars trace the beginnings of secularization to the rise of nominalism in the fourteenth century and later to sixteenth- and seventeenth-century constructions of the nature and grace relationship and the Suarezian approach to revelation. In a lecture delivered on a tour of the

United States in 1968, de Lubac explained how a sharp dichotomy between the orders of grace and nature left the field of nature open for an invasion of secularism. This theme was taken up by David L. Schindler in his critique of the culture of America, which I strongly endorse.

In adopting insights from these schools, I did not, however, become anti-Thomist. Like Aidan Nichols, I think it wrong to see Thomas and Balthasar as competitors, even enemies or logical alternatives in the manner that Balthasar and Rahner are in so many ways logical alternatives. There is much in the tradition of Thomas that Balthasar affirms.[8] I simply concluded that the ahistorical character of classical Thomism means that it is limited in the contributions that it can make to the development of a theology of culture, unless and until the Thomist tradition develops what Ratzinger and other scholars in the *Communio* circles call "the dimension of relationality." This includes an understanding of the effects of culture and history on the formation of the person. In *Principles of Catholic Theology* Ratzinger observed that "the fundamental crisis of our age is understanding the mediation of history within the realm of ontology." In short, it is a Heideggerian problematic.

I therefore concluded that those Thomists who after the cultural collapse of 1968 tried to fight a rearguard action with the artillery of Scholastic categories were in a similar situation to the Polish cavalry at the outbreak of World War II. They were right about the enemy being an enemy, right about the need to fight, absolutely heroic, but unable to meet tanks with horses. To beat Nietzsche, one has to demonstrate not that Catholicism is more *rational* than any other tradition, but rather that it is more *erotic*. Benedict XVI understands this, and Balthasar was onto it even earlier. Having immersed himself in the literature of the German Idealist tradition, Balthasar gained a deep knowledge of external perceptions of the Catholic faith. He concluded that the severance of the trinitarian relationship of the transcendentals (truth, beauty, goodness) in post-Reformation Europe meant that people now find it difficult to see the form of a Catholic culture. Without this, the faith loses its allure and becomes at best a cultural artifact in the great museums of Europe. Accordingly, the project of postconciliar Catholicism should be one not of making the faith fit into the forms of the culture of modernity, but rather of finding ways of restoring the unity of the transcendentals as they are expressed within cultural practices, so that the form of the faith again becomes visible for "plain persons" who lack the cultural capital of a Balthasar. This is not to suggest that there is only one possible form of Catholic culture. Just as Balthasar argued that there is a symphony or constellation of different spiritual missions in the life of the church and that truth itself is symphonic, there may be many different forms of a genuine Catholic culture, but what all will share is a kind of splendor based on the unity of the transcendentals in their practices.

In my doctoral dissertation I therefore suggested that part of the project of developing a theology of culture is to explore the relationships between the transcendentals, the theological virtues, and the faculties of the soul. In particular, I argued that there are important links between the faculty of memory, the theological virtue of hope, and the transcendental property of beauty; between the faculty of the intellect, the theological virtue of faith, and the transcendental property of truth; and between the faculty of the will, the theological virtue of love, and the transcendental property of goodness. I further suggested ways in which the practices operative within the cultures of modernity and postmodernity operate so as to sever these links, and thus ways in which the transposition of Catholic idioms and practices into those of the culture of modernity has the effect of undermining these evangelically vital trinitarian relationships.

In developing this area, I was influenced not only by Balthasar but also by the American Franciscan Benedict Groeschel. Groeschel has argued that people have a tendency to have a primary attraction to one or other of the transcendentals. One may argue, for example, that goodness was the primary transcendental of St. Francis of Assisi, while for Aquinas it was truth, for Augustine beauty, for Teresa-Benedicta of the Cross (Edith Stein) integrity or unity. Groeschel further suggests that it is important to understand this element of human psychology when giving spiritual direction. Some souls have a strong appetite for truth but poor formation in virtue; others have a strong appetite for goodness but no intellectual framework for directing their will; some need to see what Balthasar calls the "splendor of the form" and have a kind of inbuilt nose for it, while others seem to have suffered a beauty bypass operation, or simply live in fear of a decadent aestheticism, or have no capacity for reading between the lines, seeing the big picture, or making synthetic judgments and observations. The logic of this analysis is that one should not put all of one's apologetic energies into the basket of any single transcendental but rather should work on a number of fronts

simultaneously. With reference to the thought of Balthasar, Cardinal Marc
Ouellet expressed this conclusion thus:

> This mission [the integration of faith and culture] cannot be accomplished
> simply by speculative combat in the service of truth. It requires an investment
> of all the forces of our personal existence in the drama of fraternal love. . . . It
> is a matter here of opening up a third way, which leads beyond modernity by
> defining Christianity on its own terms instead of measuring it by the yardstick
> of critical reason.[9]

The project of defending Christianity at the bar of critical or Kantian
reason has also been subjected to criticism by Alasdair MacIntyre, Stanley
Hauerwas, John Milbank, Cardinal Scola, Cardinal Ratzinger, Archbishop
Xavier Martinez of Grenada, David L. Schindler, and numerous lesser-
known scholars in both Catholic and Protestant circles.[10] In my postdoctoral
work I have been particularly interested in approaches to ethical questions
that eschew this kind of Kantian methodology, and here the significant
Balthasarian influence has been Balthasar's critique of moralism — that is,
the reduction of Christianity to the dimensions of an ethical framework and
the substitution of casuistry for theo-drama. This has led me into the territory of the relationship between Jansenism and moralism and the related
theme of the link between sanctity and chivalry.

While Jansenism is a notoriously difficult heresy to define because it went
through various phases — some Ultramontane, some Gallican — and while
it has even been described as a mere anti-Jesuit disposition, the key element in the context of moral theology is a strongly Calvinist attitude toward
human nature and sensual pleasure. Jansenists were a sort of Catholic "fun
police." The two areas that are most affected by it are therefore sexuality and
liturgy. Jansenists have a tendency to have an instrumental attitude toward
both. Sex is for procreation; liturgy is for turning bread and wine into the
sacred species. The effect of both on the human soul, particularly the affec-
tive parts of the soul, is of no great interest. The Jansenists were actually the
original proponents of low Mass in the vernacular, and Jansenist Irish clergy
were notorious for their lack of liturgical sensibilities. In the early history of
the church in Australia, the English Benedictines who were sent to service
the pastoral needs of Irish convicts met with a hostile reaction when they
tried to introduce Gregorian chant. In the context of sexuality, a Catholic

mother with a large family once explained the fact to me by saying, "What could I do? It's a mortal sin to say no."

One of Balthasar's many original insights was precisely that such a way of thinking was a major contributing factor to the era of postconciliar dissent. Once the fear of eternal damnation had been quelled by the mixture of conciliar optimism and talk of "anonymous Christians," the motivations for obedience were no longer present or at least were far less potent. The truth is that obedience is a free act of the person, and what passed for obedience was mere outward compliance. Balthasar's point was that this kind of collapse could happen only if within the Catholic imagination morals were primarily linked to concepts such as obedience, duty, and damnation. His cousin Peter Henrici summed up the problem when he wrote that before the Council the practice of Christian life consisted largely of the performance of duties because one was obliged to do so. Christian existence was therefore viewed as a meritorious achievement that God commands and by virtue of which one is able to please him. In short, Kant had become a secret Father of the church.[11] This also accounts for why Christian living was not conceived as a synthetic development of grace or as a virtuous response to God's initiative but rather was rule dominated. Ethics became not an "I-Thou" relationship but rather an exercise in which conduct was submitted to a third person for assessment, typically a confessor who operated from a manual. Most of the postconciliar dissent in ethics, including proportionalism, was an attempt to continue this rule-based approach and justify the use of contraception. Dissent thus became a clash of wills (institutional versus personal) in which the rights of conscience were championed over what were caricatured as rigid and authoritarian calls for supine obedience.[12]

Although at first glance Kantian ethics, based upon a severance of reason and revelation and hence grace and nature, appears to be irreconcilable with the Jansenist emphasis upon the complete wreck of nature without grace, the two intellectual currents share the property of making duty and obedience to the will of a legislator the driving force behind moral action. Against the Kantian and Jansenist tendencies to place the accent on obedience and duty, and in the Kantian case, rationality divorced from human emotion, Balthasar wished to emphasize the *caritas forma virtutum* (love as the form of the virtues) and love as the form of revelation (*caritas forma revelationis*). The Jansenist opposition to devotion to the Sacred Heart is perhaps the starkest illustration of this contrast between a Kantian-Jansenist moralism and the Balthasarian emphasis on love as the form of the virtues.[13]

Benedict XVI's *Deus Caritas Est* can be read as an endorsement of this critique of moralism, especially as it is found in Balthasar's work *Love Alone Is Credible.* In the very first paragraph Benedict notes the Nietzschean claim that Christianity killed *eros,* and he acknowledges the problem with the reduction of Christian revelation to the concept of an ethical framework. He exhorts people to understand that Truth is a Person. Implicit in all that is said in the first half of the encyclical is that those who think that Christian ethics is all about duty and casuistry have got it wrong; and in particular, those who try to understand sexuality in terms of casuistry are completely missing the big picture. They do not understand sexuality because they do not understand love, and they do not understand love because they do not understand God. There has to be a better argument for a pro-life culture than "It's a mortal sin to say no." As Nietzsche insisted, if Christians want people to believe in their Redeemer, they should at least look as though they have been redeemed.

In the thought of the French writer Georges Bernanos, Balthasar sought an antidote to this type of hollow moralism. In *We the French,* Bernanos wrote,

> The more a sense of Christian honor becomes debilitated, the greater the abundance, indeed superabundance, of casuists. At the very least, the man of honor offers you the following advantage: he spares the casuist all his labor.... The moment a person feels the need to consult the casuists in order to know the amount starting from which stealing money may be considered a mortal sin ... we may say that his social value is nil, even if he abstains from stealing.[14]

Commenting on this passage, Balthasar observed that "the person who does not come to terms with his drives and whose religion risks becoming an endless struggle between duty and inclination — the threat of a Kantian Jansenism — is precisely the person who will most readily accept casuistry"; against such a "bourgeois morality and a despairing moralism, Bernanos proposed the ethos of chivalry, which for him was intimately related to the ethos of the saint."[15] Both the chivalrous person and the saint are dutiful, but they can be dutiful without consulting any manual of responsibilities. They are

motivated by a love much higher than the love of a reputation for reliability and "doing the right thing" or by the desire to avoid hell. The event of
Calvary really makes no sense if analyzed solely from within a duty-based
ethical framework. While Christ was "obedient unto death" and thus obedience has a place in Christian life and practice, this obedience operated within
a context of divine love. Balthasar therefore was opposed to any rationalistic
reduction of the logic of the cross to formulaic principles in a Kantian sense:

> For if the Cross is turned into a law which reason can grasp and administer,
> even an elastic sort of law governing the rhythm of life, then it is once again
> a law — in the Pauline sense — and absolute love is displaced and set aside
> by knowledge: this means to say that God's sovereign freedom (which could
> be quite other than what it is) is judged before the court of human reason —
> and condemned as that which it really is.[16]

Bernanos was so hostile to the project of defending the faith with reference to the court of Kantian "pure reason" that he wrote that each time
someone tries to do this, the ideas that they send out "with their little pig-
tails on their back and their basket in their hands, like Little Red Riding
Hood, get raped at the next corner by some slogan in uniform."[17] In some
of my essays I have treated the project of transposing the Catholic natural
law teaching into the idioms of natural right as an example of this kind of
strategy. Catholics end up sounding as though they are endorsing Liberal
jurisprudence while their own alternative definitions of the Liberal concepts
are simply ignored or otherwise effectively sabotaged.

In this context of the issue of the principles to be applied when considering the mode of engagement with hostile traditions, Balthasar made
a valuable observation in his essay "On the Tasks of Catholic Philosophy
in Our Time." With reference to Origen's metaphor of the *Spolia Aegypto-
rum,* he commented that any theft from the Egyptian camp that is carried
out by "genuine thinkers" (not ecclesial spin doctors) should not be a "mere
mechanical adoption of alien chains of thought with which one can adorn
and garland the Christian understanding externally."[18] There needs to be
something more than rhetorical value in a rival tradition that highlights a
lacuna within the Catholic tradition before one sets out to assimilate the
alien idea or to transpose a concept or idiom from one tradition to another.
Since traditions are handed on primarily through the medium of language,

any experimentation with different idioms is, in the words of the conciliar peritus Jean Daniélou, "an operation of extreme delicacy and difficulty."[19] Although Balthasar did not set out a systematic series of principles for discerning when and how to adopt the language and ideas of other traditions, one can nonetheless comb through his works for insights on how best this might be done.

Returning to the theme of digging the tradition out of the pit of a Kantian Jansenism, we note that a concept related to chivalry and sanctity is nobility. Balthasar addressed this in his book on Bernanos and in *A Theology of History.* Against the many materialist philosophies of history he concluded,

> Those who withdraw to the heights to fast and pray in silence are . . . the pillars bearing the spiritual weight of what happens in history. They share in the uniqueness of Christ, in the freedom of that nobility which is conferred from above; that serene, untamed freedom which cannot be caged and put to use. Theirs is the first of all aristocracies, source and justification for all the others, and the last yet remaining to us in an unaristocratic age.[20]

When I first gave a paper endorsing Bernanos and Balthasar on the theme of nobility and cited this passage, at least one member of the audience was appalled, believing that I was trying to promote the British class system. This reaction completely missed the point. While I do, as a matter of fact, support the concept of constitutional monarchy, I do not think that the British or any worldly aristocracies were uppermost in the minds of Bernanos and Balthasar when they wrote essays about the moral superiority and nobility of those with a chivalrous disposition. The fact that the mere mention of the words *aristocracy, nobility,* and *chivalry* can arouse opposition is evidence for the conclusion that egalitarianism has almost become an article of faith. This is another Kantian influence on contemporary Christian social thought of which scholars such as Robert Kraynak have been justly critical.[21] This was not, however, the argument that I was making in the context of Balthasar and Bernanos on the need for reestablishing the links between sanctity, nobility, and chivalry. My point, rather, was that if we want to give a serious response to the Nietzschean claims that Christianity has killed *eros* and is simply the morality of the herd, it does help if we explain how Christianity offers to all the possibility of ennoblement.

In this context I would argue that within Christianity there is both an aristocratic and an egalitarian dimension. The egalitarian dimension is rooted in the principle that the incarnation, crucifixion, and resurrection of Christ were for all humanity, regardless of race or class or sex. There is a universal invitation to be among the best. All are called to the heroic heights of sanctity. The aristocratic dimension, however, arises from the fact that the transcendentals are rooted in Being itself: beauty, truth, and goodness are not matters of subjective judgment. One person's idea of truth and goodness and beauty is not necessarily as valuable as another's. As Leo Strauss once put it, the opinions of the Athenian town drunk are not on the same level as those of Socrates. To the degree that different cultural practices are able to reflect transcendental properties, they exist on a scale of more or less excellence. Further, not all persons participate in the life of grace to the same degree. Aquinas acknowledged this when he argued that there are three levels in which people participate in the *imago Dei:* a kind of base level of human dignity that we all share as creatures made by God; the dignity of those who strive to live justly; and finally the dignity of those who are saints. Our own receptivity to grace is thus something for which we are, at least in part, personally responsible. We are made in the image of God to grow into the image of Christ. The drama of human life hinges on our responses to divine gifts. With reference to the novels of Bernanos, Balthasar expressed the notion thus:

> Here human nature appears like the calyx of a flower in bloom, open to grace, determined and directed by grace, summoned by grace and launched on extraordinary adventures by grace and God that surpass all human comprehension in their magnificence. These adventures are literally incomparable, which is to say, as unique and unrepeatable as God's graces are.[22]

This paragraph presents Christianity as the ultimate Romantic dream. It offers originality, individuality, nobility, and even eternal life, and the offer is made to all, regardless of class or national origin; nonetheless, it is an adventure or a quest in which some are ultimately more successful than others and in which players are offered different roles and missions. Whereas the Calvinist tradition tended to foster a "one size fits all" sort of spirituality, against which aristocratic Liberals such as John Stuart Mill understandably rebelled, the Catholic tradition as presented by Balthasar recognizes a constellation of characters around the person of Christ, each with his or her own particular mission and opportunities for heroism.

While I fully endorse the legitimate egalitarian dimensions of Christianity, I have used the ideas of Bernanos and Balthasar in a number of essays to argue that if one downplays the aristocratic dimensions, one ultimately Protestantizes Catholicism. In Protestantism there are no new saints and heroes because there is no dramatic cooperation with grace. This is the effect of Luther's reductionism: *sola gratia, sola fide, sola scriptura, solus Christus, soli Deo gloria*. In Dawsonian terms, it makes Catholic culture less erotic and more bourgeois. It thereby makes it harder for the practice of the faith to stand out as an alternative mode of being in a postmodern world. A bourgeois Catholicism blends into the mundane secular culture and offers no specific difference.

To conclude: Discovering Balthasar did not so much change my mind (in the sense of effecting a U-turn in my thinking) as to enrich my framework for considering the many contemporary theological crises faced by the church. In particular, it gave me insights into the territory of the relationship between nature, grace, and culture. It also confirmed my judgment that the postconciliar enthusiasm for dumbing down the rich devotional and intellectual life of the church with reference to the lowbrow tastes of "modern man" was a pastoral disaster. In Ratzinger's words, "A Christianity that believes it has no other function than to be completely in tune with the spirit of the times has nothing to say and no meaning to offer. It can abdicate without more ado."[23] Reading Balthasar placed this judgment into a broader theological context and provided a means for understanding much that went wrong after the Council with reference to flaws in the Baroque and other preconciliar frameworks. No one can read Balthasar and be left with a facile notion that Vatican II was a fight between progressives and conservatives. Balthasar's reading of the problems in the preconciliar traditions helps to place the debates and pastoral strategies of the Council into their historical and cultural context. In doing so, he shows that what is required is a much more multidimensional theology of culture than anything dreamed of by those who got hooked on a popularized Rahnerian notion that absolutely anything can be baptized.

Reading Balthasar is a great antidote for the kind of sadness that overcomes those who understand how much has been lost of a Catholic culture that was at once aristocratic (in the sense of refined and excellent) and popular (in the sense that participation was open to all). My favorite of all of Balthasar's many great lines is that "in this autumnal moment in Western culture" we should not "huddle up under the blankets of an eschatological pathos." Penelope was not faithful, the leaders of the generation of 1968 traded in the family silver for modish, disposable plastic junk, and the younger generations struggle to "see the form." However, Balthasar left us a treasury of scholarship in his publications where the form is clearly visible. We can therefore console ourselves plundering the spoils of Einsiedeln.

Chapter Thirteen

Hope and the Freedom of Philosophy

David C. Schindler

The name "Hans Urs von Balthasar" is a name that one rarely, if ever, hears from the mouth of a philosopher. Although his doctoral work was in *Germanistik,* and he never accepted an academic post, Balthasar was a theologian as much as it is possible, I think, for a human being to be one: he allowed every thought to be held captive to Christ; in the staggering amount of writing that he did he never tired of relating each problem that he addressed to the mystery of Christ in its Catholic fullness. It would appear, then, that Balthasar's thought would leave little room for philosophy, at least insofar as philosophy distinguishes itself from theology by approaching its problems in relative abstraction from Christian revelation, and indeed Balthasar himself resisted the name of philosopher. But this impression has seemed to me to be misguided. If it is true that Christ's divinity does not compromise but rather purifies and elevates his humanity and therefore the *humanum* in general, and if it is also true that being is illuminated in a decisive way by human being, and moreover that the natural world itself was created in, through, and for Christ, then one would have to say, at least in principle, that the centering of one's thought on Christ does not necessarily threaten the free integrity of natural reason. Quite to the contrary, the more radically one is centered in Christ, the more universal and comprehensive one can be in relation to the matters that occupy the world. In my own experience, Balthasar's thought demonstrates that exclusivity in Christ sets reason free. There are, of course, difficult details to work out in the relationship of philosophy to theology, but we can reject at the outset any a priori objection that commitment to Christianity threatens the autonomy of philosophy in principle.

Balthasar in fact "changed my mind" precisely in relation to my work in philosophy. It is not simply that Balthasar offers new philosophical concepts that are particularly compelling—though he does that as well, even if much of his "novelty" specifically in the realm of philosophy is arguably not original to him but rather is inspired in large part by his friends Ferdinand Ulrich and Gustav Siewerth and one of his mentors, Erich Przywara—but I discovered in Balthasar a new *way* of doing philosophy that is both unique (as far as I can tell) and fruitful. It is known that Balthasar's theological aesthetics and dramatic theory represents more than just a new theology; it comprises new theological method. What was persuasive to me, as I will explain below, was the realization that this method can, and ought to, be "extended" into philosophy, and that doing so reveals a first-rate significance.

"Balthasar" was a name I had heard with some regularity as I grew up intellectually, since my father collaborated with him over the course of many years with the international journal *Communio,* and *Communio* was a general presence during my student years. But the first time the name stood out in a special way among the many others that I would often hear was the announcement of his death in June of 1988, which had an immediate and dramatic effect on the atmosphere in the *Communio* office, in which I was working as an assistant. To my surprise, the announcement resulted in my father's getting directly onto a plane for the funeral in Luzerne. Clearly, this was a person of some significance. Nevertheless, at that point and indeed even after I began to "dip into" some of his theology with a certain interest toward the end of my time as an undergraduate, there was nothing about him that changed my thinking in any basic sense.

The first book that made a difference to me was one that I read during my first year of graduate theology: *Dare We Hope That All Men Be Saved?* It is an unusual place to begin with Balthasar, I suspect, and I took up the book not because I had a special interest in this particular issue, which in fact I had not given much thought to by that point, but rather because of a professor of mine who denounced the position that he believed Balthasar to espouse therein. Passionate denunciations often provoke curiosity. What I found in the book was not what I counted on finding, namely, the straightforward elaboration and defense of a theological position on this controverted topic.

Instead, I found words that changed one's heart and mind at the same time. As I read the book, I grew in the certainty that there is indeed a foundation for the hope for universal salvation, and at the same time I grew less presumptuous, and therefore more anxious and vigilant, regarding the certainty of my own salvation. One would think that these two feelings would exclude one another in principle, and yet this was the undeniable effect that the book had on me. The experience demanded further reflection.

What further reflection yielded was the first opening of an insight that has continued to sustain, inform, and inspire my own thinking. Although I cannot enter into the details of the controversy here, one thing that became quickly clear at the time was that my professor was wrong to say that Balthasar simply taught universal salvation as a certain truth (though this is not infrequently how his position has been characterized). It is a *hope* for salvation, which, as hope, is never a truth that can simply be possessed as some definitively accomplished good. Rather, the truth about salvation is in the first place *God's* truth, in relation to which we remain the recipients who are both grateful and under judgment. It is true *as* a gift, which means that presumption regarding this truth in some basic way falsifies it. In other words, it was a truth that has the peculiar property of ceasing to be true in a sense if it is received improperly. There is a paradox here, but one that is both intelligible and inspiring (as well as humbling), insofar as it seems to accord with the truth about love, which is, after all, the truth of truth.

But the great significance of this point gets lost immediately if we see it simply as a clever way of approaching the particular question of the possibility of universal salvation. Genuinely to bring about a "change of mind" as the title of the present volume understands it requires more than introducing a new way of thinking about some issue or even a set of issues, however fundamental they may be; rather, it requires the introduction of a new way of thinking *tout court*. Certainly — and this principle strikes me, in fact, as one of the great contributions of Balthasar's thought — because form and content cannot ultimately be separated, the change in one's general way of thinking will always coincide with taking a particular position with respect to certain fundamental issues, and vice versa. In any event, with regard to the issue at hand, the point is that the theological virtue of hope is relevant not just for the question of salvation, even if it is most directly ordered to this question. Rather, hope is truly a *theological* virtue; that is, it is a virtue that ought to pervade theology as a whole, because theology is itself ordered to the knowledge of God as he reveals himself, and this is in fact hope's own *telos.* It is not just the outcome of the drama of salvation that is God's truth, which we can receive only in the respectful distance of gratitude: *all* theological truth is God's truth, is ultimately a manifestation of God himself, and so all theological knowing ought to take the form of hope.

What does it mean for theology to have the form of hope? There is both a subjective and an objective dimension to the response to this question. On the subjective side, we see the root of what Balthasar famously called *knieende Theologie,* theology on one's knees, referring to the theology done during the monastic age of the church, before the advent of the first universities. According to Balthasar's reading of intellectual history, the stark impoverishment of theology in the modern age is due in large part to the separation between theology and sanctity that occurred in late Scholasticism. As a result of this separation, we are left with fragments of the Christian response to the Word of God that become sharp and crude, or soft and formless, to the extent that they lose their intrinsic relationship to one another and to the life-giving whole of which they are meant to be a part. Thus, we have rationalism in theology, and moralism and sentimentalism in spirituality. To do theology in a respectable manner requires sitting at one's desk, or indeed in front of one's computer, but when one is on one's knees, theology ceases to be the crucial thing: it is now an affair of the heart. We thus have "experts" in these — now disconnected — fields, and the tendency toward specialization manifests itself culturally in the clericalization of the church, which is itself mirrored in the secularization of the world. It is not often enough recognized that the problem of the dichotomy between nature and grace, for example, a problem with which Balthasar and the *Ressourcement* movement are generally most associated, itself lies in a way of doing theology that develops from its severance from the more straightforwardly existential dimension of sanctity. The proper response to the nature/grace dichotomy, and the subsequent evacuation of theology from the public order, requires not just a better idea of this relationship, but rather a full "change of mind" — a transformation of one's thinking. It requires, that is, a recovery of the awe and wonder necessary to see and receive what God reveals in its wholeness, of the total availability implied in the vows of poverty, chastity, and obedience that result when one places one's being unreservedly at the service of the Lord's will. This is theologizing on one's knees.

This recovery cannot be simply a moral achievement, lest it undermine in its mode precisely what it seeks to accomplish. Instead, it must itself be received in a manner appropriate to the content of what is given: the truth that the truth is a gift must itself be received *as* a gift — that is, with gratitude. But this can occur only as a response to an objective reality, namely, the integration of truth and goodness in beauty, or, to put it another way, the full mystery of being, which includes the circumincessive interrelation of the transcendentals: beauty, goodness, truth, and unity. Thus, man can respond as a whole, because that to which he responds is itself a whole and lays claim to the whole in him. There is both a metaphysical and a more strictly theological aspect of this wholeness. On the one hand is the integration of the transcendentals that I just mentioned. As Balthasar put it at one point, revelation comes by way of being. In contrast to the critics of ontotheology who seem to set the terms for much of the contemporary discussion in theology and philosophy of religion, Balthasar does not seek to free God from being and thus from the finitude and rationalism that association with being apparently implies. Instead, he opens being up, and so opens up human reason, from the inside in a way that frees being itself, allowing it to recover what turns out to be a fairly traditional "porosity" (to use William Desmond's term) to the supernatural. The intelligibility of being *is* its being revelatory of God's glory.

On the other hand is a fully Trinitarian sense of God that seeks to do justice both to the dramatic richness of the processions of the Persons as well as to God's engagement in and with the world. It is here that there emerges what strikes me as one of the most defining insights of Balthasar's thought, the insight that crystalizes the whole and gives it its distinctive color: because the Son receives all that he has from the Father and returns it all in the Spirit of loving and grateful obedience, the awe, wonder, and availability that the creature is called to have with respect to God's truth are not *simply* a function of its imperfect creaturehood, and thus something that will fall away as obsolete in the eschaton, but are in fact themselves a mark of perfection, and indeed *eternal* perfection, because they are a reflection of the Son's own reverence for the Father. To put the point in stark terms: the virtue of hope is an analogous and, to be sure, always imperfectly lived image of Divine Hope;

God's truth, in other words, is not just the object of our hope, but is itself Hope. Balthasar praises Charles Péguy's "theology of hope" for effecting "a structural shift in the whole theological edifice" of modern thought, and he points out, significantly, that it arises from what he claims to be the first ever attempt to see theology "as Trinitarian conversation." What Péguy intuits in his beautifully simple poetic style, Balthasar works out in systematic fashion through dialogue with the whole Western tradition and thus brings directly to the attention of those who are theologians by vocation.

But I wish to suggest that it ought also to claim the attention in some respect of philosophers, for this vision became especially compelling to me in my work in that field. To do so, it is helpful to compare Balthasar to Heidegger on the point just made. Heidegger ushered in a new sensibility in philosophy by recalling that wonder is not only the beginning of philosophy, but, as arch, remains its abiding and governing form. Similar in this to Balthasar, he makes the open and receptive "letting be" (*Gelassenheit*) of gratitude the highest human act: *Denken als Danken*. But why should this be ultimate? For Heidegger, the "clearing" of being in its difference from beings, its eloquently silent open space in which beings articulate themselves, in which they are given to be, withdraws from human grasping. It can "event" only in the radical receptivity of the listening that is an obedient belonging. The rationalism and pragmatism that have grown to be nearly identical with the progress of Western thought, by adhering in an exclusive way to beings, have eclipsed being itself — *Seinsvergessenheit* — and made its withdrawal, as it were, perfect. Gratitude has therefore lost its roots in the essence of humankind and become something trivial. Interestingly, one of the most decisive moments in the modern period of this history concerns the question of salvation. According to Heidegger, the anxiety over salvation that overtakes the West at the end of the Middle Ages and the rise of modernity, with the nominalist theology of God's arbitrary power and the confusion of religious conflict, is the profound origin of Descartes' search for an unfailing method to achieve certainty. We notice that the kind of vulnerability that comes with gratitude and hope is eliminated in Descartes as an imperfection and a liability. Unsurprisingly, wonder, for Descartes, gets reduced to a sometimes useful but ultimately troublesome problem to be resolved.

It is here that Balthasar's difference from Heidegger emerges in clarity. Heidegger seeks to "destroy" the closedness of Cartesian certainty, which ultimately leads to Nietzsche's "will to power" as the culmination of Western metaphysics, and proposes instead the heroic *Angst* of a sort of uncertainty. To be sure, the rather "willful" resoluteness of *Dasein,* which intoxicated Sartre in Heidegger's earlier writings, tends to cede place to the serenity of *Gelassenheit* in the later work in which being is foregrounded. But in either case, we sense a peculiar contempt for ordinary human life. Regardless of what his intentions may have been or his own feelings in this regard, such a contempt, I suggest, follows necessarily from Heidegger's conception of being. Though of course not "the highest being," being, for Heidegger, is ultimate. And it is essentially "impersonal." But if this is so, then the personal dimension of human existence cannot be what is ultimate in humankind: one cannot relate in a fully personal manner to anything but a person. The ultimacy of the impersonal leads to a fascinating dialectical opposition in Heidegger between what we could call "openness" and "closure." As I will show in a moment, the overcoming of this dialectic requires a personal relation — that is, a relation of persons, which is at once open and closed.

As impersonal, being is no-thing; letting go of beings leaves precisely nothing to hold onto and therefore precipitates a kind of dread. Facing and embracing this dread, however, requires a grand daring, a steadfastness of spirit, and heroic renunciation. It is this note, I suspect, that makes Heidegger so compelling to so many people. What he presents is the exhilaration of a sublime risk, which makes the kinds of attachment to beings that we experience, and indeed typically pursue and foster, seem petty. Attachment is bourgeois. Again, Heidegger sets before us a basic alternative: either certainty and the inauthenticity of average everydayness or uncertainty and great-souled philosophical gravitas. We see the same dialectic in Heidegger's notorious scorn for the notion of Christian philosophy, which he called "wooden iron" — that is, essentially oxymoronic. If one assents in faith to the dogma proposed by the church, one can no longer *wonder* philosophically; to affirm the truth of creation is by that very act to close the ultimate question, which must be kept open: Why is there something rather than nothing?

For Balthasar, by contrast, the doctrine of creation, far from shutting wonder off, deepens wonder by leading it beyond the already astonishing gratuity of the fact of there being a world at all, a gratuity that will never be exhausted by reasons even while it shines with intelligibility, all the way into the love itself that lies at the source of that gratuity, a love that articulates itself into the total self-giving and self-receiving of the divine Persons in the absolute unity of God. The analogy of personal love, as usual, lies closest to hand to illuminate this reality: the great sacrifice a loved one makes, unbidden, on your behalf can leave you speechless with gratitude and full of admiring wonder. You "know" why the person did it, but that knowledge only serves to quicken the wonder. There would be far less wonder, or at least it would be of a far poorer sort, if something were given without any trace of its source at all. Even the delightful surprise of a gift that arrives totally unsuspected from a "secret admirer" provokes wonder almost entirely in reference to its giver — that is, because of the unknown identity of the person who gave it. As the example suggests, what is decisive in this experience of wonder is the personal element; it is this that allows one to have knowledge and wonder at the same time.

In what seems to me to be the richest source of philosophical wonder in Balthasar's oeuvre, the dozen or so pages at the end of volume 5 of *The Glory of the Lord*, entitled "The Miracle of Being and the Fourfold Distinction," Balthasar speaks of the difference that opens up to (and in) reflection between God and worldly being, the ultimate difference (or better, the ultimate *philosophical* difference, since even this turns out to be a reflection of that difference than-which-nothing-greater-can-be-thought, namely, the difference, bridged but not closed by the Spirit of love, between the Father and the Son in their mutual regard) that lies beyond even the twofold interplay between being and beings. This is the difference of God's personal freedom, which ensures that "the finite entity is genuinely sheltered in the infinite indifference of Being." This insight arguably valorizes, to a degree that cannot but be surprising to philosophical thinking, the initial difference of the personal encounter between the mother and the child in the dawning of consciousness. Significantly, this sort of difference in and of personal love carries no weight for Heidegger. As one Heideggerian once said to me, this encounter cannot have the significance that Balthasar gives it because it is "merely ontic"; another one confessed, revealingly, that he found Balthasar's focus on the mother-child relationship "icky."

This brings us back to the point from which we started, the point that I mentioned as the one that introduced me most decisively into Balthasar's general vision: the theme of hope as the general form of theology. I would like to suggest that something like hope ought to provide the form for philosophy as well; it provides a fruitful way beyond the sterile alternatives that have seemed to be the sole possibilities on offer in contemporary thought. Hope confounds the dichotomy between certainty and uncertainty. A great hope would entail a genuine assurance that at the same time has nothing in common with the presumption of Cartesian certainty. Its difference from Descartes does not lie in the fact that it is less certain. Far from it. The difference, rather, lies in the "ground" of the certainty. For Descartes, certainty lies in the "self," insofar as it lies in the method over which the self has total control and mastery. But in hope, by contrast, certainty lies in the fidelity of the other in whom one trusts. In his philosophical volume *The Truth of the World*, Balthasar goes beyond Heidegger by insisting that *emeth*, the Hebrew word for "fidelity," stands with the Greek word *aletheia*, "unhiddenness," in the fundamental shape of truth, thus uniting the Jewish and pagan traditions in a single (Catholic) vision. In this view of truth, one can be completely certain, but without any presumption, because one becomes in a sense wholly subject to the other in one's certainty. Certainty now follows from obedience rather than from mastery. This sort of certainty, because of its other-centeredness, brings about a sort of peace that is anything but bourgeois. It should be clear that the personal element is an essential part of hope, thus understood: the relation of trust that provides the closure of certainty coincides exactly with a radical openness to what is other than the self. And it should also be clear why Heidegger, rejecting a genuine personal Other who is Lord of being, and thus forfeiting hope in any truly ontological sense, can counter certainty of the problematic sort only through some other gesture of the self, whether it be the pure spontaneity of resoluteness or the pure passivity of *Gelassenheit*. Being, for Heidegger, does not and cannot have a personal face, and thus his philosophy ultimately lacks drama.

The dialectical opposition between openness and closure that we see in Heidegger characterizes a good deal of contemporary philosophy. On the one hand, we have the "postmodern" Continental philosophy that can be traced back in some sense to Heidegger (by way of Nietzsche, as it were). Here we find various forms of a critique of "presence" — a privileging of the absent, the deferred, the undecidable and the ambiguous, the flux of becoming, temporality, the übercontextualizing of history, the multiplicity of interpretations that endlessly supplant one another, the unmasking of hidden motivations (i.e., power), the celebration of the subversive, and the absolutizing of difference and the other. We find in all of these movements the rejection of anything that has a "center": anthropocentrism, logocentrism, ethnocentrism, androcentrism, Eurocentrism, and so on. Under all of this lies the assumption that certainty necessarily takes an egocentric form: as mastery, and therefore "power *over*." On the other hand, we have the rationalism that characterizes much of analytic philosophy, namely, the total intolerance of ambiguity, so that the sorts of paradoxes that are inextricable from the deepest questions of metaphysics have to be excluded as a matter of methodological principle. As J. N. Findlay is supposed to have responded when asked why he had "converted" from analytic philosophy, these philosophers are like skaters on a winter pond: they always remain around the edges in order to stay on the surface, afraid that if they get too close to the center, they might fall in.

Notice: it is the same thing that accounts for the rejection of certainty and the exclusive embrace of it: the lack of hope. Interestingly, what is common in these two forms of "despair" is a kind of avoidance of the center, so that one might postulate a connection between having hope and aiming at the heart of things. It is almost as if one could find the best philosophical approach by mapping out the conventional possibilities in three-dimensional intellectual space and locating the empty hole in the middle. For Balthasar, what lies in this space is the illuminated and inviting openness of positive difference — positive because it is bridged, without being closed, by personal love that affirms unity and otherness at the very same time. To say it again: hope is both open and closed because, in hope, one's center lies *in* the other. To remain oneself open in this space — that is, to respond to the positive appeal of this love — is to accept the welcoming invitation into the heart of the world, the neuralgic center of reality. From a philosophical perspective, such an approach would entail (as John Paul II's *Fides et Ratio* makes clear) a basic focus on being, and in this regard we can see how the critics of ontotheology tend to fall into the same dialectical opposition between openness and closure; it would entail a metaphysics that is both ordered to and supported by a meta-anthropology, whether that latter takes the form of personalism or a renewed and resituated phenomenology; and finally it would entail giving primacy to the transcendental properties of being (beauty, truth, goodness, unity), properties that represent, as it were, the ontological expression of the personal invitation into the heart of things. It is possible to move from this philosophical wonder to the more properly theological act of adoration and worship, though it is crucial to see that there is a radical and permanent discontinuity in the analogy that lifts the mind from one to the other. However that may be, if one were to move from philosophy to theology, the invitation would become more explicitly personal, and the object of one's gaze would become itself more explicitly personal and so would cease to be a mere object, becoming instead a free subject, or indeed a perfect intersubjectivity, that calls one into communion.

In short, Balthasar changed my mind by offering the most comprehensive vision of the Christian, and indeed of the human, reality that I have encountered, without being in any way oppressively "totalizing." Quite to the contrary, I have experienced this vision, from the beginning until now, as a *liberating* comprehensiveness, which frees up the constant novelty of further development, all of which turns out not to relativize, but rather to reinforce, the central insights. In the rest of this essay I will point out what I have seen to be the fruit of this vision in more concrete terms within philosophy. This requires an initial comment on the relation between philosophy and theology.

As I mentioned at the outset, Balthasar is well known for centering the whole of his thought on the Trinitarian God of Jesus Christ. In this, he has often been compared to his friend in Basel, Karl Barth. For the very same reason, he has often been criticized by neo-Scholastic Thomists who are — rightfully, I might add — jealous of the integrity and indeed relative autonomy of reason with respect to faith. It is difficult, to be sure, to see how Barth could respond to such a criticism, since he rejects what turns out to be the ground for the integrity not only of reason but also of nature in general: the analogy of being. Barth does so, of course, because it would seem to raise a neutral concept over God and subject him to being and its created rationality, thus compromising God's absolute sovereignty. There are, of course, many issues that would have to be addressed to deal adequately with this idea, but we can observe that this rejection implies that a competition of some sort exists between God and the world, or, to use the terms of this essay, that the "closedness" of reason's own integrity stands in some tension with its openness to God's personal revelation. Ironically, the neo-Scholastic Thomists turn out, in this regard, to have more in common with Barth than Balthasar does. Like Barth, this version of Thomism tends to assume a competition between faith and reason that requires them to govern separate spheres: any overlap would represent an artificial intrusion. In this case, the closedness of integrity is affirmed *against* its internal openness to faith.

For Balthasar, as we have seen, there is, at least in principle, no such opposition. Just as certainty occurs simultaneously with expectant openness, reason finds its own natural and rational closure most perfectly precisely *within* the openness to revelation. What this means is that philosophy receives a hitherto unimaginable freedom: it is no longer the impoverished negative freedom that arises from establishing its borders against intruders, but rather is the positive freedom of enjoying, exploring, and celebrating a new depth to reality that it had not suspected before. Indeed, it is a new depth that never threatens to come to an end, and thus it is capable of provoking and sustaining an endless wonder. And because of the paradoxical connection between openness and closure, philosophy does not have to justify itself constantly to faith by pointing to its weaknesses and limitations. Instead, it is transparent to faith from the beginning and all the way through, and it never more reveals its openness to faith than when it most joyfully — hopefully — delights in its autonomy. I have not encountered any healthier view of the relation between faith and reason, any view that does more justice to the concerns of all parties to the debate, without any unsatisfying compromise. Faith reaches much further into the heart of the world than the Barthians could have demanded, and reason stands more solidly on its own than the Thomists could have desired. Balthasar's vision has been so convincing to me because it has granted a freedom to philosophy that cannot but recall the freedom that it had in its beautiful and confident naïveté, its Greek beginnings with the Presocratics, with Socrates and Aristotle, and perhaps most of all with Plato.

Among the many new fundamental insights in philosophy that Balthasar's vision offers, there are two in particular that I would like to mention in closing. Insofar as these two insights have opened up a whole range of further possibilities for the future and new responses to ancient problems, both of these insights generate what I have often referred to as a "dramatic" approach to philosophy. The first is the notion of *Gestalt,* which, to be sure, is not original with Balthasar, though the use that he makes of it in theology certainly is unprecedented. This notion, which we tend to associate in its rich sense with Goethe, has been fruitful in science (Portmann) and scientific epistemology (Polanyi) and is perhaps best known in relation to the *Gestalt* school in psychology. But its philosophical significance has yet to be pursued and developed. Representing a whole greater than the sum of its parts and at the same time a convergent integration of transcendence and immanence, history and eternity, the notion of *Gestalt* would offer an alternative to structuralism and poststructuralism, as well as to the modern variants of atomism that these seek to overcome. For Balthasar, the *Gestalt* is not a static form, as some think Plato's *eidos* is; still less is it a more pragmatic, strictly immanent shape (Dewey). Rather, it is an intelligible whole that crystalizes in the convergence of its many parts, and, while it is therefore dependent on its parts, the whole that thereby comes to expression transcends those parts and transcends the moment of their convergence. Its intelligibility thus always occurs as a kind of surprise, but one that gathers up its elements into an enduring significance that lies above history. In this respect, the *Gestalt* is dramatic; it represents a nonstatic but supratemporal order. It should be clear that making *Gestalt* the fundamental mode of intelligibility would entail a significant shift in our usual concepts of truth and reason, and it would offer the possibility of going beyond both the tendency to reduce meaning to history and tradition (McIntyre) and to eliminate or otherwise overlook the significance of history for meaning (Strauss). *Gestalt* is a perfect example of the unity of openness and closure, for it presents an intelligible whole that is always open to further integration into higher and broader perspectives, and indeed it internally demands such integration.

The second insight, related to the first, is the inherent multiplicity of all unity — one might call this an essentially dialogical (dramatic), or an essentially fruitful, notion of unity. Thomas Aquinas affirms as axiomatic that there cannot be a true unity of *acts;* for there to be unity requires one element to be active and the other to be passive (act and potency). In affirming this, Aquinas represents the common opinion of the classical tradition. Postmodern philosophy responds to this traditional opinion simply by rejecting unity as a desideratum. But Balthasar's Trinitarian thought offers an alternative: the "dramatic" unity of a *Gestalt* that arises from the (asymmetrical) unity of acts. As abstract as this point may seem, its implications are immediately concrete. It allows, for instance, a whole new way of interpreting a long series of classical dualisms: male-female, soul-body, intellect-will, mind-passions, even nature-grace, and so forth. It is not, of course, possible in the present context to think through any of these dualisms in particular, which, it is important to see, would entail a different sort of unity in each case, only analogously related to the others; however, one can see immediately that thinking of each pair as cooperating in a greater whole, and thus as in some respect reciprocally dependent on one another, without forcing the pair into the binary opposition of perfect-imperfect that Jacques Derrida was right to question, would open a new way through the difficulties that philosophy (and theology) has grown accustomed to stumbling over. Moreover, the principle of the reciprocity of acts would incline us to a more communal sense of metaphysics in which being comes to be seen as love, and a more communal sense of anthropology in which even the most intimate realities of reason and freedom reveal themselves to be constituted in the event of encounter. Balthasar's vision is so powerful because it provides a way of affirming the genuine insights in a variety of philosophies — ancient, modern, postmodern — while at the same time judging them with respect to a more comprehensive whole. Nothing good need be lost.

These two insights, which cooperate to form a "dramatic" philosophy, clearly are favorable to theology: a theory of *Gestalt* naturally suggests the gift of intelligibility "from above," and the theory of unity constituted by reciprocal activity, so that one could say that what is ultimate is reciprocity, reveals a created order that reflects a Trinitarian Creator. These both also contribute to generating a philosophy that is both confident in the reliability of its evidences and the certainty of its insights while at the same time expectantly ready and open from the inside to the revelations of the more comprehensive order of faith. They return to philosophy its original aspiration to know the whole as comprehensively as possible while never allowing it to become "totalizing," in fact discouraging this precisely by virtue of the totality of its aspiration, not by the imposition of artificial limits. In other words, they contribute to giving philosophy a form analogous to hope. At the same time, this is a form that can *belong* to philosophy as philosophy, and not simply as an instrument for theology. The radically theological vision of Balthasar creates a free space for philosophy because it rests on and is ordered to the unimaginable love within God, which is directed, as it were, wholly gratuitously to a world that remains mysteriously *other* to a God who is all in all. There can be no more solid foundation for the philosophical love of the world than that world's being loved *eis telos,* "to the end," by God himself. God's love for the world led him to "go under," to disappear in some sense beneath the world's horizon and thus to fill it full to overflowing with his generous absence. Here is the great paradox: it is when theology reaches its highest moment that it opens up in the world the place for a "natural" philosophy; philosophy and theology do not meet (extrinsically) at their borders, but each emerges at the center of the other. The Trinitarian love that frees philosophy, moreover, is the same love that provides the foundation for hope of universal dimensions. This is the spirit in Balthasar's vision that has most "changed my mind."

Chapter Fourteen

Modernity and the Nature of a Distinction

Balthasar's Ontology of Generosity

David L. Schindler

A group of theologians — Hans Urs von Balthasar, Henri de Lubac, and Joseph Ratzinger, among others — had begun plans in the early 1970s to start the journal *Communio,* and the German and Italian editions first appeared in 1972. Fr. Joseph Fessio had been a student of de Lubac and was writing his doctoral dissertation under Ratzinger on Balthasar, and he had obtained permission from these men to explore the possibility of an American edition. He contacted me to help this edition get started — he and I had been classmates in the study of philosophy at Mount St. Michael's scholasticate in Spokane, Washington — and I eventually assumed the role of assistant (or "managing") editor when this edition began publishing in 1974.[1] I attended a meeting of the German and Italian editorial boards in Munich in 1972, and there I met Balthasar for the first time, in the former library of Romano Guardini, where the meeting was being held. However, regular personal contact with him really began in 1982, when I was appointed editor of the review; and a sustained engagement with his writings — other than mostly the articles that he was writing for the review — actually began only following his death in 1988. I had become accustomed to his presence at the yearly meetings of *Communio* and having the opportunity to speak with him and ask questions. His death came as a profound shock.

The assignment here is "how Balthasar changed my mind," and thus I will focus in what follows on the significance for me of his intellectual work. But perhaps I can begin with an anecdote that expresses well what I always experienced as the personality and spirit animating that work. The incident occurred in what turned out to be my last conversation with Balthasar, at a *Communio* meeting in Madrid a month before his death in June 1988. The American *Communio* had planned a conference on "Nature, Grace, and Culture" to be held at the University of Notre Dame in 1989,[2] and my task at the Madrid meeting was to invite Balthasar to be the keynote speaker for the conference. At a coffee break, I informed him of our plans for the conference and proposed the invitation. He replied by asking what the theme of his lecture would be. Realizing then that I had not thought this through with enough precision, I said, with some embarrassment, "Well, anything you want on the theme of nature, grace, and culture." That was fine with him, and he smiled and nodded. But then he shrugged his shoulders and gently objected, "Aber ich habe keine neue Ideen" ("But I have no new ideas").[3] The self-effacing humility and graciousness expressed on this occasion characterized Balthasar in all of the conversations that I had with him. He always listened attentively, entering fully and with genuine interest into whatever it was you wanted to speak with him about. Never was he interested in speaking about himself or his work. (When I once asked him — I believe it was the year before his death — what he was working on at the moment, his face lit up and he broke into a wide smile, responding, "My last book."[4]) What most impressed me about Balthasar in the years of our contact can be summarized, in a word, in terms of how his person embodied so profoundly the content of his theology: what was emphasized in his thought was transparent in his life.

The question to be treated here, however, bears on the nature of Balthasar's intellectual achievement and of my own indebtedness to that achievement. In order to be able to state this adequately, it seems best to describe something of the history and constellation of issues and concerns that were part of my life leading up to my encounter with him. The historical narrative to follow is, of course, highly selective and fragmentary. Certainly such a brief retrospective suggests a synthetic clarity about things that was not accessible at the beginning or even along the way and brings with it an inevitable reduction and oversimplification. I offer the narrative, then, only to help clarify why that encounter was so significant for me.

I

Such a retrospective can only begin with a reference to my father. It was he who provoked questions over and over again about the state of contemporary culture by the way he lived his life. He had grown up on a farm, and he ended his formal schooling at the age of sixteen to run the farm for his father, since his older brothers by then had all moved away.[5] He used to say that all people in their work have a responsibility to make a contribution to society, and he took it as given that one was to live in accord with the teaching of the Catholic Church. Whenever any of us children wanted to participate in some social-cultural activity, it was never a good idea to try to justify such participation by saying that "everyone else is doing it." He would always insist, gently but firmly, that that was not good enough; the fact that everyone was doing something did not suffice as a good reason for doing it. And he would then offer his own reasons — most of the time why he did not think it a good idea! In any case, the lesson impressed on all of us was that the way of the dominant culture is not synonymous with a way that is good and true. The integrity of my father's way of life, and his habit always of thinking through thoroughly the patterns of life that the broader culture took for granted, provoked in me over time questions regarding those patterns of life and thought: if my father was right — and, again, his way of living seemed to me obviously a way of integrity — then why did so many others seem to follow different ways?

The point, then, is that questions about American culture, and about how to live in response to American culture, due mostly to the influence of my father, were very much a part of my early family life, albeit first experientially and only gradually in a more conscious or reflective way. Nonetheless, the questions, in a confused state to be sure, had become a more or less constant preoccupation already toward the end of my high school years, and in hindsight I can say that these questions put me on a path that eventually landed in a decisive encounter with the work of Balthasar.

II

Immediately upon graduation from high school (in 1961), I entered the Jesuit seminary of the Oregon Province in Sheridan, Oregon. After two years of novitiate, my formation entered the phase of humanistic studies, consisting especially in the study of ancient Greek and Latin culture and literature. I began early in this juniorate phase of studies (as it was called then) to read Christopher Dawson and Cardinal Newman, occupying virtually every minute of extracurricular time over the next two years reading their works.[6] This exercise led to the theme that I chose for the "senior essay" that capped our juniorate studies: the educational theories of Dawson and Newman.

The burden of the essay was to show the unity of vision that inspired these two men despite obvious differences in the character of their work. Both struggled with the question of the truth of religion, coincident with how best to read religion and culture, especially in ancient and modern Western civilization. Both were led into the Catholic faith for reasons not unrelated to the integrity of human culture generated by this faith: to the capacity of the Catholic faith to take account of humanity in all its dimensions. Dawson, with his immense historical erudition, showed that the question of God and religion lay at the heart of every human culture, and that religion and culture were thus bound up with one another from their origin and in their deepest roots. Newman demonstrated in his life and thought that the "method" adequate for reaching truth in the matter of religion and with respect to the culture had to be catholic in every sense of the word: a passionate opening with the whole of one's being — mind and heart — to the whole of reality in light of the whole God and the whole of his church. Both men turned their attention in sustained fashion to the problem of education in the modern university, and both recognized the grave failure of the latter to educate in the Catholic and catholic manner necessary to sustain a truly human civilization — recognized the failure, that is, to form men and women in the integrated and indeed God-centered habits of mind that enable intelligent resistance to the fragmentation and secularization that both perceived as the looming problem in the West.

Following the juniorate, I entered the three-year phase of studies devoted to philosophy (1965–1968). My professors, Thomists all, had been trained for the most part at the Gregorian University, the Pontifical Institute for Medieval Studies in Toronto, or St. Louis University. Two things stand out during this period. First, there was my course in metaphysics, taught by Jesuit Fr. Gordon Moreland. This class, more than any other class in my life, transformed how I approached reality. Moreland conducted the class by way of weekly lectures that are perhaps most appropriately termed "metaphysical meditations." The lectures were centered on texts from Thomas Aquinas, often supplemented by long passages from Joseph de Finance's *Être et agir dans la philosophie de Saint Thomas*. Moreland had also been deeply influenced by Gabriel Marcel. At any rate, in the lectures he advanced fourteen Thomistic theses over the fourteen weeks of the course, beginning with the Thomistic distinction between act and potency, and focusing above all on the "real distinction" between *esse* and *essentia*. We were expected to write a two-page reflection on each thesis. From the first "lecture" of this great teacher, and the writing of my first short reflection, I began to sense a new and strangely profound way of thinking about things, about the meaning of culture and indeed everything else in relation to God. It was as though my entire life was changing: for the first time I felt that a truly "explanatory" account of what was missing from modernity's picture of life was beginning to settle in upon me.

At about the same time, I began to read several other philosophers, such as Aristotle, and contemporary thinkers Yves Simon and Jacques Maritain (on politics and metaphysics), Dietrich von Hildebrand (*Transformation in Christ*), and especially Étienne Gilson (above all, *The Unity of Philosophical Experience, The Spirit of Medieval Philosophy,* and *Being and Some Philosophers*). I have always been particularly conscious of having learned from Gilson three main principles that indeed guided me in basic ways through subsequent studies in philosophy and religion, or theology. First, ontological judgments — one's notion of being, of what fundamentally makes reality real, so to speak, and hence makes life meaningful and truly worth living — operate within and thus shape one's (penultimate) judgments about *this* or *that* thing or aspect of things and thus the method and content of one's thought. Gilson's point, of course, was not that everyone has deliberately appropriated or indeed is even conscious of such judgments, but that they remain operative, whether one is aware of them or not — indeed, in a sense all the more so when one is unaware of the implication of their presence in one's conscious acts. In a word, for Gilson, the human being "by his very nature . . . is a metaphysical animal," and it was only in retrieving being in its wholeness *qua* being[7] that one could take adequate account of the whole of reality. A proposition that has always stayed with me in this connection is a famous statement in Gilson's *Unity of Philosophical Experience:* "Philosophy [i.e., metaphysics] always buries its undertakers." That is, if one denies metaphysics or feels capable of making claims about this or that aspect of reality without somehow implying metaphysical claims (about the nature or logic of reality), the result will be not that one successfully avoids such claims, but rather only that one is now being controlled by presuppositions of which one remains unaware.

But, second, this teaching of Gilson was tied to another judgment, regarding the significance of the "real distinction" between *esse* and *essentia,* and indeed, in this connection, of the primacy of *esse.* Herein lay the heart of Gilson's sustained criticism of the "essentialism" that he took to be characteristic of the dominant tradition of modern (i.e., Cajetanian) Scholasticism. *Esse* was not merely the act that actualized essence, simply signifying the fact that essence existed; *esse,* on the contrary, was the act of acts, the perfection of act that, as such, had primacy in accounting first or absolutely for the richness and density of the thing in its "transcendental" truth, goodness, and beauty.[8]

Third, the question of the distinction between *esse* and *essentia* for Gilson at once presupposed and evoked the question of God and creation. Gilson resolutely insisted on the enduring distinction between faith and reason. At the same time, his historical studies revealed to him the ways in which, for example, the philosophy of the great thinkers of the Middle Ages differed from that of the Greeks, that is, by virtue of the intervening historical revelation of God in Jesus Christ, and of the articulation of that revelation in the Creed and its doctrines of creation and redemption. Gilson argued that Aquinas's sense of the distinction between *esse* and *essentia,* and his introducing thereby a significantly new meaning into Aristotle's duality of act and potency, could not be properly understood except in light of Aquinas's faith in the Christian God of creation. Gilson argued, in a word, for a distinctly Christian philosophy, a philosophy that remained essentially or formally philosophy even as it acknowledged the internal influence of faith on philosophy in the concrete order of existence or exercise.[9]

Here is not the place to enter into the controversy that arose around these distinctive claims of Gilson. It suffices only to emphasize how Gilson's Thomistic philosophy opened up being and the intelligibility of being — of being in its inner constitution and its inner rationality as such — to what may be called their historical and transformal dimensions. Mystery, for example, is not merely the unknown lying beyond or "underneath" what was known, but rather is the excess of intelligibility implicit in every act of knowing and in every cognitive content of being. Furthermore, Gilson showed how, through the "real distinction" of Aquinas, the question of God and creation was implicitly present at the heart of all other questions about the nature of things.

Among the many things I learned from Gilson, then, was that the questions of being and its intelligibility as such were deepened within the life of faith and thus within the call to holiness. The human being was at once, most basically, a metaphysical and a religious animal; and this teaching had common roots in Augustine and Bonaventure and Aquinas, despite significant differences in the philosophical articulations of each of these thinkers. In language I became more accustomed to using later, Gilson's position as expressed in the foregoing three points showed how and why being in its structural roots was a matter of gift and love in relation to God.

In 1970, and now having left the seminary, I began doctoral studies at Claremont Graduate School in southern California, enrolling in a program called Philosophy of Religion and Theology. I decided upon this program at Claremont because of, among other reasons, what appeared to me from the catalog the breadth of study that it afforded in theology, philosophy, and culture, and also because of the strong tradition of classical political philosophy that was available in Claremont's department of government.[10] My time at Claremont, however, was dominated by an encounter with the person and theological work of John Cobb, a Methodist theologian deeply influenced by Alfred North Whitehead and Charles Hartshorne. Cobb, a man of remarkable simplicity, humility, and generosity, took up theology with a deep and concrete passion for the truth and concern for the crisis that he saw developing in modern Western culture. My classes with him and our conversations together over four years constantly gravitated back toward discussion of what he was convinced was a modernity afflicted by dualisms (between God and the world, the soul/mind and the body, the mind and reality, etc.) and consequent reductionisms, as inspired by, for example, Descartes and seventeenth-century philosophy and science generally. Cobb's politics were radical — radically different from those of the Straussians, for example — and his politics were driven by what was palpably a gospel-centered, Beatitude-centered, concern for human beings. It was impossible not to be deeply drawn to this man with his great love and compassion for others.

Cobb insisted that what lay at the heart of the modern West's liberal culture was a lack of a truly relational understanding of reality, one that at its core implied a centeredness in God. In this insistence, of course, Cobb, as I said, had been influenced by Whitehead and Hartshorne, and so it was not surprising that he took the notion of substance as such, that is, already beginning with Aristotle and not only with the seventeenth century, to be a major source of the problem. This became a matter of friendly but vigorous discussion between us over four years, because it seemed to me then, as it still does today, that Whitehead and Hartshorne had conflated what were in fact fundamentally different ideas of substance: Aristotle's substance is simply not static in the way that, say, the Lockean substance is static. Then there was Aristotle's understanding of the human being as naturally social, and as naturally-dynamically inclined to seek the truth about being (metaphysics) and God (natural theology). I defended Aristotelian substance against Whitehead's criticisms, supported by Gilson and in light also of Thomist philosophers such as Fr. Norris Clarke and especially Frederick Wilhelmsen (e.g., *The Paradoxical Structure of Existence*); and I thus defended Aristotle in terms of the philosophical deepening provided by Aquinas. Above all, it was through Aquinas's metaphysical distinction between *esse* and *ens,* conceived in light of the Christian doctrine of creation, that I was able to see how every being could — must — be fundamentally related to God and to other beings in God, that is, in a way that did not attenuate, but on the contrary presupposed, the notion of substance.[11]

Through the sustained discussions with Cobb, it became ever more profoundly clear to me that Aquinas's "real distinction" was the key to coming to terms both reasonably and Christianly with the dualisms and reductionisms, and consequent fragmentation, that Cobb took to be the greatest threat to the future of Western — and global — civilization, and indeed to Christianity itself. This four-year period of study ended with my writing a dissertation, under Cobb, on the "methodological" aspects of the issues raised here, that is, on how Christian faith deepened the metaphysical understanding necessary to deal adequately with theological-cultural problems.[12]

Cobb's criticisms of modernity, with Whitehead in the background, were much involved with issues in modern science and technology. As a consequence, my conversations with Cobb prompted much reading in the philosophy of physics and biology and indeed psychology.[13] It was some years after leaving Claremont, when I began (in 1979) to teach in the University of Notre Dame's Program of Liberal Studies, and offered a course called "Concepts of Man," that I read an article by theoretical physicist David Bohm.[14] What immediately interested me was Bohm's concern to recover a "realistic," or ontological, sense of physical order in the universe, an order requiring some version of interior causes such as Aristotle's form and finality — or again some significant sense of the simultaneity of necessity and nonnecessity for any adequate understanding of causality — and some nonreductive version of the wholeness of things, and indeed of a relationality among cosmic entities that would permit us truly to affirm a universe (i.e., a *uni-verse:* a genuine turning of the many toward unity). The burden of Bohm's work, in a word, was to challenge the mechanistic patterns of thought that he took to characterize the basic science of modernity, physics, and thereby to play a fundamental role in modern culture generally. Bohm insisted that an adequate sense of physical order entailed recuperation of an adequate notion of eternity and infinity, of the indispensability of such notions for understanding time and the finite properly.

After reading this article, I wrote a review of Bohm's just-published book, *Wholeness and the Implicate Order.* I sent a copy of the review to him, while inviting him to a conference to be sponsored by *Communio* and held at Notre Dame.[15] Bohm sent a response to my review and accepted the invitation to the conference, and this began a conversation between us that continued with some regularity until the time of his death in 1992. At the heart of our discussions was the question, from his side, of how to develop an ontological interpretation of modern physics (e.g., quantum theory) — the problem of deterministic versus nondeterministic order in the physical universe — and, from my side, of how the Thomistic notion of being, rooted in the distinction between *esse* and *ens,* and opening dynamically into the Christian understanding of the God-world relation, could account for all that Bohm wanted to correct in the modern conception of order in the physical universe, that is, while enabling one to avoid what seemed to me the problems involved in Bohm's proposed idea of the "implicate order."[16] During this time and through the 1980s, I was assisted much by the writings of Kenneth Schmitz on the structure of being as gift, metaphysical interiority, and the philosophy of Hegel and Aquinas.

During a sabbatical from Notre Dame spent in France during the fall semester of 1983, and while beginning to write a book on modernity and the metaphysics of love,[17] I read Balthasar's book on de Lubac and books by de Lubac himself, though I had of course read articles by Balthasar written for *Communio,* the American edition of which, as mentioned above, I had been appointed editor of the year before.[18] At any rate, when I returned to Notre Dame, I set aside this manuscript, judging now, in light of the reading of Balthasar and de Lubac that I had begun, and indeed as the fruit of some days of retreat spent at the end of my sabbatical, that the argument on which I had embarked needed more explicit and comprehensive theological integration.

III

Although, as I said at the outset, my reading of Balthasar had thus begun in the early 1980s, it was only in the time immediately following his death in 1988 that I began to study his work in sustained fashion. My experience in reading him at this time was much like that undergone in my course in metaphysics, except that the reading continued steadily over several years.[19] I was being drawn into a "new" vision of reality, one that gathered up and restored in radically deepened and transformed ways all that I had learned — or struggled to learn — to that point, with respect to this basic and abiding question: What does it mean to live, simultaneously and with integrity, the truth of reality, of the church, and of God *at the heart of the world*?

But the problem, again, as it continued to seem to me, was that modernity in its pervasively liberal articulation rendered living the truth in this comprehensive way impossible. Reality and reason were one thing; the church and God, and indeed the love associated with both, were something else. Modernity had its way of distinguishing or, better, separating, and at the same time reducing these. Science as conceived in its dominant academic disciplinary modes gives us the meaning of reason, of reality as accessible to reason. Politics and economics in their dominant liberal democratic-capitalist mode circumscribe for us what counts as a legitimately *public* exercise of reason, and hence as public "realism." Fundamental to reason and reality as conceived in both science in its dominant modern disciplinary form, and politics and economics in their dominant Anglo-American liberal form, is abstraction from God, church, and love. Not that these latter might not be granted by scientists and persons in liberal institutions to have even decisive importance in life, but that this importance was granted only in terms of piety, moral intentionality, or faith, now conceived voluntaristically, and for life in "private" — that is, not in terms of what was judged reasonable or realistic in the proper sense, or meant for life in "public."

This abstraction of scientific-public reason and reality from God, church, and love, however, cannot be squared with the God of the Bible and Christian revelation — or so at least it had seemed to me through years of formative guidance by Christian thinkers such as Dawson and Newman and Gilson, as well as Augustine and Aquinas. If God is truly the Creator of all things, if all things were made through the Word (John 1:3); if all things were created in Christ, the image of the invisible God (Col. 1:15–16); if we know and love God implicitly (*implicite*) in all that we know or love (Thomas Aquinas, *De veritate*, 22, 2, 1); if it is in his very revelation of the Father's love that Christ reveals the meaning of humankind, and through humankind, of all flesh and hence of all the matter of the cosmos (Vatican II, *Gaudium et Spes*, no. 22; John Paul II, *Dominum et Vivificantem*, no. 50); if this Christian revelation of God's Fatherly-Trinitarian love abides sacramentally in the (Marian-Petrine) church, then God and the love of God revealed in Christ through the church must make a difference to everything — to every entity and every act, including every human cognitive and voluntary act, all the time. Nothing in the cosmos is or can be indifferent to God or indeed to love — finally, to the love of God as revealed in Jesus Christ through the church. The point, then, vis-à-vis modernity with its fragmented and reductionistic patterns of thought, is that God — Christ, church — love, carry *their own way of making distinctions among, and unifying or integrating, all creaturely entities.*

Here, then, is the heart of what Balthasar communicated to me with an unequaled comprehensiveness and depth: *God in his creative and redemptive love — in his love as imaged in creation, as embodied hypostatically in the person of Jesus Christ, and as present sacramentally in the (Marian-Petrine) church — reveals the proper and most basic terms of all distinctions and all unities in the cosmos.* In a word, God and love penetrate to the innermost meaning and form of all "worldly" being and cognition.

To be sure, "worldly" being and knowing and acting and making have their own autonomy; they have a lawful "logic" of being proper to themselves as distinct natural entities. Indeed, that is just the crucial point to be made relative to modern patterns of thought: not that this autonomy is to be denied or short-circuited — after all, human nature was not absorbed (*non perempta*) but rather was assumed (*assumpta*) by the Son of God (Vatican II, *Gaudium et Spes,* no. 22), and thus the incarnation presupposes the integrity of nature as created — but that creaturely autonomy is on the contrary preserved and deepened, albeit now precisely *from within* and *by virtue* of the relation of generous love by which God gives the creature being and sustains the creature in being in the first place. Creaturely being and knowing and acting, to realize their rightful autonomy or distinctness or difference, need not, and indeed finally cannot, remain, even for a moment, indifferent toward God or the love that images God.

This, it seems to me, is the burden of Balthasar's lifelong emphasis on the relation between theology — or, more comprehensively stated, the order of reason and reality — and sanctity, expressed emblematically in his 1948 article of that title.[20] It also lies at the core of his lifelong work regarding the lay state of consecrated life — the consecrated life that remains at the heart of the world — and at the core of his decision, with Adrienne von Speyr, to begin the Community of St. John: to go to the heart of the world in order to take every thought and action, every aspect of every reality, captive to Jesus Christ (2 Cor. 10:5), so that God might be "all in all" (1 Cor. 15:28), beginning here and now and on earth, and hence including "worldly" public order.[21]

It is this catholicity coincident with the Catholicity of Balthasar's life and theological work that led to reconfiguring in new and more profound and comprehensive ways all that I had learned from the authors and teachers mentioned earlier. For present purposes, I will limit myself to sketching only the basic contours of how Balthasar reconceives the nature of distinction and unity within and among all cosmic entities, in the orders both of being and of cognition — how he does so, that is, vis-à-vis modern culture's fragmented-reductionistic way of distinguishing and uniting, and in terms of the call to sanctity that is formed in the love that says "forever" in response to God.

IV

From within the dominant liberal-modern patterns of thought, which are operative both outside of Catholic institutions and often within them, this formulation of the problem of modernity, and of how I understand the center of Balthasar's thought in relation to modernity, may seem too general or simplistic, academically unserious, or even politically dangerous, and in any case an invitation to confusion. The characteristic achievements of modernity, with the latter's affirmation of the autonomy of the creature that is itself taken to be the fruit of the Christian idea of creation, seem to presuppose and demand just the proliferation of distinctions within and among things, as well as of specialized forms of study and methodological abstraction, that Balthasar at once objects to and reconfigures. But what Balthasar proposes, in my judgment, is not fewer or less precise distinctions, but rather distinctions made differently: that is, made in the manner of one who loves and in terms of the thing itself understood as a matter innermostly of love. In other words, Balthasar accepts the real contributions of modernity while transforming them in terms of God-centered love.

This objection, then, goes to the heart of concerns that need to be faced, precisely to avoid the kind of reductionism ruled out by the catholicity of Catholicism. Initially, let me say only that the God-centered, and love-centered, understanding of reality developed by Balthasar does not collapse distinctions into premature unities. On the contrary, he conceives cosmic-creaturely distinctions and unities in terms of a God/Christ/church-centered and, so to speak, being-centered *analogy of love.* In contrast, modernity conceives cosmic-creaturely distinctions and unities in an equivocal way that in fact expresses a kind of inverted univocity (in a sense to be shown below) — a paradoxical equivocity-*cum*-univocity that is informed by a forgetfulness of God and being and that consequently drains the reasonable-real universe of love. To put it another way, Balthasar conceives cosmic-creaturely distinctions and unities in terms of a universal-catholic *community* of being and of meaning or reason, while modernity conceives these distinctions and unities in a way that leads at every turn to a reduction of community to an aggregate of individual entities — that is, logically, even if typically unintentionally. Let me now attempt a brief sketch of what is meant by modernity's fracturing of authentic community, first in terms of modernity and then in terms of Balthasar's thought.

Consider the various dualities that are commonly invoked in one way or another in accounting for our experience of things: God and the world; the order of reality and the order of knowing; the soul/mind and the body; the self as individual and the self as social; rights and duties; the private and the public; state and society; the human and the subhuman; object (or objective) and subject (or subjective); freedom and necessity; love, or freedom, and intelligence; faith and reason; obedience and creativity; the holy and the secular; the inner-ecclesial (e.g., liturgy and sacrament) and the inner-worldly; experience and idea; the living and the nonliving; analysis and integration or synthesis; part and whole; singular and universal; the theoretical/contemplative and the practical; fact and value — the list goes on and on. Needless to say, each of these dualities raises issues specific to itself. Nevertheless, each of the dualities at the same time invokes the problem of relation in some way — invokes, that is, the problem of a distinction between a one and an other, between x and non-x.

Modern culture's approach to this problem of relation and distinction is exposed paradigmatically in the work of Descartes. The clarity and distinctness sought by Descartes as the condition for an idea's reasonability, and hence for something's being affirmed as certainly present in reality or in the objective world, require that there be no trace of an implication of non-x in x. The straight lines of (abstract) geometry serve the important function for Descartes of indicating the way in which x and non-x, lying on opposite sides of the line from each other, are thus cleanly outside of one another, and hence indicating that there is nothing — no implication — of non-x in x, and vice versa. The clarity and distinctness required for the intelligibility and reality of x demand the closure of the identity of x to the identity of non-x, and vice versa. Again, clarity and distinctness demand conceiving x and non-x first in terms of each one's externality relative to the other. And, lacking any order *from within itself toward* non-x, the identity of x cannot but be logically self-centered, even as non-x then appears to x first as available for use in the self-centered interests of x.

All of this bears profound consequences for how one can then reasonably conceive any subsequent relation between x and non-x. The key is the original mutual indifference between x and non-x. Given this indifference, the relation between x and non-x can remain external in nature and hence a matter merely of *addition* — and just so far what is properly termed a dualistic relation. On the other hand, insofar as the relation becomes "real" — that is, insofar as x truly reaches inside non-x — that relation cannot but be forceful and intrusive, because any relation between x and non-x, given the original indifference just indicated, is *eo ipso* adventitious: the relation is one for which there is no already given interior order *in* x or non-x. The significance of this can be stated in various terms: any "real" relation of x to non-x entails an *external* movement that can only be *outward* and *without a center* — *without an anterior-interior centering in either x or non-x*— a movement, therefore, that is simply *dispersive* in nature (from *dispergere*, "to scatter"). Again, the adventitious and thus forceful character of any "real" relation of x to non-x entails that that relation, always and everywhere, be a matter most basically of coercive power and thus of violence (from *violo*, "to violate, injure").

This understanding of reason and reality, mediated as it is by the presupposition of an originally indifferent relation of x to non-x, and vice versa, lies at the root of modernity's characteristic ways of conceiving the various dualities mentioned above. Thus we have modernity's dominant religious positivism, whereby relation to God is not so much constitutive of humankind's being as initially posited by humankind. We have social contractualism, whereby the relation between the self and the other is first contracted. We have a human dignity founded on what one achieves, or self-determination, and not (also) on one's being as constitutively *given / received*. We have constitutively self-centered or self-interested rights, whereby responsibilities of the self toward the other, and vice versa, tend at best toward a mutual instrumentalism or self-interest. We have the tendency toward nominalism, according to which the many bear no inner unity in terms of a one, or again the one bears no inner-inclusive openness toward the many in their manyness. We have the tendency toward Pelagianism, according to which x's relation to non-x is conceived first in terms of the power construed as somehow native to x alone — that is, not of a power that is anteriorly *given* to x and thus of a power that is *originally participated in* by x. We have a body that lacks any immaterial or interior center within itself, and hence matter as inert stuff. We have a causality consisting primarily in external "efficient" relations of force rather than in the communication of meaning via the interiority of form and finality or purpose.[22] We have the separation of the true from the good, or again, of fact from value. We have the technological approach to cosmology and the scientific knowledge of nature that views the world exhaustively as an *instrument:* nature is no longer a matter of "being born" (*nascor*) but rather of an object ready to hand for making; nature is no longer good *qua ens* but only *quia factum.* We have extroverted patterns of life consisting in endless outwardly directed movement and activity. We have voluntarism — and moralism — according to which freedom, or the will, operates without anterior mediation by intelligence.[23] We have rationalism — and mechanism — whereby intelligibility is coerced out of an x whose identity has in principle been analytically closed.[24]

In the academy, we have the abstractions (from *abstrahere,* "to pull out, drag away") characteristic of the modern disciplines, according to which what is abstracted is treated *methodologically* as though it were, or could be, *indifferent* toward what is left aside in the act of abstraction; or again, as though the *limited aspect* of an entity "pulled out" in an abstraction were, or could be, indifferent to what lies "outside" or beyond what is pulled out, in the concrete world of "real" being.[25]

Recalling the language of equivocity and univocity used above, then, we see that, in accord with the modern Cartesian ontology of identity and distinction/relation, every x is logically simply different from non-x, resulting in what appears to be, and in a significant sense is, a radical pluralism. And yet every x is different from non-x by virtue of a *single idea* of identity and distinction/relation, and hence modernity's radical pluralism takes the form at once of a radical monism. There is a radical fragmentation that presupposes a nominalist equivocity of being and meaning, even as, at the same time, this fragmentation is mediated by a univocal conception of being and meaning — of x alone and of x in its distinction from/relation to non-x.

It thus does not seem improper, echoing Nietzsche, to characterize modern patterns of thought in terms of a kind of nihilism — a nihilism of the surfaces (from *superfacies,* "staying on or along the surface") — or indeed, as Nietzsche also says, in terms of "homelessness." We conceive both x and non-x in terms of an identity lacking the depth and interiority that alone can establish each as an order of inherent meaning and worth; and we consequently conceive any relation between x and non-x in terms of a movement that can now only be dispersive, without end. It is just this end-lessness — this identity and this movement that are without an interior *center* and thus without ordered relation to, and hence ability to rest in, any end — that promotes the *distraction from the depths* of things (from *distrahere*, "to draw away or divert") characteristic of modernity's peculiar nihilism. It is also what constitutes the peculiarly modern form of homelessness: the lack of a capacity really to indwell the familiar and the here and the now, investing it with life-giving passion.

What is crucial to notice here, in sum, is the way in which modernity's dominant Cartesian ontology of distinction affirms a mechanical identity of x and of non-x, and consequently an original "negative" relation of mutual indifference between x and non-x that can then unfold into "positive" relations only of arbitrariness and force. Modernity's characteristic pluralism thus of its inner nature hides, and just so far imposes or "dictates," a monism, resulting in the double nihilism whereby the identity of x lacks the interior depth and order that give meaning, even as x, when it relates or moves, can then only simply disperse. The modern nihilism of mechanical identity, in other words, opens of its inner dynamic into the postmodern nihilism of dispersal, though, as we can now see, the "post" in postmodernity signals what is in fact only the later arrival of what is structurally implied already in modernity's characteristic Cartesianism.

V

The patterns of modern thought as sketched here are, from the point of view of Balthasar, best understood in terms of an absence of an ontology of generosity, and indeed my reading of those patterns is reasonable only on the presupposition of such an ontology. By "ontology of generosity" I mean an ontology according to which what is naturally given (x) bears within it, precisely coincident with its own identity as such, an order of relation, or an ordered relation, toward and indeed from others. This relation is a matter first not of forceful power but rather of the power proper to love, or, in the case of nonspiritual beings, of a power that participates in an analogical way in love.[26] The key to understanding the relation of x to non-x first in terms of love and not forceful power lies above all in the recognition that the relation is *given in and with the constitution* of x's identity as such and hence as a matter of the original-natural order of x — and non-x.[27]

The point, then, is that the Christian understanding of creation entails this constitutive relationality of each entity — to the Creator God, who is a God of love, and indeed to all other creatures in and through their common relation to God. The being of everything that is, is a *being-given* in and by love, above all by God's love, but also by the love of all creatures structured naturally into the universe itself by virtue of their creation in the image of, or as analogically conceived signs or symbols of, God's love.[28]

The ontology of generosity indicated here, once again, does not simply reject *any* of the distinctions that modernity has deemed necessary and indeed that undergird and render possible its characteristic — and genuine — achievements. On the contrary, such an ontology recuperates all of these distinctions, precisely in *the relational-analogical way demanded by a universal community of being and meaning under God.*

Although, as I said earlier, thinkers such as Dawson and Newman and Gilson, and professors such as Moreland and Cobb, and behind them, Aquinas and "neo-Thomism" and indeed Greek thought generally, had led me toward the reading of modernity sketched above, it was Balthasar who reconfigured from the inside out, and immeasurably deepened, what is referred to here as an ontology of generosity. The terms of this ontology were, of course, reached only gradually and after many years of reading and reflecting upon his work. What Balthasar showed me, in his life and his work, was the indissoluble unity — or convertibility — of being and love in relation to God, and thereby what is meant by living the catholicity entailed in Catholicism down into the heart of every being, thus in a way that spans the cosmos in its entirety. This formulation, however, still expresses things in a short-handed way, hence still too abstractly. How, exactly, does Balthasar distinguish between and relate God and the world, such that being and love are convertible inside this relation between God and the world? As noted earlier, fundamental for Balthasar is the idea that God and love indicate their own manner of making distinctions, in a way that affects the original and most basic logic of all distinctions and relations of whatever sort anywhere in the cosmos. How are we to understand this?

As mentioned above, Balthasar emphasized throughout his life the inner link between theology — the order of reason and reality — and sanctity, a link that lies at the heart of his lifelong engagement with the form of consecrated life that remains in the world. The depths of this link between theology and holiness can be seen by pointing out now how it is holiness itself that brings to completion the claim that being and love are convertible, in relation to God. The meaning of being as love, in other words, can be realized fully and properly only in persons: substances possessing the capacities of intelligence and freedom. Sanctity, if you will, is but the personal-subjective realization — the realization in and by a human subject — of the objective convertibility of being and love in relation to God. To be sure, and once again, Balthasar's argument is that this convertibility obtains analogically all the way down through the entire order of created being. It is important, then, to see how the very content of this claim of convertibility — namely, that all of being participates in a genuinely analogical way in love — presupposes that every being is a *subject,* in the sense that every being bears some metaphysical immateriality or interiority, again, analogically conceived.[29] It is, however, only in beings possessing spirituality, and thus in human beings, that there exists a subject, or subjectivity, in the full and proper sense. What we are terming a saint, then, is the human being who realizes in a profound and proper way the objective meaning of being as a subject ordered toward and called to participate in God-centered love: ordered toward and called to participate in the grateful love or worship of God and the love of all other creatures in relation to God.

Here, then, we see in all its radicality Balthasar's C(c)atholicity: all of created being and meaning is ordered in its depths toward participation in sanctity, in and through the human persons, who alone among the beings of the cosmos realize sanctity in the proper sense.

But we must take this further. Sanctity realizes the proper creaturely response both to God's gift of the creature to itself that constitutes the act of creation and to God's gift of himself to the creature in Jesus Christ that constitutes the creature's re-creation (justification). This double gift of God to the creature takes the form of a covenant, or promise of unfailing fidelity to the creature. This covenant of God with the creature — with humankind and with all other creatures in relation to humankind[30] — comes to fulfill-ment in Jesus Christ and thus in the church, where Christ continues to abide sacramentally. What is crucial for Balthasar is to see that the incarnation of the Son of God in Jesus Christ, and thereby the beginning of what becomes a sacramental-ecclesial community in Christ, elicits and presupposes a re-sponse on the part of a creature, a response given its primordial form in the *fiat* of the virgin-mother Mary; and indeed to see further that Christ's founding of his sacramental-ecclesial community is completed when Christ, from the cross, unites Mary's love with that of Peter, that is, in and through the love of John that has always abided.

The point here, then, is twofold. First, God's covenant indicates God's total gift of himself to creatures, a gift that affirms the inherent dignity and worth of the creature in his integrity as such, that is, by virtue at once of God's act of creation and of God's willingness himself to suffer death and abandonment in his incarnate Son on behalf of the creature. Thus we might say, in light of the covenant, that God desires to appear to the world as the whole God, and he desires at the same time that the world appear as the whole world within the appearance of the whole God. God in Jesus Christ desires to be all in all, such that each being can simultaneously be all *it* is, at once in itself and in God. In Jesus Christ and his covenant, the center of God is revealed to be open to the heart of the world, even as the heart of the world is now seen to be opened to the center of God.[31]

Second, this total gift of God expressed in the covenant — in Jesus Christ and his sacramental church — elicits and presupposes a total gift of self on the part of creation, in and as grateful response to God's total gift. This grateful response, which is first and above all that of Christ as the Son (Col. 1:15–18), as the firstborn among creatures, is, from the side of the creature, embodied in Mary (the virgin-mother) and sacramentalized in the church upon Christ's death in and through the mediation of John (the first son in the Son, so to speak). The point, then, is that God's love makes its entry into the cosmos in and through his Son, Jesus Christ, and, from the side of the creature, in and through Mary as his mother and John as the first son in the Son. But what is crucial for present purposes to see is that, though the feminine-motherly love of Mary and the masculine-filial love of John both give primordial form in Jesus Christ to the Petrine sacramental church, they do so *while remaining in the world,* and thus *while giving form to the meaning of creatureliness as such.* Mary and John give primordial form to the *church* not as (objective) office but rather as (subjective) state — as the lay state.[32] And, retaining their lay character, Mary and John simultaneously also give the *world* its most basic form in Jesus Christ.

The point, then, in a word, is that Mary and John, for Balthasar, provide the privileged, or archetypal, form of the sanctity to which the world *as world,* in and through human persons in Jesus Christ, is called from its original creation. And what is that form? A gift of self that is total — *of the whole self* and *forever — in and as obedient, grateful response* to God's total gift of self expressed in his covenant that is sacramentalized in Christ's church. As Balthasar says, total love can only be given once, and thus it is ordered toward taking a vow,[33] and thus toward a state of life. It is this total love as state, as embodied in the form of a vow, that defines the most proper meaning of the sanctity to which the whole of creation, in and through human persons in Jesus Christ, is called. It is from inside this sanctity, in other words, that the whole God in Jesus Christ becomes present in the world, coincident with the world's appearance in its own wholeness *as world,* such that God can now, in Jesus Christ, be all in the allness of all. It is essential, for Balthasar, to see that Mary, precisely as mother, and John, precisely as son — and thus the reality of both in their virginal-familial-spousal relations — are the creaturely point of intersection between this mutual, albeit radically asymmetrically actualized, appearance in Jesus Christ of God's love in the world and the world's love in grateful response to God's love.

In sum, the whole world is ordered from and toward the sanctity of God himself in Jesus Christ that abides sacramentally in Peter (church as office), in and through the form of that sanctity as personalized above all in Mary and John (church as state).

Needless to say, this brief discussion of the sanctity — the realization of the unity of being and love in relation to God — to which the world as world is ordered from its creation carries an abundance of further presuppositions that bring into play all the major themes of Balthasar's theology. It will nevertheless suffice for our purposes now to provide a sketch of the ontology implied in the foregoing account: to indicate how the world in its given creaturely being as such is ordered from and toward a God-centered love that takes its proper "worldly" form in human persons, a form whose perfection is realized in sanctity.

VI

First, since our question concerns the heart of the world, we must go to the world's first and last word about itself, so to speak: that it *is*. We must go to the world in its primitive revelation as *being*. Here Balthasar follows Aquinas, and his different contemporary interpreters such as Étienne Gilson and Ferdinand Ulrich, in affirming that being (*ens*), which takes its name from the existential act of being (*esse*), is the word that articulates first and most basically the meaning of the world. *Esse,* as Aquinas says, is the act of acts and thus perfection of all acts. It is *esse* that makes be the whole of the what that is. *Esse* makes things be from the inside out, makes being be from its depths to its surfaces. Nothing falls outside of *esse; esse* is what is innermost in a thing.

Second, in this context, however, Balthasar follows Ulrich in making central Aquinas's dictum that *esse* is *completum et simplex sed non subsistens:* that is, *esse* is complete and simple, hence "perfect" in the sense just indicated, but nevertheless is so, paradoxically, only as *esse* itself is nonsubsistent, not itself existent in the proper sense. On the contrary, *esse,* in the very act by which it makes things be, depends for its proper existence on the very things that it makes be. *Esse,* so to speak, gives itself away, lends its wealth or perfection as act of being to the things that it makes be only by way of emptying itself into those things and thus becoming poor. At the same time, the things that *esse* makes be, originally poor in their utter need for the act of being, themselves contribute a wealth of content to that act of being coincident with their enactment by the latter.

In short, *esse* and *essentia* (the what that being is) each give themselves to the other, such that it is in and as, and only in and as, the composition of the two — of what is and the act by which it is — that either *esse* or *essentia* subsists. One might say that the concrete being that subsists is the fruit of the mutual gift of these two principles — the act of existence and what is. The problem, however, is that *esse* and *essentia* subsist only in and through and hence in exhaustive dependence upon the other, and consequently neither *esse* nor *essentia,* nor the composition of the two, can finally be said to exist in the proper sense.

The language of mutual gift used here with respect to the structure of being, of course, appears unacceptably anthropomorphic, since principles of being do not exercise agency. Only actual beings — beings already composed of *esse* and essence, and indeed composed of these in a personal-spiritual way — exercise agency properly in the sense of gift-giving and receiving. Use of such language, however, is not anthropomorphic; on the contrary, it is an analogical use of language serving simply to indicate that the structure of being itself anticipates what is finally fulfilled only in persons.

Third, Balthasar thus undertakes his own discussion of what is termed the "real distinction" between *esse* and *essentia* — or again the ontological difference between Being and beings — in terms of a personal relationship, indeed in the form of the mother-child relation, and thus we come to the third point. For Balthasar, the "real distinction" between *esse* and *essentia* can be sustained in its full and proper meaning only, as it were, by being rendered personal, indeed in the form of parental love.

Thus, for Balthasar, the mother's smile at her newborn child reveals being as gift, and the smile thereby sets in motion what will gradually become a conscious wonder in the child, a grateful response confirming being as gift. The child grasps itself as recipient of the gift of being permitted to be. And yet in time the child comes to see that the mother, like itself, is also the recipient of the gift of being permitted to be, indeed that all beings are in this same condition. The Being that shares itself with all beings, that gives its act of being to all beings, and that is thus transcendent of beings, itself exists only in and as those beings: that is, such that Being appears to reduce to beings, even as beings threaten to absorb Being into themselves. Either beings are some form of explication of Being, or Being is some form of projection by beings, or both. In either case, there is an oscillation within the structure of Being/beings in their mutual relation that threatens to drain the world as a whole of the giftedness that called forth gratitude and that seemed, originally and most deeply, in the mother-child relation, to constitute the reality of the world as such — that is, the reality of its giftedness coincident with the giftedness of its reality.

Fourth, insofar as we would sustain all the way through and with consistency the originary experience of the child in relation to its mother, then, we are led reasonably, in and through the distinction between Being and beings in light of this originary experience, to affirm that Being itself subsists (*Esse* as such subsists) and indeed at the same time that this Subsistent Being somehow must be generous, in the sense that it can (in its transcendence) give beings their being while (in its simultaneous immanence) staying with that being and caring for it — that is, somehow in the manner that a mother or father does in her or his parental love for the child. We are led reasonably to the conclusion that Subsistent Being must somehow be personal in the way expressed in such love.

And yet it is just here that we have already begun to cross a threshold. We are led necessarily — that is, reasonably — to conclude that Subsistent Being must exist and must somehow be a personal, or parental, lover, but we cannot conceive properly or fully how this is so. In other words, we reach the point where the ontological difference must become in turn, albeit *at the same time,* the difference between God and the world, and thus the metaphysical act must become at once a theological act. But it is important to be clear here: reason, reflecting on the implications of what it finds in being itself as it appears in the world, is led in an intrinsic way to God — that is to say, the metaphysical act is led into what may be termed a natural theological act. It is important to stress this; otherwise we slip into a fideism rejected by Balthasar. At the same time, however, precisely from inside its logical movement that has "naturally" reached to the reality of God, reason must await God's own self-revelation as (tri-Personal) love. This is to say, reason must remain open — in Marian fashion — to the theological-Christian act properly speaking.[34]

In sum, being is created for love, even as the fullness of this love for which being is created cannot finally be conceived or sustained on its own. On the contrary, the very structure of being entails a "waiting" for the Being (Subsistent *Esse*) that makes it be to reveal itself as a lover, one who can be provident for it and look after it and share life with it in the intimate fashion of a parent. The revelation of being as a gift calling forth wonder and gratitude, which takes place above all in the relation between mother and child, awaits the revelation of divine Being itself — Subsistent *Esse* — as creator-giver of the gift of being in his Son, Jesus Christ.

This, then, is what it means for the metaphysical (or natural theological) act to break open to the theological (or Christian) act, which goes beyond even as it contains and presupposes the metaphysical (or natural theological) act. Thus, as Balthasar sums up:

> The fundamental metaphysical act is love within the Ontological Dif-ference...; the fundamental Christian act is love within the God-world

distinction...: in each case love means here the total human act which comprehends the totality of mind and body and, in particular, percipient intelligence. As metaphysical intelligence, it perceives the relation of the existent and Being which defies formulation and, as Christian intelligence, it perceives God's free word of absolute love which utters itself as a medium within this relation. But we must guard here against both false distinctions and false equations. We are following the right path when we genuinely locate the metaphysical act within the Ontological Difference—even if it naturally points to God as its depths—and understand the Christian act as a new response to the new word of God which, of course, contains the metaphysical act within itself and, beyond that, contributes also to its fulfilment.[35]

And again:

Only this much can be said: in the love between human beings a mystery already operative at the origin is foreshadowed, because the loving persons (in whom the all-encompassing Being of reality prevails) never close themselves off from one another. On the contrary, they are open to the original mystery of Being in their (always conditioned) fruitfulness. The fruitfulness they share, rooted in nature, (as when a child is conceived) indeed remains an important but still limited parable of this fruitfulness of love, which at the most archetypal level must have some inexpressible analogue within the divine identity.[36]

The radical comprehensiveness finally intended by Balthasar here is captured in the following summary formulations:

The non-subsistence of the *actus essendi* is the creative medium which suffices for God to utter His kenotic word of the Cross and of glory and to send it as His Son into the world to experience death and resurrection.[37]

The incarnation and the cross have their "place" where the *actus completus non subsistens* is at work in created reality, which is realized only in individual beings. The Son of God in no way replaces this act. But if "everything in heaven and on earth has its being in him," then he is the head of everything that has been created from that identity. And the free assumption not only of human nature but also of its alienation can ensue only "above" or "beneath" the situatedness of all natural beings.[38]

Thus from the very core of being as such there is an opening to love. Everything that is, and insofar as it is, participates in this logic of love, even as this logic is adequately and properly expressed only in and through personal-spiritual beings. Being as gift, to have its full meaning as such realized, must pass through — must be brought home to itself, as it were — through the interior acts of giving and receiving, the wonder- and gratitude-filled fruitfulness, proper to human lovers who have become saints.

In short, the point for Balthasar is that all human beings are meant to recapitulate personally the meaning of being as such, to perform the metaphysical act. Human persons are ordered in their constitutive reality as such to the gathering up of the being of the cosmos in its entirety and recapitulating it in love, in their total gift of self — lending the cosmos their own gift of self, as it were; and they must do this in openness to the Christian act that goes beyond this metaphysical act even as it contains and fulfills the latter. In other words, metaphysical love must finally be taken up within and comprehended by — through participation in — God's act of love in Jesus Christ, expressed in the total gift of his self in death and abandonment, a death and abandonment, again, that recapitulates and fulfills in an utterly new and inconceivable way the original meaning of being as such in its dual unity of *esse-essentia*! And again, this "upward" participatory love, which enables even as it is comprehended by God's "descending" love, receives its archetypal form in the Marian and Johannine love that remains in the world even as it mediates Christ's love as expressed sacramentally in the office of Peter.

The foregoing, then, reveals the burden of Balthasar's work: that the heart of the whole God of love in Jesus Christ appear at the heart of the whole world in the integrity of its worldly being and meaning; and that the heart of the whole world be opened to the heart of the whole God of love in Jesus Christ in the integrity of his divine Being and meaning. God's reality as a total gift of self in Jesus Christ makes its entry into the world precisely coincident with, and indeed from inside or "beneath" and as the ground for, the world's recovery of its own inner meaning as ordered to a total gift of itself in and through the saints to God.

VII

Balthasar's C(c)atholic ontology is thus fulfilled and recapitulated in a sanctity that takes every reality and every thought "captive" in Jesus Christ, *generously:* in a way that "assumes," while thus not "absorbing" but rather gathering up and "perfecting" every being and meaning of the cosmos in its singular creaturely integrity as such. It is love inside the double distinction between *esse* and *essentia / ens* (the ontological difference) and between God and the world (the Christian difference) that gives all cosmic identities, distinctions, and relations their most basic (onto)logic and thereby establishes the cosmos as a whole and in each of its parts as an analogically conceived generous community of being and meaning under God and as a participatory sign of God's presence. It is the horizon set by love inside this double distinction, then, that enables us for the first time fully to understand what has been termed a Cartesian ontology of identity and distinction/relation. This Cartesian ontology of identity, which is both rooted in and serves to bring about a forgetfulness of Being and of God, expresses even as it promotes the failure (however unintended) to live and think reality as a matter of love — or, a fortiori, sanctity as a matter of the "perfection" of being.

In conclusion, I note briefly how Balthasar's position stands with respect to two major alternative streams of Catholic thought in response to modernity.

First, viewed in light of Balthasar as presented above, the dominant stream of modern Catholic theology and philosophy, even when harshly critical of modern patterns of life and thought, has nevertheless left intact the root assumptions of those patterns as reflected in a Cartesian ontology of identity. Modern Catholic thought has itself typically taken the identity of x to be originally-conceptually *closed to* non-x or to any implication of the presence of non-x in x. That is to say, much of modern Catholic thought has itself presupposed just the structural indifference between x and non-x that, on Balthasar's understanding as outlined above, lies at root of the modernity that mechanizes the order and intelligibility of things even as it (then) moralizes — voluntarizes: conceives as arbitrary and just so far not integral to the order and intelligibility of things — relation and love and religious piety. Catholic thought in the modern period, in a word, has had its own version of modernity's forgetfulness of Being (in relation to beings) and of God (in relation to the world), thus its own version of modernity's forgetfulness of love *in its ontological meaning* as signified and expressed in this double distinction.

The stream of Catholic thought referred to here is above all that of modern, or Cajetanian, Scholasticism. Much is often made of the question of how Balthasar stands with respect to the thought of Thomas Aquinas. In fact, Aquinas is a pivotal figure for Balthasar as well as for modern Scholasticism. The issue between Balthasar and Scholasticism bears rather on what each takes to be the basic achievement of Aquinas. And this question turns finally on what each takes to be the Thomistic ontology of identity and distinction: how each conceives the double distinction between *esse* and *essentia* (the ontological difference) and between God and the world (the Christian difference), and how each consequently understands the relation between being and love under God. Modern Scholasticism's assumed, even if unintended, Cartesian ontology of identity manifests itself in Scholasticism's construal of these two distinctions in terms of what amounts to an original-structural indifference of *essentia* in relation to *esse* and the world in relation to God. That is, Scholasticism overlooks the significance of *esse* in its constitutive implications for being and also the significance of God in his constitutive implications for the world, and thus misses the significance of love in its constitutive implications for the world — the world in the dual sense of its being created, hence its originally being-given, and of its being invited, simultaneous with its being created, to share in God's own love as revealed in Jesus Christ.[39]

The point, then, is that Scholasticism lacks just the ontology of generosity ordered to sanctity whose absence is the bane of modernity, an ontology that Balthasar takes to be implied in the symphony of all great Catholic theologian-saints. Balthasar reads Aquinas, and indeed grants him his pivotal place, within this symphony. Key for Balthasar is Aquinas's articulation of the ontological difference, which eliminates Cartesian (mechanistic) identity at its source even as it restores identity in its genuinely catholic sense as warranted by the Christian doctrine of creation rightly understood.

Cajetanian Scholasticism customarily insists that inscribing generosity within the original logic of being and meaning leads to relativism. Such a fear, however, from the point of view argued above in the name of Balthasar, overlooks the crucial fact that it is the *very relation to God* by which the creature is constituted in existence that gives the creature its substantial *identity* in the first place. Relationality and identity are constitutively, thus simultaneously, given. It follows that each presupposes even as it always already shapes the original and proper meaning of the other. The relationality of the individual creature to God — and indeed thereby the transcendental

relationality of the individual creature to all other creatures in God[40] — on
the one hand, and the substantial identity of the individual creature, on the
other hand, can never be simply juxtaposed or simply opposed to each other.
Identity and relation, in a word, are *both* integral to the original-constitutive
order of being and intelligibility. This is why the identity of things can never
be most basically mechanistic, even as relationality can never consist most
basically in arbitrary or forceful movement. And this is why, further, the
proper intelligibility of things, which necessarily presupposes a conceptual
identity just so far subject to power and control, is *simultaneously* a matter *also* of *mystery* — the mystery entailed by an identity that is generously
conceived.

Regarding the problem of relativism, then: the burden of the earlier
criticism of modernity's Cartesian ontology was that the latter's originally
assumed mechanistic, and just so far closed, identity of x is what first gave
rise to, and indeed required, the idea that relations between x and non-x
were arbitrary and dispersive and thus a matter of *relativism* — or indeed
better, for the reasons adduced earlier, relativistic *nihilism.* In sum, it is Balthasar's originally generous identity that alone enables us reasonably to reject
relativism, while on the contrary, Scholasticism's mechanistic identity of its
inner logic generates, dialectically, the very relativism that it is Scholasticism's
intention to oppose.[41]

Here, then, we can see the difficulty also with a second stream of Catholic thought that has emerged in recent decades, as a kind of "postmodern"
response to modernity, including modernity in the above Scholastic form.
Thus certain Catholic thinkers argue that love and God are, strictly speaking, beyond or other than being. Such a position, however, itself continues
to presuppose modern patterns of thought, that is, *precisely coincident with,*
and in a way that thus, *eo ipso,* anteriorly shapes, what is intended as a fundamental postmodern criticism of these patterns. For what we should now
be able readily to see is that love — or God — needs to be placed "beyond"
or "without" being only insofar as one has already, however tacitly and unintentionally, assumed that being in its original-proper meaning as such lacks
generosity; insofar as one already presupposes that the being of the world in
its constitutive identity is not interiorly-anteriorly open to God and the love
that images God; in a word, insofar as one continues, however contrary to
one's intention, to presuppose the Cartesian ontology of identity whereby x

is not properly *open* to non-x *coincident with* x's substantial self-identity *as x.* In short, the Catholic postmodern claim that love — or God — is "beyond" being is in fact but the later arrival of what is already logically implied in modernity's characteristic Cartesianism.

The difficulty with both modern Catholic Scholasticism and its post-modern Catholic alternative, in a word, is that both, albeit from opposite directions, are simultaneously too modern and too antimodern. They both remain caught in the dialectic that is the bane of the modern cultural situa-tion: between an identity that is mechanistic, on the one hand, and relations that are (consequently) purely arbitrary and dispersive, on the other.

It is crucial, then, in light of these two Catholic responses to modernity, to see that Balthasar's own response, expressed in what has been termed his catholic ontology of generosity, is one that shares the assumptions neither of modernity nor of postmodernity — or better, one that adopts the assump-tions of both modernity and postmodernity but only as it transforms these. As I have repeatedly insisted, the identity of modernity and the relationality of modern postmodernity[42] both need to be recuperated, *precisely in terms of the community* of x and non-x that originally constitutes the order of reality as love and love as the order of reality, under God and in the image of God — in creation, hypostatically in Jesus Christ, and sacramentally in the church.

But here, in conclusion, I need to emphasize what has been implied all along: this recuperation, which is finally realized only in and through the lives of the saints, necessarily involves, in the one order of history that is weighted with sinfulness, a transformation at the heart of which stands the cross. "Worldly" identities, all of which are disfigured by the sin of the first human persons, are restored in their originally given and intended meaning through the total-personal gift of self: first and above all through Christ's total gift of self, which is then truly symbolized in and through the saint's total gift of self, which lends its own total gift of self to the cosmos, thereby gathering the cosmos itself up into the love of God revealed in Christ and in his saints.

The point, then, is that all identities of every age, in their real and their cognitive being, are always to be recuperated and never simply rejected, but only from within the dynamic toward love that, in the one order of history, involves a crucifying conversion: involves following Christ into his suffer-ing death and abandonment on the cross. This following is realized in the saints, precisely as they extend themselves in an embrace of the cosmos in its entirety, in its unity and in each of its parts, so that the cosmos as a whole may be drawn up into its needed conversion into love.

It is just here, then, and finally only here, that we can understand rightly what it means to affirm *in love* the identity peculiar to being in each of its epiphanies in every time and place of history, including modern Western history.

♦ ♦ ♦

Let us summarize. What, according to Balthasar, we need to see today — need to see in all cultures, but especially in our modern liberal-technological culture whose hallmark is to deny it — is this: that, in identifying *this* or *that* or distinguishing between *this* and *that,* in life (reality) or in thought (concept), we necessarily invoke *an ontology of creation.* We invoke, at least implicitly and however unconsciously, some view of what constitutes the meaning of being, of a one in relation to a many, *ultimately* — originally and finally — and hence some response to the question of the nature and existence of God.[43] In the one concrete order of history, this necessarily implied view bears the further implication of some response to God as he has revealed himself in Jesus Christ and remains sacramentally present in the church, whose primordial form, in Christ by the Holy Spirit, is given in Mary and John, as state, and Peter, as office, of holiness. It is to this holiness that all "worldly" being, in and through the human persons whose meaning is archetypically embodied in Mary and John, is called.

The point, then, is that every being in the cosmos, "real" or cognitive, realizes its perfection finally only from within the love whose katalogical-analogical meaning is revealed in the Christian doctrine of creation and redemption. Sanctity, then, in realizing this love, alone liberates being into its deepest and most proper identity as such — as ordered toward the depths of God himself.

This, then, is the truly catholic and Catholic burden of the work of Balthasar, the burden that, it seems to me, articulates well the core meaning of the Second Vatican Council in its renewed sense of the Trinitarian God- and Christ-centered church's mission of love to the heart of the world.[44]

Postscript: An Ontology of Generosity and Christ's "Descent into Hell"

I have not mentioned Balthasar's teaching regarding Holy Saturday and the nature of Christ's descent into hell, which requires more discussion than is appropriate for the present context focusing on Balthasar's ontology of creation. It is not quite true to say that the theology of Christ's descent represents the core of Balthasar's thought, as critics often assert. On the contrary, what lies at the heart of his thought is the love embodied in Jesus Christ as the revealer of the Trinitarian God, and the call to beings created in that love to follow Christ unconditionally. Failure to acknowledge that the decisive core of Balthasar's thought is God-centered love as revealed in Christ — and hence failure to read his speculative account of Holy Saturday as an attempt to draw out the final implications of God's generosity to creatures — can only lead to a serious *petitio principii*. Balthasar's theology of Christ's descent presupposes an understanding of creaturely being in terms of a love centered in Christ as the revelation of the Trinitarian God, and it is in that context that he portrays Christ's redeeming love as a suffering solidarity with sinners that reaches all the way into hell.

The point here is not that acceptance of the fundamentality of God-centered love and generosity in our understanding of the structure of reality *eo ipso* resolves all the questions regarding Balthasar's theology of Holy Saturday — indeed, Balthasar himself, in his customary Catholic spirit, presumed that the church would over time evaluate the speculative elements of this theology. The point, rather, is that it is impossible to interpret his account fairly without situating it within his articulation of what I have termed here an "ontology of generosity."[45] Indeed, the significance of this point is heightened if we recognize that perhaps the core teaching of the Second Vatican Council lies in its affirmation that Christ, in his very revelation of the Father and his love, reveals the meaning of humankind to itself, and thereby the entire order of the cosmos in humankind. I am unaware of any criticism of Balthasar's theology of Christ's descent that takes adequate account of the ontology of generosity that is presupposed in that theology and indeed that, arguably, lies at the heart of the renewal indicated by the Second Vatican Council, as carried forward in the pontificates of John Paul II and Benedict XVI.

I offer the following three comments, then, to help bring into relief some principles or affirmations that would have to be treated in any non-question-begging criticism of Balthasar's theology of Holy Saturday.

First, already in Balthasar's ontology of creation we have a basic principle for approaching the question of the seriousness of human freedom, and indeed the problem of sin and eternal damnation. The key is the infinite generosity of God. This implies that freedom (participation in generosity) is really given to creatures. But it also implies both that creatures matter "infinitely" to God, and that serious abuse of freedom in relation to God bears infinitely serious implications: infinitely offends God. But, because and insofar as creaturely abuse of freedom involves *infinite* offense, the creature by definition is unable to justify itself before God. It would seem to follow, then, that the real possibility of eternal damnation (hell) is implied in the infinite generosity characteristic of the act of creation itself. It is this real possibility alone that can reveal the true — that is, infinite — magnitude of, and indeed drama implicit in, a serious offense against the infinitely generous God. In short, God's infinite generosity and the possibility of eternal damnation seem to be not inversely related, but rather directly related.

Second, God's infinite generosity, however, raises at the same time a crucial second consideration, evoked in light of God's revelation in Christ, of the further implications of that generosity: his willingness to suffer with the sinner until the very end. Or better: the Son of God judges, or redeems, the sinner only while bearing, in and with the sinner, the consequences of sin — the sinner's forsakenness. What is meant by this is indicated in several statements by Benedict XVI in his book *Jesus of Nazareth:*

> [Jesus' descent] is a descent into the perils besetting mankind, for there is no other way to lift up fallen humanity. Jesus has to enter into the drama of human existence, for that belongs to the core of his mission; he has to penetrate it completely, down to its uttermost depths, in order to find the "lost sheep," to bear it on his shoulders, and to bring it home. The Apostles' Creed speaks of Jesus' "descent into hell." This descent not only took place in and after his death, but accompanies him all along his entire journey. He must recapitulate the whole of history from its beginnings — from Adam on; he must go through, suffer through, the whole of it, in order to transform it.[46]
>
> Jesus' Baptism... is understood as a repetition of the whole of history, which both recapitulates the past and anticipates the future. His entering

into the sin of others is a descent into the "inferno." But he does not descend merely in the role of a spectator, as in Dante's *Inferno*. Rather, he goes down in the role of one whose suffering with others is a transforming suffering that turns the underworld around, knocking down and flinging open the gates of the abyss.... [The evil one] is overcome and bound by one yet stronger, who, because of his equality with God, can take upon himself all the sin of the world and then suffers it through to the end — omitting nothing on the downward path into identity with the fallen. This struggle is the "conversion" of being that brings it into a new condition, that prepares a new heaven and a new earth.[47]

The understanding of the great mystery of expiation is... blocked by our individualistic image of man. We can no longer grasp substitution because we think that every man is ensconced in himself alone. The fact that all individual beings are deeply interwoven and that all are encompassed in turn by the being of the One, the Incarnate Son, is something that we are no longer capable of seeing. When we come to speak of Christ's crucifixion, we will have to take up these issues again.[48]

As we have seen, Jesus must suffer through these temptations to the point of dying on the Cross, which is how he opens the way of redemption for us. Thus, it is not only after his death, but already by his death and during his whole life, that Jesus "descends into hell," as it were, into the domain of our temptations and defeats, in order to take us by the hand and carry us upward.[49]

Third, the concrete meaning for the everyday lives of Christians of the drama between God and the creature implied by my first and second comments is well exhibited in Georges Bernanos's *Diary of a Country Priest*, with its portrayal of the utter magnitude and objective seriousness (order of justice) of sin simultaneous with the utterly profound suffering-solidarity (mercy) that sin evokes from the infinitely gracious God in Christ ("Tout est grâce"). Bernanos's portrayal of the country priest's sense of justice and mercy seems entirely consistent with that developed theologically in John Paul II's *Dives in Misericordia*. It accurately depicts what is also the view of Balthasar.[50]

In sum, the point here is not that considerations such as these, in and of themselves, warrant acceptance of all aspects of Balthasar's theology of the "descent into hell," but rather only that we need to come to terms with what is affirmed in these considerations as a necessary condition for evaluating that theology — for assessing whether, for example, in light of the infinite generosity of God as indicated, there are grounds for truly hoping that every human heart (which heart, it should be recalled, bears naturally-constitutively in its depths a passionate restlessness for God's own generosity [cf. Augustine]) might in the end be responsive to God. Questions such as these — as well as the nature of Holy Saturday itself — cannot be answered in a non-question-begging way relative to Balthasar's theology, or indeed in an authentically Catholic manner, without taking adequate account of God's infinite generosity, or indeed the ontology of generosity, as suggested in the present essay.

Chapter Fifteen

Every Thought Captive to Christ

How Balthasar Changed My Mind
about Faith and Philosophy

Adrian Walker

Introduction:
Confessions of a Limping Balthasarian

The book of Genesis recounts how God appears one night to the patriarch Jacob in the guise of a mysterious man who challenges him to a wrestling match (Gen. 32:24–32). The text tells us that the man struggles with Jacob all through the night but is unable to defeat him. Towards daybreak, the man, realizing that he cannot win the bout, resorts to the trick of dislocating his opponent's thigh. Yet even then, Jacob refuses to release him without receiving his blessing. The man accedes to Jacob's demand and departs. Jacob, it seems, has won. In fact, the man even acknowledges that Jacob is the victor in the struggle. And yet, this acknowledgment occurs in the context of a remarkable dialogue in which it becomes clear that the question of who has defeated whom in this nocturnal battle is not at all so simple as it might appear at first.

Jacob has begun to suspect that there is something out of the ordinary about his opponent; otherwise, he would hardly ask for the man's blessing. Significantly, the man responds to Jacob's demand by asking Jacob to reveal his name. Having been told that it is "Jacob," the man promises him a new name, "Israel." The man then attaches an explanation to this promise: Jacob will be called "Israel" because he has striven with God and with men and

For John and Margaret McCarthy, in friendship.

has prevailed. With these words, the man acknowledges Jacob as the victor, yet this acknowledgment is accompanied by a gesture — the bestowal of a new name — that reveals that even in defeat he is more powerful than his vanquisher. The man possesses Jacob's name and future, but not vice versa. Thus, when Jacob asks the man's name, he gets an evasive answer that anticipates the manifestation of the divine name to Moses at the burning bush (see Exod. 3:14): "Why do you ask my name?" says the man (Gen. 32:29). Jacob receives the man's blessing, to be sure, yet he obtains it only as it begins to dawn on him that he has seen God face-to-face but has not died. At this point, the dislocation of Jacob's thigh turns out to be something more than a failed attempt to defeat him by trickery. It proves, quite to the contrary, to be a sign that Jacob's victory is, on a deeper level, a defeat that penetrates to the core of his being and, precisely in doing that, bestows blessing. This seems to be the point of the story's concluding remark: Jacob emerges from his wrestling match with a limp, and "to this day the Israelites do not eat the sinew of the hip which is upon the hollow of the thigh, because he touched the hollow of Jacob's thigh on the sinew of the hip" (Gen. 32:32).

I would like to interpret the man in Genesis 32:24–32 as a prefigurement of Christ. If I am right about that, the story of his nocturnal combat with Jacob would perhaps have something like the following "tropological" sense. God's defeat on the cross is actually his victory. We tend, of course, to resist God's at first counterintuitive-seeming method of vanquishing his foes. It appears to be so unnecessarily, so wastefully, and so painfully roundabout, to say the least. This very resistance of ours, however, can be a prelude to the sudden insight that God's method of winning through defeat, while as unexpected as the man's blow to the thigh was to Jacob, turns out, in retrospect, to have been the one most befitting the godliness of God — the most *theoprepes,* as the Greek Fathers used to say. Like the man who dislocates Jacob's thigh, God, in his defeat, gets underneath our defenses and convinces us inwardly that "the foolishness of God is wiser than men, and the weakness of God is stronger than men" (1 Cor. 1:25). This inward conviction, moreover, is so intimate that it actually opens up to us interior depths in ourselves whose existence we at most dimly suspected before (see 1 Cor. 2:9–10); God's victory-through-defeat on the cross wins us over from "deeper inside us than we are to ourselves."[1] Thus, whereas we at first resisted the invitation to share in this "logic of the cross" (see 1 Cor. 1:18), because it seemed at first to be so alien to us, we now willingly embrace it as the key to the deepest truth about ourselves:

> Nay in all that toil, that coil, since (seems) I kissed the rod,
> Hand rather, my heart lo! lapped strength, stole joy, would laugh, cheer.
> Cheer whom though? The hero whose heaven-handling flung me, foot trod
> Me? or me that fought him? O which one? is it each one? That night, that year
> Of now done darkness I wretch lay wrestling with (my God!) my God.[2]

I suspect that, like Jacob, all serious Christians sooner or later find themselves struggling with the crucified God in the night. If they remain Christians, it is because just when they think that they have beaten him with watertight arguments, he surprises them with an unexpected move. They suddenly catch sight of the glory shining in his despised and humiliated countenance, and that is enough to dissipate all their objections in a single blaze of light. At any rate, this is a pattern that I detect when I reflect on my own twenty-year experience as a Christian and as a Catholic. More than anyone else, Hans Urs von Balthasar has taught me to discern and to accept this pattern. For Balthasar, as for the two great patrons of his thought, John the Evangelist and Ignatius of Loyola, the glory of God's love shines in the darkness of the cross. Abasement and exaltation are inextricably interwoven, and Christ's godforsaken death coincides with his most intimate union with the Father and the paternal will "that all men be saved and come to a knowledge of the truth" (1 Tim. 2:4). The intertwining of humiliation and exaltation that reaches its apex on the cross is, for Balthasar, the key to the figure — the *Gestalt* — of Christ, which enjoys a kind of radiance and coherence that cannot be exhaustively accounted for in this-worldly terms (however much the Christ-form includes the worldly).

It has become something of a conferencier's cliché to repeat Balthasar's strictures against an "aesthetic theology," but it is easy to forget that these strictures reflect his own keen awareness that the beauty of the Christ-form is an unwonted one that is satisfying precisely because it includes what at first sight is unbeautiful: the bloody death of the Lord of glory on a criminal's gibbet. Balthasar knows that there is something scandalous about his proposal, and he does not try to minimize the scandal, but actually insists on it emphatically. I do not always find this emphasis immediately easy to accept, and so I struggle sometimes with Balthasar, even though he has been such a pivotal figure in my life. A daybreak always seems to come, though: the sudden realization that I am struggling not with Balthasar but rather with the core of Christianity itself, which, strange as it may seem, does make sense after all. With dislocated thigh, I am happy to confess myself a Balthasarian, if only a "limping" one.

Breaking the Faith-Reason Synthesis?

What is it about Balthasar's theology, though, that sometimes provokes resistance? In my experience, the sticking point is his emphasis on the need for unconditional surrender to the paradoxical "logic" of victory in defeat and of glory in abasement that I talked about just now — that is, on the need for obedience. But why should this Balthasarian emphasis on obedience be problematic?

The answer, I think, has something to do with the fact that Balthasar assigns a certain ultimacy to obedience. Obedience, on his account, is not just a stage on the way to the beatific vision, but rather it corresponds to something inherent in the nature of final beatitude itself. Not only are Christians sons in the Son called to spend eternity growing into filiation and not out of it, but also, as Adrienne von Speyr puts it, even the Son himself eternally "lets himself be generated."[3] This "letting himself be generated," which is the transcendent foundation of what the Son lives as obedience in the economy of his incarnation, does not imply any subordination of being or diversity of will on his part with respect to the Father. Rather, it highlights how the Son, being "God from God," is beyond the dialectic of independence and dependence, of autonomous self-possession and relation. The Son, von Speyr is telling us, receives the divine being from the Father, even as he is the being he receives:[4] He *is* his act of receiving himself from the Father, at once as *autotheos*,[5] God on his own account, and *ab alio*[6] as *Deus genitus*.[7]

At this point, the Thomist (and there is one in me) rises in protest. For Thomas does not obviously elevate obedience to any kind of ultimacy, however carefully qualified that elevation (as it is in Balthasar). A much more plausible candidate for such ultimacy in Thomas Aquinas's work would in fact be intellectual contemplation. As I read the *Summa theologiae*, at any rate, one of the central subplots of the work is the story of how the ideal of philosophical contemplation is fulfilled in the beatific vision, which in turn is a participation in the eternal generation of the Word, God's self-contemplation in person.[8] This fulfillment seems to be the key to what might be called the Catholic synthesis of reason and revelation. If, then, Balthasar really does elevate obedience to such an ultimate height, does he not call this synthesis into question? Does he not give ammunition to Leo Strauss, who argues that there can be no honest synthesis between Athens and Jerusalem, only an uneasy standoff, because their respective principles are simply heterogeneous? For Strauss, the believer's loving obedience to God's Word (and to its human mediators) and the philosopher's "love of wisdom" are two mutually exclusive first principles for governing the conduct of a whole human life:

> No alternative is more fundamental than this: human guidance or divine guidance. The first possibility is characteristic of philosophy...the second is presented in the Bible. The dilemma cannot be evaded by any harmonization or synthesis. For both philosophy and the Bible proclaim something as the one thing needful, as the only thing that ultimately counts, and the one thing needful proclaimed by the Bible is the opposite of that proclaimed by philosophy: a life of obedient love versus a life of free insight. In every attempt at harmonization, in every synthesis however impressive, one of the two opposed elements is sacrificed, more or less subtly but in any event surely: philosophy, which means to be the queen, must be the handmaid of revelation or vice-versa.[9]

It should be apparent from the foregoing that I do not think that Balthasar and Thomas are mutually exclusive. On the one hand, obedience, for Balthasar, is not the abolition of insight, or even of its ultimate status, but rather is its "communionalization" in light of the Trinitarian nature of Ultimate Reality; on the other hand, Thomas is open in many ways to just this "communionalization," as some of the texts that I cited above seem to suggest. Rather than focus on the comparison between Thomas and Balthasar, however, I want to focus on the comparison between Balthasar and Strauss, for Strauss puts his finger on what I consider to be the nub of the difficulty with any faith-reason synthesis, which consists in the fact that Christianity thinks of God both as a First Principle and as a living Person who says, "I am who I am" (Exod. 3:14). If Strauss is a tough opponent of the reason-revelation synthesis, it is because, he, unlike Heidegger, sees the idea that God is personal — an identifiable Someone — as the oppo-site, rather than as the culmination, of Greek philosophy's discovery of the primacy of nature. In what follows, I want to defend the possibility of faith-reason synthesis, although that will require, as we will see below, a critique of the notion of synthesis that serves the discovery of an even deeper kind of unity between them.

But what has all this got to do with Balthasar and his emphasis on what a Straussian might think is only the half of Strauss's either-or: *Liebesgehorsam,* the obedience of love, to use Balthasar's own oft-repeated term? As the fore-going discussion already suggested at least indirectly, Balthasar's theology of obedience is interwoven with his own account of the Christian synthesis between the personal and the principal, nature and freedom, which, in my opinion, is the only one in twentieth-century theology that can stand toe-to-toe with Strauss's critique of that synthesis. In what follows, I first will sketch this account against the backdrop of philosopher Thomas Prufer's re-flections on Strauss in his small masterpiece *Recapitulations,* which shows a lot of surprising parallels to Balthasar.[10] This will be the work of the next two sections of the essay. Having done that, I will go on in the section following those two to use Balthasar's understanding of the Christian synthesis of the personal and the principal as a platform for briefly defending the thesis that is implied in the title of this essay: christological obedience is not the op-posite of philosophy; rather, it is the embodiment of the inmost ground of stringent philosophical argumentation. In the final section, I will conclude with a few words about how obedience so understood has changed, and goes on changing, my mind as a Christian philosopher. In this connection, I will focus on what it means for me that the freedom of philosophy lies in the captivity of its every thought to Christ (see 2 Cor. 10:5).

Two caveats. First, this essay is just that: an essay, neither an exhaus-tive treatise — if there is such a thing in the first place — nor a work of scholarship. This explains why I cite selectively and only for the purposes of illustration. The reader should therefore not expect anything even ap-proaching a complete account of Prufer, Strauss, Balthasar, or indeed any of the other authors whom I occasionally cite (such as Plato). Quite frankly, I am to a large extent ignorant of all these authors; if I venture to discuss them here, it is only because what I do know of all three has produced some reflections that might be of interest to my readers, even without the benefit of scholarly completeness.

Second, although this is an essay appearing as a chapter in a book called *How Balthasar Changed My Mind,* what follows is not an autobiography, since I do not wish to bore anyone with my life story. That said, this essay does represent a distillation of a modest experience of life as a Christian philosopher. While not autobiographical, then, it is personal, especially in the concluding section.

Philosophical Reverberations of Divine Freedom

In the introduction to *Recapitulations,* Prufer says that he is going to tell two overlapping "stories": the story of being and the story of nature.[11] Let us start with the second story, whose beginning Prufer locates in the discovery of the primacy of nature over artifice and convention. As Prufer tells it, however, the story does not remain there, but takes a decisive turn with Socrates, who widens the scope of the philosophical question "What is it?" to include not only the natural, but also the artificial and the conventional. So far, then, Prufer's characterization of the "Socratic turn"[12] squares with Strauss's. It is just at this point, though, that a decisive question arises on which Prufer will part ways with Strauss while nonetheless "recapitulating," in the context of the doctrine of *creatio ex nihilo,* Strauss's central insight about the primacy of nature in a new framework. The question is this: does "the articulation of being into the natural, on the one hand, and into the conventional, on the other hand" exhaust the "senses of being"?[13]

Strauss, as far as I can tell, seems to answer this question in the affirmative, in the sense that, for him, the philospher's horizon (my word) is what he calls "the whole," which on his view does articulate itself into the natural, on the one hand, and the conventional-artificial, on the other. Prufer agrees with Strauss that the "whole" so articulates itself. Nevertheless, his agreement occurs in the context of a larger disagreement, for Prufer, unlike Strauss, thinks that philosophy culminates in reflection on the nonultimacy of the "whole." For Prufer, in fact, the very being of the "whole" depends asymmetrically on a Principle that was neither originally a part of nor paired with the "whole." On Prufer's account, moreover, this is a properly philosophical insight, which, however, is recapitulated in the Christian revelation of God as free, personal Creator. God is Principle and Person in one simple act of being.

For Prufer, the ontological independence of divine nature from the "whole" coincides with God's freedom to create or not to create: "Nature, in the secondary sense, is creatures created by God; but nature in the primary sense is God—whether He choose to create or not to create, and therefore whether or not there be creatures at all, whether or not there be nature in the secondary sense."[14] Since, however, the creation of the world is not the overcoming of a lack for God,[15] the actual decision to give it existence is not a more or less arbitrary option for one of two more or less equally attractive alternatives within an already existing framework. It is, rather, a wholly un-owed yet not at all arbitrary production of the being of the framework—of the world, of the "whole"—in the first place. The "whole" is intelligible because its very being is a liberally, but not arbitrarily, bestowed gift.

Against this backdrop Prufer tackles (in chapter 7 of *Recapitulations*) Strauss's insistence on the "incompatibility between philosophy and taking creation to be true."[16] Prufer explains, "For Strauss, this incompatibility is based on a rejection of raising contingency and community, understood in a certain way, to a level higher than necessity and self-sufficiency, understood in a certain way (or ways)."[17] Although Prufer frankly and justly acknowledges and admires Strauss's genius,[18] he argues, in essence, that Strauss (for whatever reason) remains too much within the perspective of the worldly "whole." Consequently, Prufer says, Strauss tacitly treats the intraworldly antithesis between nature and artifice-convention, which here translates into that between necessity and contingency, as the ultimate framework. To the extent that such a framework is assumed to be ultimate, however, the freedom of creation asserted by Christianity almost inevitably ends up getting confused with intraworldly contingency, hence, with a subphilosophical randomness.[19]

By contrast, Prufer holds that the primordial divine unity of freedom and nature relativizes the distinction between nature and artifice (which turns out to be secondary)[20]—and just so grounds the intelligibility of intraworldly nature. For God's creative act produces precisely the "whole" in its very being, inclusive, then, of the basic intraworldly distinction between nature and artifice (though God's creative power also extends to intraworldly artificing as well). This means — to unfold the implications of Prufer's position in my own words — that while the Creator is the artificer of natures, he does not thereby rob them of the (relative) "primordiality" that Aristotle saw in them or reduce them to the status of arbitrary brainstorms.[21] God is indeed an artisan, or better, an artist, but he and he alone is the one artist who can create something endowed with a reality, indeed, a life of its own that all other art then "subcreatively," as Tolkien says, imitates. God creates natures, including natures like ours that are capable of "subcreation" in their own right.

This brings us to what I think is the core of Prufer's response to Strauss. Given the internal intelligibility, yet nonultimacy, of the worldly "whole," something like a gratuitous but nonrandom act posited by a Source at once necessary and free is actually the best, most philosophically respectable explanation of the being and intelligibility of the "whole" in the first place. But a Source like this can ultimately only be a creator *ex liberalitate*[22] of the kind revealed in the Bible. The knowledge of creation out of nothing, then, however acquired, is not subphilosophical, but rather is the highest and deepest fulfillment of philosophical *eros* itself:

> Philosophy, as eros for nature and for the whole, is not less itself (a) for moving from a less primary sense of nature, nature2, to the most primary sense of nature, nature1, most primary because of its eternity and necessity, self-sufficiency and intelligibility, and (b) for moving from the whole to the principle of the whole, the principle that is not itself part of the whole.[23]

"The Place of Glory in Metaphysics"[24]

Although Prufer does not say so explicitly, the foregoing sketch (which far from exhausts the richness of his book) shows that *Recapitulations* actually tells three stories, and not just two. The third story is about how the Christian sense of God's personal freedom "reverberates"[25] in the history of philosophy. It is this third story, I think, that is really what is most deeply at issue in Prufer's discussion with Strauss in chapter 7 of the book. In the terms of the third story, Strauss's claim that holding the truth of creation is unphilosophical means that the idea of God's personal freedom in Christianity (or Judaism and Islam) is a relapse behind or below philosophy's breakthrough to nature, a relapse into mythology. Translated into the same terms of the third story, Prufer's answer to Strauss's objection means that the Christian revelation of God's personal freedom, far from being a subphilosophical relapse into mythology, is a confirmation, delivered in a surprising context, of what some of the greatest philosophers, starting with Plato, have glimpsed about the nonultimacy of the "whole." God is Principal and personal at once. But this means that if we are going to deal adequately with our question of the synthesis between faith and reason — and the issue of the unity of personhood and principality is central to it — then we have to delve more deeply into the nonultimacy of the "whole." It is at his point that Prufer's first story, the story about nature, overlaps with his second story, the story about being. The breakthrough to God as Principle and Person goes hand in hand with a breakthrough to a properly metaphysical sense of being that is both immanent in and transcendent of the "whole."

From this point, it is a short step to Balthasar, who, for his part, is fascinated by the question of how God can be a person acting freely in history without losing his status as First Principle. This concern runs, for example, throughout the entire trilogy, but I would like to focus on the two volumes on metaphysics in *Herrlichkeit* because he formulates the question there in terms of the relationship between philosophy and mythology. This way of formulating the question makes it easier to see how Balthasar's account of God as at once Personal and Principial goes beyond Strauss's either-or between loving obedience and free philosophical insight while at the same time doing justice to the legitimate concerns behind Strauss's refusal of any honest synthesis between them.

Balthasar, like other thinkers in the German tradition, is unwilling simply to jettison the experience of the sacred reflected in Greek mythology, which he understands broadly as a kind of fusion of art and religion. Balthasar solves the problem, though, not by turning Christ into a cipher for the mythic sacred, but rather by opting for something like C. S. Lewis's idea that Christ is the fulfillment of mythology, the true myth. At the same time, Balthasar insists that this true myth is not a relapse below the level of philosophy. The Christian God is a personal divinity acting freely in history — so far Christianity agrees with mythology. Yet when the free, personal God acts in history, he makes it perfectly clear that he transcends history. He is free and personal, but he is also the First Principle. Conversely, his personal freedom fulfills what the philosophers glimpsed, or could have glimpsed, of his Principality, precisely by removing it once and for all from any idea of a natural or necessary pairing of God and the world in some "last whole."[26] For Balthasar, then, the personal aspect of God is bound up with what the Bible means by God's "glory," his one-of-a-kind "godliness," even as this "glory" is something that the philosophers glimpsed, or could have glimpsed, obliquely in their speculation about the First Principle: the fact that God is radically independent from the world and yet therefore radically immanent in it, *superior summo* and therefore *interior intimo*[27] with respect to the "whole." With all this in mind, Balthasar, much like Prufer, then asks this: What is it about the way the worldly "whole" is structured that enables God to manifest his distinctive glory in it by freely becoming what by nature he is not: a part of the "whole"? Where is the "place of glory in metaphysics"?

Balthasar's most sustained treatment of this question in the metaphysics volumes of *Herrlichkeit* appears toward the end of the second volume under the title "The Wonder of Being and the Fourfold Difference."[28] In what follows, I want to focus on how Balthasar handles the question of the philosophical "reverberation" of the revelation of God's personal freedom. As we will see, Balthasar's thesis is parallel to Prufer's: the free self-revelation of the Christian God, in its formal quality as personal and free, while never deducible from the "subject matter of metaphysics," nonetheless contains the fulfillment of what philosophical contemplation of that "subject matter" has glimpsed, or should be able to glimpse, about being in relation to its "Principle." Indeed, precisely because it is underivable from beings, this revelation can touch them from the inside without therefore having to be one of their immanent parts or principles. The strange and surprising event of Christ thus turns out, in retrospect, to be what the whole creation was waiting for without knowing it.

Balthasar begins his reflection on the "fourfold difference" on a distinctly metaphysical note: wonderment over the very being of anything at all.[29] For Balthasar, however, this wonderment over being is not only the beginning, but also the end, of philosophy. Put another way, wonderment, for Balthasar, is not just a function of a temporary ignorance destined to be dissolved into the light of understanding; it is the touchstone of true understanding in the first place. This claim seems to me to be borne out experientially. We begin to wonder, in the sense of being amazed, precisely when we get the point of something. The necessity with which we see the initially disparate elements suddenly converge into unity is never simply banal or obvious, but rather is always something of a surprise.[30] This is why, as I read him, Aristotle can maintain an analogy between logical syllogism and natural organism that then erects a bridge to Balthasar's insight that the beauty of a living *Gestalt* is the paradigm of the kind of surprising necessity that we find already in the sphere of logic. The (relative) primacy of the aesthetic in the trilogy does not undermine, but rather grounds, the integrity of the logical (which, from another point of view, can also claim a certain primacy).

Wonderment is not only the beginning, but also the end, of philosophy. For Balthasar, this claim makes sense only if logical necessity includes surprise, which in turn makes sense only if being, on which logical necessity is based, is a combination of necessity and surprise. Being must be intelligible, but without being banal; it must be gratuitous, but without being arbitrary. In short, it must be gift. And, if it is a gift, it must flow from a Giver who is endowed both with intelligence and freedom (the gift is not necessary, but chosen) and with the fullness of being (the gift is not some arbitrarily chosen object, but is nothing less than the very being of things). Wonderment is both *arche* and *telos* of philosophy because the being that it wonders over is gift, and being is gift because it flows from a divine Source who is at once Principal and Personal.[31]

Balthasar, like Prufer, uses the Thomistic "real distinction," enriched with phenomenology, to make the unity of Principle and Person in God plausible. As the passage from the third to the fourth difference makes clear, Balthasar, also like Prufer, interprets the "real distinction" as a distinction not only between *esse creatum* and *essentia creata* within each created *ens,* but also between both *esse creatum* and *essentia creata* in their interplay and God, which is why created *ens* is created in the first place.[32] Balthasar, once again like Prufer, stresses that the unity of created being is one cut through by a dyad of *esse* and essence;[33] it rests in itself only to the extent that it "floats" (*schwebt*) between "poles" of the dyad.[34] These poles support each other but do not ultimately originate each other. Rather, each of the " 'pole[s]' has to seek and find its 'salvation' in the other: Being comes to itself as subsistence only in the essence; essence comes to its actuality . . . only by participation in being."[35] A final parallel between Prufer and Balthasar: this structure of created reality points upward to a Source that enjoys not only the unity of essence and *esse,* but also the requisite freedom "that neither being (as nonsubsistent) nor the existent essence (insofar as it always already finds itself as the essence it is) could have."[36] It needs to be borne in mind that, for Balthasar, this upward pointing is just that: a *pointing.* By the very nature of the case, this "subsisting freedom of absolute being"[37] cannot be constructed "from below." This is how Balthasar puts it in *Epilog:*

> The real "identity" of God . . . lies, to speak in the language of Plato . . . *epekeina tou ontos,* above and beyond what we are still able to imagine as "being-ness." Only from this Above, which points to God's absolutely uncapturable freedom from all intra-worldly laws of being, can he sovereignly avail himself of the most comprehensive thing that we know, being — not in order to define himself ("I am being"), but to designate his ungraspably free turning to us ("I will be who I will be"), which contrasts with the idols, who are all "identities" constructed by human thought.[38]

Wonderment is not just the beginning of philosophy, but also the end. Balthasar does not deny, of course, that wonderment entails a question that can be answered: what is the origin of the being of the "whole"? Nevertheless, precisely because the answer to this question involves an Origin that is at once Person and Principle, the answer to it only deepens the original question, though without ever ceasing to be a real answer. The answer to the great philosophical question "Why is there something rather than nothing?" thus entails for Balthasar a kind of rationality that neither dissipates wonder nor undermines thought, but rather leads to an ever more thoughtful wonderment over the fact that being itself is a wondrous combination of necessity and freedom, intelligibility and surprise, form and event, and that it is because its Source, Principal and Personal as it is, wondrously combines these things as well. By the same token, Balthasar thinks that God's free self-revelation, which fully unveils what it means for him to be Principle and Person (this unveiling is what the doctrine of the Trinity is about), is not so much an answer to the philosophical question about the being of the "whole" as it is a (surprising) recapitulation of how all viable philosophical answers to this original question deepen it in the way I suggested just now that Balthasar thinks it does. Similarly, the revelation of God's personal freedom, while not in any way derivable from a philosophical consideration of created *ens,* does recapitulate what the philosophers glimpsed, or could have glimpsed, of created *ens* in relation to its Principle:

> This mystery of the self-outpouring light of being, which Plato and Plotinus glimpsed, is the only thing that explains the possibility of a world.... It does not become fully transparent, though, until absolute freedom (as God's intellectual and personal character) shines in from the biblical domain, though not as if the personal God encountered man as one delimited being does another (as one might think if one interpreted the Old Covenant without philosophy). Rather, the personal, free depth of self-donating absolute being is what first brings the mystery of creation, the "fourth difference" into the clear light of day. God is the Wholly Other only as the *Non-aliud,* the non-other.[39]

The "Spiritual Rereading" of Philosophy

I began with Leo Strauss's objection to the possibility of an honest synthesis between biblical faith and philosophy. I then tried to connect this objection to a seeming difficulty with the personal, free character of the God of the Bible, which on the surface can appear to have little to do with Universal Reason. Finally, I enlisted the help of two Christian masters of thought in order to dissipate the prima facie impression that the freedom of the God of the Bible is somehow subphilosophical. The revelation of God's freedom, which is not the arbitrariness of an individual subjectivity but rather coincides with a love that is personal but never merely individual, is not the negation, but rather is the superabundant fulfillment, of what philosophy glimpsed, or could have glimpsed, of the inmost nature of being in its flowing forth from its Principle. This fulfillment lies in a double recapitulation.

The first recapitulation is a rereading of nature in the light of nonsubsistent *esse.* This rereading opens up — or discovers — an *interior* with respect to nature's own *intimo,* out of which the light of God's creative freedom can shine in such a way as to deepen, rather than to undermine, the inner intelligibility of nature whose discovery, according to Strauss, is the starting point of philosophy. In more directly Balthasarian terms: nature is *Gestalt,* a coherent whole held together from within by an inexhaustible luminosity. The interplay of light and form within the *Gestalt* is at once its own immanent mystery and an intracreaturely image of the immanence and transcendence of God within the world. By the same token, *Gestalt* is the place where the recapitulation of nature in light of the being that is "in" and "above" it opens up to the second of the two recapitulations that I mentioned: the rereading of the *esse*-nature relation in light of the enfleshment of the Son of God.

This second recapitulation is an event analogous to the "spiritual reading" of the Old Testament in light of the New Testament: a shift that shows itself to be such "by preserving what" it shifts from ("The new is inscribed over the old; the old is legible beneath the new; palimpsest"[40]). This "spiritual reading" is, of course, liable to the same criticism that Jews will level against the christological reading of the Old Testament: "You are co-opting our texts and doing violence to them to boot." This, apparently, was the reaction of Porphyry on hearing Origen use Greek sources in his lectures about Christianity.[41] Although space does not permit it, I think it would be possible to show — for example, through a careful reading of Plato's *Phaedo*[42] — how Socrates images, but without yet "incarnating" in a Christian sense, the self-effacing power of the middle that holds together initial premise and conclusion in a unity of necessity and surprise. Socrates, on this interpretation, prefigures how Christ is the embodiment of the foundation of the stringency of argument (where the embodiment is actually intrinsic to the foundation), and never more so than in his obedience, which Balthasar interprets as the sheer exposition of the binding power of the "middle," the naked fullness of the logical "ought" in the blank of Holy Saturday.

But we can go even further. The inaugurator of the second recapitulation is Christ himself. The Son of God, receiving himself as man from the Virgin Mary in the primordial act of obedience, simultaneously does three things. First, he relives the philosophical ascent from nature through being to the personal principle of both — he is the primordial philosopher. Second, he embodies two times over the inner necessity-*cum*-surprise that gives the argumentative dimension of that ascent — indeed, all argument — its stringency: as personal divine principle of the gift of being and as virtual recapitulation of the being that is thus given. Third, he is for both these reasons the philosophical ascent in person.[43] The *Gestalt* of Christ, which indissolubly unites the personal principle of the gift of being, the gift itself, and the creaturely receiver of it (and ties together the four sides of the fourfold structure mentioned above), embodies both the foundation of philosophical

reason and the unsurpassable practice of it in the philosophical life par excellence — person and principle fusing so fully that we can say, *Ipse Christus philosophia.*

In this sense, Strauss is both right and wrong. He is right, though perhaps not for the reasons he thinks, in refusing a synthesis or harmonization
of faith and philosophy. These terms are in fact inadequate to capture the
nature of the relation between revelation and philosophical thinking. This
revelation involves something at once more intimate and more respectful
of philosophy's integrity than the words harmony and synthesis can convey
(at least if they are not explained properly): a recapitulation of philosophy in
light of Christ — a recapitulation whose best analogate is not the combining
of elements into a larger whole but rather a "spiritual rereading" of the sort
that Christians bring to the Old Testament when they read it in light of the
New Testament. Moreover, Strauss is also right that this spiritual rereading
involves a certain capitulation of philosophy to revelation: Christ is Lord,
and there is no other. Where Strauss seems to me to go wrong, however,
is in the reason that he gives, or seems to give, for the impossibility of any
synthesis between Christ and philosophy. As I read him, he takes obedient
love to be a foreign body that threatens the integrity of philosophy. Here,
too, Strauss is not completely wrong, for Christ, and the obedient love that
he embodies, does transcend philosophy: he is *superior* to its *summo.* But
that is what allows him to be *interior* to its *intimo.* Christ is not a foreign
body threatening philosophy's integrity from the outside; rather, he comes
to it from under (and over) its inside-outside divide, and so he obliges it
to relive even more deeply its own experience of the immanence and transcendence of the Principle (this experience is the essence of wonderment).
Conversely, this experience makes the autonomy of philosophy a relative
one lying beyond the antithesis of independence and dependence — a foreshadowing (we see in retrospect) of the unity of freedom and obedience
in Christ, which in turn expresses in time the unity of self-reception and
self-subsistence characterizing his eternal filial being in the Trinity.

Christ has a more than external or accidental pertinence to philosophy. Nevertheless, he does not achieve this pertinence by entering into
competition with philosophy, or becoming a premise or a conclusion of
philosophical argumentation, or offering some system for more or less auto-
matically generating philosophical conclusions. All of these methods come

too late, so to speak, because he already *is* philosophy. And there is more, for Christ is philosophy not only by supereminently containing it; rather, just as he both contains and depends on Mary, he extends this same mystery of containment-*cum*-dependence to his relation with philosophy. For him to be philosophy, then, means for him to contain and, in so doing, to receive himself from philosophy — as the Marian womb of the spiritual rereading of it that he himself inaugurates and is: *philosophari in Maria.* Strauss saw correctly that philosophy, like everything else, is called to surrender to Christ; what he did not see is that, at that very moment, Christ also surrenders to *it* in a different way as a condition of the possibility of his own incarnation (and of the spiritual rereading of philosophy in light of that incarnation).

The obedience of faith — acceptance of Christ's *Gestalt* in his humiliation — is a gift to philosophy from beyond its own resources, yet which enables it to attain a deeper rediscovery of its own integrity, which was always a paradoxical unity of self-possession in self-dispossession (*eros*) in the first place. The evidence of the Christ-form is hidden and it yields its "blessing" for thought only in the conclusion of a nocturnal struggle, but that is as it should be. For only thus can philosophy, like Jacob, emerge from the struggle transformed and precisely thereby restored even more deeply to its true self. Who can claim to limit a priori the fruitfulness of the old-new vision that results from this paradoxical experience of death and resurrection?

How Balthasar Keeps Changing My Mind

The foregoing is, of course, not a refutation of Strauss, but rather is the statement of an account of the faith-philosophy relation from the Christian and Balthasarian point of view that in my opinion responds to the sorts of concerns that Strauss had about the integrity of philosophy. For the upshot of the previous discussion is this: Balthasar, along with many Balthasarians, has helped me to see that philosophy's native recognition of its own relativity is the key to what might be called its "subordinate priority" (to borrow a term from David Crawford) even with respect to theology and is also the immanent principle that allows it to receive its proper starting point anew from revelation without being alienated from itself. In a word, Balthasar has taught me (sometimes through Jacob-like struggles) that the freedom of philosophy consists precisely in the captivity of its every thought to Christ. But how, exactly, has this lesson about Christian obedience as the recapitulation of philosophy changed my mind, and how does it keep on doing so?

Let me begin by noting that, for Ignatius of Loyola, who in some sense is the father of Balthasar's theology, Christian obedience is the preference of God's will to one's own. In this sense, it is the practice of what Ignatius calls "indifference," the subordination of one's own spontaneous preferences to God's preferences. Ignatian indifference has been much criticized as a kind of voluntaristically enforced suppression of desire. Of course, it is indisputable that it does include a certain distance from one's spontaneous desires. It is also indisputable that Ignatius, being a realistic observer of the human condition, fully expects this distancing to require of sinful humankind an ascetic struggle in which effortful willing necessarily plays a part. In reality, though, indifference is anything but a voluntaristic attack on desire; rather, it is the basic willingness to extend my desire to things whose desirability — whose status as a worthwhile good — God sees, but for whatever reason (good or bad) I may not immediately see. Indifference, as the readiness to desire, so to speak, from God's point of view is not at all the suppression of human desire, but rather is its assumption, at once transformative and fulfilling, into the desire with which God (in his sovereign condescension) ardently desires all the things that he has made.

We could put the same thing another way and say that indifference has to do with a thankful reception of *everything* as a gift, even of what I do not, or would not, immediately prefer. In number 233 of his *Spiritual Exercises,* for example, Ignatius implicitly situates indifference between gratefulness, on the one hand, and an ability to love God in all things, on the other: "The second [point] is to ask what I want: here it will be to ask for internal knowledge of so much good received so that, entirely grateful, I am able to love and serve his divine majesty in everything." Seen in this way, indifference is bound up with the acknowledgment that my whole existence, from top to bottom, is a gift flowing from a Source that is sheer paternal goodness unshadowed by disordered passion or arbitrariness. By the same token, indifference is the acceptance of the call to become what I am: a being whose subsistence is gratitude by virtue of its participation in the eternal Son, whose eternal being is to let himself be generated ("entirely grateful"). Christian obedience is not in the first instance a negative rejection, even though it may concretely demand sacrifices, but rather is first and foremost the supremely affirmative act of letting God give us the whole world in the light of Christ's sonship.

It is true, of course, that obedience, by rigorously making our every thought about the world captive to Christ, does create a certain distance between us and the world. What I have learned from Balthasar, and from many Balthasarians, however, is that precisely this distance turns out, in retrospect, to coincide with a deeper proximity to the world than is possible outside of the rigor of Christian obedience (at least that is my experience). And this proximity-in-distance includes (at least for me) the gift of a new experience of the starting point of philosophy. We have already seen that the core of obedience, Ignatian indifference, creates proximity-in-distance vis-à-vis the world by letting God assume our desire into his burning love for all things. My point here is that philosophy includes an analogous kind of indifference. Under the impulse of wonderment, in fact, philosophy revisits initial opinions or presuppositions, not primarily to prove them false (except insofar as they happen to be false), but rather in the first instance to test them against, and make them transparent to, the one and only absolute presupposition: all is gift.[44] In this sense, the rigor of obedience, far from leading away from philosophy, recapitulates awareness of the sheer gift-character of being (which, in my interpretation, is ultimately what awakens and sustains wonderment) and so retrieves the foundation of philosophical rationality in the first place.

As David C. Schindler has argued, Socrates embodied philosophy's relative ultimacy by stepping beyond discourse into something like a "martyrdom" that was not so much a single philosophical act as it was an incarnation of the foundation of all philosophical acts *tout court*. For Balthasar, Christian obedience retrieves this "Socratic moment" within the following of him whose forerunner Socrates was; it fuses the Christian philosopher's whole existence and thought into a unity by pouring them out into the crucible of a stable form or state of life whose content is the obedient following of the Lord.[45] Of course, Balthasar makes no secret of the fact that the demands of the state of life oblige the Christian philosopher to accept the painful truth that philosophy is not everything. What I have tried to show in this essay, though, is that Balthasar's vision of the *sequela Christi* has another implication as well: precisely by teaching Christian philosophers that philosophy is not everything, the state of life also teaches them that everything can none-theless become philosophy. How does the state of life do this? By catching the Christian philosopher's whole existence into a *Gestalt* that makes of it an incarnation of the principle of all philosophical reasoning — on the analogy of, and by way of participation in, the incarnation of the Logos. If Baltha-sar has changed my mind, it is mainly because he has taught me this lesson and has shown me that the all-encompassing form of a life held in obedi-ent readiness for God is a three-dimensional proof of the truth that gives the world its intelligbility: *Non coerceri maximo, contineri minimo, divinum est.*[46]

Notes

Chapter Two / Martin Bieler

1. Letter from July 8, 1975: "Sehr geehrter Herr Bieler, vielleicht kommen Sie einmal vorbei (im Juli noch) man redet besser über solche Dinge. Die *Möglichkeit* des Doppelten Ausgangs ist *für uns* notwendig. Aber *wir* als Christen dürfen eine *unbeschränkte* Hoffnung haben, dass alle, für die Gott gelitten hat, gerettet werden. Gott verliert seine Schlachten nicht. Ihr Problem ist tausendfach in der christl. Geschichte durchdacht worden, aber meist falsch. Lesen Sie die Kleine Theresia. Ich würde auch gern einmal kurz über Ihren Studienort reden. Herzliche Grüsse Ihr H. U. v. Balthasar."

2. *www.holocaust-history.org/works/stroop-report/htm/intro 001.htm.*

3. Bonaventure, *Collationes in Hexaemeron* 11.6.

4. Hans Urs von Balthasar, *Die Wahrheit ist symphonisch: Aspekte des christlichen Pluralismus* (Einsiedeln: Johannes Verlag, 1972), 59.

5. Hans Urs von Balthasar, *Pneuma und Institution* (Einsiedeln: Johannes Verlag, 1974), 444.

6. Hans Urs von Balthasar, *Theodramatik,* vol. 3, *Die Handlung* (Einsiedeln: Johannes Verlag, 1980), 461–62.

7. Hans Urs von Balthasar, *Mysterium Paschale,* in *Mysterium Salutis: Grundriss heilsgeschichtlicher Dogmatik,* vol. 3.2, *Das Christusereignis: Zweiter Halbband,* ed. Johannes Feiner and Magnus Löhrer (Einsiedeln: Benziger, 1969), 246–48. Note also a similar thought expressed by C. S. Lewis: "And Christ, because He was the only man who never yielded to temptation, is also the only man who knows to the full what temptation means — the only complete realist" (*Mere Christianity,* 21st ed. [Glasgow: Fount, 1985], 123).

8. See David Lauber, *Barth on the Descent into Hell: God, Atonement and the Christian Life* (Aldershot: Ashgate, 2004).

9. Balthasar, *Pneuma und Institution,* 408.

10. Among contemporary exegetes, Wilhelm Thüsing is the one who comes closest to Balthasar's method. See Wilhelm Thüsing, *Die neutestamentlichen Theologien und Jesus Christus: Grundlegung einer Theologie des Neuen Testaments,* 2nd ed., 3 vols. (Münster: Aschendorff, 1996–1999).

11. Balthasar told me that he was particularly fond of the writings of Martin Hengel ("Hengel has so much common sense"), whom he considered the

best contemporary biblical scholar. Balthasar even asked him to write a book on Christ's atoning death for the Johannes Verlag, but Hengel declined because he felt committed to the J. C. B. Mohr publishing house.

12. See Gilbert Narcisse, *Les raisons de Dieu: Argument de convenance et esthétique théologique selon saint Thomas d'Aquin et Hans Urs von Balthasar* (Fribourg: Editions universitaires, 1997).

13. Bonaventure, *Collationes in Hexaemeron* 9.2.

14. See Martin Bieler, "The Theological Importance of a Philosophy of Being," in *Reason and the Reasons of Faith,* ed. Paul J. Griffith and Reinhard Hütter (New York: T & T Clark International, 2005), 295–326.

15. See Martin Bieler, "Braucht es ein Amt in der Kirche? Erwägungen zur Neufassung der Kirchenordnung der Evangelisch-reformierten Landeskirche des Kantons Zürich im ökumenischen Kontext," *Rivista Teologica di Lugano* 3 (2003): 491–507.

16. I am grateful to Adrian Walker for his helpful comments and his assistance in matters of grammar and style.

Chapter Four / Raymond Gawronski, SJ

1. In these concerns, the theology of Karl Rahner poses real challenges. Friedrich Heer observes, "The development of dogma in the fourth century, which set the direction (as in the 'Jewish problem') for the next fifteen hundred years: the problems arising from that have still not been fully solved by the Roman Catholic Church. K. Rahner [in *Schriften zur Theologie IV*] says that the real problem has been deliberately passed over. In all questions of dogma the pressure of the superstitious masses played an important role. Rahner pleads with modern theologians to work against this 'popular' form of piety, which dominated church councils and controversies on dogma in the fourth and nineteenth centuries. Hans Küng calls for a historical approach, which considers church dogma itself as a historical phenomenon" (*God's First Love: Christians and Jews over Two Thousand Years,* trans. Geoffrey Skelton [New York: Weybright & Talley, 1970], 455–56, note to page 34, chapter 5).

2. Balthasar's conversion story, in a forest outside Basel, bears a strikingly similar feel to that of Luther, although, significantly, Balthasar knew no thunderstorm but rather a strong spiritual movement.

3. Anyone familiar with the origins of the Orthodox Church in America or of the Polish National Catholic Church in America will understand some of this long-standing problem of failure in cross-cultural understanding.

4. My master's thesis in philosophy was a first attempt to deal with the question of form, and of particular being: "The Role of Sensible Beings in Knowledge of the Real for Jacques Maritain" (master's thesis, Gonzaga University, 1983).

5. Norman Davies writes, "Americans may or may not be flattered to learn that this po-faced purveyor of mystical metaphysics [Hegel] awarded America 'the final embodiment of the Absolute Idea, beyond which no further development would be possible' " (*Europe: A History* [New York: HarperPerennial, 1996], 790). This may help explain the deep-seated Germanophile traditions in American academia. This may also help explain why American Catholic theology has so favored Continental theologies steeped in German philosophy in general.

6. The phrase "Form is emptiness, emptiness is form" from the *Mahaprajna-paramita Hridaya,* the "Heart Sutra," daily chanted in Zen life, supplied me with the question that I brought to Balthasar, who, in a response to a letter, wrote to me, "The question is: does selflessness mean 'emptiness' [Zen] or [trinitarian] love?"

7. Hans Urs von Balthasar, *Epilog* (Einsiedeln: Johannes Verlag, 1987), 8 (translation mine).

8. Hans Urs von Balthasar, *The Glory of the Lord: A Theological Aesthetics,* vol. 1, *Seeing the Form,* trans. Erasmo Leiva-Merikakis (San Francisco, Ignatius Press, 1982), 216.

Chapter Five / Michael Hanby

1. I gather that there are numerous causes for this both internal and external to theology, though the distinction is somewhat artificial inasmuch as external factors affect the internal shape of modern theology and the marginal place that it has come to occupy within modern life. Nevertheless, some of the difficulty, particularly within Protestant theology, can be attributed to the sense that the more "particularist" categories of Christology and ecclesiology are to be favored over that of creation. I do not wish to suggest, however, that these can be separated in the end. Christologies and ecclesiologies that fail to do justice to the doctrine of creation in all its depth are ultimately deficient precisely as christological and ecclesiological.

2. That is to say that the fundamental problem with "materialism" is not its one-sided emphasis on matter but rather the conception of matter that it privileges.

3. I say a "debased" form of *techne* because traditionally *techne* was not concerned with the endless manipulation of an inherently plastic nature but rather was ordered toward the goods of a craft, which implies a teleological conception of nature.

4. Joseph Cardinal Ratzinger, *Introduction to Christianity* (San Francisco: Ignatius Press, 1990), 58.

5. Hans Urs von Balthasar, *The Glory of the Lord: A Theological Aesthetics,* vol. 1, *Seeing the Form,* trans. Erasmo Leiva-Merikakis (San Francisco: Ignatius Press, 1982), 18. On the aesthetics as a deliberate protest against theological rationalism, regarded as a species of rationalism more generally, see Hans Urs von Balthasar, *Theo-Drama: Theological Dramatic Theory,* vol. 1, *Prolegomena,* trans. Graham Harrison (San Francisco: Ignatius Press, 1988), 16.

6. Balthasar, *Seeing the Form*, 25. This is the second of Balthasar's fundamental aesthetic principles, and one should take "antecedent" in both a historical and an ontological sense. One should therefore read the priority of form not as the absolute priority of the vertical over the horizontal, which would obviate the entire "dramatic" horizon of Balthasar's thought, but rather as a relative priority that thus encompasses the horizontal, as we see in his christological reconciliation of *mythos* and *logos* (Balthasar, *Seeing the Form*, 141–55). Transposed into the biological realm, Balthasar's understanding holds fascinating possibilities for overcoming the impasse between a so-called typological conception of species favored by premodern biology and the purely historical, post-Darwinian conception.

7. Ibid., 151.

8. "Polarity means that the poles, even as they are in tension, exist strictly through each other" (Hans Urs von Balthasar, *Theo-Logic: Theological Logical Theory*, vol. 1, *The Truth of the World*, trans. Adrian J. Walker [San Francisco: Ignatius Press, 2000], 105).

9. This is partly what Balthasar means by the "freedom" of the object. It is the freedom of the object to communicate its interior depths exteriorly in phenomenal appearance that is by no means identical to those depths. See Balthasar, *The Truth of the World*, 84.

10. Balthasar, *Seeing the Form*, 26.

11. Balthasar, *The Truth of the World*, 81.

12. Balthasar, *Seeing the Form*, 152–53.

13. Instructive here is Balthasar's use of Mozart's *The Magic Flute* to demonstrate how a proper understanding of creative freedom and beauty renders the theodical question of "best possible worlds" nonsensical. See Hans Urs von Balthasar, *Theo-Drama: Theological Dramatic Theory*, vol. 2, *The Dramatis Personae: Man in God*, trans. Graham Harrison (San Francisco: Ignatius Press, 1992), 269 n. 40.

14. "We have learned that truth involves freedom, in that it transcends the predetermined outlines of nature" (Balthasar, *The Truth of the World*, 131).

15. Balthasar, *Seeing the Form*, 18. "If *verum* lacks that splendor which for Thomas is the distinctive mark of the beautiful, then the knowledge of truth remains both pragmatic and formalistic. The only concern of such knowledge will then merely be the verification of correct facts and laws, whether the latter are laws of being or laws of thoughts, categories and ideas. But if the *bonum* lacks that *voluptas* which for Augustine is the mark of its beauty, the relationship to the good remains both utilitarian and hedonistic: in this case the good will involve merely the satisfaction of a need by means of some value or object" (ibid., 152).

16. Balthasar continues, "It then becomes manifest that what I have known — really, not just seemingly known — was a mystery. Before I knew it, I was unaware of this mystery. Now that I have come to know it, my knowledge is richer because it has gained a [permanent] mystery" (*The Truth of the World*, 131–32).

17. I regard this as a category mistake because the demand for theology to supply a mechanism for the being of the world violates the metaphysics proper to *creation ex nihilo,* which leads Aquinas to define creation simply as a nonreciprocal relation. In short, the absence of such a mechanism means that there can be no explanation conforming to the request for one. I have written about this elsewhere, but much of what I am saying at this point in the essay is a corrective addition to those earlier efforts.

18. Ratzinger, *Introduction to Christianity,* 77.

19. Han Urs von Balthasar, *The Glory of the Lord: A Theological Aesthetics,* vol. 5, *The Realm of Metaphysics in the Modern Age,* trans. Oliver Davies et al. (San Francisco: Ignatius Press, 1991), 619. All of the claims of this section I take to be entailed in Balthasar's treatment of the fourfold distinction.

20. "Modern science, which strives to investigate the order of the world more and more deeply, has its ready-made metaphysics in Aquinas's doctrine of order and relation, presupposing of course, that science does not absolutise, in essentialist fashion, the laws it discovers but lets them rest on a profound creaturely proportion between existence and essence and thus be in suspension in relation to the absolute freedom of God" (Han Urs von Balthasar, *The Glory of the Lord: A Theological Aesthetics,* vol. 4, *The Realm of Metaphysics in Antiquity,* trans. Brian McNeil et al. [San Francisco: Ignatius Press, 1989], 411).

21. Balthasar, *The Dramatis Personae: Man in God,* 262.

22. The list of predicates is from Bonaventure, *Itinerarium* 5.6, though it could be found in any number of sources.

23. Balthasar, *Prolegomena,* 548.

24. Ibid.

25. Ibid., 546.

26. Balthasar, *The Realm of Metaphysics in Antiquity,* 393–412.

27. Balthasar, *Prolegomena,* 591.

28. Ibid., 645.

29. Hans Urs von Balthasar, *Love Alone Is Credible,* trans. D. C. Schindler (San Francisco: Ignatius Press, 2004), 143.

30. This, of course, begs the question of why he refers to "philosophy" here rather than theology or what Balthasar means by philosophy as distinct from theology. This is beyond our scope here. Let it suffice to say first that he is eager to preserve the distinction and the integrity of each of its poles, and second that the inter-Trinitarian difference is the ontological basis for the self-revelation of created being, which thus provokes a genuinely philosophical *eros,* which presses on toward its own fulfillment that can only be supplied from beyond its own resources in the fulfillment of what is other than created being. Philosophy thus finds its own integrity in its relation to theology in analogous fashion to the way creation finds its own integrity in relation to God.

31. Balthasar, *The Dramatis Personae: Man in God*, 258.

32. Ibid., 261.

33. Ibid., 258.

34. Ibid., 259.

35. Ibid., 261.

36. Ibid., 266.

37. Hans Urs von Balthasar, *Mysterium Paschale: The Mystery of Easter*, trans. Aidan Nichols (San Francisco: Ignatius Press, 2000), 13.

38. By "constitute," obviously, I am not suggesting the God is somehow the being of the world; instead, I refer to the sense in which Christ's dereliction from the Father constitutes for Balthasar the hell of godlessness, but this dereliction is itself made possible for Balthasar only by the positive difference inherent in God as love. See Balthasar, *Mysterium Paschale*, 168.

39. I mean this in the quite literal sense that I am not yet settled on how far I can follow him here.

40. Balthasar, *Seeing the Form*, 18.

41. Balthasar, *The Dramatis Personae: Man in God*, 260.

Chapter Six / Nicholas J. Healy

1. David L. Schindler, "Sanctity and the Intellectual Life," *Communio* 20, no. 4 (1993): 653.

2. Hans Urs von Balthasar, *The Glory of the Lord: A Theological Aesthetics*, vol. 1, *Seeing the Form*, trans. Erasmo Leiva-Merikakis (San Francisco: Ignatius Press, 1982), 158.

3. Hans Urs von Balthasar, *My Work: In Retrospect*, trans. Brian McNeil (San Francisco: Ignatius Press, 1993), 108.

4. Charles Péguy, *Le mystère de la charité de Jeanne d'Arc*, in *Œuvres poétiques complètes* (Paris: Gallimard, 1975), 392.

5. For an outstanding reflection on the relation between the Eucharist and the theologian's task of interpreting and handing on the tradition, see Adrian Walker, "Love Alone: Hans Urs von Balthasar as a Master of Theological Renewal," *Communio* 32, no. 3 (2005): 517–40.

6. Pope Benedict XVI, "I Wished to Show the Humanity of Faith," address to a meeting organized by the Pontifical Council "Cor Unum," January 23, 2006 (*http://zenit.org/article-15085?l=english*).

7. Ibid.

8. Hans Urs von Balthasar, *The Glory of the Lord: A Theological Aesthetics*, vol. 5, *The Realm of Metaphysics in the Modern Age*, trans. Oliver Davies et al. (San Francisco: Ignatius Press, 1991), 643.

9. Ibid., 644.

10. Hans Urs von Balthasar, *Theo-Logic: Theological Logical Theory,* vol. 2, *The Truth of God,* trans. Adrian J. Walker (San Francisco: Ignatius Press, 2000), 61.

11. Thomas Aquinas, *De potentia Dei,* q. 1, a. 1.

12. Thomas Aquinas, *In Dionysii de divinis nominibus,* c. 4, lect. 9.

13. Hans Urs von Balthasar, "Erich Przywara," in *Tendenzen der Theologie im 20. Jahrhundert: Eine Geschichte in Porträts,* ed. Hans Jürgen Schultz (Stuttgart: Kreuz-Verlag, 1966), 355.

14. Thomas Aquinas, *Summa theologiae,* Ia, q. 4, a. 3.

15. Thomas Aquinas, *In sententiae,* I, *Prooemium.*

16. Han Urs von Balthasar, *The Glory of the Lord: A Theological Aesthetics,* vol. 4, *The Realm of Metaphysics in Antiquity,* trans. Brian McNeil et al. (San Francisco: Ignatius Press, 1989), 20.

17. Ibid., 17.

18. Balthasar, *The Realm of Metaphysics in the Modern Age,* 648–49.

19. Balthasar, *My Work,* 77.

20. Ibid., 83.

21. Cited in Han Urs von Balthasar, *The Glory of the Lord: A Theological Aesthetics,* vol. 3, *Studies in Theological Styles: Lay Styles,* trans. Andrew Louth et al. (San Francisco: Ignatius Press, 1986), 407.

22. Ibid.

23. Charles Péguy, *Œuvres en prose 1898–1908* (Paris: Gallimard, 1959), 192–93 (cited in Balthasar, *Studies in Theological Styles: Lay Styles,* 445).

24. Charles Péguy, *Œuvres en prose 1909–1914* (Paris: Gallimard, 1957), 495 (cited in Balthasar, *Studies in Theological Styles: Lay Styles,* 458).

25. Charles Péguy, *The Portal of the Mystery of Hope,* trans. David Louis Schindler (Grand Rapids: Eerdmans, 1996), 76.

26. Ibid., 81.

27. Ibid., 72–73.

28. Péguy, *Œuvres en prose 1909–1914,* 1400 (cited in Balthasar, *Studies in Theological Styles: Lay Styles,* 464).

29. Péguy, *The Portal of the Mystery of Hope,* 92–93.

30. Ibid., 3.

31. Ibid., 136–37.

32. Balthasar, *Studies in Theological Styles: Lay Styles,* 494.

33. Ibid., 506.

34. Balthasar discusses von Speyr's seminal account of "the mystery of our being represented on the Cross by the Son, and how, in the future, the Father will be able to contemplate and evaluate the world solely through the Son" (Hans Urs von Balthasar, *First Glance at Adrienne von Speyr,* trans. Antje Lawry and Sergia Englund [San Francisco: Ignatius Press, 1981], 61).

35. Hans Urs von Balthasar, *Theo-Drama: Theological Dramatic Theory,* vol. 4, *The Action,* trans. Graham Harrison (San Francisco, Ignatius Press, 1994), 391–92.

36. St. Ephrem, *Sermo IV in Hebdomadam Sanctam.*

37. Henri de Lubac, *The Splendor of the Church,* trans. Michael Mason (San Francisco: Ignatius Press, 1999), 133.

38. Origen, *Homilies on Leviticus* 7.5 (cited in Hans Urs von Balthasar, *Theo-Drama: Theological Dramatic Theory,* vol. 5, *The Last Act,* trans. Graham Harrison [San Francisco, Ignatius Press, 1998], 382–83).

39. Origen, *Homilies on Leviticus* 7.2.

40. Hans Urs von Balthasar, "*Communio:* A Program," *Communio* 33, no. 1 (2006): 167.

41. Hans Urs von Balthasar, *Unless You Become Like This Child,* trans. Erasmo Leiva-Merikakis (San Francisco: Ignatius Press, 1991), 64.

Chapter Seven / Rodney A. Howsare

1. Flannery O'Connor, "The Violent Bear It Away," in *Collected Works* (New York: Library of America, 1988), 401.

2. Wendell Berry, *Life Is a Miracle: An Essay against Modern Superstition* (Washington, DC: Counterpoint Press, 2000). A good Enlightenment thinker, Wilson tries to offer an account of all reality through the lens of empirical science. As such, he makes an effort to reconcile C. P. Snow's two cultures of the humanities and the sciences without realizing that his reconciliation is actually already a reduction of the humanities to the sciences. As Berry puts it, "Like a naïve politician, Mr. Wilson thinks that he has found a way to reconcile two sides without realizing that his way is one of the sides" (*Life Is a Miracle,* 99).

3. O'Connor, "The Violent Bear It Away," 343.

4. Ibid., 341–42.

5. Rowan Williams, *Grace and Necessity: Reflections on Art and Love* (Harrisburg, PA: Morehouse, 2005).

6. Michael Polanyi, *Personal Knowledge: Towards a Post-Critical Philosophy* (Chicago: University of Chicago Press, 1962), 354.

7. This is the only explanation that I can see for Rahner's aversion for any notion of vicarious substitution; he can only see such substitution as being heteronomous to the subject. If, on the other hand, there are already mysterious ways in which we are all related in our common belonging in being, then there is no other (much less Christ!) who is simply external to me.

8. Hans Urs von Balthasar, *Theo-Logic: Theological Logical Theory,* vol. 1, *The Truth of the World,* trans. Adrian J. Walker (San Francisco: Ignatius Press, 2000), 29.

9. If we look, for instance, at the area of soteriology, it is not as if the church had sufficiently worked through the sorts of issues raised by Augustine in his anti-Pelagian writings. There was still a sense that even if the church was uncomfortable

with Augustine's double predestination, it had not yet come up with an answer to it that was not guilty of some variety of at least semi-Pelagianism.

Chapter Eight / Francesca Murphy

1. Hans Urs von Balthasar, *Theo-Logic: Theological Logical Theory*, vol. 1, *The Truth of the World*, trans. Adrian J. Walker (San Francisco: Ignatius Press, 2000), 42.

2. Ibid., 77–78, 119–20.

3. Joseph Cardinal Ratzinger, "Wounded by the Arrow of Beauty: The Cross and the New 'Aesthetics' of Faith," in *On the Way to Jesus Christ*, trans. Michael J. Miller (San Francisco: Ignatius Press, 2005), 36–37.

4. Balthasar, *The Truth of the World*, 272.

5. Hans Urs von Balthasar, "Theology and Sanctity," in *Word and Redemption*, trans. A. V. Littledale and Alexander Dru (New York: Herder & Herder, 1965), 49–86.

Chapter Nine / Danielle Nussberger

1. For Balthasar's discussion of the nonantagonistic relationship between the physical and spiritual senses, see *The Glory of the Lord: A Theological Aesthetics*, vol. 1, *Seeing the Form*, trans. Erasmo Leiva-Merikakis (San Francisco: Ignatius Press, 1982), 365–425. See specifically pp. 406–7, where he alludes to how the body and soul are never separated, how the incarnation brings God into the sphere of the senses, and how one goes through the process of mystical kenosis where the senses are emptied and filled spiritually by God.

2. See Hans Urs von Balthasar, *Prayer*, trans. Graham Harrison (San Francisco: Ignatius Press, 1986), 108–26. This earlier work by Balthasar presents the same material as the first volume of *The Glory of the Lord*, but in a much simpler fashion.

3. Balthasar, *Seeing the Form*.

4. Ibid., 10–130.

5. See ibid., specifically pp. 131–425 for the subjective evidence, and pp. 429–683 for the objective evidence. Also consult, in its entirety, Hans Urs von Balthasar, *Prayer*, trans. Graham Harrison (San Francisco: Ignatius Press, 1986).

6. Balthasar, *Seeing the Form*, 435.

7. Hans Urs von Balthasar, *The Glory of the Lord: A Theological Aesthetics*, vol. 7, *Theology: The New Covenant*, trans. Brian McNeil (San Francisco: Ignatius Press, 1989), 287.

8. Hans Urs von Balthasar, *The Glory of the Lord: A Theological Aesthetics*, vol. 5, *The Realm of Metaphysics in the Modern Age*, trans. Oliver Davies et al. (San Francisco: Ignatius Press, 1991), 48–140.

9. Balthasar remains in dialogue with both ancient and modern philosophical permutations throughout volumes 4 and 5 of *The Glory of the Lord*. See Hans Urs von Balthasar, *The Glory of the Lord: A Theological Aesthetics*, vol. 4, *The Realm of*

Metaphysics in Antiquity, trans. Brian McNeil et al. (San Francisco: Ignatius Press, 1989). The precise wording of the creaturely posture toward the Absolute as a "non-reciprocal dependence relation" is found in Sara Grant's lectures on her encounter with the Hindu theologian Sankara: *Toward an Alternative Theology: Confessions of a Non-Dualist Christian* (Notre Dame, IN: University of Notre Dame Press, 2002), 40.

10. Balthasar, *The Realm of Metaphysics in the Modern Age,* 572–90.

11. See David Tracy's introduction to Jean-Luc Marion's *God without Being: Hors-Texte,* trans. Thomas A. Carlson (Chicago: University of Chicago Press, 1991), xii.

12. Marion, *God without Being,* 75–78.

13. Ibid., 25–52.

14. Ibid., 22–23.

15. These three saintly qualities are the touchstone of Balthasar's christological hermeneutic in *Theology: The New Covenant,* 217.

16. Ibid., 208–43.

17. Ibid., 208–9.

18. Ibid., 257–58.

19. Hans Urs von Balthasar, *Theo-Drama: Theological Dramatic Theory,* vol. 2, *The Dramatis Personae: Man in God,* trans. Graham Harrison (San Francisco: Ignatius Press, 1990), 14.

20. Hans Urs von Balthasar, *Theo-Drama: Theological Dramatic Theory,* vol. 3, *The Dramatis Personae: Persons in Christ,* trans. Graham Harrison (San Francisco: Ignatius Press, 1992), 270.

21. Han Urs von Balthasar, *Truth Is Symphonic: Aspects of Christian Pluralism,* trans. Graham Harrison (San Francisco: Ignatius Press, 1987).

22. Hans Urs von Balthasar, *Two Sisters in the Spirit: Thérèse of Lisieux and Elizabeth of the Trinity,* trans. Donald Nichols, Anne Elizabeth Englund, and Dennis Martin (San Francisco: Ignatius Press, 1992).

23. Ibid., 81–96, 385–419.

24. Hans Urs von Balthasar, *The Glory of the Lord: A Theological Aesthetics,* vol. 2, *Studies in Theological Style: Clerical Styles,* trans. Andrew Louth, Francis McDonagh, and Brian McNeil (San Francisco: Ignatius Press, 1984), 144–210, 260–362. See also Hans Urs von Balthasar, *The Glory of the Lord: A Theological Aesthetics,* vol. 3, *Studies in Theological Style: Lay Styles,* trans. Andrew Louth et al. (San Francisco: Ignatius Press, 1989), 105–71, 353–99, 400–517.

25. Balthasar, *Two Sisters in the Spirit,* 420.

26. Ibid., 9–12.

27. Ibid., 9.

28. Hans Urs von Balthasar, "Liberation Theology in the Light of Salvation History," trans. Erasmo Leiva, in *Liberation Theology in Latin America,* ed. James V. Schall (San Francisco: Ignatius Press, 1982), 131–46.

29. Balthasar, *The Dramatis Personae: Man in God,* 14.

30. See Gustavo Gutiérrez, *We Drink from Our Own Wells: The Spiritual Journey of a People,* trans, Matthew J. O'Connell (Maryknoll, NY: Orbis Books, 1984); Juan Luis Segundo, *The Christ of the Ignatian Exercises,* trans. John Drury (Maryknoll, NY: Orbis Books, 1987); Jon Sobrino, *Spirituality of Liberation: Toward Political Holiness,* trans. Robert R. Barr (Maryknoll, NY: Orbis Books, 1988).

Chapter Eleven / Russell Reno

1. Alyssa Lyra Pitstick and Edward T. Oakes, "Balthasar, Hell, and Heresy: An Exchange," *First Things* 168 (December 2006): 25–32.

2. Hans Urs von Balthasar, *Explorations in Theology,* vol. 1, *The Word Made Flesh,* trans. A. V. Littledale and Alexander Dru (San Francisco: Ignatius Press, 1989), 152.

3. Hans Urs von Balthasar. *Test Everything: Hold Fast to What Is Good,* trans. Maria Shrady (San Francisco: Ignatius Press, 1989), 52.

4. Quotations from Joseph Wilhelm and Thomas Scannell, *A Manual of Catholic Theology: Based on Scheeben's Dogmatik,* vol. 1 (London: Kegan Paul, 1890), 59.

5. Hans Urs von Balthasar, *Mysterium Paschale: The Mystery of Easter,* trans. Aidan Nichols (San Francisco: Ignatius Press, 2000), 37.

6. Ibid., 36.

Chapter Twelve / Tracey Rowland

1. Alasdair MacIntyre, "Aquinas's Critique of Education," in *Philosophers on Education: New Historical Perspectives,* ed. Amélie Oskenberg Rorty (London: Routledge, 1998), 96.

2. See Aidan Nichols, *The Word Has Been Abroad: A Guide through Balthasar's Aesthetics* (Edinburgh: T & T Clark, 1998); *No Bloodless Myth: A Guide through Balthasar's Dramatics* (Edinburgh: T & T Clark, 2000); *Say It Is Pentecost: A Guide through Balthasar's Logic* (Edinburgh: T & T Clark, 2001); *Scattering the Seed: A Guide through Balthasar's Early Writings on Philosophy and the Arts* (Washington, DC: Catholic University of America Press, 2006).

3. Aidan Nichols chose this phrase as the title for the second of his books introducing the thought of Balthasar. It comes from a line in a poem by Geoffrey Hill.

4. John Milbank, *The Suspended Middle: Henri de Lubac and the Debate Concerning the Supernatural* (Grand Rapids: Eerdmans: 2005), 15.

5. Aidan Nichols, *Christendom Awake: On Re-energising the Church in Culture* (London: T & T Clark, 1999), 59.

6. E. Michael Jones, *Living Machines: Bauhaus Architecture as Sexual Ideology* (San Francisco: Ignatius Press, 1995), 42.

7. Paul VI, general audience address, November 26, 1969 (published in *L'Osservatore Romano*, December 4, 1969). Nothing in this paragraph is intended to convey the impression that I am opposed to organic liturgical developments. I fully endorse the principles contained in Joseph Cardinal Ratzinger, *The Spirit of the Liturgy*, trans. John Saward (San Francisco: Ignatius Press, 2000); *A New Song for the Lord: Faith in Christ and Liturgy Today*, trans. Martha M. Matesich (New York: Crossroad, 1996). I make reference to this particular speech of Paul VI because it is an excellent illustration of the way in which leaders of the conciliar generation made decisions for pastoral reasons without reference to the many complex issues that are now being considered under the umbrella of the theology of culture.

8. On this topic, see Aidan Nichols, "A Coda on Thomas," in *Scattering the Seed*, 250–52.

9. Marc Ouellet, "Hans Urs von Balthasar: Witness to the Integration of Faith and Culture," *Communio* 18, no. 1 (1991): 118, 122.

10. For Ratzinger's full frontal attack on Kantian "pure reason," see his address to the bishops of Mexico at Gaudalajara in 1996, published as "The Current Situation of Faith and Theology," *L'Osservatore Romano* no. 45–46 (November 1996): 7.

11. Peter Henrici, "Modernity and Christianity," *Communio* 17, no. 2 (1990): 140–51.

12. I am indebted to Brett Doyle for this insight about the continuance of preconciliar moralism in the postconciliar proportionalist and consequentialist systems.

13. I am indebted to Russell Hittinger for drawing my attention to this dimension of Jansenist history.

14. Quoted in Hans Urs von Balthasar, *Bernanos: An Ecclesial Existence*, trans. Erasmo Leiva-Merikakis (San Francisco: Ignatius Press, 1996), 298–99.

15. Ibid.

16. Hans Urs von Balthasar, *Love Alone Is Credible* (San Francisco: Ignatius Press, 2005), 114.

17. Quoted in Hans Urs von Balthasar, "The Fathers, the Scholastics, and Ourselves," *Communio* 24, no. 2 (1997): 347–96.

18. Han Urs von Balthasar, "On the Tasks of Catholic Philosophy in Our Time," *Communio* 20, no. 1 (1993): 155–56.

19. Jean Daniélou, *The Lord of History: Reflections on the Inner Meaning of History* (London: Longmans, 1958), 57.

20. Hans Urs von Balthasar, *A Theology of History* (San Francisco: Ignatius Press, 1994), 125.

21. See, for example, Robert P. Kraynak, *Christian Faith and Modern Democracy: God and Politics in a Fallen World* (Notre Dame, IN: University of Notre Dame Press, 2001).

22. Balthasar, *Bernanos: An Ecclesial Existence*, 32.

23. Joseph Cardinal Ratzinger, *Principles of Catholic Theology* (San Francisco: Ignatius Press, 1987), 57.

Chapter Fourteen / David L. Schindler

1. Though I should say that I hesitated for a long while. I had little familiarity with the work of Balthasar at the time, and I had heard almost nothing of Joseph Ratzinger, though of course I was familiar with de Lubac. My hesitation had to do with whether Balthasar, and thus whether the journal being founded, would engage the problems of the culture sufficiently in their ontological roots! What follows, of course, makes clear why this hesitation was ill informed. Fortunately, Fr. Fessio was insistent that I make a decision and get on with the work.

2. The conference papers were published as *Catholicism and Secularization in America: Essays on Nature, Grace, and Culture,* ed. David L. Schindler (Huntington, IN: Our Sunday Visitor; Notre Dame, IN: Communio Books, 1990).

3. I have always wished I had had the presence of mind at the moment to tell him that his old ideas would do just fine.

4. My recollection is that the book was *Epilog*, the conclusion to his great trilogy. On another occasion, during the afternoon break at a one-day conference on his thought being held prior to a *Communio* meeting, Balthasar came into the coffee shop of the hotel where we were all staying and sat down. We asked him how the conference was going. He replied, in his humility, that the papers were going on and on about his thought, and that it was "langweilig" (boring).

5. After our family moved to the West Coast, and during my high school years, my father started Nelco Corporation, an electrical equipment manufacturing company, and later started Baden Sports, a manufacturer of athletic balls. When I once asked him why he chose manufacturing companies, he replied that only if he were able to control what went into a product from the beginning could he stand completely behind the quality of the product when marketed. He insisted that the phrase "Remember, quality is important" appear on every piece of paper with the Baden letterhead. (The phrase was replaced within months after his death.) When I asked my father why he did not use his own name when naming the companies, he said that they were not about him but rather about making an objective contribution to society.

6. The two-volume biography by Meriol Trevor, *The Pillar of the Cloud* (New York: Doubleday, 1962) and *Light in Winter* (New York: Doubleday, 1963), was especially helpful in guiding me in the reading of Newman.

7. It was just this openness to being in its wholeness, grounded above all in Aquinas's distinction between *esse* and *essentia,* that indicated for Gilson the singular greatness of Aquinas's achievement (see the third of the three points on Gilson in the present discussion in the main text).

8. For a discussion of how this "Gilsonian" understanding of Thomism was modified and deepened by Balthasar and the philosopher Ferdinand Ulrich, see section VI in the main text.

9. Gilson's notion of Christian philosophy is clearly affirmed in John Paul II's encyclical *Fides et Ratio* (see nos. 74, 76).

10. Leo Strauss, who was listed in the catalog at the time I applied, and with whom I was interested in studying, unfortunately had departed for St. John's in Annapolis by the time I began my studies the following September, though I was able to take classes from two of his disciples, Harry Neuman and Harry Jaffa. Also during this time, I read the major works of political philosopher Eric Voegelin (e.g., *Order and History*). All of this helped me to deepen an understanding of the characteristic differences between ancient (classical Greek) and modern culture, especially in terms of social-political order.

11. That is, the substantial identity granted to each creature in the act of creation was the necessarily presupposed term (the "what") *of* the constitutive relation to God established in and by that act.

12. Against the background of issues arising, for example, in connection with the historical-critical method, hermeneutics, the "quest for the historical Jesus," the nature of reason and rationality as conceived in the modern (Catholic) academy, and so on. The thesis was entitled, not entirely unpretentiously, "Knowing as Synthesis: A Metaphysical Prolegomenon to a Critical Christian Philosophy."

13. Most important here, probably, were the writings of philosopher-physical chemist Michael Polanyi and my introduction, through Cobb, to the person and work of Hans Jonas—for example, *The Phenomenon of Life*.

14. David Bohm, "The Implicate Order," in *Mind in Nature: Essays on the Interface of Science and Philosophy,* ed. John B. Cobb and David Ray Griffin (Washington, DC: University Press of America, 1978), 37–42.

15. The conference, "Beyond Mechanism: The Universe in Recent Physics and Catholic Thought," took place March 29–31, 1984, and the proceedings were published under the same name (Lanham, MD: University Press of America, 1986).

16. Perhaps chief among these problems is an inadequate sense of the analogy of being, which would, for example, afford a more satisfactory view of finite entities in their singular integrity. See David L. Schindler, *Heart of the World, Center of the Church: Communio Ecclesiology, Liberalism, and Liberation* (Grand Rapids: Eerdmans; Edinburgh: T & T Clark, 1996), 173–75, n. 51.

17. Based on the Thomistic metaphysics of *esse* and the distinction between *esse* and *ens.* Interestingly, I suggested in a letter to Bohm during this time that it seemed

to me that the argument that he was making could be summed up as an effort to interpret the basic order and activity in the (physical) universe in terms of love. He replied (in essence), "Yes, of course, but I can't use such language with physicists." And some years later, in a conversation that we had at a meeting in Zurich, he said that he had decided to replace the term "implicate order" with the term "generative order," but I am unaware whether or where this change was made in print. I should say about Bohm that he was a man of profound humility and compassion and was in fact quite shy, though his being and manner exuded a genius and passion for inquiry after the truth in all of its mystery that were the equal of any person I had ever met.

18. I believe that I also had read some of de Lubac long before this — for example, his writings on nature and the supernatural, on Pierre Teilhard de Chardin, and *The Discovery of God*.

19. Perhaps I should say that my reading of Balthasar was often accompanied also by a reading of Joseph Ratzinger, and later of the encyclicals of John Paul II. I was first introduced to Cardinal Ratzinger, by Balthasar, at a celebration hosted by Ratzinger, in September of 1985 at Castel Sant'Angelo in honor of Balthasar's eightieth birthday, following a conference on Adrienne von Speyr held at the request of Pope John Paul II.

20. Hans Urs von Balthasar, "Theology and Sanctity," in *Explorations in Theology*, vol. 1, *The Word Made Flesh*, trans. A. V. Littledale and Alexander Dru (San Francisco: Ignatius Press, 1989), 181–209. This translation of the article includes Balthasar's 1960 revision and expansion.

21. Perhaps it should be stated in this connection that love, rightly understood, carries its own answer to the problem of political integralism — that is, its own way of distinguishing state and society — a problem that may be suggested by the reference to public order. But treating this falls outside the scope of the present essay (in this connection, see David L. Schindler, "Multiculturalism and the Liberal State" [*Communio*, forthcoming]; "The Way of Love in the Church's Mission to the World," in *The Way of Love: Reflections on Pope Benedict XVI's Encyclical "Deus Caritas Est*," ed. Livio Melina and Carl A. Anderson [San Francisco: Ignatius Press, 2006], 29-45; an expanded version of the latter article is "Charity, Justice, and the Church's Activity in the World," *Communio* 33, no. 3 [2006]: 346-67).

22. See David C. Schindler, "Truth and the Christian Imagination: The Reformation of Causality and the Iconoclasm of the Spirit," *Communio* 33, no. 4 (2006): 521–39.

23. To be sure, rightly understood, the intelligence's mediation of freedom itself presupposes, in a different order, freedom's own mediation of intelligence. See Thomas Aquinas, *Summa theologiae*, I, 82, 4.

24. Compare in light of this paragraph Balthasar's suggestion that the deepest theme of modern thought lies in "the divorce between spirit and life, between the

theoretical and practical reason, between Apollo and Dionysus, idea and existence, between [modernity's] conception of the spiritual world as valuable but impotent, and of the practical world as one of power but spiritual poverty. This dualism in philosophy has prevailed at least since Kant" (Balthasar, "Theology and Sanctity," 193–94).

25. The methodological abstractions of the modern disciplines are, of course, both necessary and legitimate. How they are to be conceived, however, in terms of the Christian doctrine of creation, rightly understood, is a matter requiring qualification — that is, when and insofar as the God of creation is understood to be a God of Trinitarian love.

26. A power, in other words, rooted in metaphysical interiority. See, for example, Hans Urs von Balthasar, *Theo-Logic: Theological Logical Theory,* vol. 1, *The Truth of the World,* trans. Adrian J. Walker (San Francisco: Ignatius Press, 2000), 84ff.; Kenneth L. Schmitz, *The Gift: Creation* (Milwaukee: Marquette University Press, 1982); "Immateriality Past and Present," in *The Texture of Being: Essays in First Philosophy,* ed. Paul O'Herron (Washington, DC: Catholic University of America Press, 2007), 168–82.

27. It is crucial here to see that the character of being "in itself" that is necessary for x's identity must not be set in opposition to x's being simultaneously "for," or "from," another. Indeed, x is "*in* itself" and thus bears an interiority or "within" and indeed is also *for itself* and *from itself,* precisely *coincident with* and *by virtue of* its being constituted *by* another — a constitutive relation given its first and "transcendental" meaning in the act of being created by God. There is no identity, or "in itselfness," without the constitutive relation *from* and *toward* another that creates the "within" of x presupposed in x's being "*in* itself" in the first place. Relationality rightly understood, then, does not attenuate but, on the contrary, enables and deepens the identity of x rightly understood. Compare here the link discussed above between an identity construed originally mechanistically and the relative order of such an identity toward dispersal.

28. See Adrian J. Walker, "Personal Singularity and the *Communio Personarum:* A Creative Development of Thomas Aquinas' Doctrine of *Esse Commune,*" *Communio* 31, no. 3 (2004): 457–80.

29. A center or a "within" is required for something to be at all, and it is this center or "within" that establishes something as a subject. Which is to say, a pure object, or an exhaustively objective being, does not properly exist. See Balthasar, *The Truth of the World;* Schmitz, *The Gift: Creation;* "Immateriality Past and Present."

30. Genesis 9:8–14: "God spoke to Noah and his sons, 'See, I establish my covenant with you, and with your descendants after you; also with every living creature to be found with you, birds, cattle and every wild beast with you: everything that came out of the ark, everything that lives on earth. I establish my covenant with you: no thing of flesh shall be swept away again by the waters of the flood.... Here

is the sign of the covenant I make between myself and you and every living creature for all generations...a sign of the covenant between me and the earth.'"

31. See in this connection the important work of Orthodox theologian Alexander Schmemann on sacramentality and the symbolic nature of the world, particularly in *For the Life of the World: Sacraments and Orthodoxy* (Crestwood, NY: St. Vladimir's Seminary Press, 1997); *The Eucharist: Sacrament of the Kingdom* (Crestwood, NY: St. Vladimir's Seminary Press, 2003); *The Journals of Father Alexander Schmemann, 1973–1983* (Crestwood, NY: St. Vladimir's Seminary Press, 2000). See also Nicholas J. Healy, *The Eschatology of Hans Urs von Balthasar: Being as Communion* (Oxford: Oxford University Press, 2005).

32. Of course, John, in uniting Mary and Peter, shares in both lay state and office.

33. See Han Urs von Balthasar, *The Glory of the Lord: A Theological Aesthetics,* vol. 5, *The Realm of Metaphysics in the Modern Age,* trans. Oliver Davies et al. (San Francisco: Ignatius Press, 1991), 654.

34. "And just as in giving her assent to Gabriel's word, Mary lost nothing of her true humanity and freedom, so too when philosophy heeds the summons of the Gospel's truth its autonomy is in no way impaired. Indeed, it is then that philosophy sees all its enquiries rise to their highest expression. This was a truth which the holy monks of Christian antiquity understood well when they called Mary 'the table at which faith sits in thought.' In her they saw a lucid image of true philosophy and they were convinced of the need to *philosophari in Maria*" (John Paul II, *Fides et Ratio,* no. 108).

35. Balthasar, *The Realm of Metaphysics in the Modern Age,* 637.

36. Hans Urs von Balthasar, *Epilogue* (San Francisco: Ignatius Press, 1991), 57.

37. Balthasar, *The Realm of Metaphysics in the Modern Age,* 631–32.

38. Balthasar, *Epilogue,* 120.

39. Contemporary Scholastic thinkers not infrequently accuse Balthasar of a theological reduction: a precipitous move from the order of nature and reason to that of faith and the supernatural. In point of fact, however, these critics typically make this accusation while also presupposing a metaphysics different from that of Balthasar, in the way already suggested in the text. That is, they read differently from Balthasar the distinction *esse* and *essentia / ens,* with all that this distinction implies for Balthasar in terms of the inner openness of being to God, and indeed for the nature of being, in its given structure as such, as gift. Balthasar's argument, in other words, shows being to be open already in its natural philosophical meaning (in the one concrete order of history) to God-related love and generosity. The charge that Balthasar's understanding of the world in terms of God-centered love or generosity implies *eo ipso* a precipitous move to the order of faith and the supernatural thus begs what Balthasar himself takes to be *also* the crucial *philosophical* issue: the relation between *esse* and *essentia / ens.* Balthasar holds that this issue is necessarily invoked in any theological account of the world-God difference. The Scholastic charge of

a theological reduction on Balthasar's part, then, in a word, misses the crucial fact that the difference between Scholasticism and Balthasar regarding the meaning of being in its relation to God-centered love is a matter simultaneously of a properly philosophical *and* a properly theological argument. Such a charge, therefore, to be sustained in a reasonable and non-question-begging fashion, must defend itself also in philosophical terms, by providing an account of the "real distinction" relative to Balthasar's account of this distinction.

40. See Walker, "Personal Singularity and the *Communio Personarum.*"

41. The point, in other words, is that, while modern Scholasticism has clearly insisted on the truth of Catholic dogma, precisely against modern, or modern liberal, forms of relativism, it has done so typically while failing to provide any adequate opening in the *structure of being* to relationality to God and God's love. Catholic dogma, then, that is, insofar as it speaks of God and God's love, can only appear to be, and be, an *arbitrary-adventitious imposition from without* on reality and reason in their naturally given logic.

42. And thus, for example, the subjectivity and history that are characteristic achievements of the modern era.

43. This in fact is one of the two main points of Pope Benedict XVI's lecture to the faculty of the University of Regensburg, delivered on September 12, 2006, which emphasizes that the West needs to see that reason of its inner logic is open to God even as the major religions of the world (e.g., Islam) need to see that God is innerly open to reason — that God is reasonable.

44. It seems difficult, then, not to see the work of Balthasar as of a piece with that of the constellation of Catholic thinkers — for example, Henri de Lubac, John Paul II, and Benedict XVI — who have influenced and guided the church in and since the Second Vatican Council, insisting that the Council's basic teaching is rightly understood in these terms of Christ's revelation of the mystery of the love of the Father (Vatican II, *Gaudium et Spes*, no. 22; see John Paul II, *Dives in Misericordia*, no. 1). Balthasar's work demonstrates that the renewal of the church and the church's relation to the world, as conceived at the Council and in the pontificates of John Paul II and Benedict XVI, is a matter of ontology and thus of reason and reality, and not merely of moral or spiritual intentionality. Compare in this connection the Council's new, or renewed, understanding of Christ's revelation of divine Trinitarian love as the key to understanding the reality of the church (the idea of the church as *communio*), and the developments since the Council regarding humankind, the body, and the world (the ideas of *communio personarum*, the "nuptial" attribute of the body, and humankind as a unity within distinctness of *eros* and *agape*), and regarding the laity and the call to live sanctity at the heart of the world (on the latter, see Hans Urs von Balthasar, "The Council of the Holy Spirit," in *Explorations in Theology*, vol. 3, *Creator Spirit*, trans. Brian McNeil [Ignatius Press, 1993], 245–67).

45. See, for example, Juan M. Sara, "*Descensus ad inferos,* Dawn of Hope: Aspects of the Theology of Holy Saturday in the Trilogy of Hans Urs von Balthasar," *Communio* 32, no. 3 (2003): 541–72; Adrian J. Walker, "Love Alone: Hans Urs von Balthasar as a Master of Theological Renewal," *Communio* 32, no. 3 (2003): 517–40.

46. Pope Benedict XVI, *Jesus of Nazareth: From the Baptism in the Jordan to the Transfiguration,* trans. Adrian J. Walker (New York: Doubleday, 2007), 26.

47. Ibid., 20.

48. Ibid., 159–60.

49. Ibid., 161.

50. See Hans Urs von Balthasar, *Bernanos: An Ecclesial Existence,* trans. Erasmo Leiva-Merikakis (San Francisco: Ignatius Press, 1996).

Chapter Fifteen / Adrian Walker

1. See Augustine, *Confessions,* III, 11.

2. Gerard Manley Hopkins, "Carrion Comfort," in *The Oxford Authors: Gerard Manley Hopkins,* ed. Catherine Phillips (Oxford: Oxford University Press, 1991), 168.

3. Adrienne von Speyr, *Die Welt des Gebetes* (Einsiedeln: Johannes Verlag, 1992), 41. On the legitimacy, even the necessity, of using the work of von Speyr to illuminate that of Balthasar, see Balthasar's own emphatic testimony in Hans Urs von Balthasar, *Unser Auftrag: Bericht und Entwurf* (Einsiedeln: Johannes Verlag, 1984), 11.

4. See Thomas Aquinas, *Summa theologiae,* I, 27, 2, ad 3.

5. Francis Turretin, *Institutes of Elenctic Theology,* trans. George Musgrave Giger, vol. 1 (Phillipsburg, NJ: P & R Publishing, 1992), 291.

6. See, for example, Thomas Aquinas, *Summa theologiae,* I, 32, 3.

7. See, for example, Thomas Aquinas, *Summa theologiae,* I, 34, 2, ad 4.

8. On the beatific vision as the fulfillment of philosophical *eros,* see, among other texts, Thomas Aquinas, *Summa theologiae,* I, 12, 1, where Thomas insists that, without the beatific vision, the *natural* desire to know the effect on seeing the cause would be frustrated, even though he says just a few articles later that humankind cannot attain the beatific vision by its own natural powers (*Summa theologiae,* I, 12, 4–5). On the connection with the generation of the Word, see, for example, Thomas Aquinas, *Summa theologiae,* I, 22, 2 (the Word as the subsistent self-conception of the divine being); I, 43, 5 (our assimilation to the Son in his Word- or intellect-character). Of course, not every school of Thomism would accept my reading of Thomas on the relation between the supernatural grace of the beatific vision and the *eros* of human nature. This is not the place, however, for showing why the position that I adumbrate here is textually, philosophically, and theologically the most adequate.

9. Leo Strauss, *Natural Right and History* (Chicago: University of Chicago Press, 1953), 74–75. In his essay "How to Begin to Study Medieval Philosophy" (in *The Rebirth of Classical Political Rationalism: An Introduction to the Thought of Leo Strauss,* ed. Thomas L. Pangle [Chicago: University of Chicago Press, 1989], 221–24), Strauss does acknowledge that Christianity, as a religion, has an *ex professo* interest in philosophy that Judaism and Islam as (on his account) law-based religions do not. At the same time, he holds that, for precisely this reason, philosophy in the Christian polity is fated to become part of a public orthodoxy, whereas philosophy in the medieval Islamic polity (whether practiced by Muslims or by Jews) preserved philosophy's character as esoteric inquiry that is essentially different in kind from, and even downright dangerous to, any public orthodoxy. This seems to me to amount to a subtler restatement of the same position represented by the citation from *Natural Right and History.*

10. Thomas Prufer, *Recapitulations: Essays in Philosophy* (Washington, DC: Catholic University of America Press, 1993).

11. Ibid., xiii.

12. Ibid., xii.

13. Ibid.

14. Ibid., 32.

15. Ibid., 34, 68.

16. Ibid., 36.

17. Ibid.

18. Ibid., 35.

19. Ibid, 39–41.

20. This distinction turns out to be a typically intraworldly one, which therefore does not apply *tel quel* to God, who is neither originally a part of nor paired with the world. God does not articulate himself into nature and artifice/convention; he is not simply a repetition of the "whole" on a higher level. If he does any articulating at all — but the term "articulating" is actually inappropriate to his simplicity — it is into the three Persons, who, according to Christian teaching, are the one divine nature in the eternal act of exchanging it among themselves. See ibid., 34.

21. Even within the world, nature can be thought of without artifice, but not vice versa (even though this thought presupposes a being who in some way distinguishes itself from nature and knows that it is doing so). Aristotle saw this. Accordingly, in *Physics* B, 1 he conceived of the distinction drawn between nature and artifice as a *basic* distinction. This implies, in turn, that nature as such is essentially different, and ontologically-logically prior to, fabricable machines. Nature is rather a ground resting on no further ground of the same order: an intraworldly image of God as unoriginated origin.

22. Prufer, *Recapitulations,* xii.

23. Ibid., 42.

24. Hans Urs von Balthasar, *Herrlichkeit: Eine theologische Ästhetik*, vol. 3.1, *Im Raum der Metaphysik* (Einsiedeln: Johannes Verlag, 1965), 943. Although in English translation, as well as in later German editions, this has appeared as two separate books, in the original edition, from which I will be citing here, all the matter later divided into two volumes appeared under one cover.

25. Prufer, *Recapitulations*, xii.

26. Ibid., 40.

27. Augustine, *Confessions*, III, 11.

28. Balthasar, *Im Raum der Metaphysik*, 943–57.

29. Ibid., 943. This single wonderment is for him inherently dual: it includes a double wonderment over the being of the wonderer and over the being of the "whole" of which the wonderer is and is not a part. For Balthasar, this two-in-one wonderment over being has its archetype in the child's awakening to itself in its mother's arms, an event in which the mother gives the wonderer to himself in giving him access to the the "whole" in light of the being. In so doing, the mother mediates being's letting be of both self and world, even as this very letting be simultaneously depends on her mediation. The dual unity of wonderer and "whole" is thus held together in its turn by a double mediation of mother and being. Since neither mother nor being — nor, again, self or world — is absolute, the whole fourfold structure therefore points upward to a source of at once immanent in, yet transcendent of, the structure in its entirety. Moreover, because this source is the simultaneous origin of being, of the wonderer, and of the "whole," and the mother, it must be at once personal and principial. Balthasar then analyzes this original fourfold structure into four interlocking differences that together point upward as a whole to such a personal and principal source.

30. Take the conclusion of a valid argument. It closes the argument with rigorous necessity, but in doing so it completes the argument as a luminous form or *Gestalt* whose evidence rises up from a depth that is not exhaustibly capturable by the premises, the conclusion, or their interplay taken simply on their own level. However trivial the conclusion may be as a proposition in its own right, the "ought-ness" with which it follows from the initial premise is not just necessity, but rather a necessity that rises up spontaneously from a bottomless depth with all the force of a revelation, and so it produces, or ought to produce, unceasing wonderment.

31. Balthasar is careful to remove from God's subsisting freedom any all-too-anthropomorphic traits that would compromise his status as First Principle of being. But Balthasar operates this remotion within a larger option. Precisely because he thinks that God cannot be constructed "from below," he refuses to let either anthropomorphism or the often all-too-human desire to overcome it ultimately set the terms on which God can appear as God within the world. Just as humankind is both a "part" of the "whole" and bigger than the "whole," the free personal God is neither humanlike nor an impersonal negation or absorption of the human. Rather,

as Maximus the Confessor — an important source of Balthasar's theology — puts it, "God and man are paradigms for each other. Moreover, God is humanized for man out of love for man to the same extent that man has divinized himself for God by the power of charity, and man is snatched up noetically by God to the object of *gnosis* to the same extent that man has through the virtues manifested the God who is invisible by nature" (*Ambigua*, 10 [PG 91 1113b]). Of course, it takes the risen Jesus to show us fully how humankind can image what divine personhood is like. The resurrection spiritualizes humankind, not to take away physicality, but rather to free it from a "mere individuality" doomed to die, and so to complete humankind's imaging of divine personhood in the context of deathless triune eternity.

32. Note the following passage from Prufer: "Aquinas...makes a shift to *esse commune* (*completum et simplex sed non subsistens*), which falls within 'the subject (matter) of metaphysics' although not identical with *ens qua ens*...and to *esse ir-receptum subsistens*, 'the principle of the subject (matter) of metaphysics'" (Prufer, *Recapitulations*, xii–xiii). See also p. xii, n. 6, where Prufer acknowledges his debt to the work of Ferdinand Ulrich, who is also a source of Balthasar's account of the real distinction. Ulrich has explored in depth the meaning of Thomas Aquinas's "definition" of the "to be" of beings as *aliquid completum et simplex, sed non subsistens* (see Thomas Aquinas, *Quaestiones disputatae de potentia Dei*, 1, 1) — that is, complete and simple, but not subsistent. See, for example, Ferdinand Ulrich, *Homo Abyssus: Das Wagnis der Seinsfrage*, 2nd ed. (Freiburg: Johannes Verlag, 1998).

33. Balthasar, *Im Raum der Metaphysik*, 955.

34. Balthasar does not mean that the unity of being is itself a third element that somehow stands by itself apart from, or between, *esse* and essence. His knows perfectly well that *ens* is a unit, and that this unit is "composed" only of *esse* and essence, and nothing more. Balthasar's point in talking about "floating" here (an alternative translation would be "oscillation") is simply this: the very fact that the unit *ens* is "composed" of two coprinciples implies that its unity is simultaneously on both sides of the *esse*-essence distinction. This affirmation in turn has two implications. On the one hand, the unity of *ens* really is on each side of the essence-*esse* distinction, albeit in a different way appropriate to the metaphysical character of the respective coprinciple. Thus, the assertion of a "floating" or "oscillating" quality to the unity of *ens* does not mean that this unity is, as it were, tantalizingly withheld from *ens;* Balthasar would be the last person to deny that the gift of being, and of the unity that comes with it, is truly *given*, once and for all. On the other hand, though, there is a second implication that we need to keep in mind to balance out the first one. While the unity of *ens* is really in each one of the coprinciples of *ens*, it is so only insofar as the one coprinciple is always indwelt by the other, not after the fashion of a component, but rather by way of a noninvasive mutual immanence (the "real distinction" between *esse* and essence thus never disappears). Putting together both implications at once, we get the whole picture that Balthasar is trying to draw

for us. On the one side, being, and the unity that comes with it, is not withheld, but rather is given once and for all; on the other side, this unity is not a simple, self-contained identity, but rather includes a one-of-a-kind "perichoresis" between *esse* and essence characterized by a noninvasive mutual indwelling that "constitutes" the indwelt beyond the logic of whole and part (*esse* and essence are [analogously speaking] cocomponents of *ens,* but not of each other). This noninvasive mutuality in its turn reflects, and extends, the way God constitutes the creature by being noninvasively immanent in it (once again beyond the whole-part logic). One of the novelties of Balthasar's thought is that he tries to read the mutual dependence of *esse* and essence within being's unity not only as an imperfection, but also as a perfection, as the way in which the oneness of being in itself is always more than itself: fruitfulness. The unity of being includes a difference beyond division, so that, rereading it spiritually in the light of revelation, we can discern in it an *imago Trinitatis* that serves as a creaturely basis for the intrinsic unity of creation and redemption. (I am grateful to Martin Bieler for stimulating me to develop the points laid out in this note.)

35. Balthasar, *Im Raum der Metaphysik,* 955.

36. Ibid., 954.

37. Ibid., 955.

38. Hans Urs von Balthasar, *Epilog* (Einsiedeln: Johannes Verlag, 1987), 72. It should be borne in mind that Balthasar is sharply critical of Jean-Luc Marion's thesis of "God without being." See Hans Urs von Balthasar, *Theologik,* vol. 2, *Wahrheit Gottes* (Einsiedeln: Johannes Verlag, 1985).

39. Balthasar, *Im Raum der Metaphysik,* 955f.

40. Prufer, *Recapitulations,* xii.

41. See Robert Louis Wilken, *The Christians as the Romans Saw Them* (New Haven: Yale University Press, 2003), 129.

42. For the elements of this, see Prufer, *Recapitulations,* 1–5. See also the important work of David C. Schindler on Socrates as an image of the Good who embodies the ground of rationality.

43. Here I add a few brief words about the metaphysics of this. The Son of God, *esse subsistens ab alio receptum et se recipiens* (subsistent *esse* received and receiving itself from another), assumes human nature at the point where *esse non subsistens in et ab alio receptum* (nonsubsistent *esse* received in and by another) normally exercises its paradoxical quasi-formality for nature: making it be while simultaneously depending on it to give it the subsistence that it does not have in itself. The point is not that the Son assumes a created *esse* in addition to his uncreated one; it is rather that he recapitulates *virtute* the gift-character and gift-causality of created *esse* within his eternal hypostatic *esse.* In this sense, he both archetypically relives the philosophical ascent from nature through being to the personal principle of being

and is the principle of the intelligbility of that ascent twice over, both as the personal principle itself and as the "virtual" recapitulation of *esse creatum* as gift.

44. Philosophy, or at any rate classical philosophy, begins its reflection by sifting through current opinions, which it recognizes are not all necessarily true, but without concluding fallaciously from this that they are therefore all necessarily false. For the essential difference between philosophy and prephilosophical opinion is not the same as the difference between truth and falsity; rather, it coincides with the difference between understanding why and not yet, or not yet explicitly, understanding why. (I owe this point to David Tye.)

45. There are two such forms of life in the church: either consecration or marriage. David Crawford has shown how Balthasar's emphasis on the centrality of the consecrated life nonetheless is compatible with, even implies, an "intrinsic analogy" or "circumincession" of both states of life that bestows on marriage a "subordinate priority" over consecrated virginity as a way to holiness.

46. Epigraph to Friedrich Hölderlin's book-length poem *Hyperion:* "Not to be constrained by the greatest, yet to be contained by the smallest — that is divine."

Contributors

Robert Barron is Professor of Theology at the University of St. Mary of the Lake, Mundelein Seminary, Mundelein, Illinois.

Martin Bieler is a privatdozent in systematic theology at the University of Berne, Switzerland. He is also an ordained pastor of the Swiss Reformed Church.

Larry S. Chapp is Professor of Theology at DeSales University, Center Valley, Pennsylvania.

Anthony DiStefano teaches theology at Xavier College Preparatory School, Phoenix, Arizona.

Raymond Gawronski, SJ, is Professor of Theology at St. John Vianney Theological Seminary, Denver.

Michael Hanby is Assistant Professor of Biotechnology and Ethics at the Pontifical John Paul II Institute for Studies on Marriage and the Family, Catholic University of America, Washington, D.C.

Nicholas J. Healy is Assistant Professor of Philosophy and Culture at the Pontifical John Paul II Institute for Studies on Marriage and the Family, Catholic University of America, Washington, D.C.

Rodney A. Howsare is Associate Professor of Theology at DeSales University, Center Valley, Pennsylvania.

Francesca Murphy is Professor of Theology at the University of Aberdeen, Scotland.

Danielle Nussberger is Assistant Professor of Theology at Marquette University in Milwaukee.

Cyril O'Regan is the Huisking Professor of Theology at the University of Notre Dame, South Bend, Indiana.

Russell Reno is Professor of Theological Ethics at Creighton University, Omaha, Nebraska.

Tracey Rowland is Associate Professor of Theology at the Pontifical John Paul II Institute for Studies on Marriage and the Family, East Melbourne, Australia.

David C. Schindler is Associate Professor in the Department of Humanities, Villanova University, Philadelphia.

David L. Schindler is the Academic Dean and Edouard Cardinal Gagnon Professor of Fundamental Theology at the Pontifical John Paul II Institute for Studies on Marriage and the Family, Catholic University of America, Washington, D.C. He is also the editor of the American edition of *Communio: International Catholic Review.*

Adrian Walker is a prolific translator and scholar, who currently resides near Freiburg, Germany. He is also the co-editor of the American edition of *Communio: International Catholic Review.*

Of Related Interest

Kevin Mongrain
THE SYSTEMATIC THOUGHT
OF VON BALTHASAR
An Irenaean Retrieval

"This important study is, as far as I know, the best comprehensive account of von Balthasar's thought in any language. Von Balthasar's oeuvre is immense, sprawling, varied, and often difficult. Finding an organizing system that makes coherent sense of the whole requires great conceptual creativity; doing so in a way von Balthasar himself might have approved demands meticulous scholarship. This clear, interesting, and balanced work delivers on both counts."

— **George Lindbeck,** Professor Emeritus, Yale University,
author of *The Nature of Doctrine: Religion and Theology
in a Postliberal Age*

"Mongrain's interpretation of von Balthasar is deep, fertile, and persuasive. This highly original reading is not simply a footnote to current scholarship — it challenges and even displaces it, showing the systematic unity of von Balthasar's thought and challenging the 'either-or' interpretations that pit von Balthasar against, for example, Karl Rahner or political theology. This comprehensive, erudite, and sophisticated study is one of the best published works on the subject in any language."

— **Cyril J. O'Regan,** Professor of Theology, University of
Notre Dame, author of *The Heterodox Hegel* and
Gnostic Return in Modernity

0-8245-1927-2, paperback

crossroad

Of Related Interest

Christopher Steck
THE ETHICAL THOUGHT OF
HANS URS VON BALTHASAR

*Winner of the Book of the Year Award
from the College Theology Society*

In contemporary theology, the thought of Hans Urs von Balthasar (1905–1988) exerts ever-greater influence, as readers discover
that his thought is too subtle and rich to be pigeonholed into
categories as simple as "neopatristic" or "conservative." In the
emerging discussion of his contributions to key themes in theology, however, surprisingly little attention has been paid to his
view of ethics. In this remarkable study, the first of its kind in any
language, Christopher Steck uncovers the ethical dimension of
von Balthasar's thought, showing its relation to other key issues in
his works, and to key figures such as Ignatius Loyola, Karl Barth,
and especially Karl Rahner. Steck shows both the importance of
ethics in von Balthasar's thinking and how it exposes limitations
of current ethical reflection. This clear, authoritative introduction is indispensable for von Balthasar scholars and students of
contemporary Catholic theology, as well as all interested in major
trends in contemporary conversations about religious ethics.

0-8245-1915-9, paperback

Check your local bookstore for availability.
To order directly from the publisher,
please call 1-800-707-0670 for Customer Service
or visit our Web site at *www.cpcbooks.com.*
For catalog orders, please send your request to the address below.

THE CROSSROAD PUBLISHING COMPANY
16 Penn Plaza, Suite 1550
New York, NY 10001

crossroad